空知英秋

Hideaki Sorachi

Thanks to your support, I've made it to twenty volumes. I feel like I've been walking a tightrope since about the third volume, but I've made it this far, so I'll keep doing my best until somebody cuts the rope!

Hideaki Sorachi was born on May 25, 1979, and grew up in Hokkaido, Japan. His ongoing series, *GIN TAMA*, became a huge hit when it began running in the pages of Japan's *Weekly Shonen Jump* in 2004. A *GIN TAMA* animated series followed soon after, premiering on Japanese TV in April 2006. Sorachi made his manga debut with the one-shot story *DANDELION*.

GIN TAMA VOL. 20
SHONEN JUMP ADVANCED Manga Edition

STORY & ART BY HIDEAKI SORACHI

Translation/Kyoko Shapiro, Honyaku Center Inc.
English Adaptation/Lance Caselman
Touch-up Art & Lettering/Avril Averill
Design/Ronnie Casson
Editors/Jann Jones & Mike Montesa

Printed in Canada

Published by VIZ Media, LLC
P.O. Box 77010
San Francisco, CA 94107

10 9 8 7 6 5 4 3 2 1
First printing, November 2010

www.viz.com

THE WORLD'S MOST CUTTING-EDGE MANGA
www.shonenjump.com

GIN TAMA

Vol. 20
The Best Part of Summer Vacation Is Before It Begins

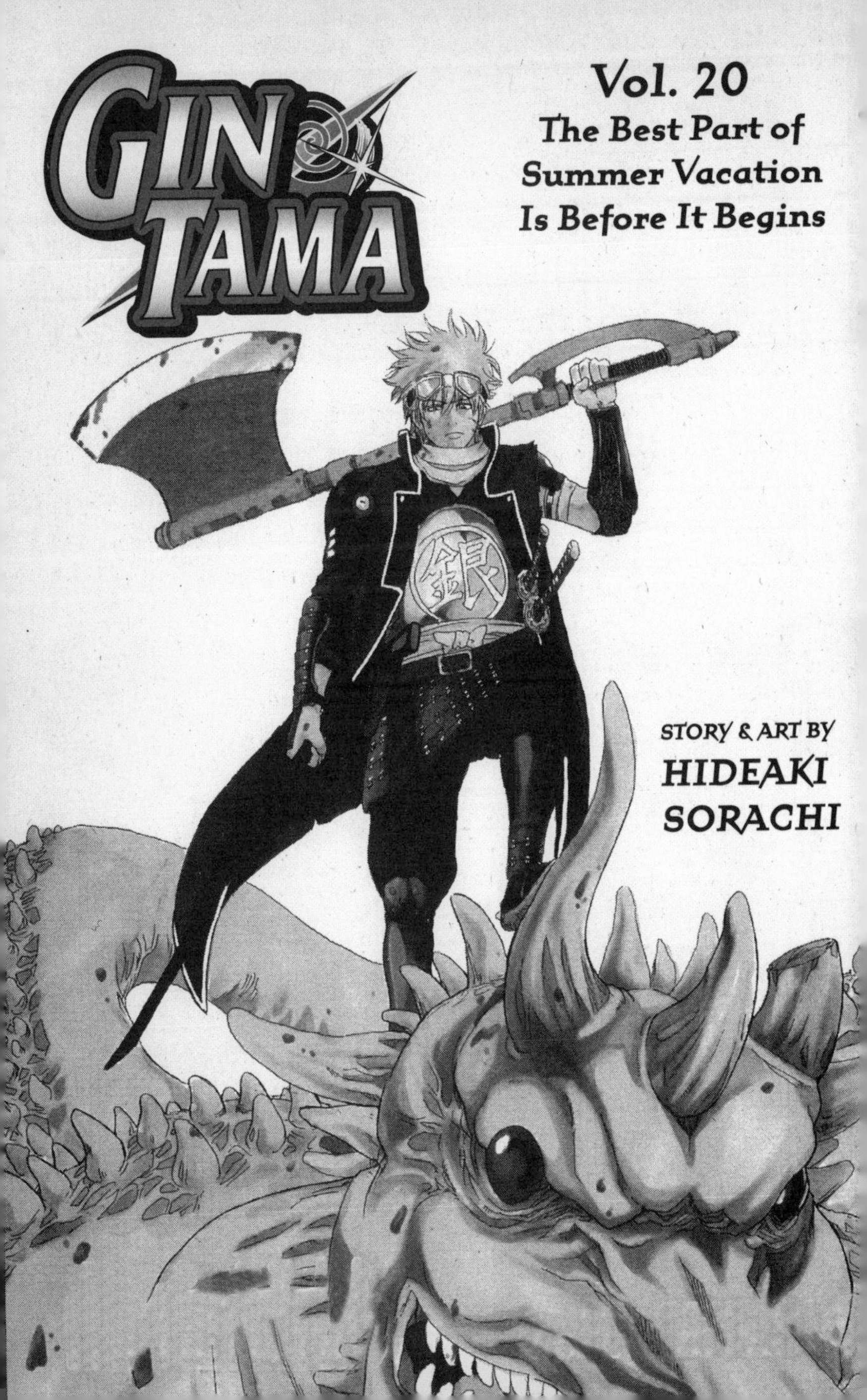
銀

STORY & ART BY
HIDEAKI SORACHI

Cast of Characters

Yorozuya Members

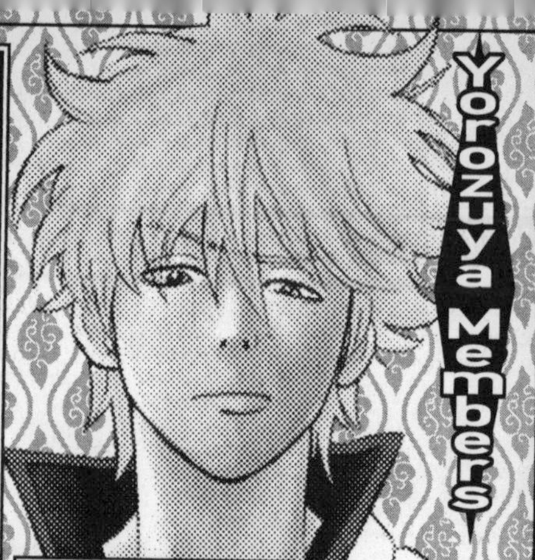

Gintoki Sakata

The hero of our story. If he doesn't eat something sweet periodically he gets cranky—really cranky. He boasts a powerful sword arm, but he's one step away from diabetes. A former member of the exclusionist faction that seeks to expel the space aliens and protect the nation.

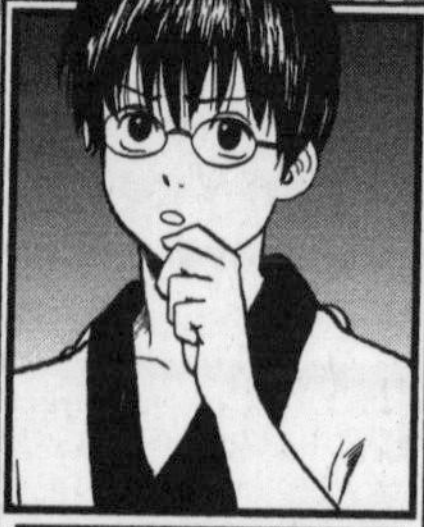

Shinpachi Shimura

Works under Gintoki in an attempt to learn about the samurai spirit but has often come to regret his decision recently. President of the Tsu Terakado Fan Club.

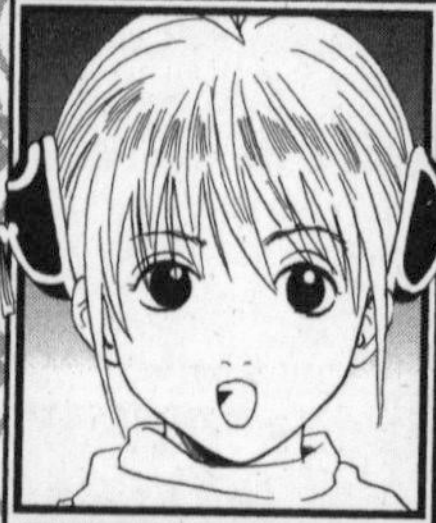

Kagura

A member of the Yato Clan, the most powerful warrior race in the universe. Her voracious appetite and alien worldview lead frequently to laughter…and sometimes contusions.

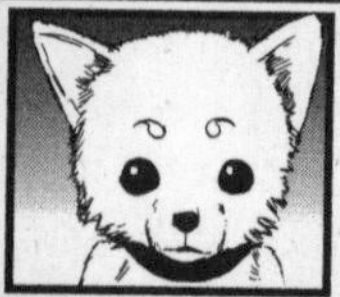

Sadaharu

A giant space creature turned office pet. Likes to bite people (especially Gin).

Shinsengumi Members

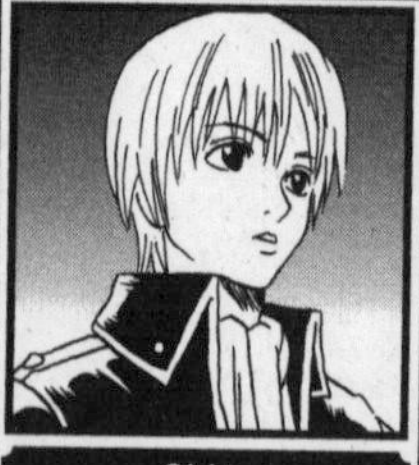

Okita

The Shinsengumi's most formidable swordsman. Behind a facade of amiability, he tirelessly schemes to eliminate Hijikata and usurp his position.

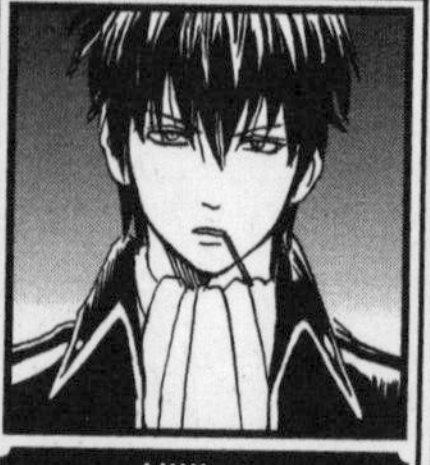

Hijikata

Vice chief of the Shinsengumi, Edo's elite counter-terrorist police unit. His air of detached cool transforms into hot rage the instant he draws his sword…or when someone disparages mayonnaise.

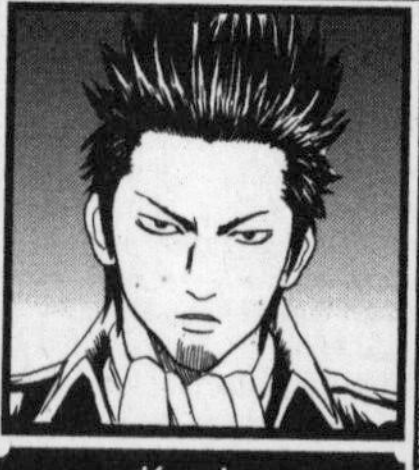

Kondo

The trusted chief of the Shinsengumi (and the remorseless stalker of Shinpachi's older sister Otae).

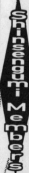

Other Characters

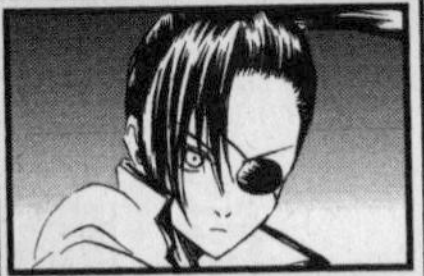

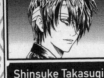

Kyube Yagyu

Crown prince of the famous Yagyu family of swordsmen and Otae's former fiancé. Only this prince has no scepter.

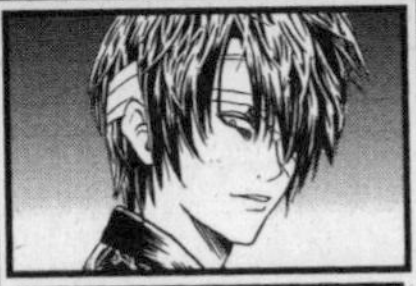

Shinsuke Takasugi

A samurai who fought beside Gintoki and Katsura before going over to the dark side.

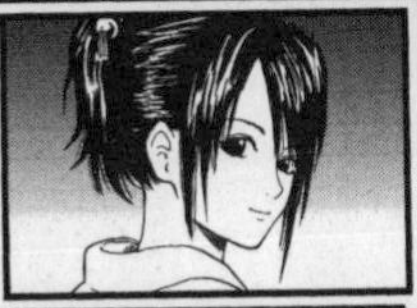

Otae Shimura

Her demure manner hides the heart of a lion. Though employed at a hostess bar, she ruthlessly guards her virtue and plots to revive the family fortunes.

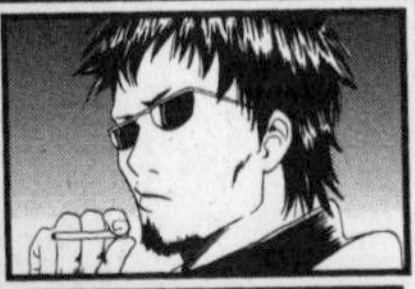

Taizo Hasegawa

Formerly a high official in the Bakufu government, his life has become one long slide into despair.

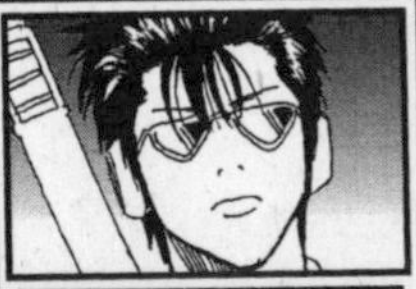

Bansai Kawakami

A Kiheitai swordsman whose nickname is the "Manslayer." He's a music producer on the side.

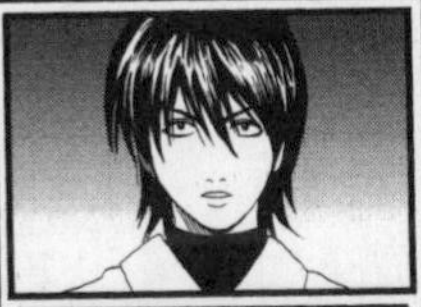

Sagaru Yamazaki

A member of the Shinsengumi who works as an observer (spy). His favorite pastime is badminton.

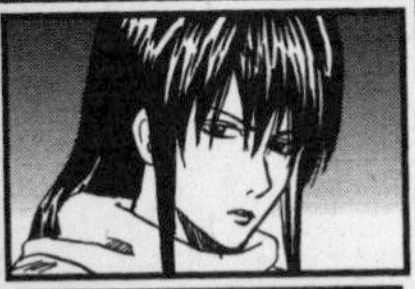

Kotaro Katsura

The last surviving holdout of the exclusionist rebels, and Gintoki's pal. Nickname: Zura.

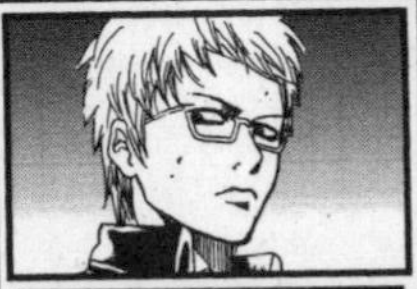

Kamotaro Ito

A new Shinsengumi member who wants to take over the organization. He got Hijikata suspended and planned Chief Kondo's assassination.

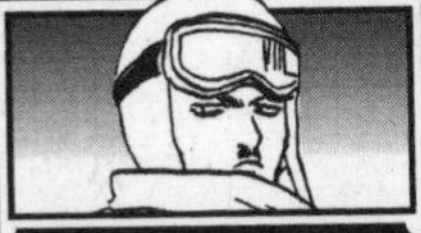

Umibozu

Kagura's father, the mightiest alien-buster in the galaxy.

The story thus far

In an alternate-universe Edo (Tokyo), extraterrestrials land in Japan, and the new government issues an order outlawing swords. The samurai, who have reached the pinnacle of power and prosperity, fall into rapid decline.

Twenty years hence, only one samurai has managed to hold on to his fighting spirit: a somewhat eccentric fellow named Gintoki "Odd Jobs Gin" Sakata. A lover of sweets and near diabetic, our hero sets up shop as a *yorozuya*—an expert at managing trouble and handling the oddest of jobs.

Joining Gin in his business is Shinpachi Shimura, whose sister Gin saved from the clutches of nefarious debt collectors. After a series of unexpected circumstances, the trio meet a powerful alien named Kagura, who becomes—after some arm-twisting—a part-time team member.

New Shinsengumi member Ito Kamotaro, driven by ambition, allies himself with the Kiheitai and betrays his comrades! A fierce battle erupts as the Shinsengumi splits into rival factions, and the yorozuya trio find themselves fighting to save Kondo and the Shinsengumi! As the battle builds to its furious climax, Gin finds himself entangled in Bansai Kawakami's deadly strings!

WHAT THIS MANGA'S FULL OF
vol. 20

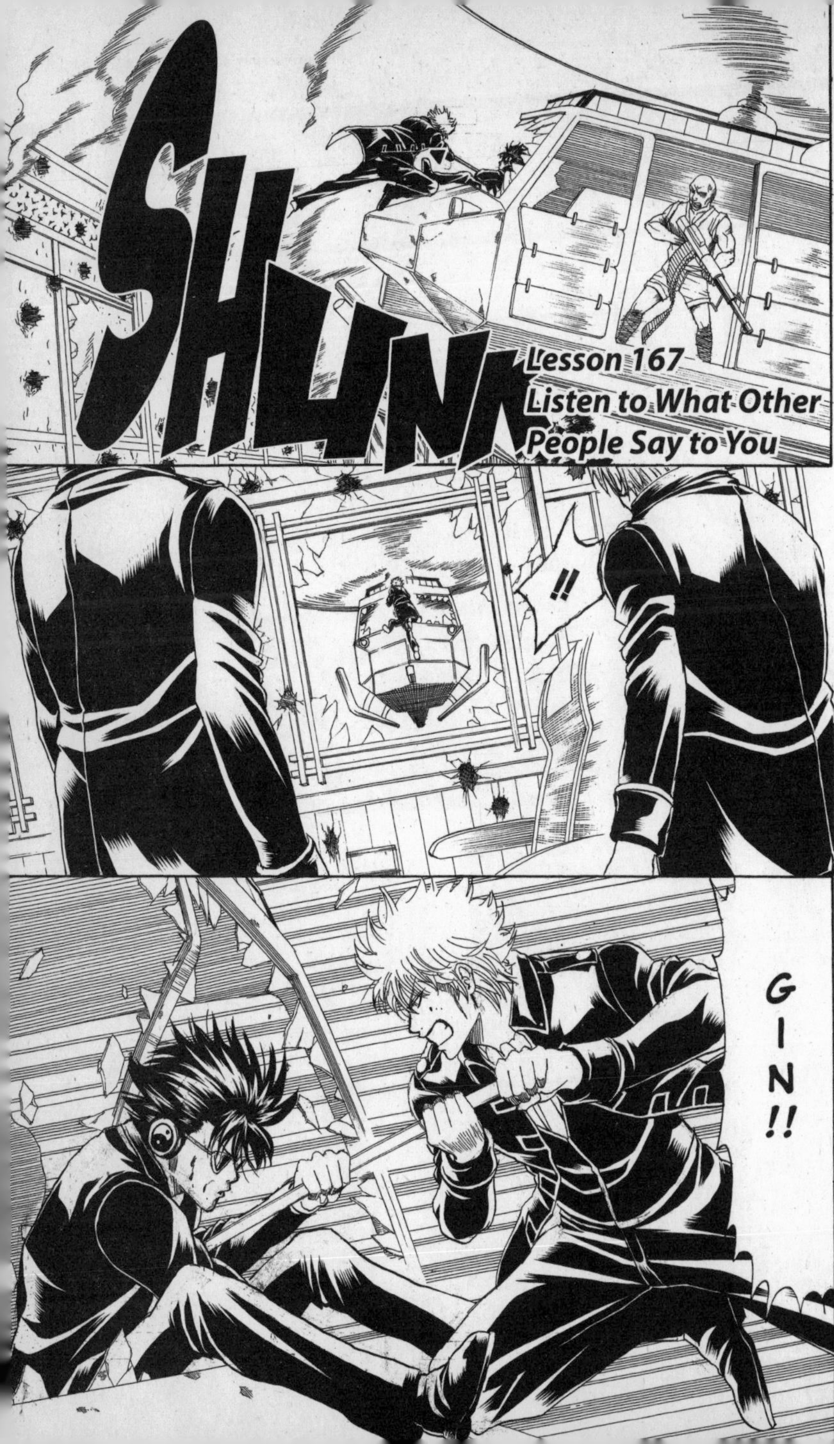
SHUNK
Lesson 167
Listen to What Other People Say to You
!!
GIN!!

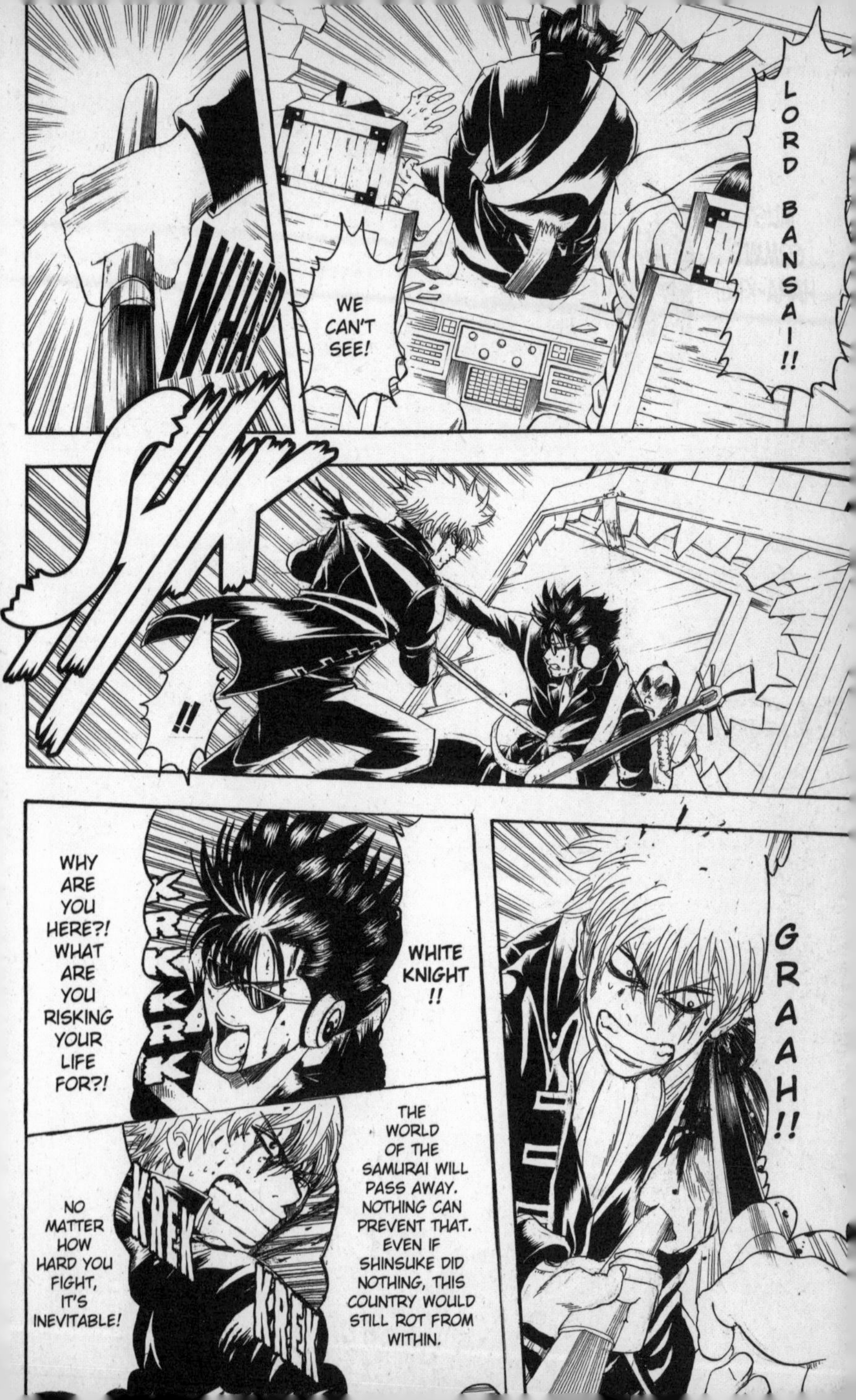
LORD BANSAI!!
WE CAN'T SEE!
WHAP
!!
GRAAH!!
WHITE KNIGHT!!
WHY ARE YOU HERE?! WHAT ARE YOU RISKING YOUR LIFE FOR?!
KRK KRK KRK
THE WORLD OF THE SAMURAI WILL PASS AWAY. NOTHING CAN PREVENT THAT. EVEN IF SHINSUKE DID NOTHING, THIS COUNTRY WOULD STILL ROT FROM WITHIN.
NO MATTER HOW HARD YOU FIGHT, IT'S INEVITABLE!
KREK
KREK

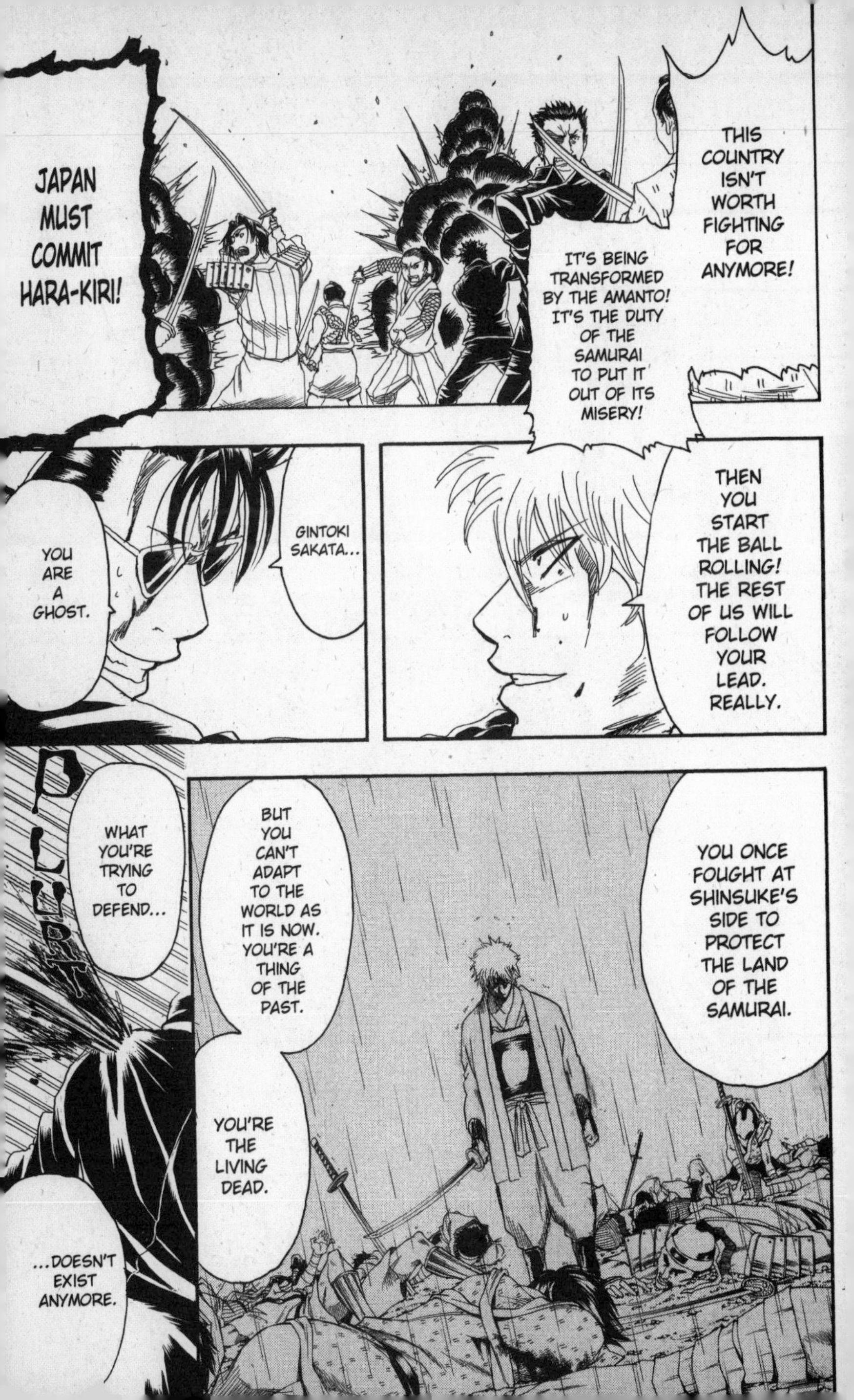
THIS COUNTRY ISN'T WORTH FIGHTING FOR ANYMORE!
IT'S BEING TRANSFORMED BY THE AMANTO! IT'S THE DUTY OF THE SAMURAI TO PUT IT OUT OF ITS MISERY!
JAPAN MUST COMMIT HARA-KIRI!
THEN YOU START THE BALL ROLLING! THE REST OF US WILL FOLLOW YOUR LEAD. REALLY.
GINTOKI SAKATA...
YOU ARE A GHOST.
YOU ONCE FOUGHT AT SHINSUKE'S SIDE TO PROTECT THE LAND OF THE SAMURAI.
BUT YOU CAN'T ADAPT TO THE WORLD AS IT IS NOW. YOU'RE A THING OF THE PAST.
YOU'RE THE LIVING DEAD.
PLURT
WHAT YOU'RE TRYING TO DEFEND...
...DOESN'T EXIST ANYMORE.

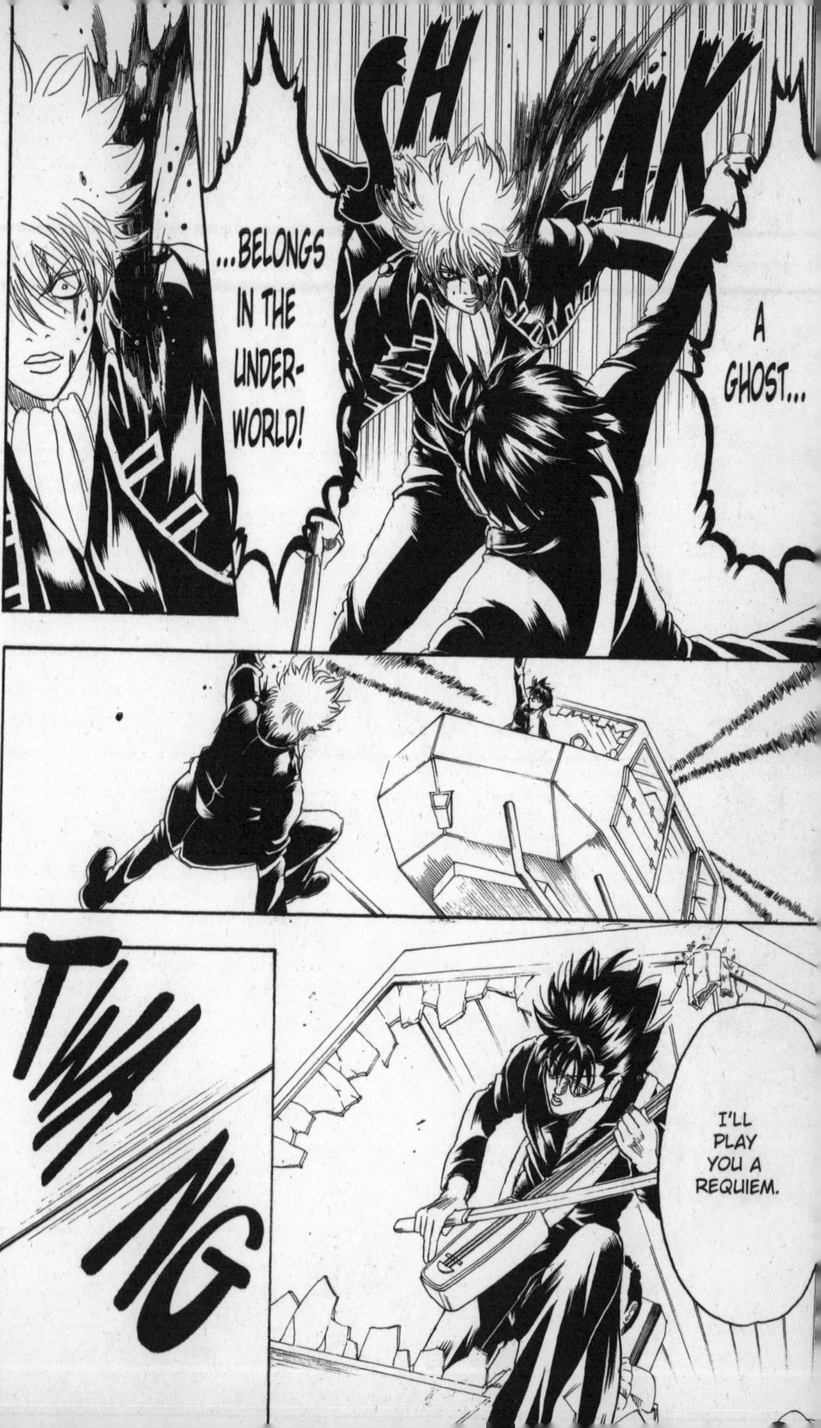
SHAAK
A GHOST...
...BELONGS IN THE UNDER-WORLD!
I'LL PLAY YOU A REQUIEM.
TWANG

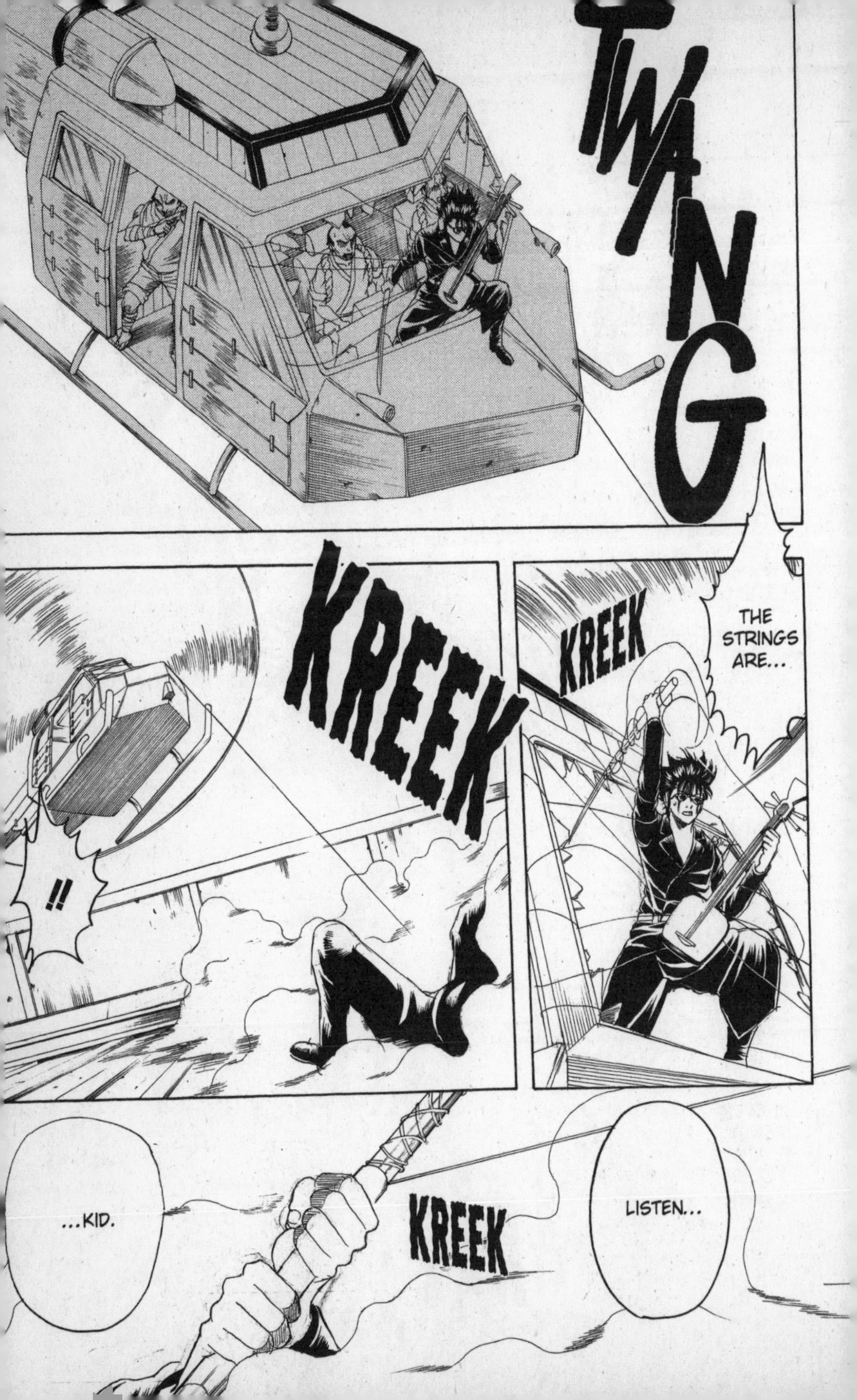
TWANG
THE STRINGS ARE...
KREEK
KREEK
!!
LISTEN...
KREEK
...KID.

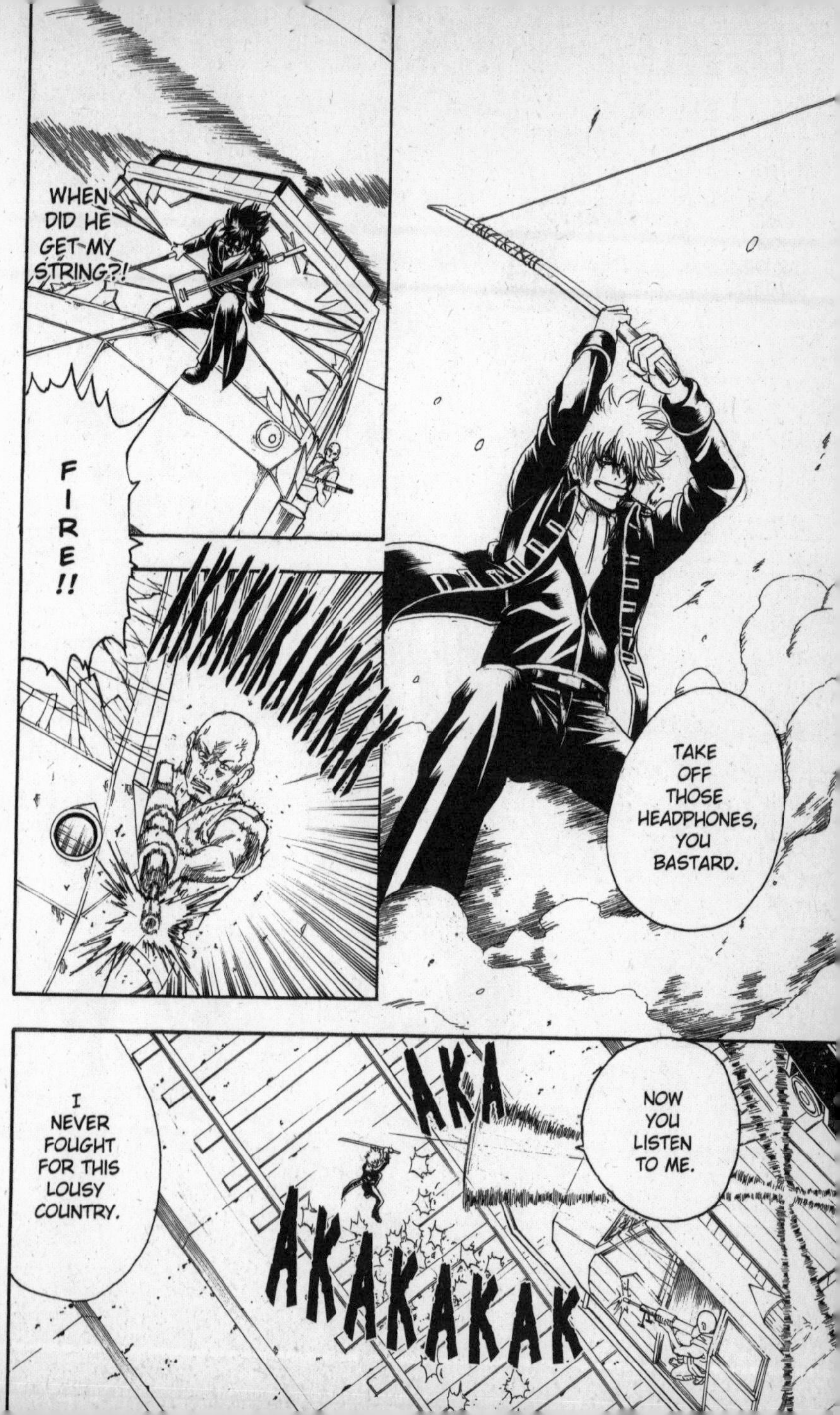
TAKE OFF THOSE HEADPHONES, YOU BASTARD.
WHEN DID HE GET MY STRING?!
FIRE!!
AKAKAKAKAKAKAK
NOW YOU LISTEN TO ME.
AKA
I NEVER FOUGHT FOR THIS LOUSY COUNTRY.
AKAKAKAK

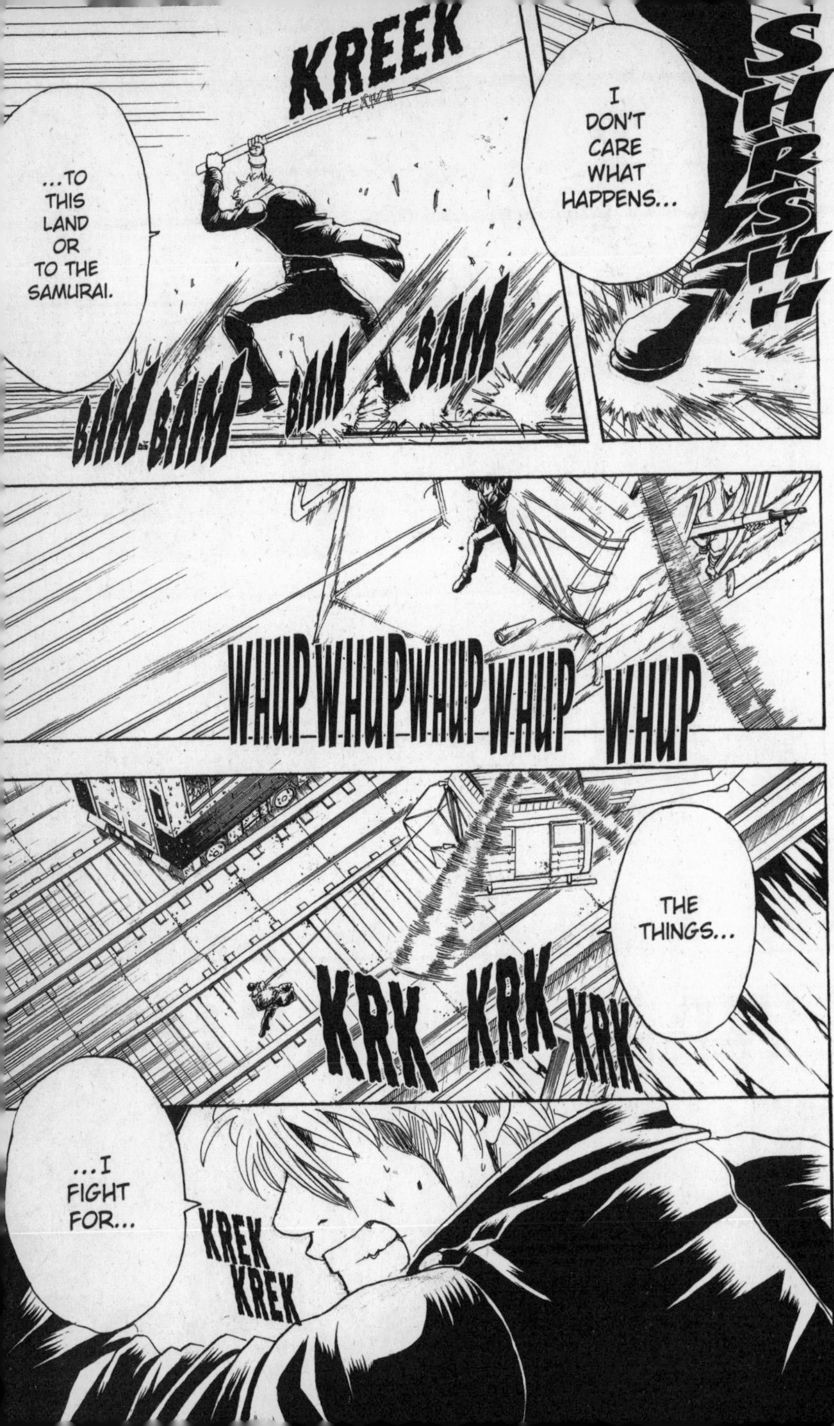

I DON'T CARE WHAT HAPPENS...
SHRSHH!!
KREEK
...TO THIS LAND OR TO THE SAMURAI.
BAM BAM BAM BAM BAM
WHUP WHUP WHUP WHUP WHUP
THE THINGS...
KRK KRK KRK
...I FIGHT FOR...
KREK KREK

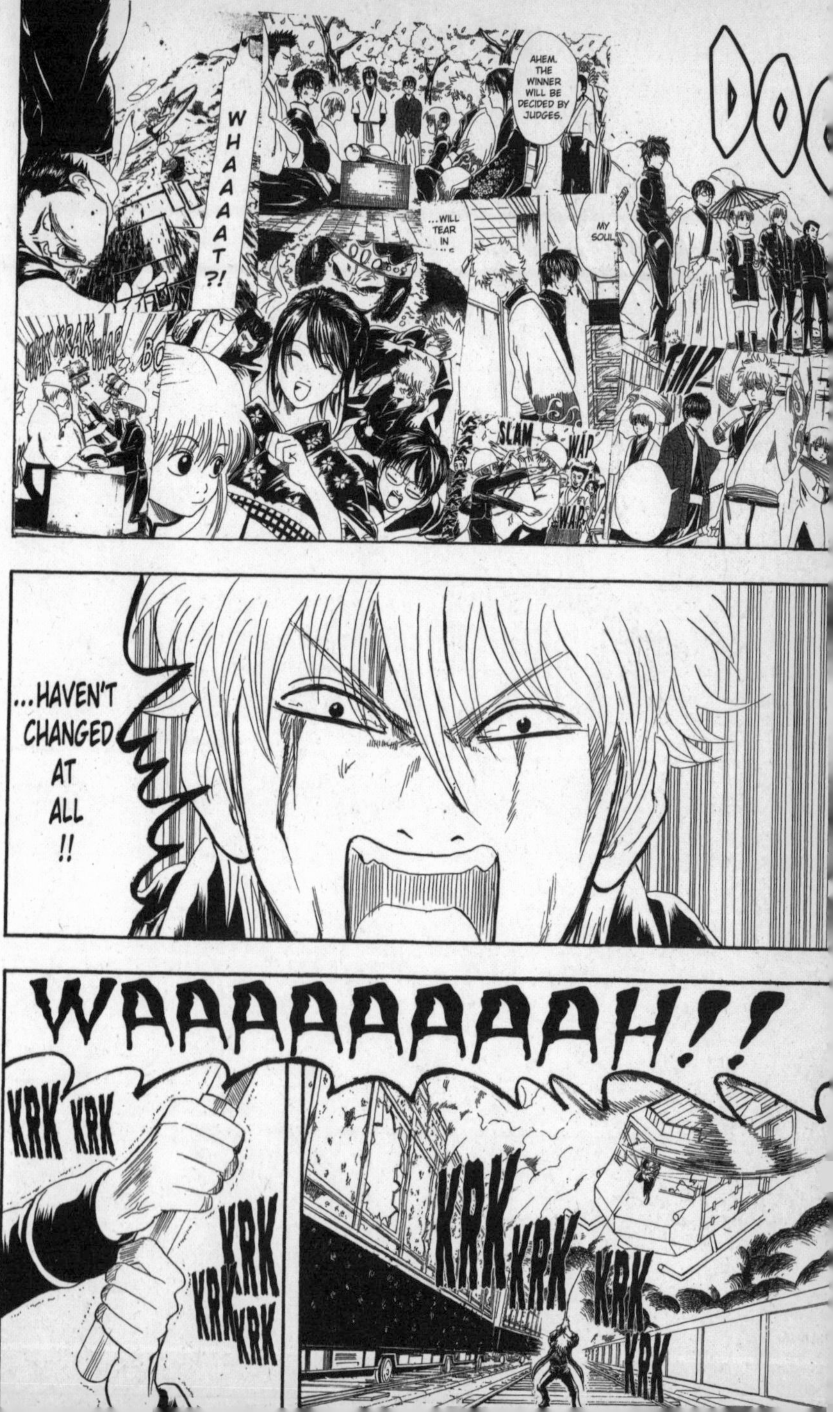
AHEM. THE WINNER WILL BE DECIDED BY JUDGES.
MY SOUL
...WILL TEAR IN
WHAAAAAT?!
THP
WAP
WAP
SLAM
WAK KRAK WAP
...HAVEN'T CHANGED AT ALL !!
WAAAAAAAAH!!
KRK KRK
KRK KRK
KRK KRK
KRK KRK KRK KRK

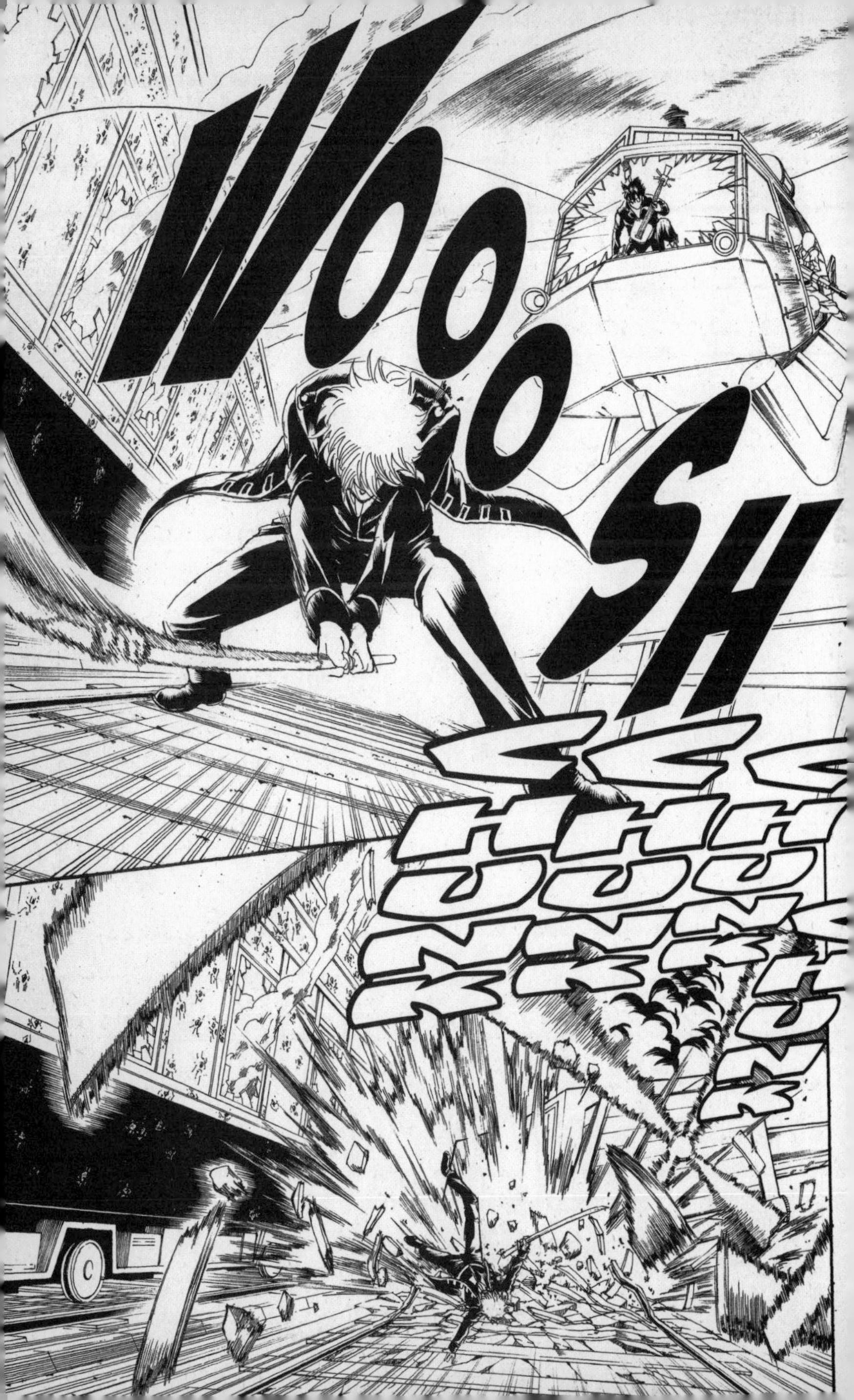
WOOOSH
CHUNK

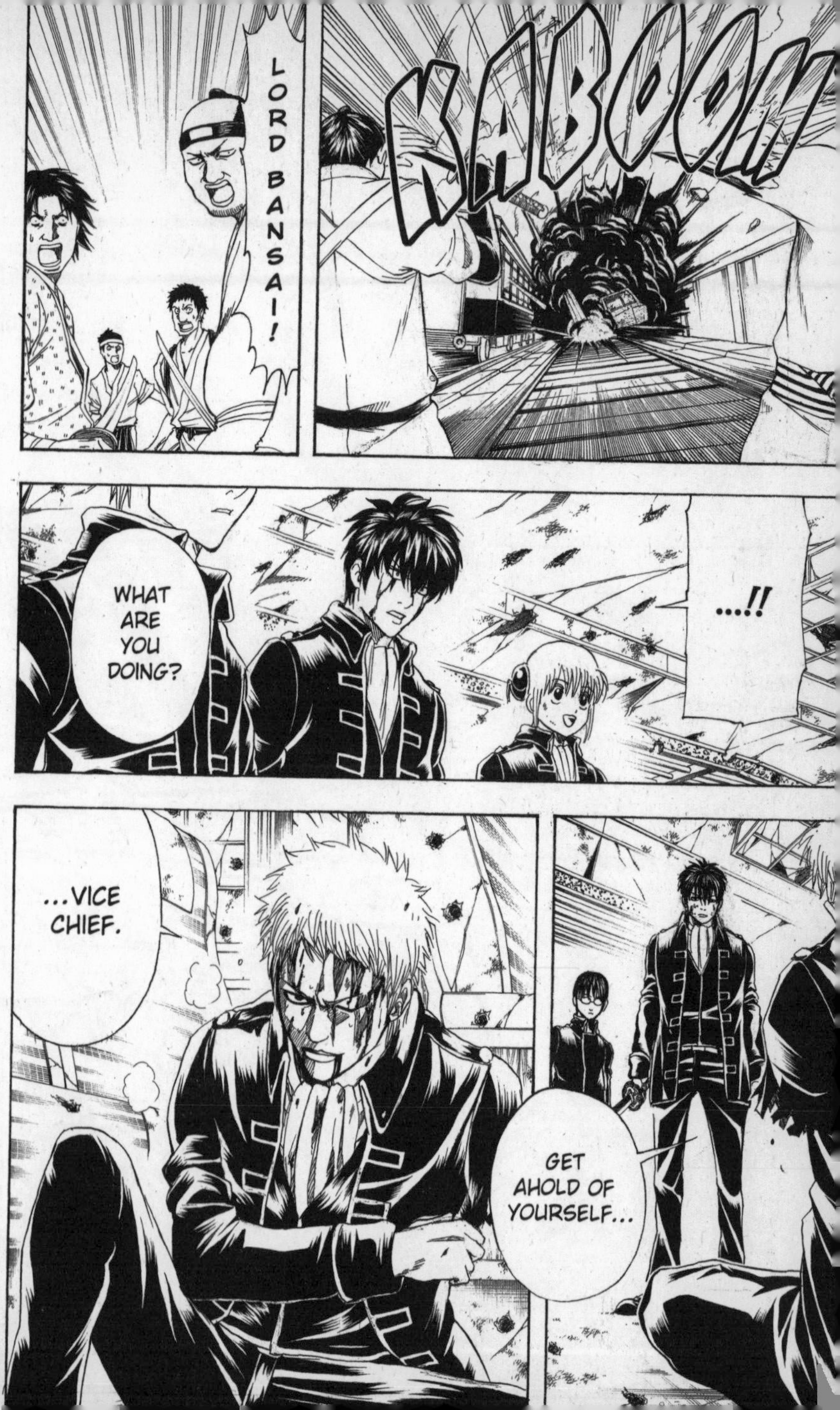
KABOOM
LORD BANSAI!
...!!
WHAT ARE YOU DOING?
GET AHOLD OF YOURSELF...
...VICE CHIEF.

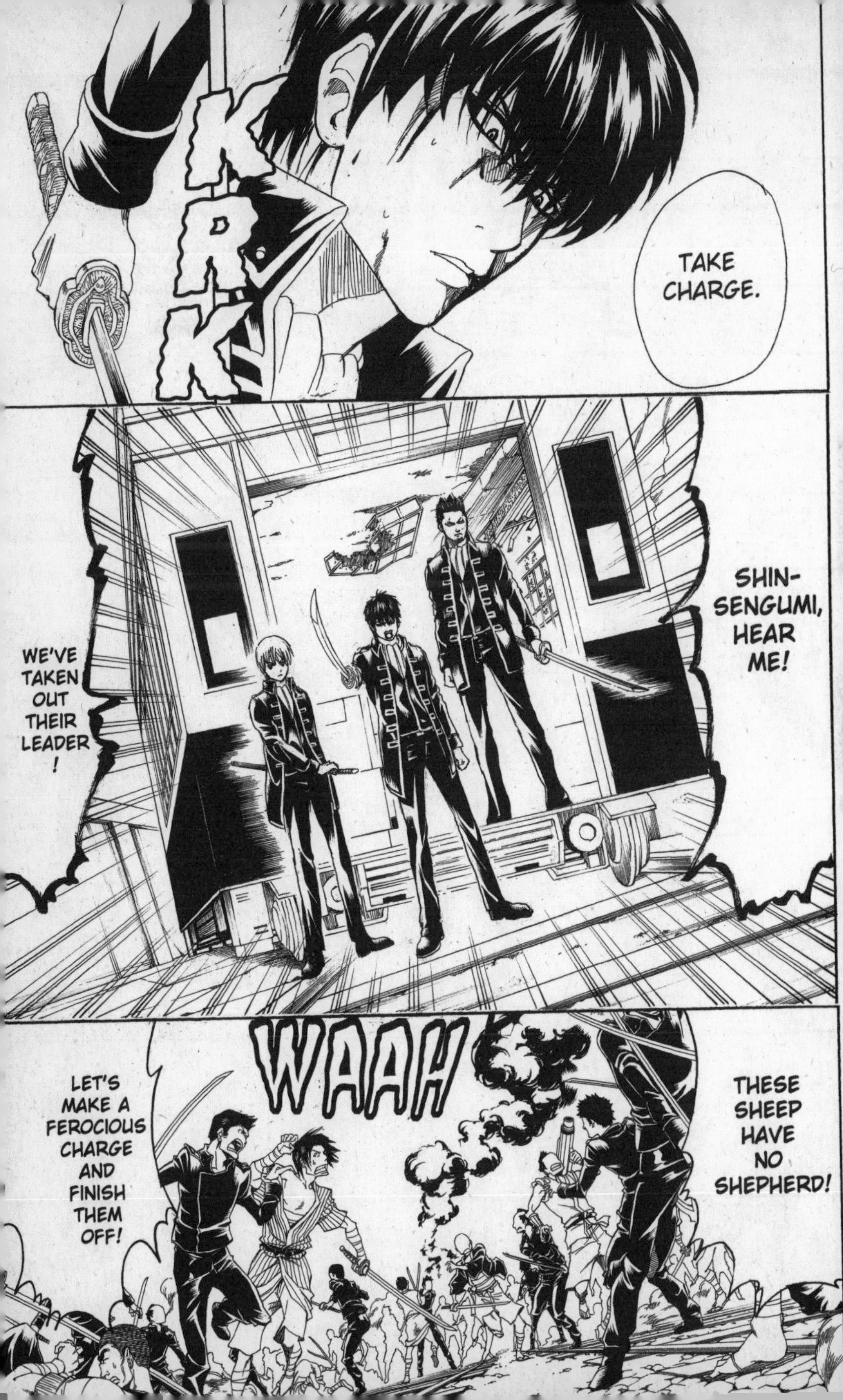

TAKE CHARGE.
KRK
SHIN-SENGUMI, HEAR ME!
WE'VE TAKEN OUT THEIR LEADER!
THESE SHEEP HAVE NO SHEPHERD!
WAAH
LET'S MAKE A FEROCIOUS CHARGE AND FINISH THEM OFF!

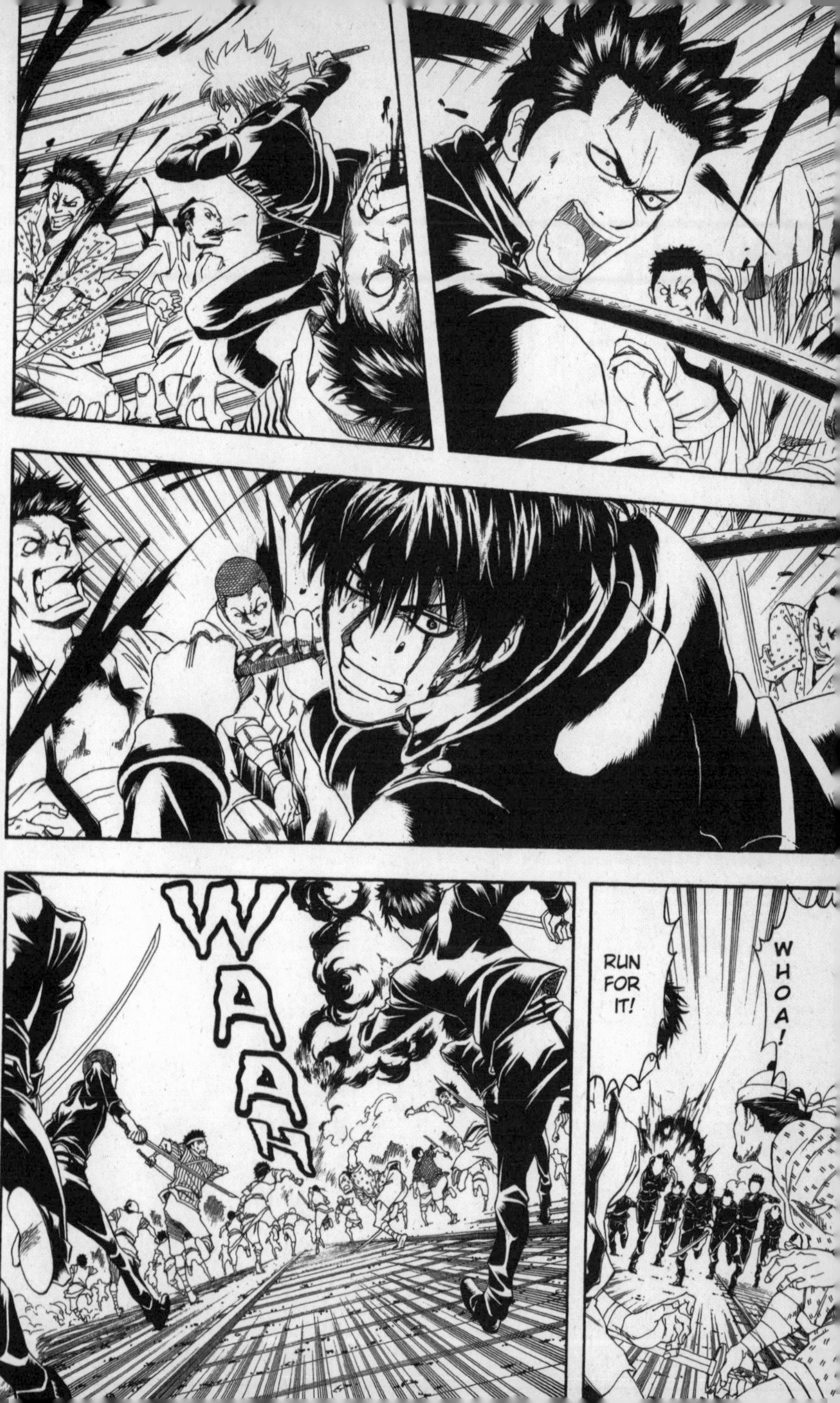
WHOA!
RUN FOR IT!
WAAAH

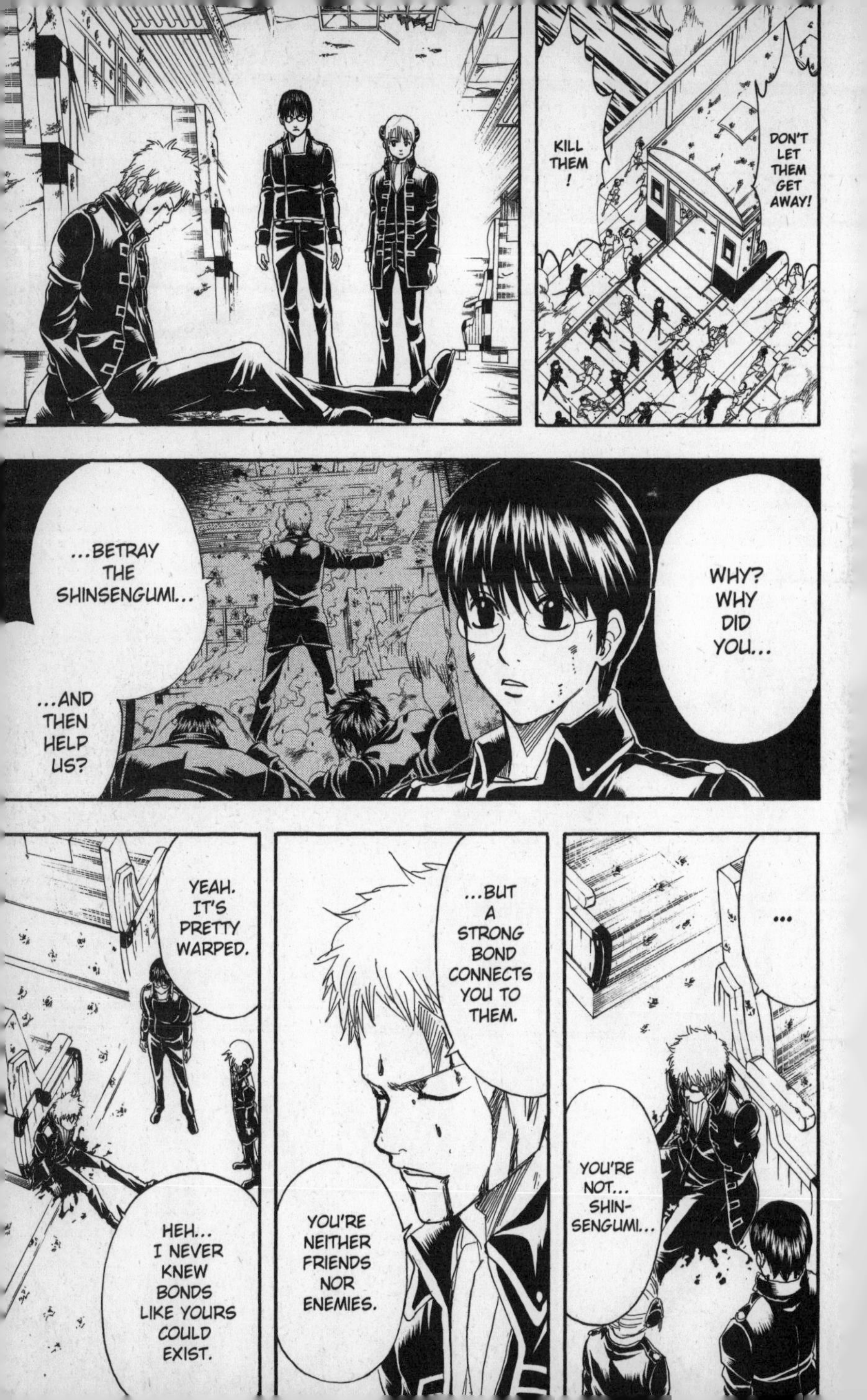
DON'T LET THEM GET AWAY!
KILL THEM !
WHY? WHY DID YOU...
...BETRAY THE SHINSENGUMI...
...AND THEN HELP US?
...
YOU'RE NOT... SHIN-SENGUMI...
...BUT A STRONG BOND CONNECTS YOU TO THEM.
YOU'RE NEITHER FRIENDS NOR ENEMIES.
YEAH. IT'S PRETTY WARPED.
HEH... I NEVER KNEW BONDS LIKE YOURS COULD EXIST.

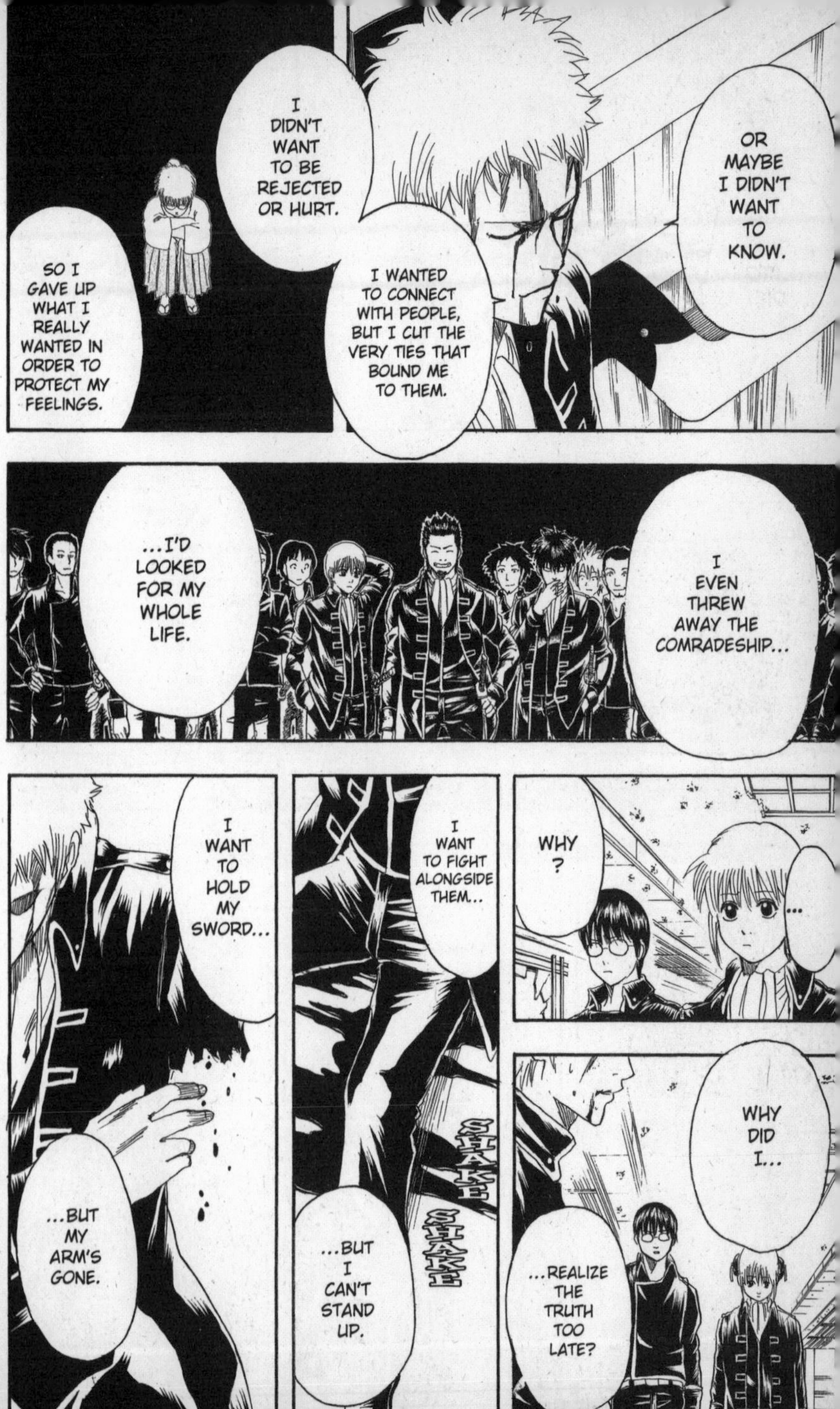
OR MAYBE I DIDN'T WANT TO KNOW.
I DIDN'T WANT TO BE REJECTED OR HURT.
I WANTED TO CONNECT WITH PEOPLE, BUT I CUT THE VERY TIES THAT BOUND ME TO THEM.
SO I GAVE UP WHAT I REALLY WANTED IN ORDER TO PROTECT MY FEELINGS.
I EVEN THREW AWAY THE COMRADESHIP...
...I'D LOOKED FOR MY WHOLE LIFE.
...
WHY?
WHY DID I...
...REALIZE THE TRUTH TOO LATE?
I WANT TO FIGHT ALONGSIDE THEM...
SHAKE
SHAKE
...BUT I CAN'T STAND UP.
I WANT TO HOLD MY SWORD...
...BUT MY ARM'S GONE.

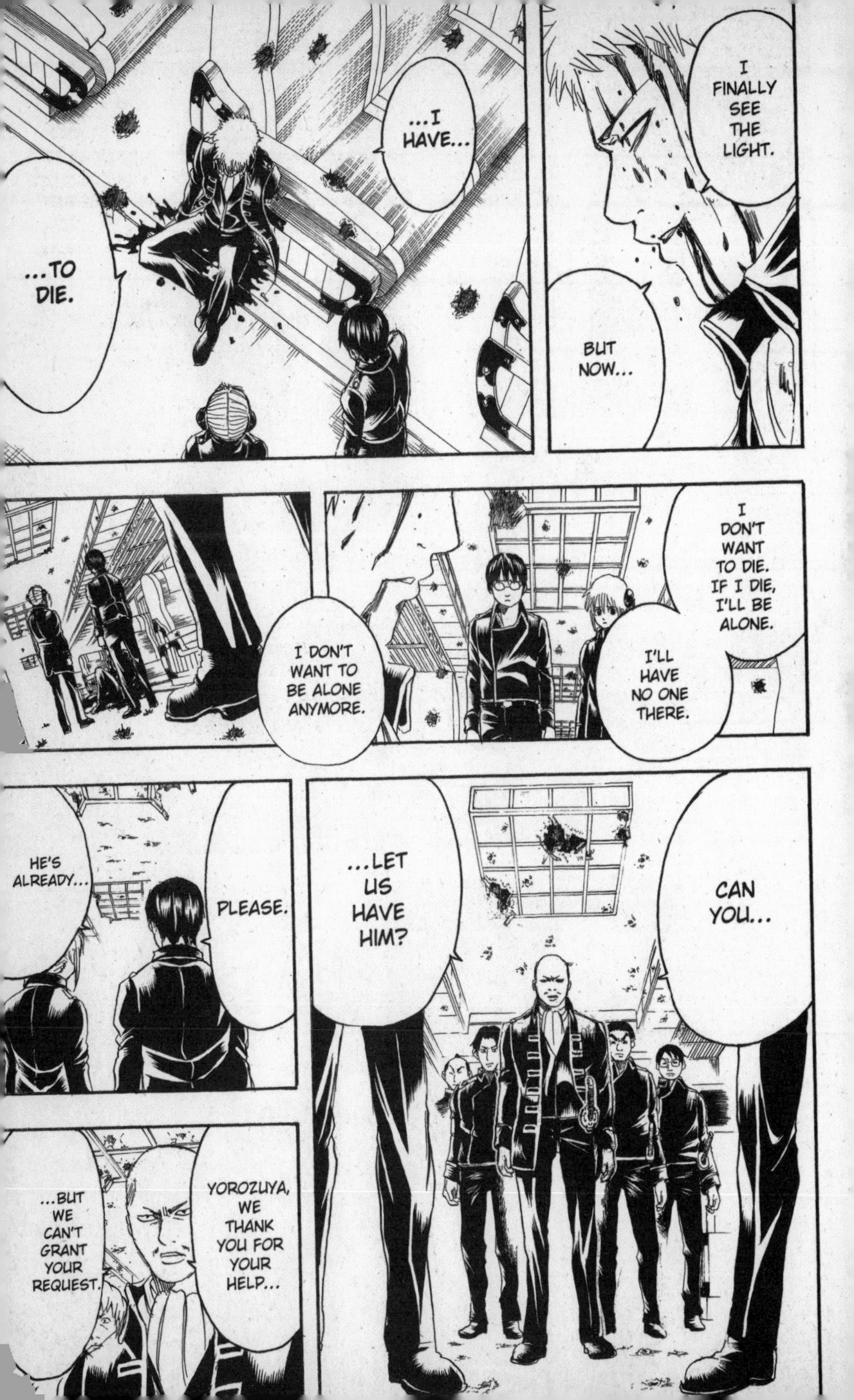
I FINALLY SEE THE LIGHT.
BUT NOW...
...I HAVE...
...TO DIE.
I DON'T WANT TO DIE. IF I DIE, I'LL BE ALONE.
I'LL HAVE NO ONE THERE.
I DON'T WANT TO BE ALONE ANYMORE.
CAN YOU...
...LET US HAVE HIM?
PLEASE.
HE'S ALREADY...
YOROZUYA, WE THANK YOU FOR YOUR HELP...
...BUT WE CAN'T GRANT YOUR REQUEST.

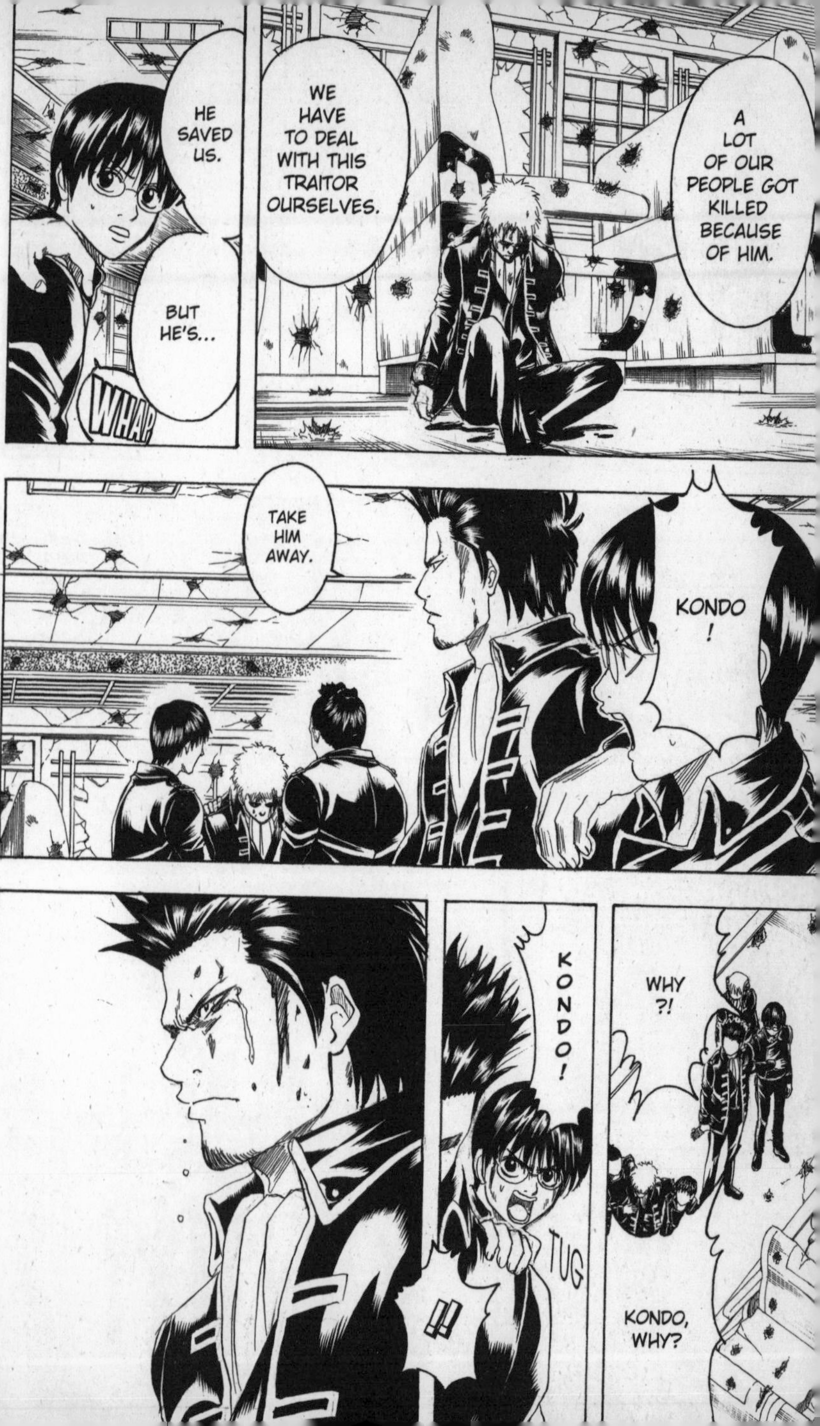
A LOT OF OUR PEOPLE GOT KILLED BECAUSE OF HIM.
WE HAVE TO DEAL WITH THIS TRAITOR OURSELVES.
HE SAVED US.
BUT HE'S...
WHAP
KONDO!
TAKE HIM AWAY.
WHY?!
KONDO, WHY?
KONDO!
TUG
!!

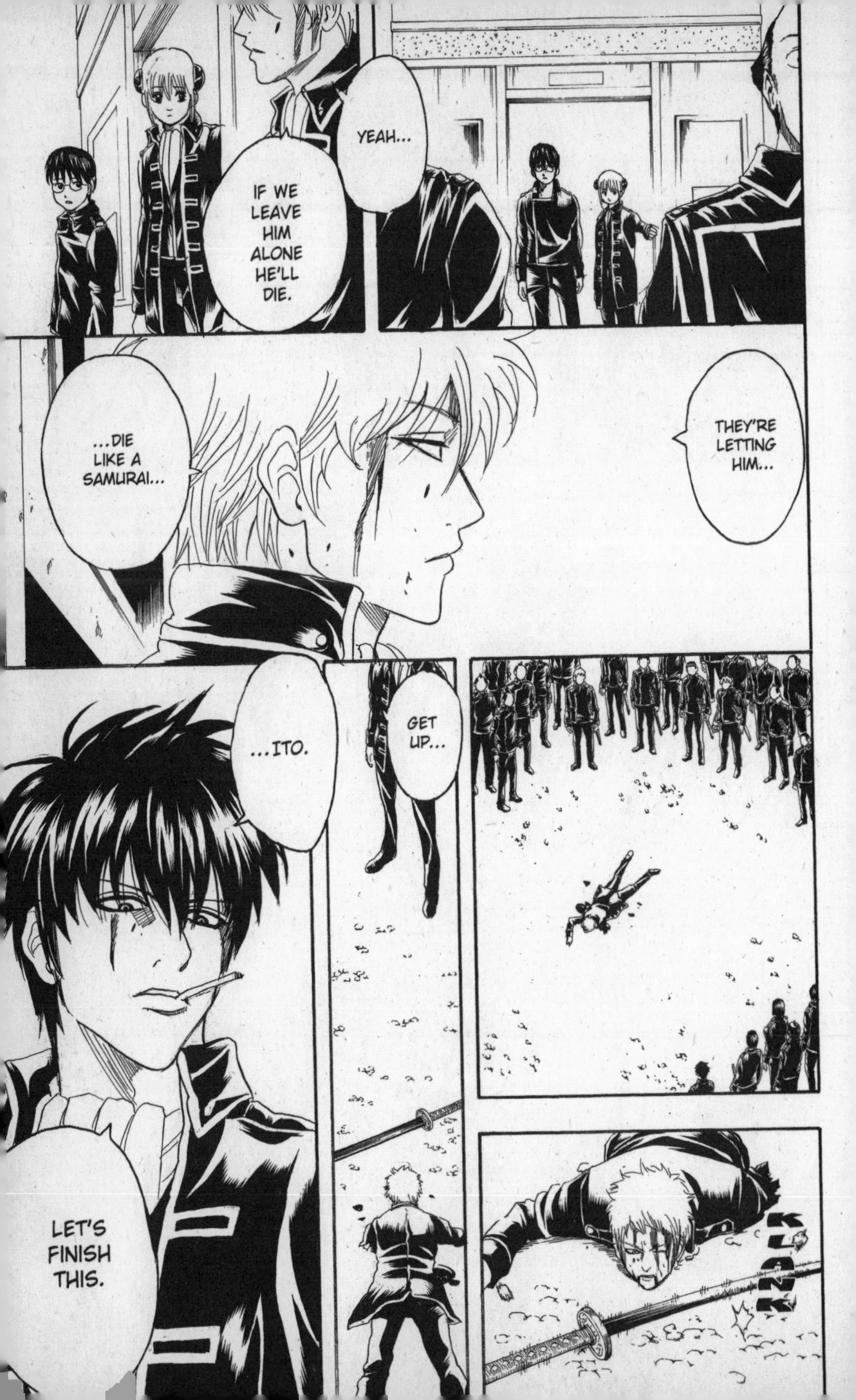
YEAH...
IF WE LEAVE HIM ALONE HE'LL DIE.
THEY'RE LETTING HIM...
...DIE LIKE A SAMURAI...
KLANK
GET UP...
...ITO.
LET'S FINISH THIS.

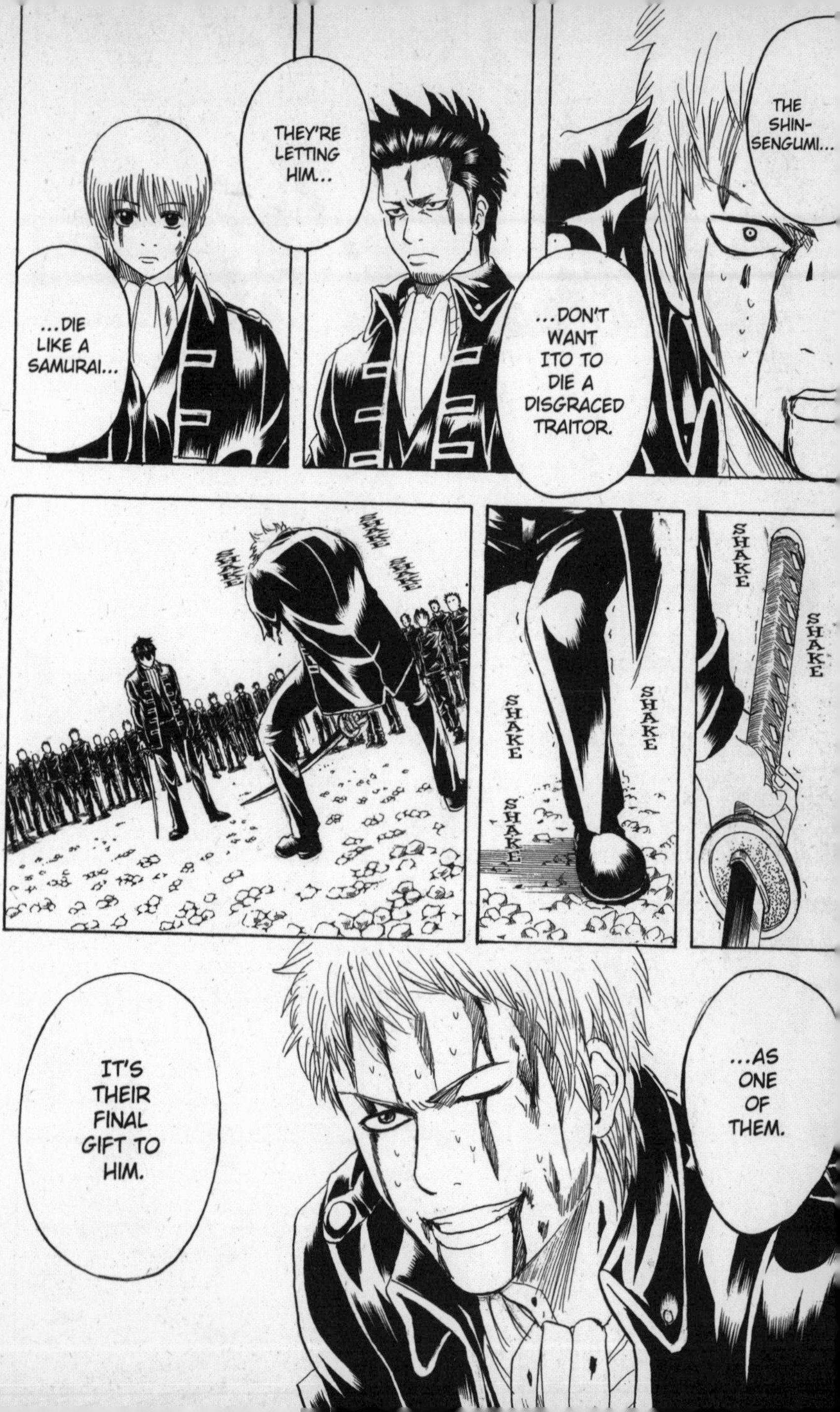
THE SHIN-SENGUMI...
...DON'T WANT ITO TO DIE A DISGRACED TRAITOR.
THEY'RE LETTING HIM...
...DIE LIKE A SAMURAI...
SHAKE
SHAKE
SHAKE
SHAKE
SHAKE
SHAKE
SHAKE
SHAKE
...AS ONE OF THEM.
IT'S THEIR FINAL GIFT TO HIM.

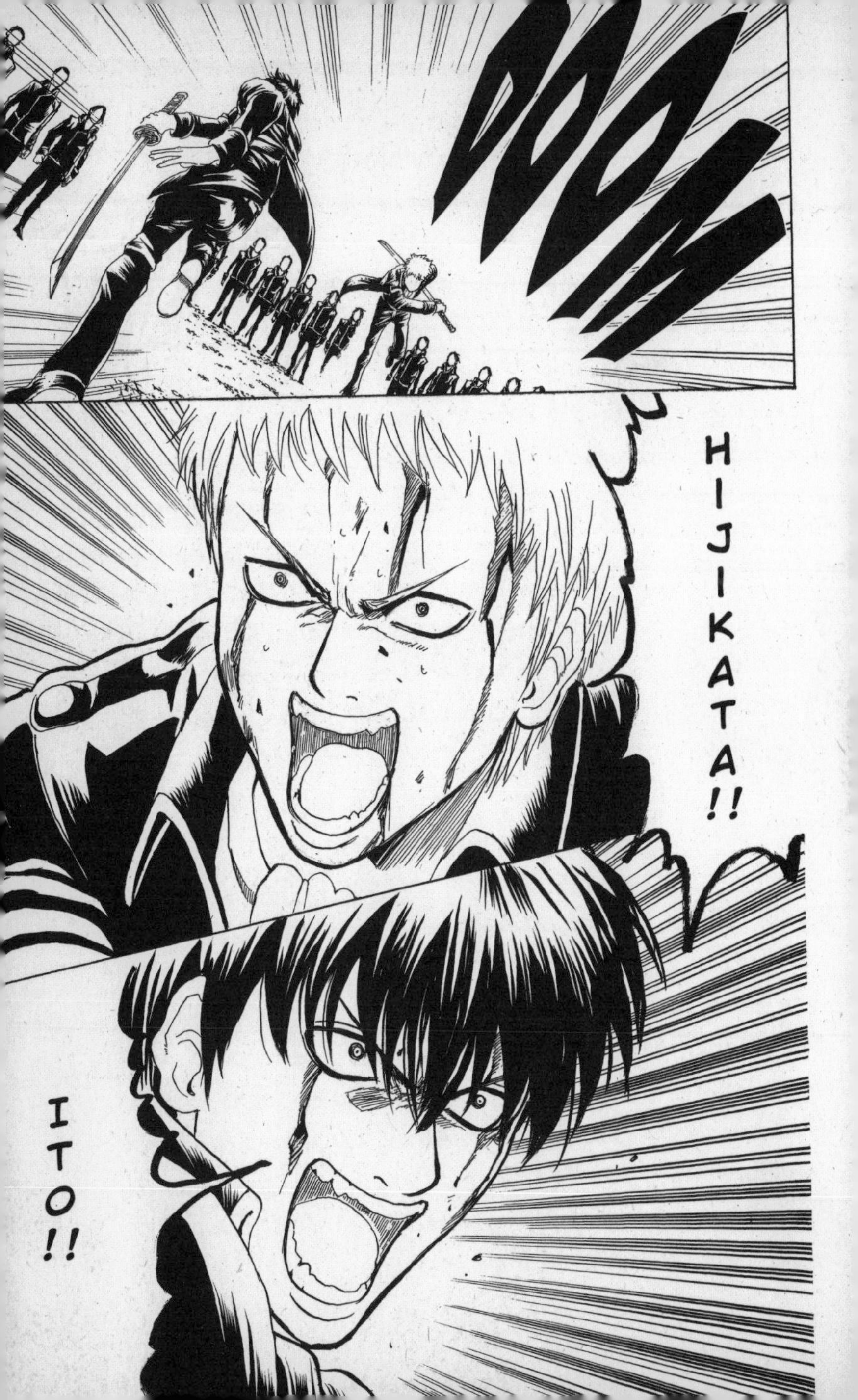
HIJIKATA!!
ITO!!

Thank you for purchasing *Gin Tama* Volume 20. One of my editors appears as Konishi in the 169th chapter in this volume. I actually drew that episode for Editor Oonishi's wedding reception because Yoshida, the editor who was organizing it, said to me, "Can you do something for him, Sorachi?" Yoshida came to the company the same year Oonishi did. He's a shrewd, good-looking guy who's edited *Death Note* and *D.Gray-man*. But apparently he only cares about manga he works on because he had the audacity to ask me, "Can you do an episode where Oonishi proposes to his fiancée in *Gin Tama*?" I said, "Hold on. I could, but the readers don't know Oonishi. It would just be a big inside joke for the staff." I thought this was a reasonable reply, but he just said, "It'll be okay. It's *Gin Tama*." People who were born in 1978 really are no good. On top of that, I was working on another story, the one about Ito and the Shinsengumi, and Yoshida wanted me to drop everything and do it so that they could present it at the wedding reception. Basically Yoshida was trying to obstruct my business. Seriously, people born in 1978 should be glad I don't have the *Death Note*.

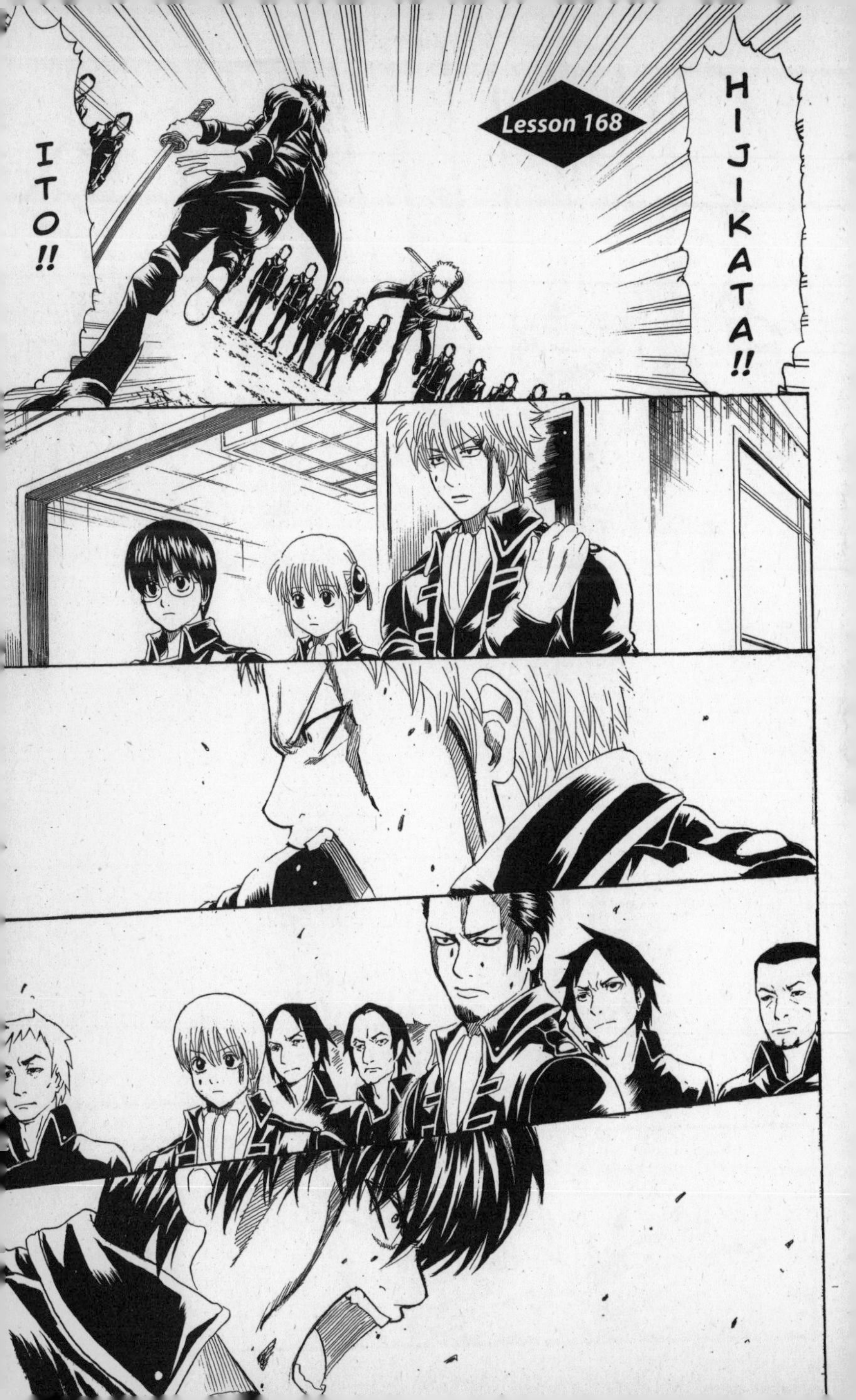
HIJIKATA!!
Lesson 168
ITO!!

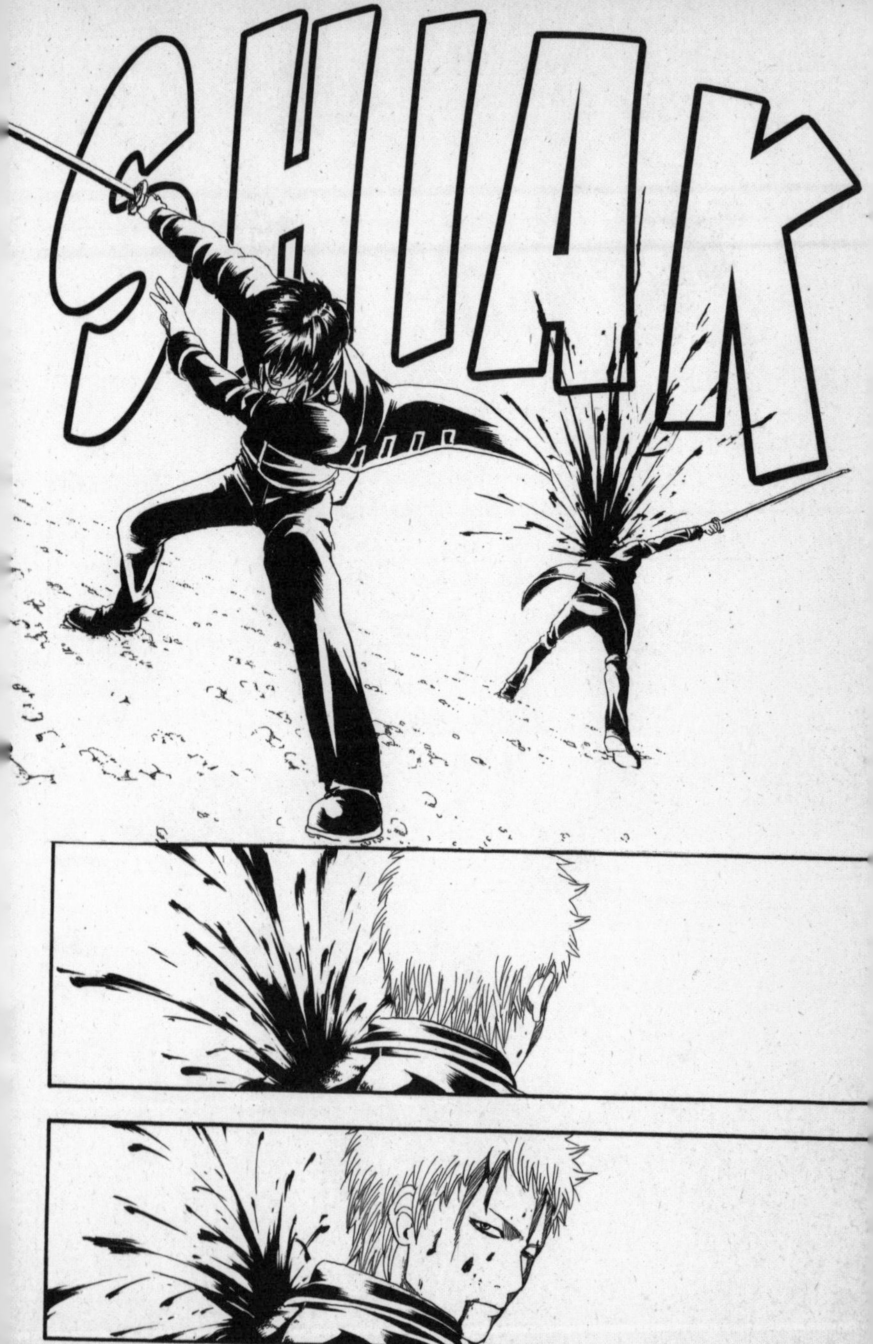
SHIAK

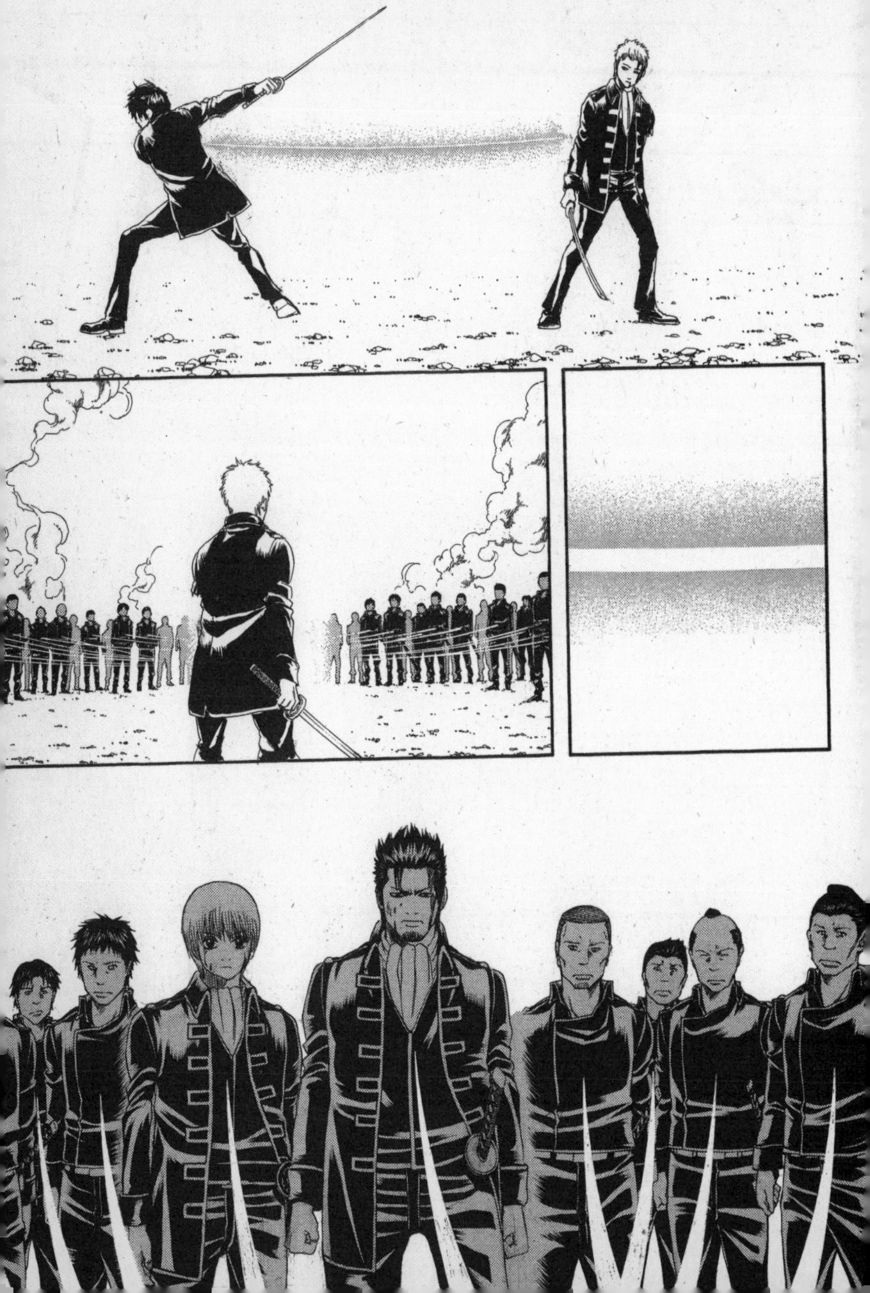

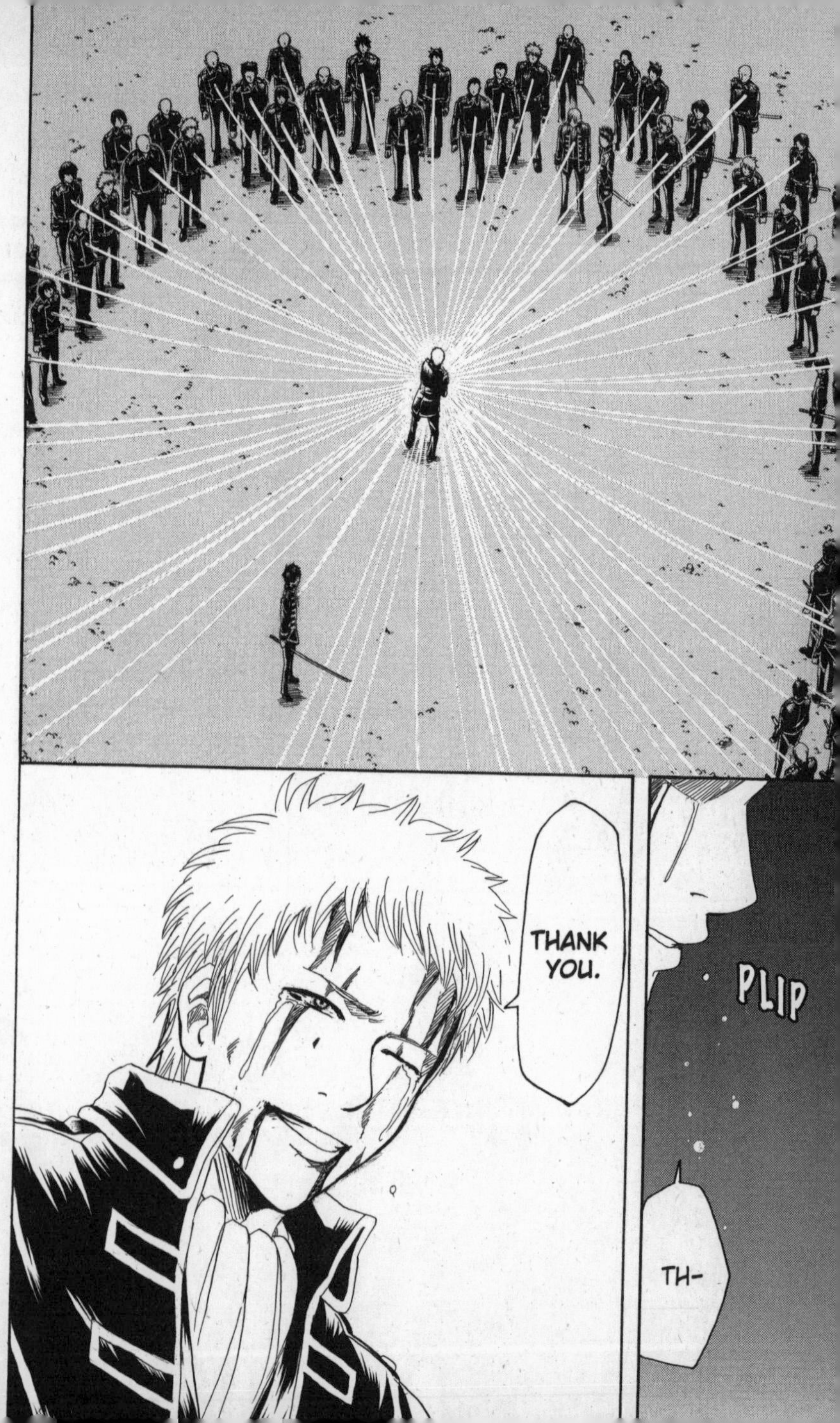
PLIP
TH-
THANK YOU.

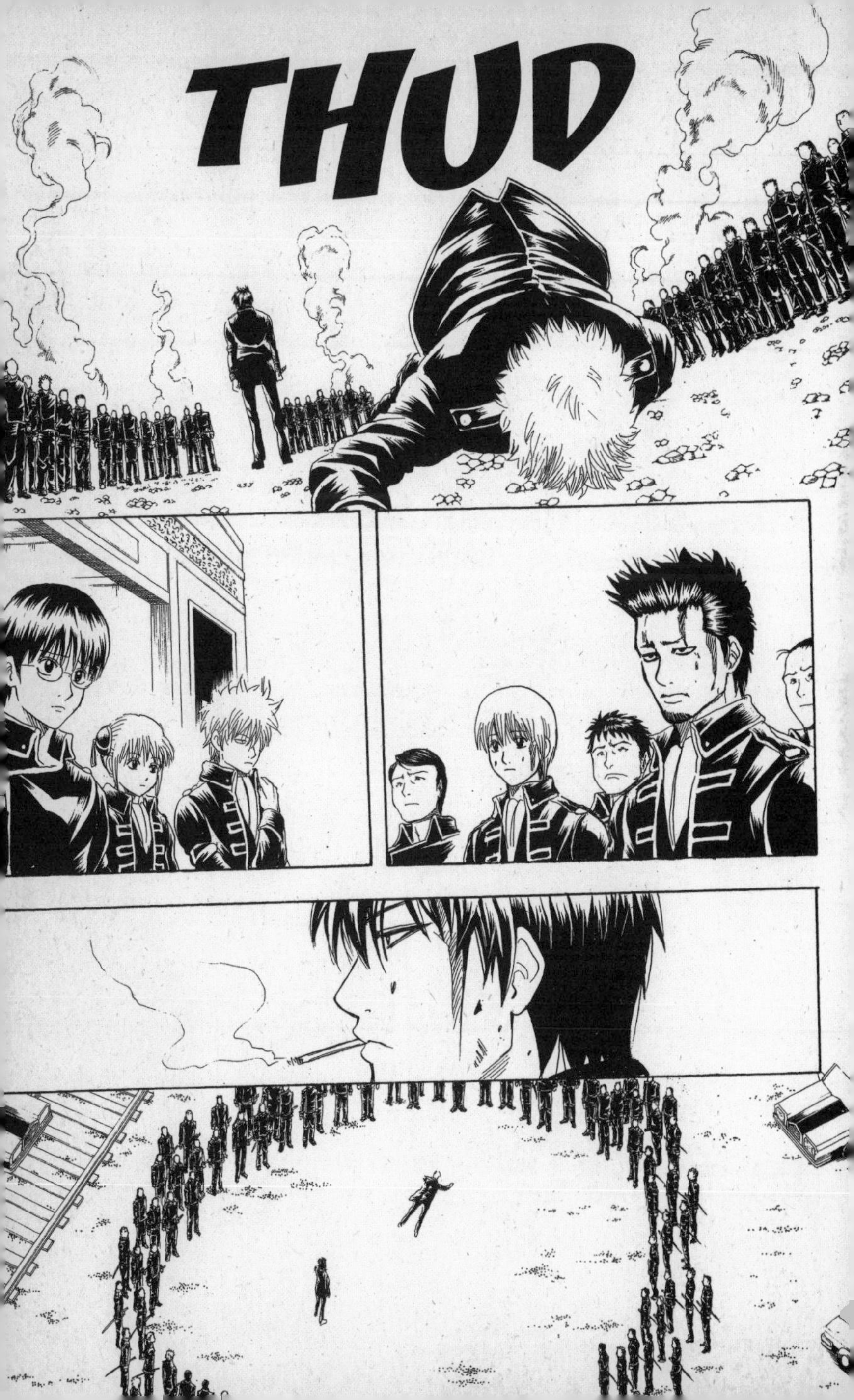
THUD

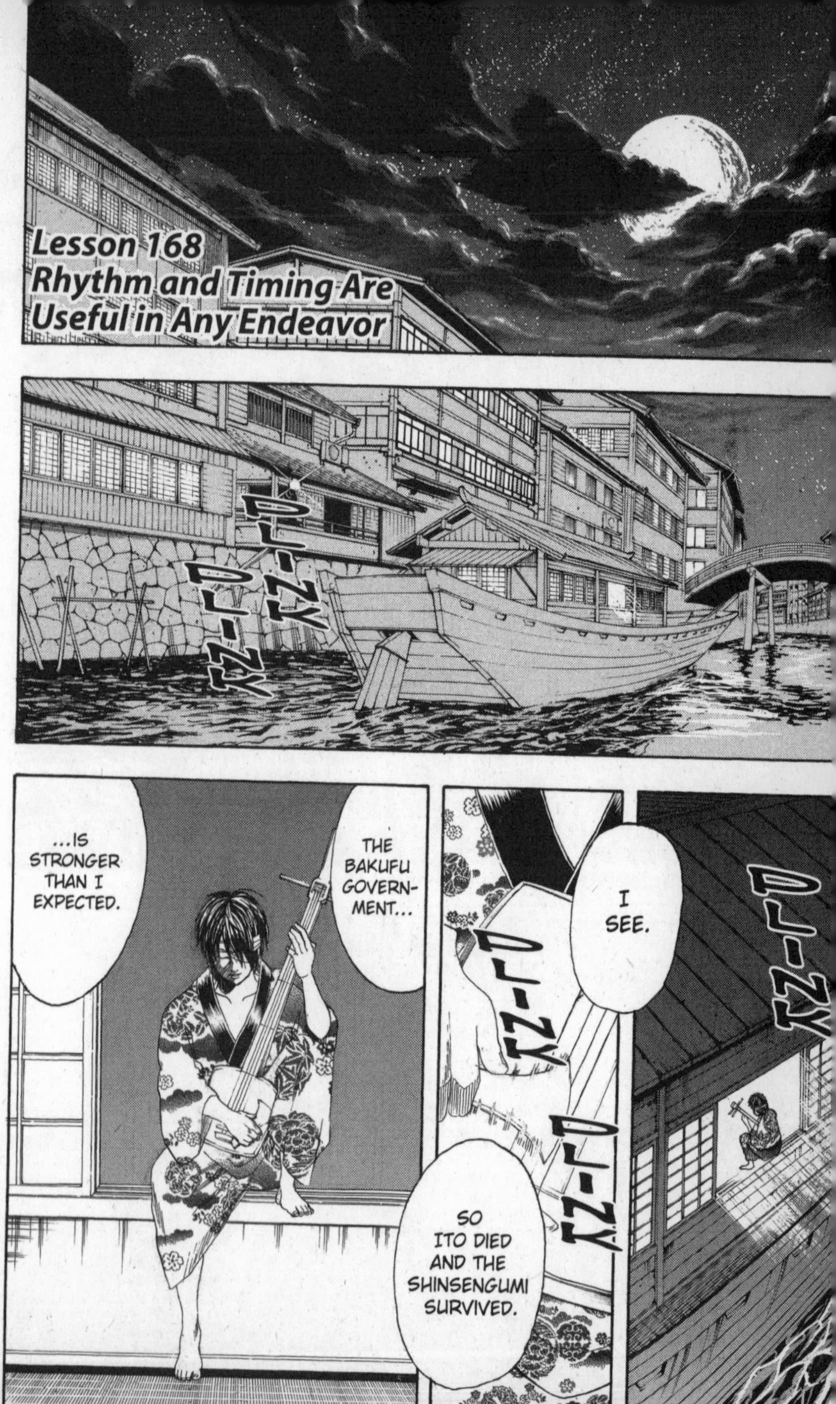
Lesson 168
Rhythm and Timing Are Useful in Any Endeavor
PLINK
PLINK
PLINK
I SEE.
PLINK
PLINK
SO ITO DIED AND THE SHINSENGUMI SURVIVED.
THE BAKUFU GOVERNMENT...
...IS STRONGER THAN I EXPECTED.

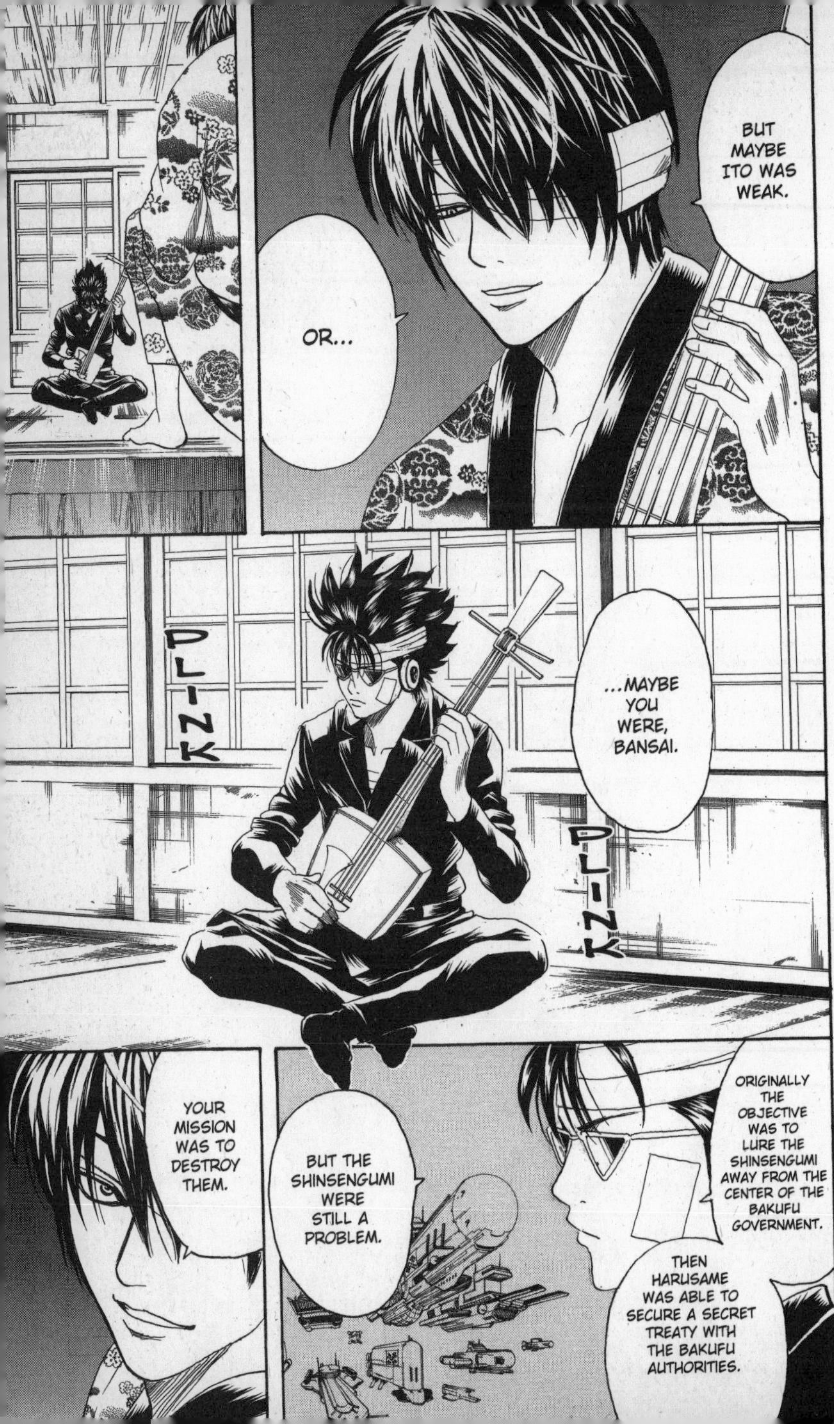
BUT MAYBE ITO WAS WEAK.
OR...
...MAYBE YOU WERE, BANSAI.
PLINK
PLINK
ORIGINALLY THE OBJECTIVE WAS TO LURE THE SHINSENGUMI AWAY FROM THE CENTER OF THE BAKUFU GOVERNMENT.
THEN HARUSAME WAS ABLE TO SECURE A SECRET TREATY WITH THE BAKUFU AUTHORITIES.
BUT THE SHINSENGUMI WERE STILL A PROBLEM.
YOUR MISSION WAS TO DESTROY THEM.

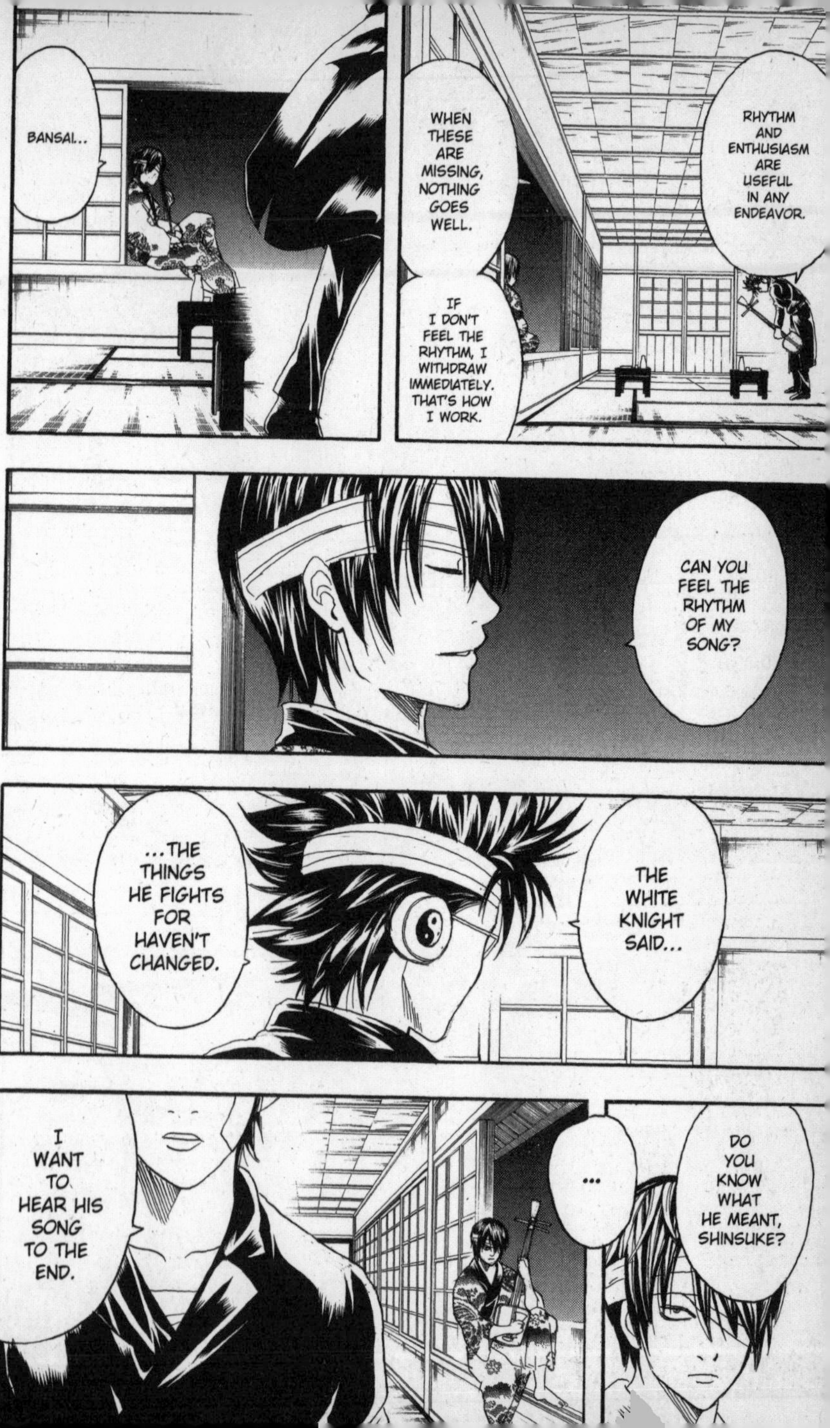
RHYTHM AND ENTHUSIASM ARE USEFUL IN ANY ENDEAVOR.
WHEN THESE ARE MISSING, NOTHING GOES WELL.
IF I DON'T FEEL THE RHYTHM, I WITHDRAW IMMEDIATELY. THAT'S HOW I WORK.
BANSAI...
CAN YOU FEEL THE RHYTHM OF MY SONG?
THE WHITE KNIGHT SAID...
...THE THINGS HE FIGHTS FOR HAVEN'T CHANGED.
DO YOU KNOW WHAT HE MEANT, SHINSUKE?
...
I WANT TO HEAR HIS SONG TO THE END.

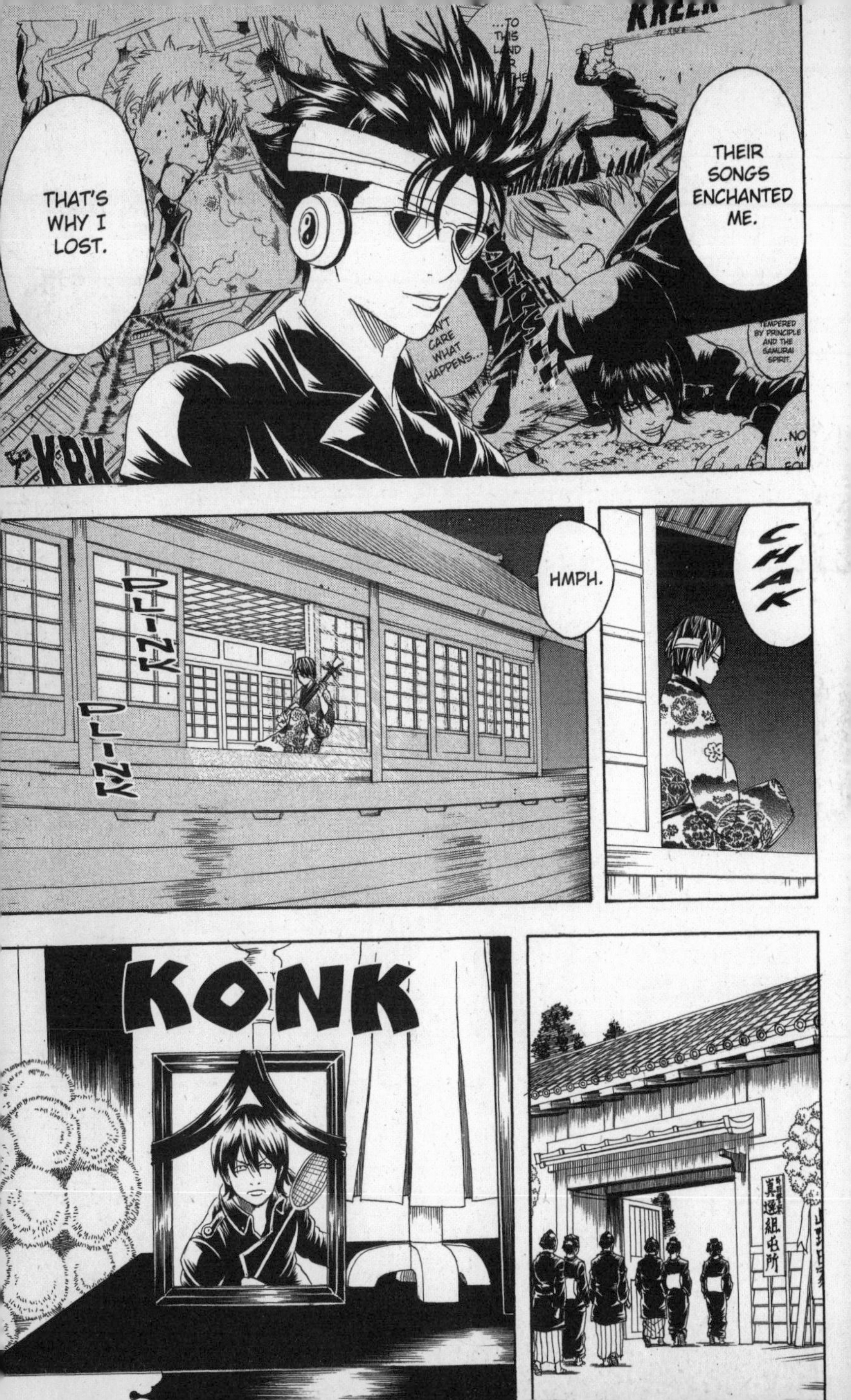
THEIR SONGS ENCHANTED ME.
TEMPERED BY PRINCIPLE AND THE SAMURAI SPIRIT.
THAT'S WHY I LOST.
KRK
CHAK
HMPH.
PLINK
PLINK
真選組屯所
KONK

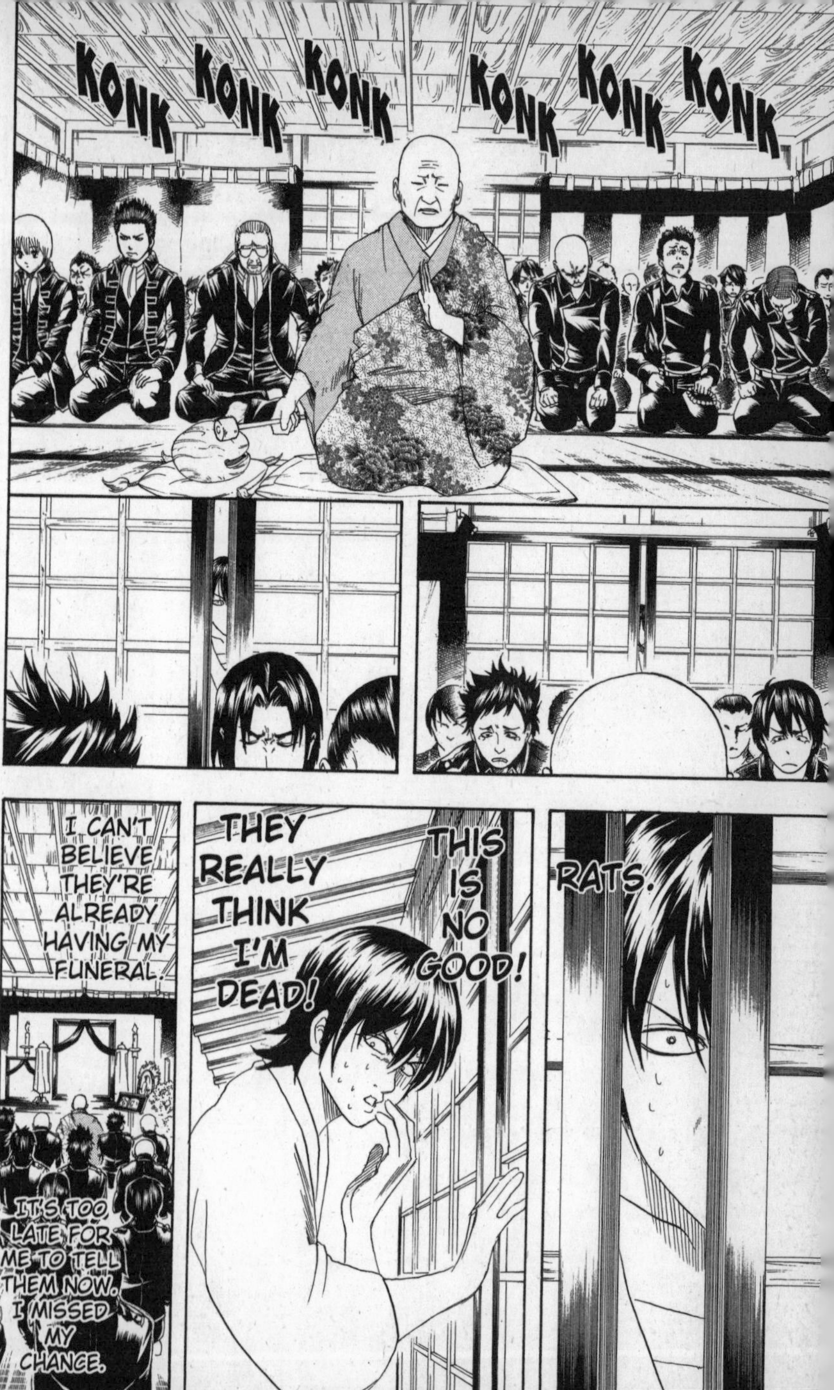
KONK KONK KONK KONK KONK KONK
RATS.
THIS IS NO GOOD!
THEY REALLY THINK I'M DEAD!
I CAN'T BELIEVE THEY'RE ALREADY HAVING MY FUNERAL.
IT'S TOO LATE FOR ME TO TELL THEM NOW. I MISSED MY CHANCE.

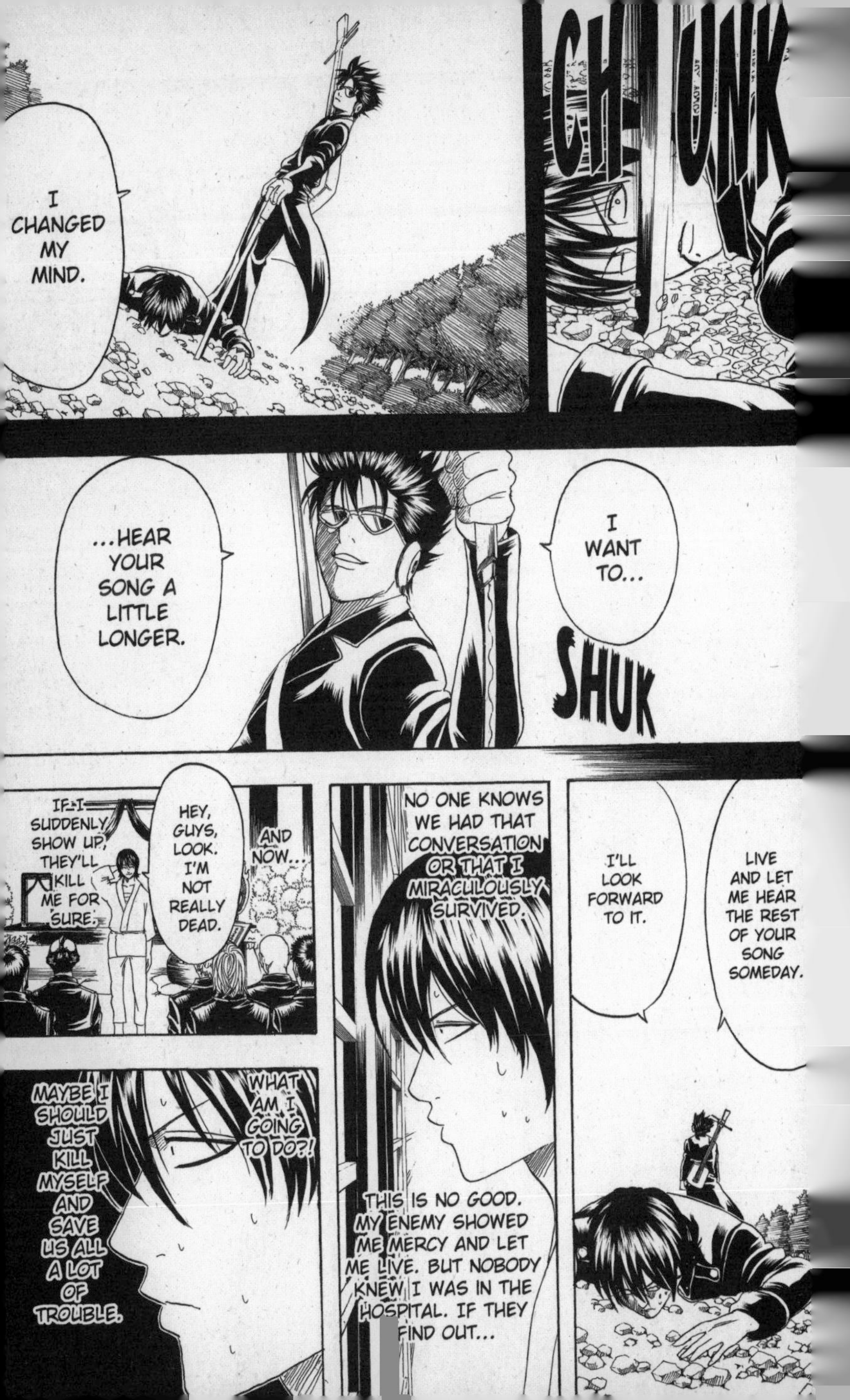

CHUNK
I CHANGED MY MIND.
I WANT TO...
...HEAR YOUR SONG A LITTLE LONGER.
SHUK
LIVE AND LET ME HEAR THE REST OF YOUR SONG SOMEDAY.
I'LL LOOK FORWARD TO IT.
NO ONE KNOWS WE HAD THAT CONVERSATION OR THAT I MIRACULOUSLY SURVIVED.
THIS IS NO GOOD. MY ENEMY SHOWED ME MERCY AND LET ME LIVE. BUT NOBODY KNEW I WAS IN THE HOSPITAL. IF THEY FIND OUT...
AND NOW...
HEY, GUYS, LOOK. I'M NOT REALLY DEAD.
IF I SUDDENLY SHOW UP, THEY'LL KILL ME FOR SURE.
WHAT AM I GOING TO DO?!
MAYBE I SHOULD JUST KILL MYSELF AND SAVE US ALL A LOT OF TROUBLE.

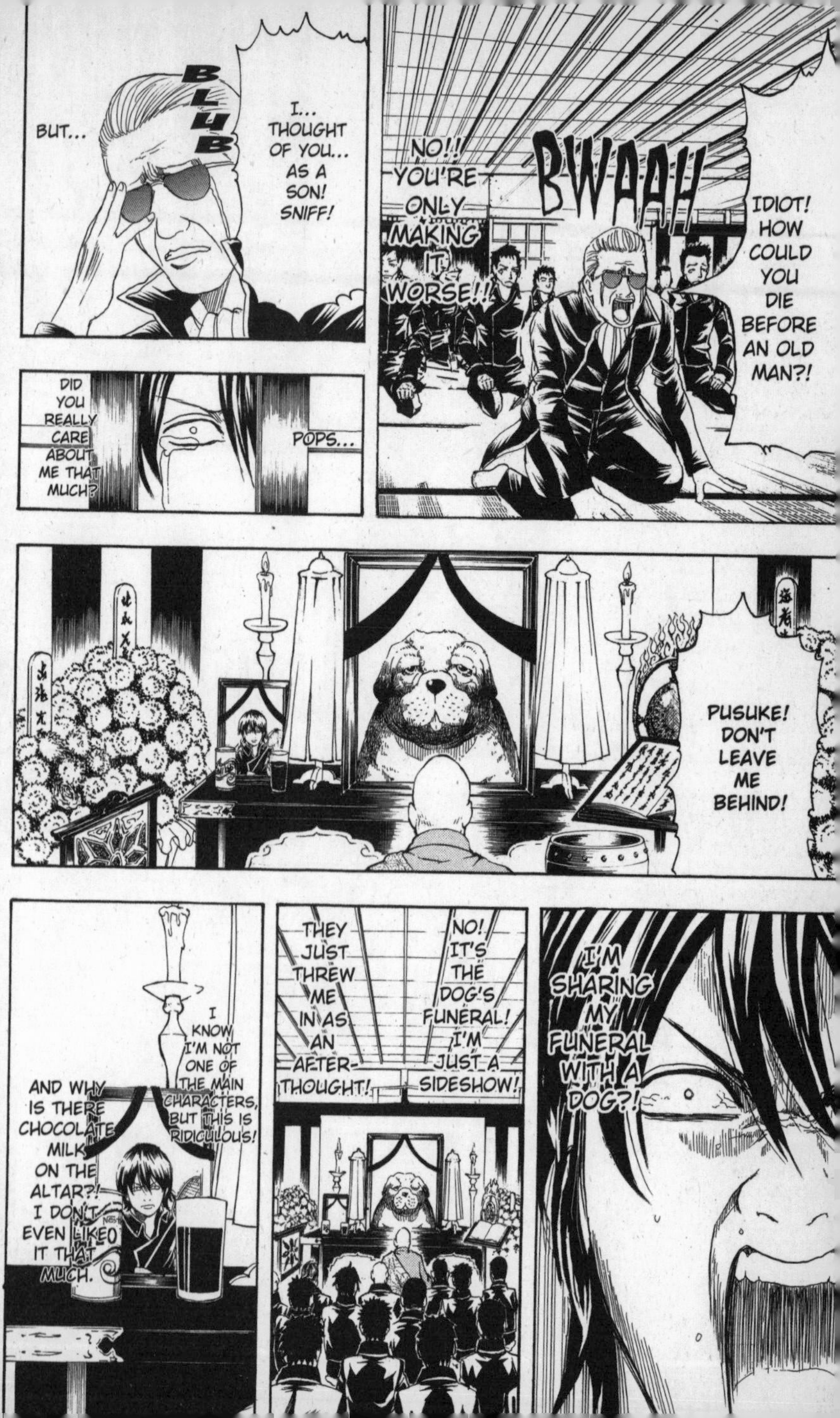
IDIOT! HOW COULD YOU DIE BEFORE AN OLD MAN?!
BWAAH
NO!! YOU'RE ONLY MAKING IT WORSE!!
I... THOUGHT OF YOU... AS A SON! SNIFF!
BLUB
BUT...
POPS...
DID YOU REALLY CARE ABOUT ME THAT MUCH?
PUSUKE! DON'T LEAVE ME BEHIND!
I'M SHARING MY FUNERAL WITH A DOG?!
NO! IT'S THE DOG'S FUNERAL! I'M JUST A SIDESHOW!
THEY JUST THREW ME IN AS AN AFTER-THOUGHT!
I KNOW I'M NOT ONE OF THE MAIN CHARACTERS, BUT THIS IS RIDICULOUS!
AND WHY IS THERE CHOCOLATE MILK ON THE ALTAR?! I DON'T EVEN LIKE IT THAT MUCH.

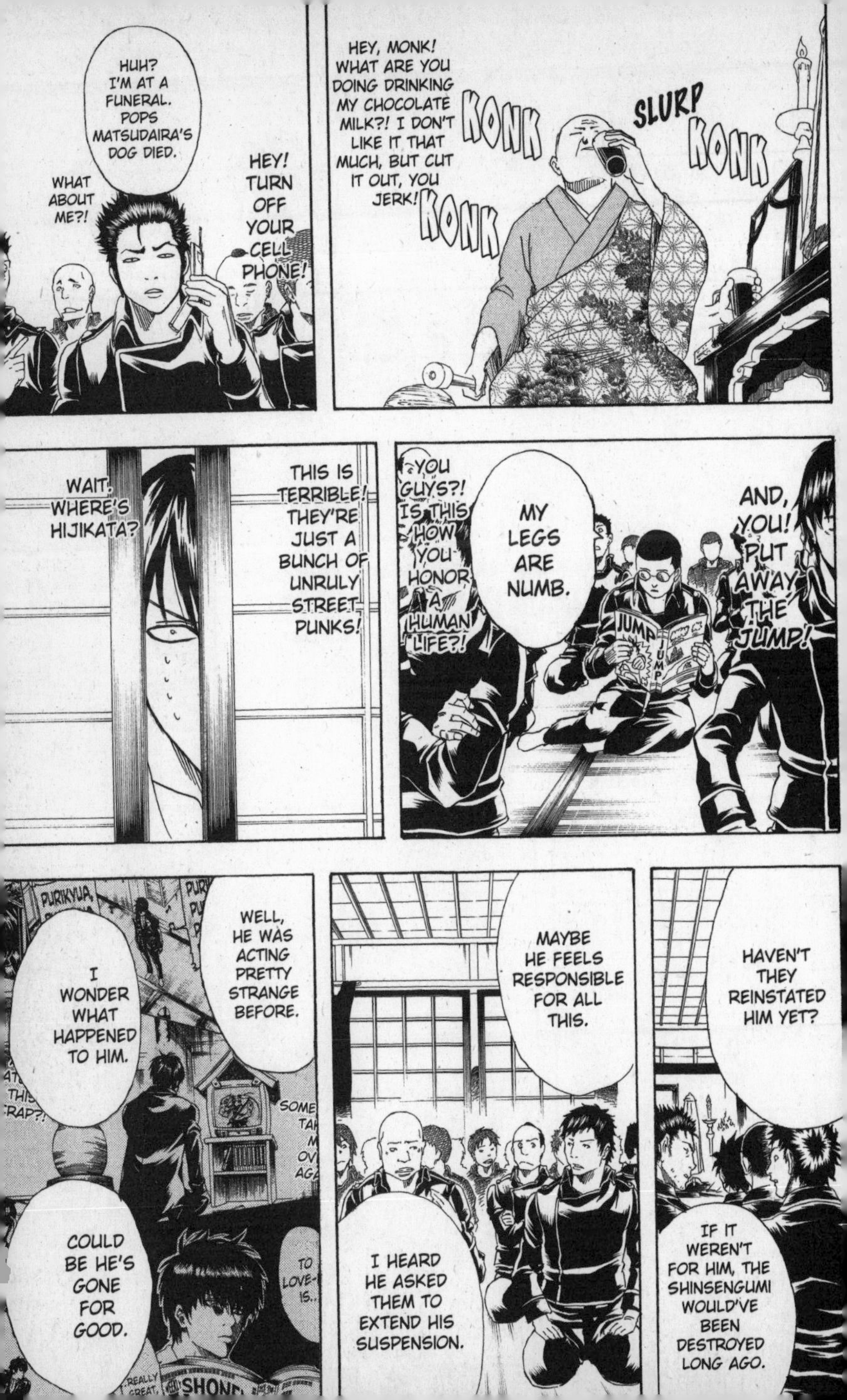
HEY, MONK! WHAT ARE YOU DOING DRINKING MY CHOCOLATE MILK?! I DON'T LIKE IT THAT MUCH, BUT CUT IT OUT, YOU JERK!
KONK
SLURP
KONK
KONK
HUH? I'M AT A FUNERAL. POPS MATSUDAIRA'S DOG DIED.
HEY! TURN OFF YOUR CELL PHONE!
WHAT ABOUT ME?!
AND, YOU! PUT AWAY THE JUMP!
MY LEGS ARE NUMB.
YOU GUYS?! IS THIS HOW YOU HONOR A HUMAN LIFE?!
JUMP
THIS IS TERRIBLE! THEY'RE JUST A BUNCH OF UNRULY STREET PUNKS!
WAIT! WHERE'S HIJIKATA?
HAVEN'T THEY REINSTATED HIM YET?
IF IT WEREN'T FOR HIM, THE SHINSENGUMI WOULD'VE BEEN DESTROYED LONG AGO.
MAYBE HE FEELS RESPONSIBLE FOR ALL THIS.
I HEARD HE ASKED THEM TO EXTEND HIS SUSPENSION.
WELL, HE WAS ACTING PRETTY STRANGE BEFORE.
I WONDER WHAT HAPPENED TO HIM.
COULD BE HE'S GONE FOR GOOD.

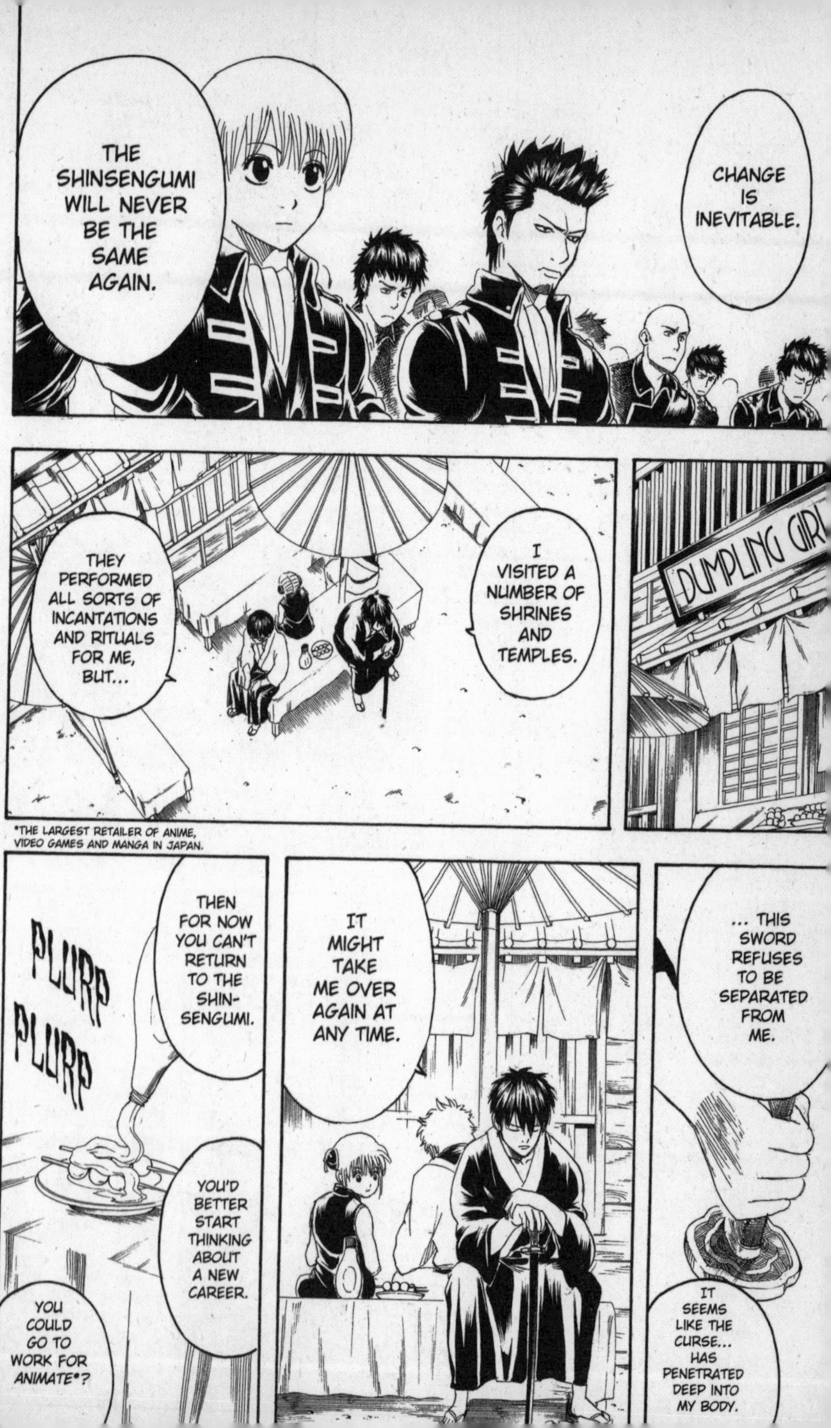
CHANGE IS INEVITABLE.
THE SHINSENGUMI WILL NEVER BE THE SAME AGAIN.
DUMPLING GIRL
I VISITED A NUMBER OF SHRINES AND TEMPLES.
THEY PERFORMED ALL SORTS OF INCANTATIONS AND RITUALS FOR ME, BUT...
... THIS SWORD REFUSES TO BE SEPARATED FROM ME.
IT SEEMS LIKE THE CURSE... HAS PENETRATED DEEP INTO MY BODY.
IT MIGHT TAKE ME OVER AGAIN AT ANY TIME.
THEN FOR NOW YOU CAN'T RETURN TO THE SHIN-SENGUMI.
PLURP PLURP
YOU'D BETTER START THINKING ABOUT A NEW CAREER.
YOU COULD GO TO WORK FOR ANIMATE*?

*THE LARGEST RETAILER OF ANIME, VIDEO GAMES AND MANGA IN JAPAN.

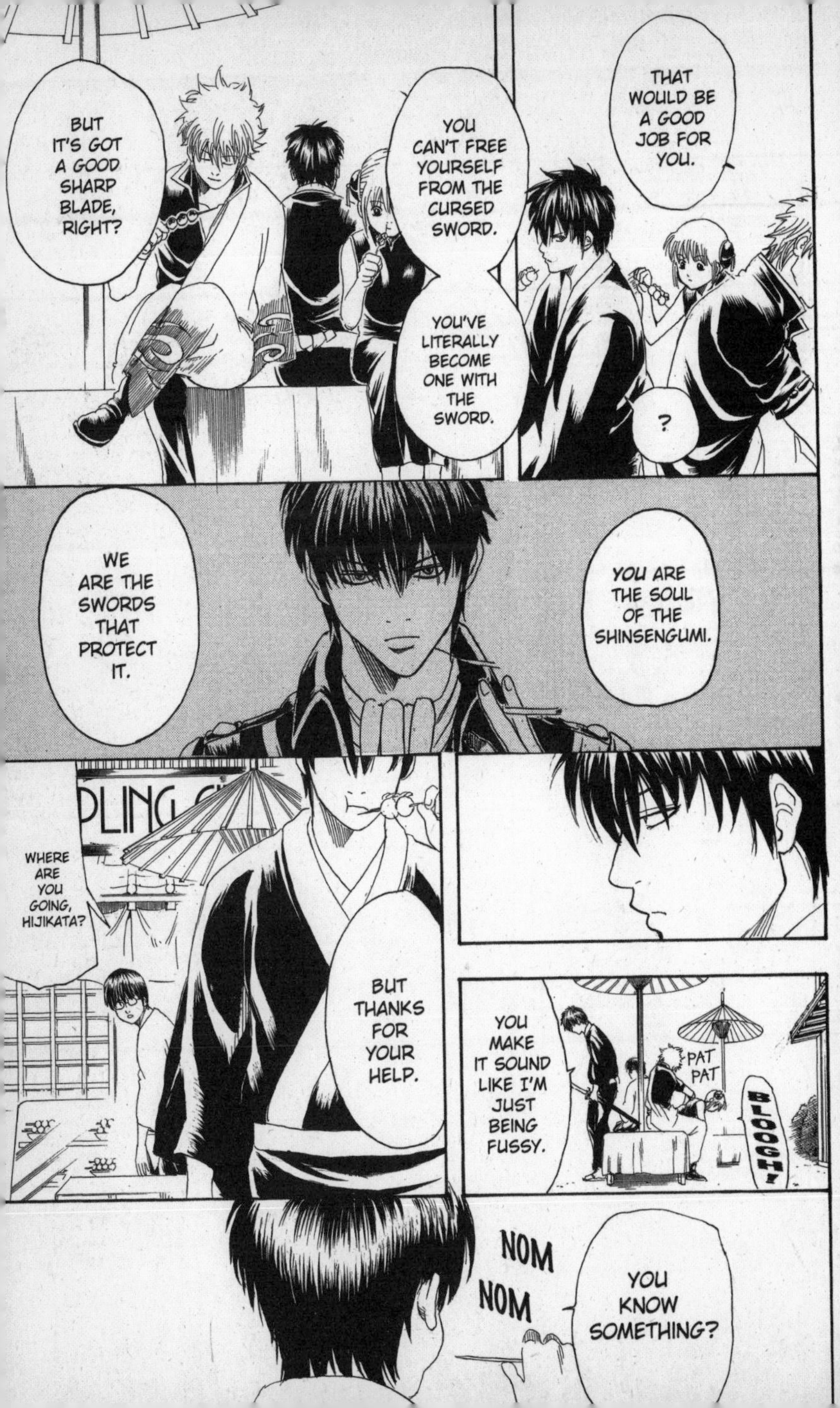
THAT WOULD BE A GOOD JOB FOR YOU.
?
YOU CAN'T FREE YOURSELF FROM THE CURSED SWORD.
YOU'VE LITERALLY BECOME ONE WITH THE SWORD.
BUT IT'S GOT A GOOD SHARP BLADE, RIGHT?
YOU ARE THE SOUL OF THE SHINSENGUMI.
WE ARE THE SWORDS THAT PROTECT IT.
YOU MAKE IT SOUND LIKE I'M JUST BEING FUSSY.
PAT PAT
BLOOGH!
BUT THANKS FOR YOUR HELP.
WHERE ARE YOU GOING, HIJIKATA?
NOM NOM
YOU KNOW SOMETHING?

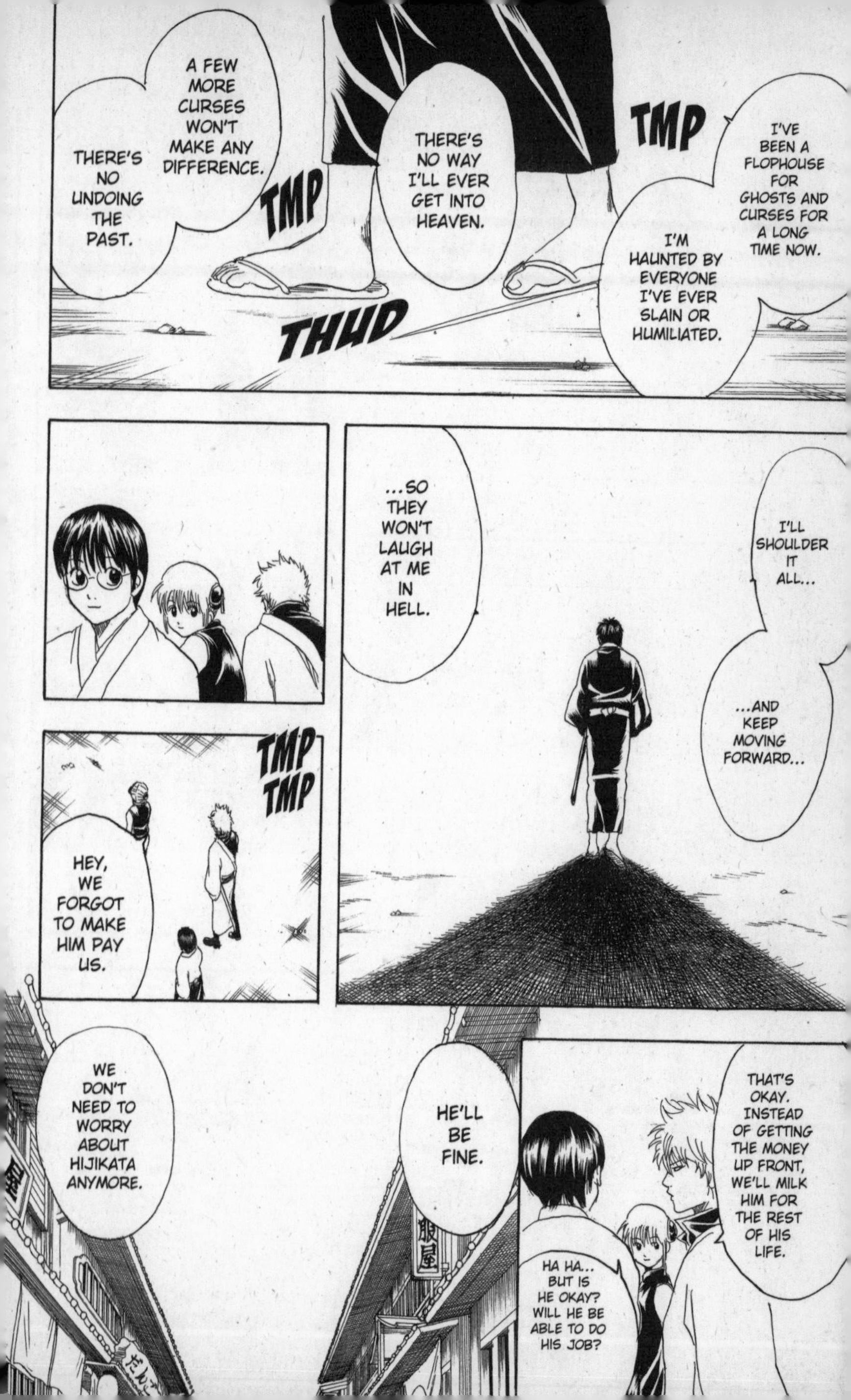
I'VE BEEN A FLOPHOUSE FOR GHOSTS AND CURSES FOR A LONG TIME NOW.
I'M HAUNTED BY EVERYONE I'VE EVER SLAIN OR HUMILIATED.
TMP
THUD
THERE'S NO WAY I'LL EVER GET INTO HEAVEN.
TMP
A FEW MORE CURSES WON'T MAKE ANY DIFFERENCE.
THERE'S NO UNDOING THE PAST.
I'LL SHOULDER IT ALL...
...AND KEEP MOVING FORWARD...
...SO THEY WON'T LAUGH AT ME IN HELL.
TMP TMP
HEY, WE FORGOT TO MAKE HIM PAY US.
THAT'S OKAY. INSTEAD OF GETTING THE MONEY UP FRONT, WE'LL MILK HIM FOR THE REST OF HIS LIFE.
HA HA.. BUT IS HE OKAY? WILL HE BE ABLE TO DO HIS JOB?
HE'LL BE FINE.
WE DON'T NEED TO WORRY ABOUT HIJIKATA ANYMORE.

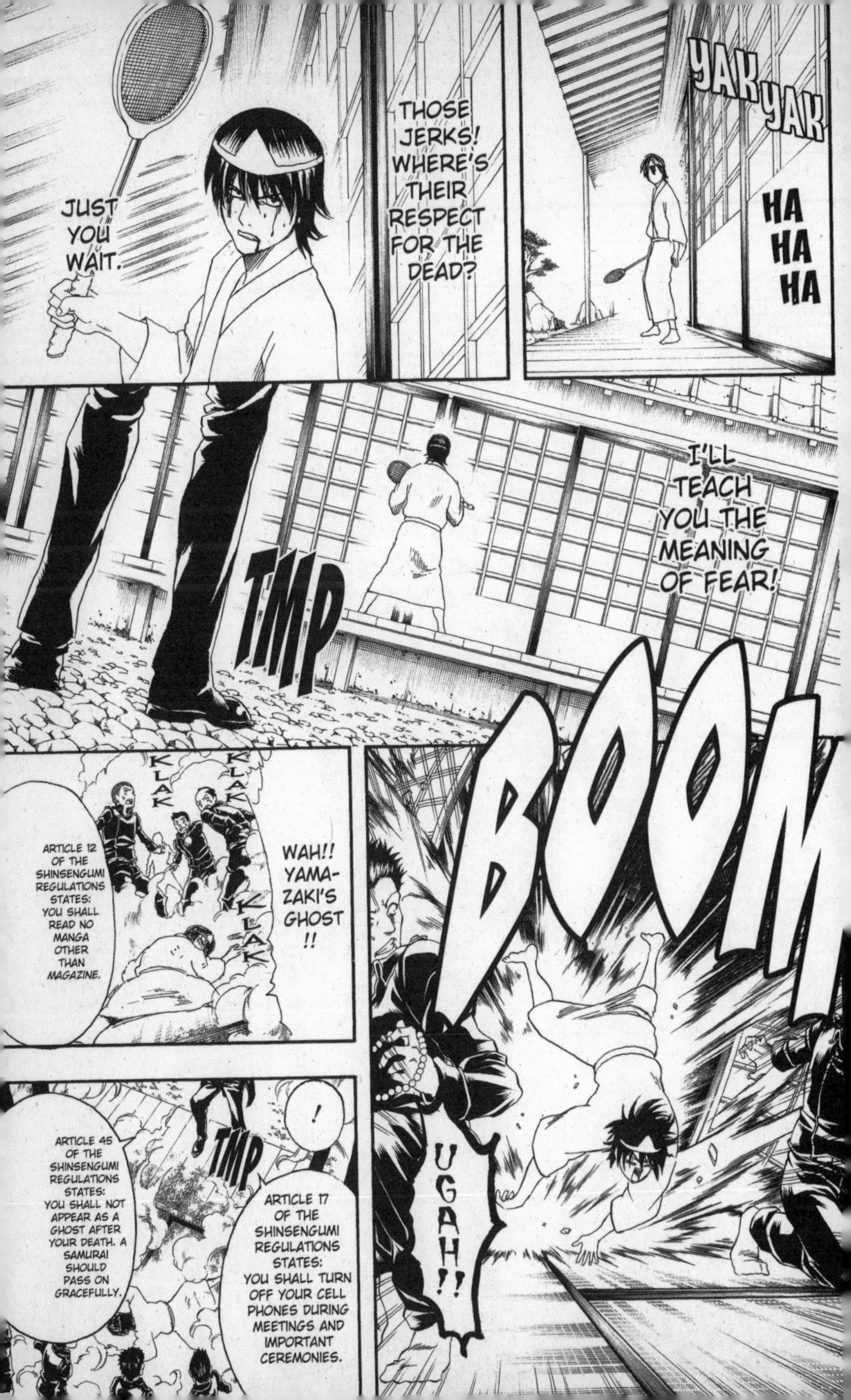
YAK YAK
HA HA HA
THOSE JERKS! WHERE'S THEIR RESPECT FOR THE DEAD?
JUST YOU WAIT.
I'LL TEACH YOU THE MEANING OF FEAR!
TMP
BOOM
UGAH!!
KLAK KLAK KLAK KLAK
WAH!! YAMAZAKI'S GHOST!!
ARTICLE 12 OF THE SHINSENGUMI REGULATIONS STATES: YOU SHALL READ NO MANGA OTHER THAN MAGAZINE.
!
TMP
ARTICLE 17 OF THE SHINSENGUMI REGULATIONS STATES: YOU SHALL TURN OFF YOUR CELL PHONES DURING MEETINGS AND IMPORTANT CEREMONIES.
ARTICLE 45 OF THE SHINSENGUMI REGULATIONS STATES: YOU SHALL NOT APPEAR AS A GHOST AFTER YOUR DEATH. A SAMURAI SHOULD PASS ON GRACEFULLY.

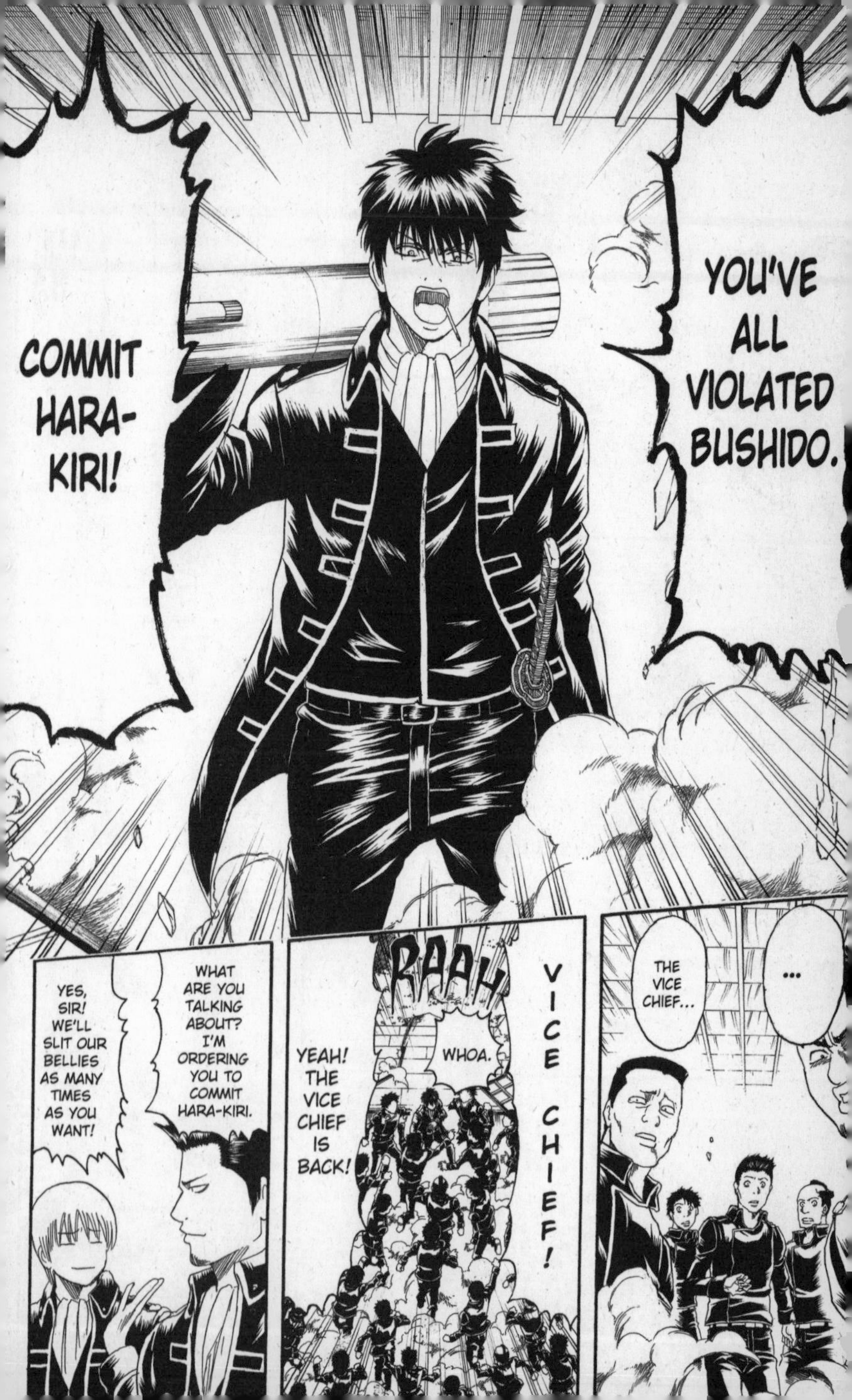
YOU'VE ALL VIOLATED BUSHIDO.
COMMIT HARA-KIRI!
...
THE VICE CHIEF...
VICE CHIEF!
RAAH
WHOA.
YEAH! THE VICE CHIEF IS BACK!
WHAT ARE YOU TALKING ABOUT? I'M ORDERING YOU TO COMMIT HARA-KIRI.
YES, SIR! WE'LL SLIT OUR BELLIES AS MANY TIMES AS YOU WANT!

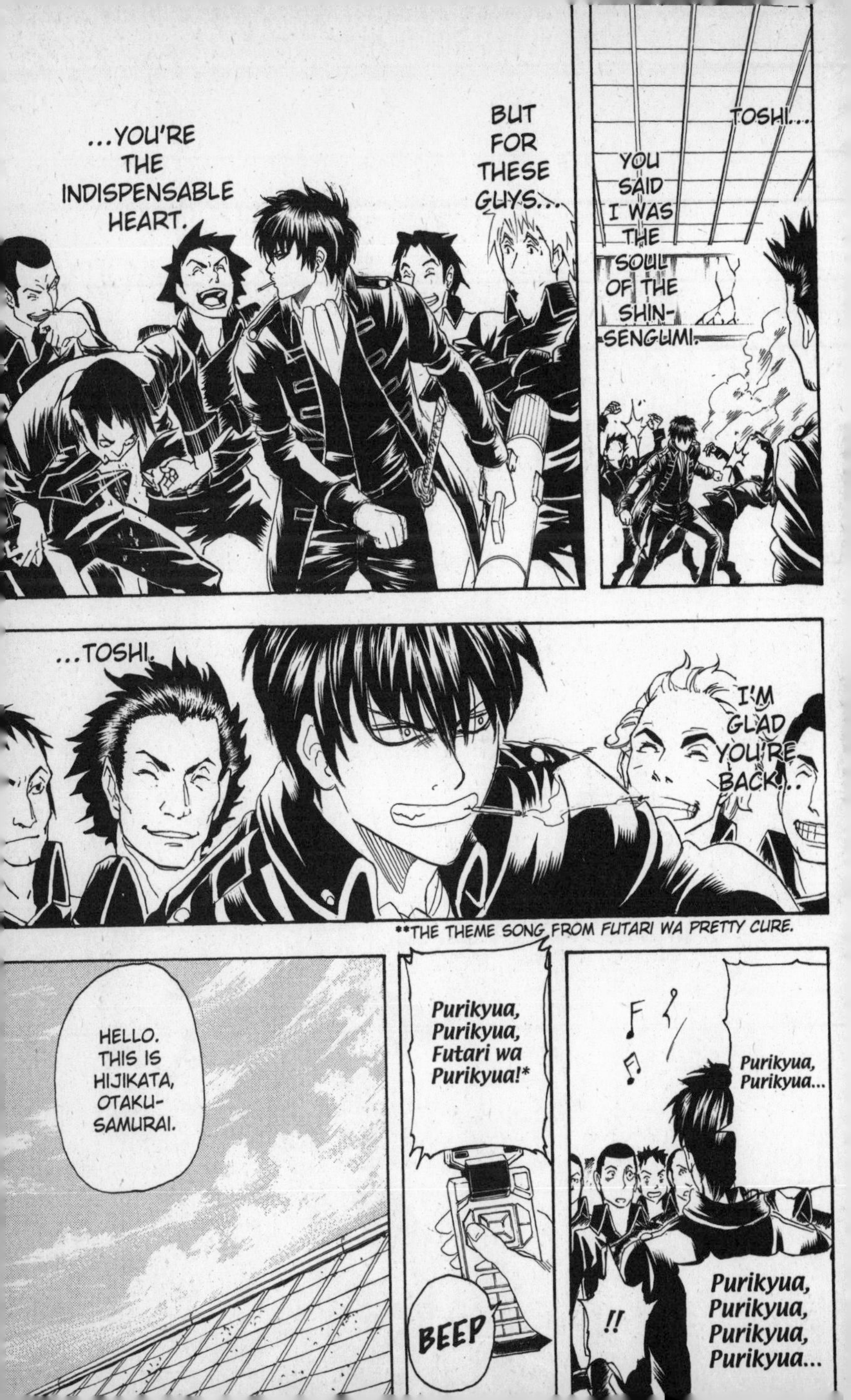
TOSHI...
YOU SAID I WAS THE SOUL OF THE SHIN-SENGUMI.
BUT FOR THESE GUYS...
...YOU'RE THE INDISPENSABLE HEART.
I'M GLAD YOU'RE BACK...
...TOSHI.
Purikyua, Purikyua...
!!
Purikyua, Purikyua, Purikyua, Purikyua...
Purikyua, Purikyua, Futari wa Purikyua!*
BEEP
HELLO. THIS IS HIJIKATA, OTAKU-SAMURAI.

**THE THEME SONG FROM FUTARI WA PRETTY CURE.

● Published in the vol. 22 & 23 joint issue
of *Shonen JUMP Weekly*, 2007

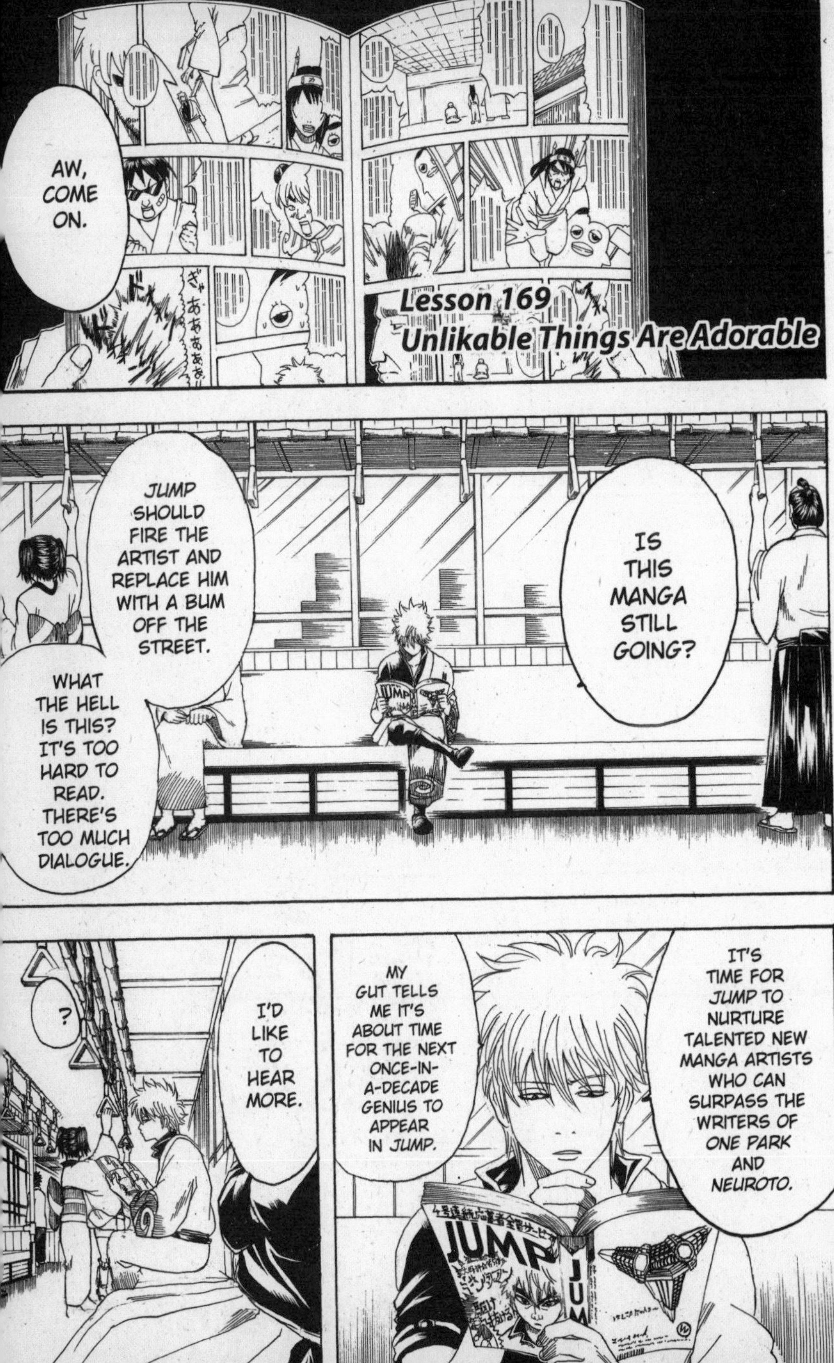
Lesson 169
Unlikable Things Are Adorable
AW, COME ON.
IS THIS MANGA STILL GOING?
JUMP SHOULD FIRE THE ARTIST AND REPLACE HIM WITH A BUM OFF THE STREET.
WHAT THE HELL IS THIS? IT'S TOO HARD TO READ. THERE'S TOO MUCH DIALOGUE.
IT'S TIME FOR JUMP TO NURTURE TALENTED NEW MANGA ARTISTS WHO CAN SURPASS THE WRITERS OF ONE PARK AND NEUROTO.
MY GUT TELLS ME IT'S ABOUT TIME FOR THE NEXT ONCE-IN-A-DECADE GENIUS TO APPEAR IN JUMP.
I'D LIKE TO HEAR MORE.
?
JUMP

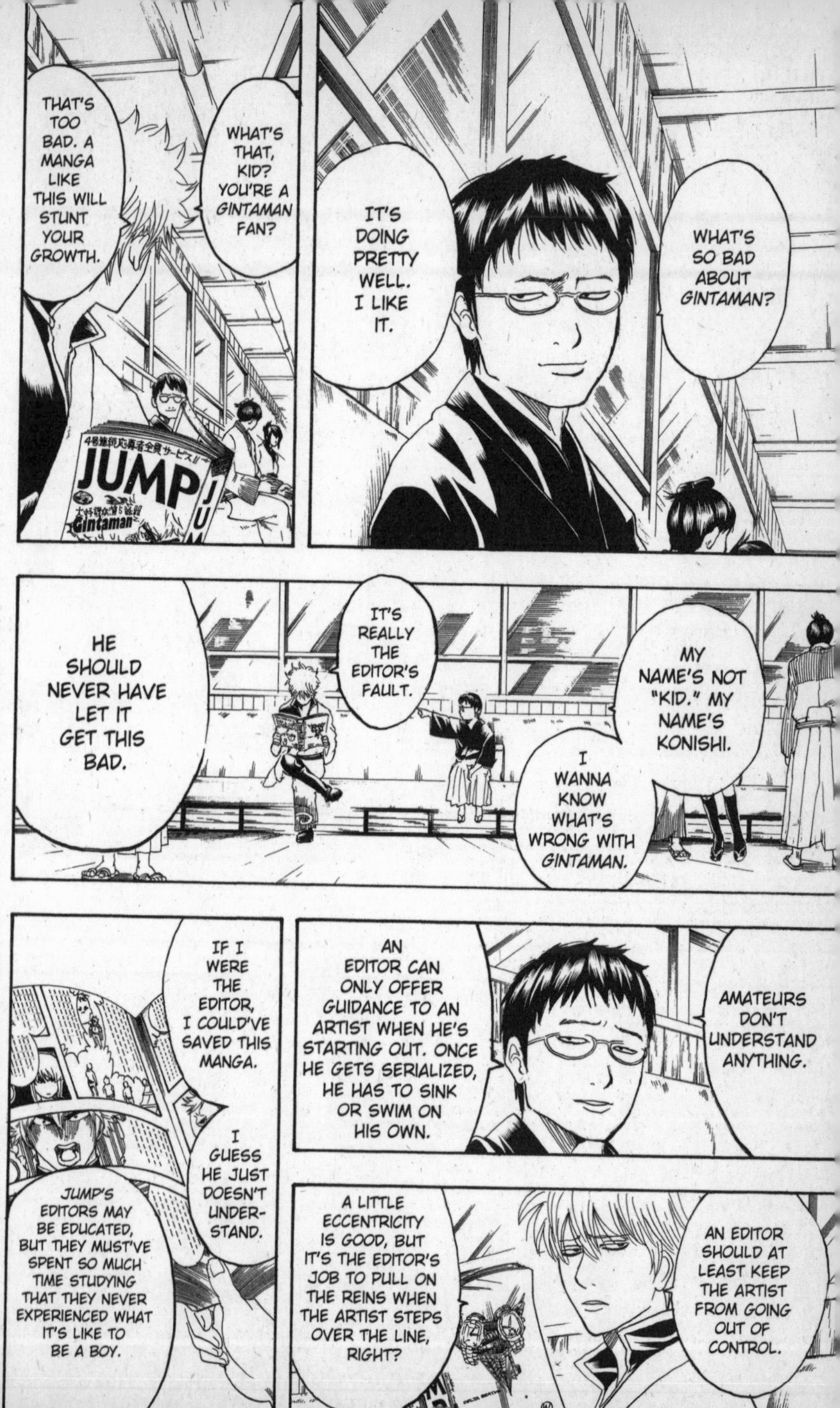
WHAT'S SO BAD ABOUT GINTAMAN?
IT'S DOING PRETTY WELL. I LIKE IT.
WHAT'S THAT, KID? YOU'RE A GINTAMAN FAN?
THAT'S TOO BAD. A MANGA LIKE THIS WILL STUNT YOUR GROWTH.
JUMP
Gintaman
MY NAME'S NOT "KID." MY NAME'S KONISHI.
I WANNA KNOW WHAT'S WRONG WITH GINTAMAN.
IT'S REALLY THE EDITOR'S FAULT.
HE SHOULD NEVER HAVE LET IT GET THIS BAD.
AMATEURS DON'T UNDERSTAND ANYTHING.
AN EDITOR CAN ONLY OFFER GUIDANCE TO AN ARTIST WHEN HE'S STARTING OUT. ONCE HE GETS SERIALIZED, HE HAS TO SINK OR SWIM ON HIS OWN.
AN EDITOR SHOULD AT LEAST KEEP THE ARTIST FROM GOING OUT OF CONTROL.
A LITTLE ECCENTRICITY IS GOOD, BUT IT'S THE EDITOR'S JOB TO PULL ON THE REINS WHEN THE ARTIST STEPS OVER THE LINE, RIGHT?
IF I WERE THE EDITOR, I COULD'VE SAVED THIS MANGA.
I GUESS HE JUST DOESN'T UNDER-STAND.
JUMP'S EDITORS MAY BE EDUCATED, BUT THEY MUST'VE SPENT SO MUCH TIME STUDYING THAT THEY NEVER EXPERIENCED WHAT IT'S LIKE TO BE A BOY.

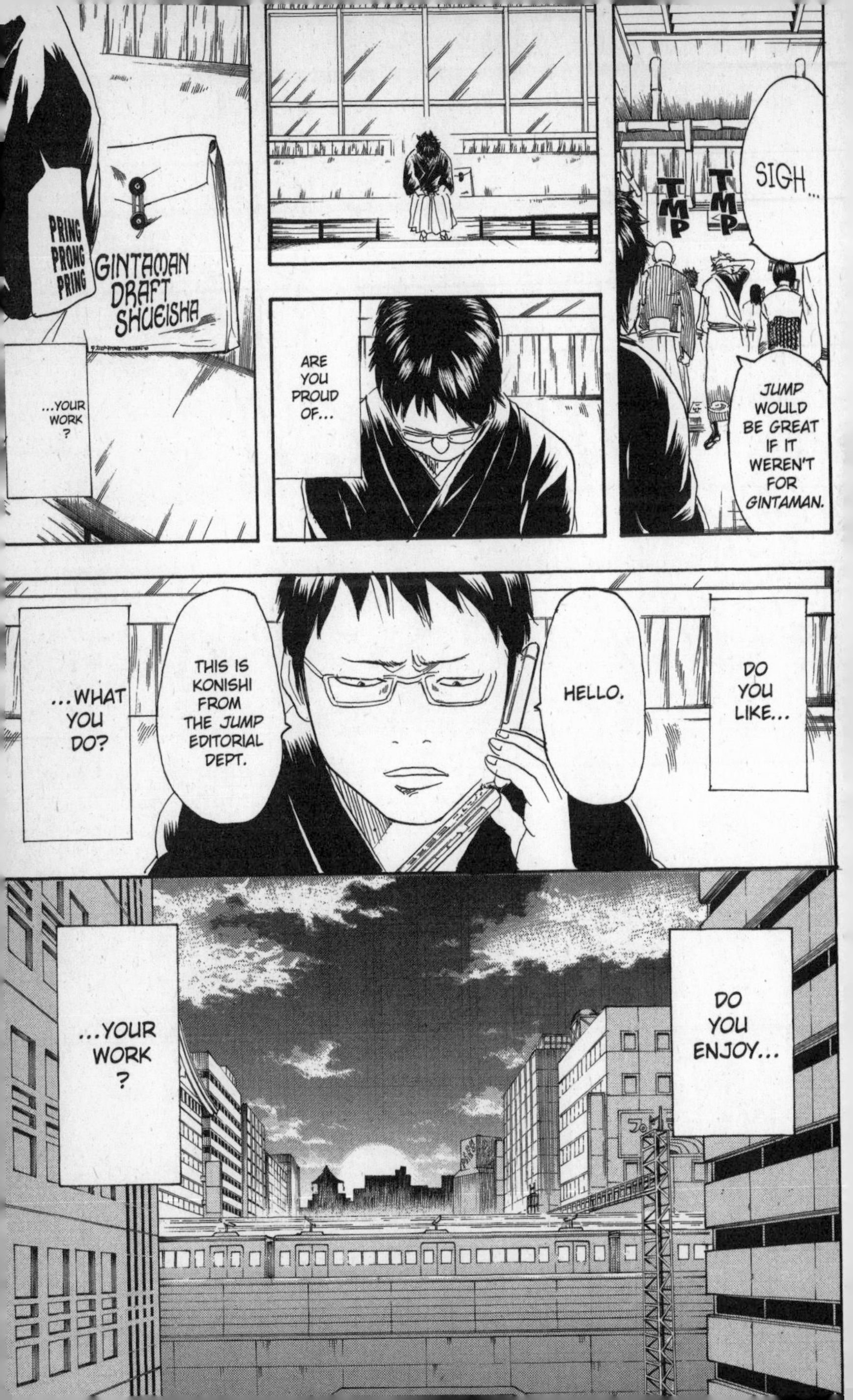

SIGH...
TMP TMP
JUMP WOULD BE GREAT IF IT WEREN'T FOR GINTAMAN.
ARE YOU PROUD OF...
PRING PRONG PRING
GINTAMAN DRAFT SHUEISHA
...YOUR WORK ?
DO YOU LIKE...
HELLO.
THIS IS KONISHI FROM THE JUMP EDITORIAL DEPT.
...WHAT YOU DO?
DO YOU ENJOY...
...YOUR WORK ?

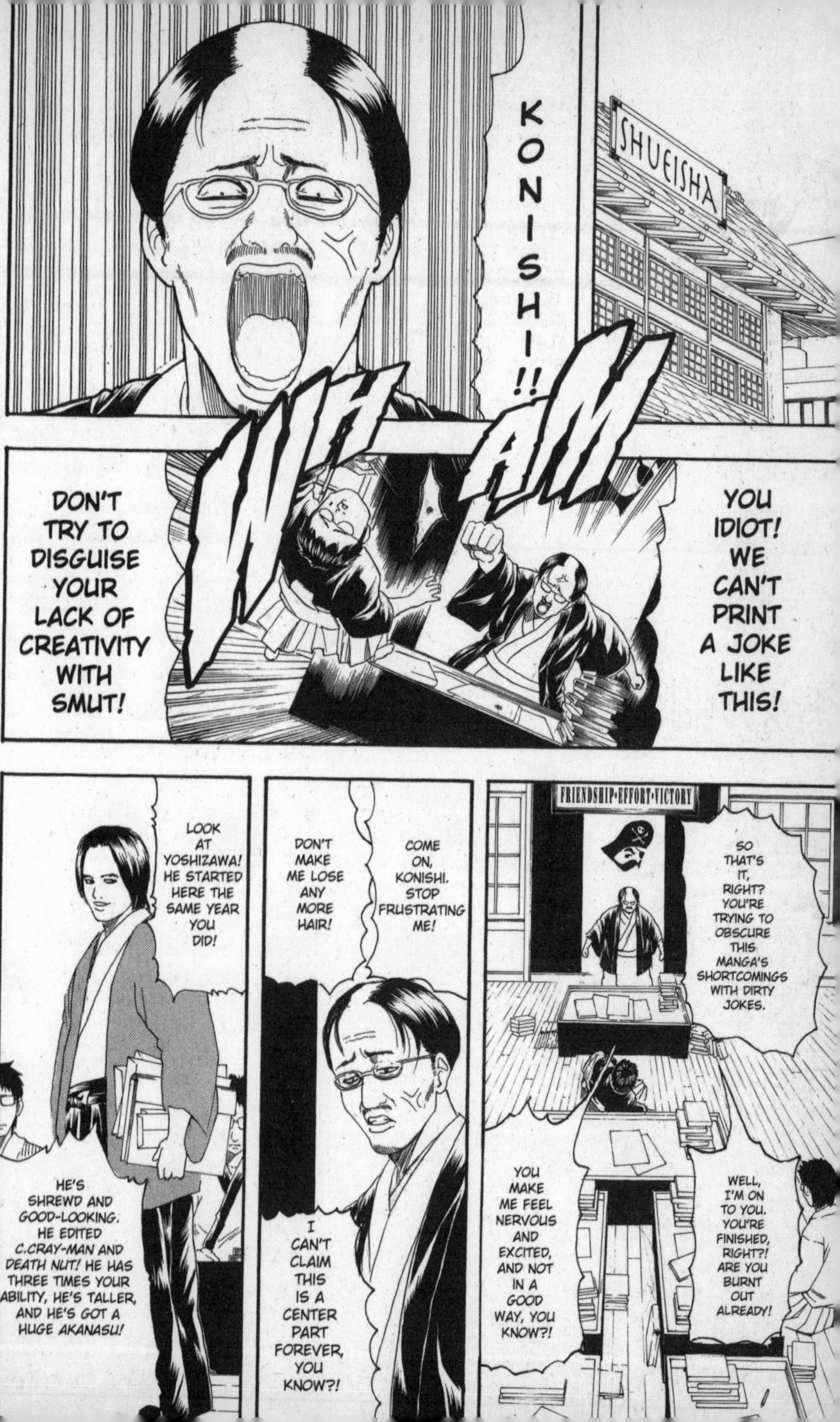
KONISHI!!
SHUEISHA
WHAM
YOU IDIOT! WE CAN'T PRINT A JOKE LIKE THIS!
DON'T TRY TO DISGUISE YOUR LACK OF CREATIVITY WITH SMUT!
FRIENDSHIP·EFFORT·VICTORY
SO THAT'S IT, RIGHT? YOU'RE TRYING TO OBSCURE THIS MANGA'S SHORTCOMINGS WITH DIRTY JOKES.
WELL, I'M ON TO YOU. YOU'RE FINISHED, RIGHT?! ARE YOU BURNT OUT ALREADY!
YOU MAKE ME FEEL NERVOUS AND EXCITED, AND NOT IN A GOOD WAY, YOU KNOW?!
COME ON, KONISHI. STOP FRUSTRATING ME!
DON'T MAKE ME LOSE ANY MORE HAIR!
I CAN'T CLAIM THIS IS A CENTER PART FOREVER, YOU KNOW?!
LOOK AT YOSHIZAWA! HE STARTED HERE THE SAME YEAR YOU DID!
HE'S SHREWD AND GOOD-LOOKING. HE EDITED C.CRAY-MAN AND DEATH NUT! HE HAS THREE TIMES YOUR ABILITY, HE'S TALLER, AND HE'S GOT A HUGE AKANASU!

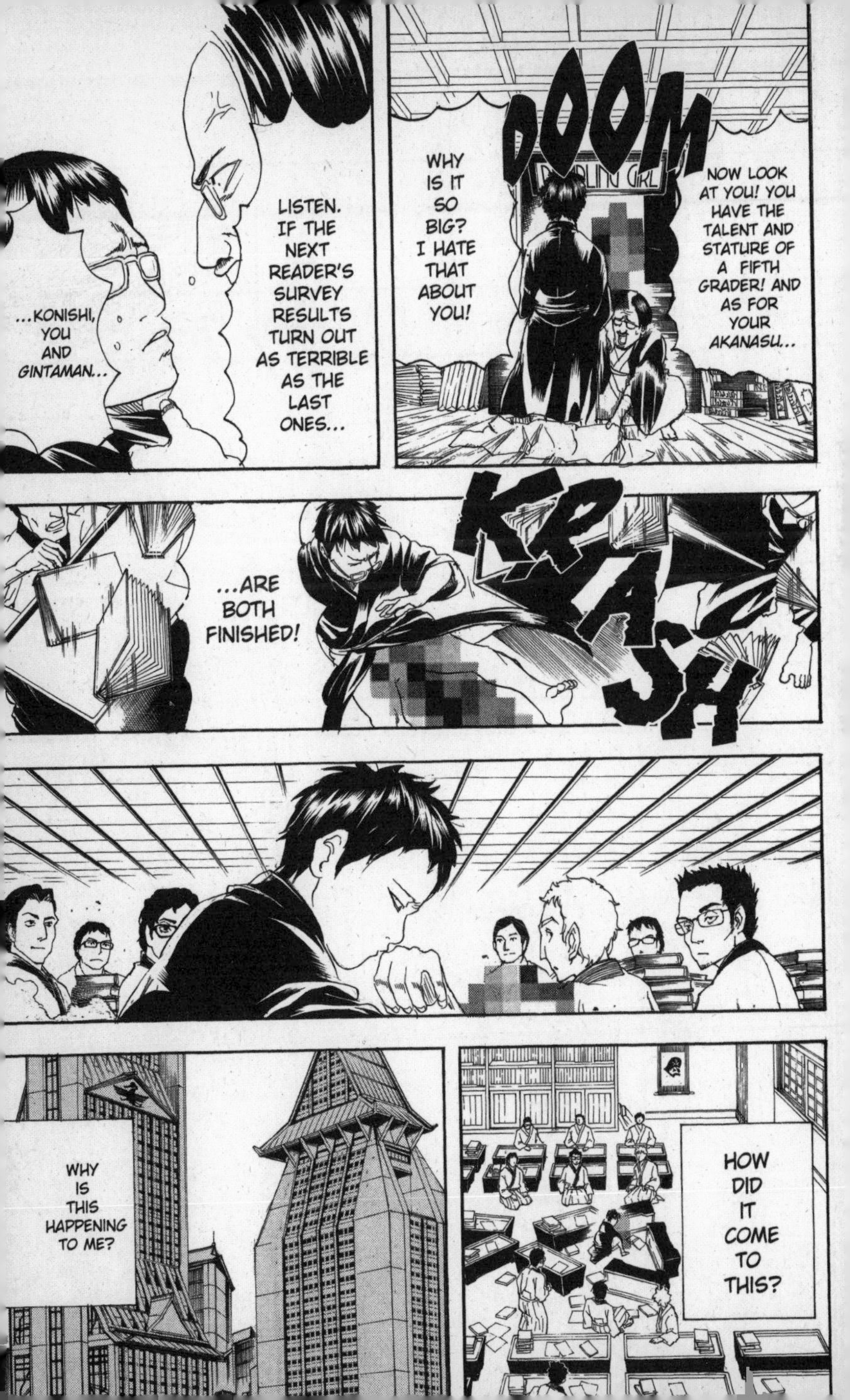
DOOM
NOW LOOK AT YOU! YOU HAVE THE TALENT AND STATURE OF A FIFTH GRADER! AND AS FOR YOUR AKANASU...
WHY IS IT SO BIG? I HATE THAT ABOUT YOU!
LISTEN. IF THE NEXT READER'S SURVEY RESULTS TURN OUT AS TERRIBLE AS THE LAST ONES...
...KONISHI, YOU AND GINTAMAN...
KRASH
...ARE BOTH FINISHED!
HOW DID IT COME TO THIS?
WHY IS THIS HAPPENING TO ME?

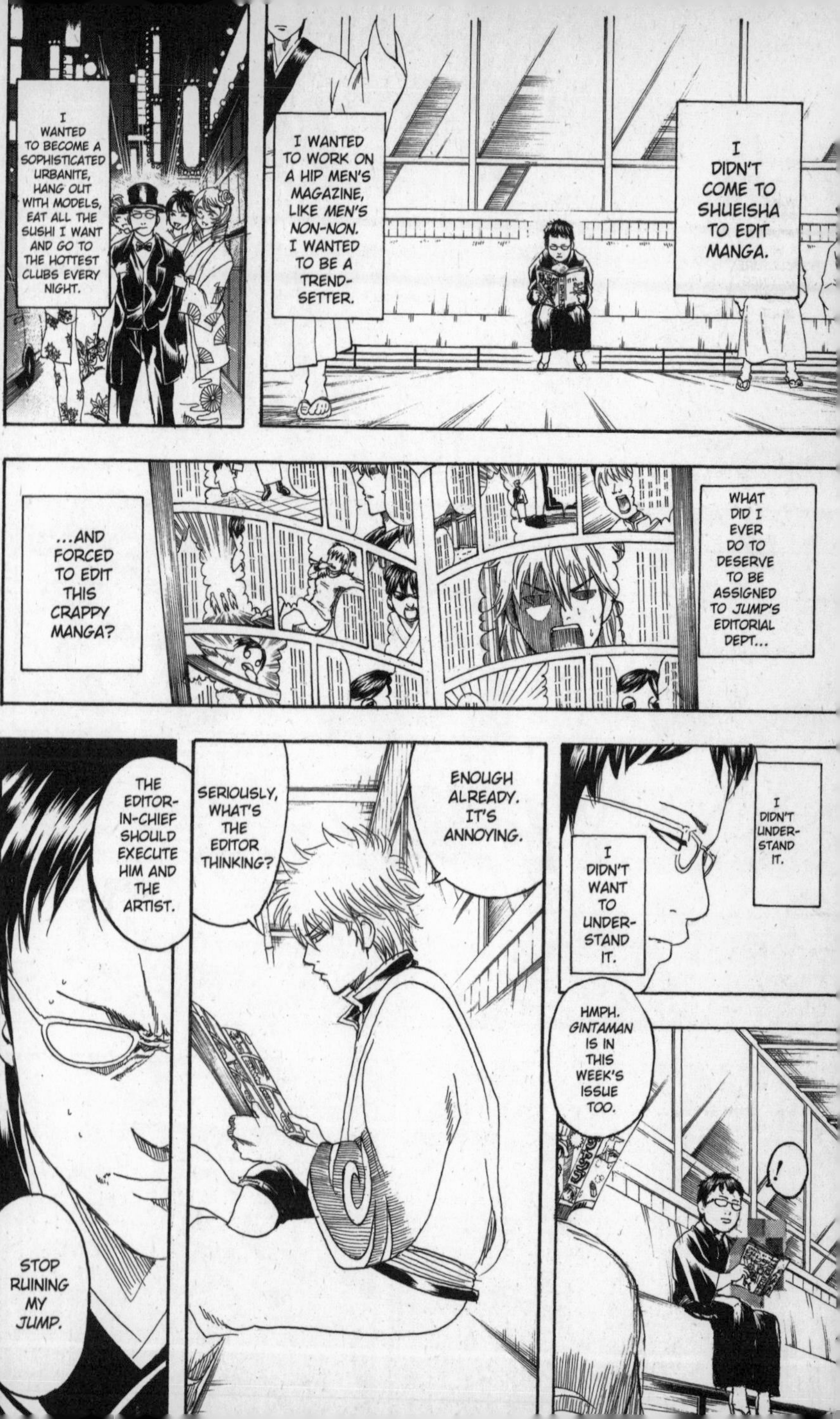
I DIDN'T COME TO SHUEISHA TO EDIT MANGA.
I WANTED TO WORK ON A HIP MEN'S MAGAZINE, LIKE *MEN'S NON-NON*. I WANTED TO BE A TREND-SETTER.
I WANTED TO BECOME A SOPHISTICATED URBANITE, HANG OUT WITH MODELS, EAT ALL THE SUSHI I WANT AND GO TO THE HOTTEST CLUBS EVERY NIGHT.
WHAT DID I EVER DO TO DESERVE TO BE ASSIGNED TO JUMP'S EDITORIAL DEPT...
...AND FORCED TO EDIT THIS CRAPPY MANGA?
I DIDN'T UNDER-STAND IT.
I DIDN'T WANT TO UNDER-STAND IT.
HMPH. *GINTAMAN* IS IN THIS WEEK'S ISSUE TOO.
!
ENOUGH ALREADY. IT'S ANNOYING.
SERIOUSLY, WHAT'S THE EDITOR THINKING?
THE EDITOR-IN-CHIEF SHOULD EXECUTE HIM AND THE ARTIST.
STOP RUINING MY JUMP.

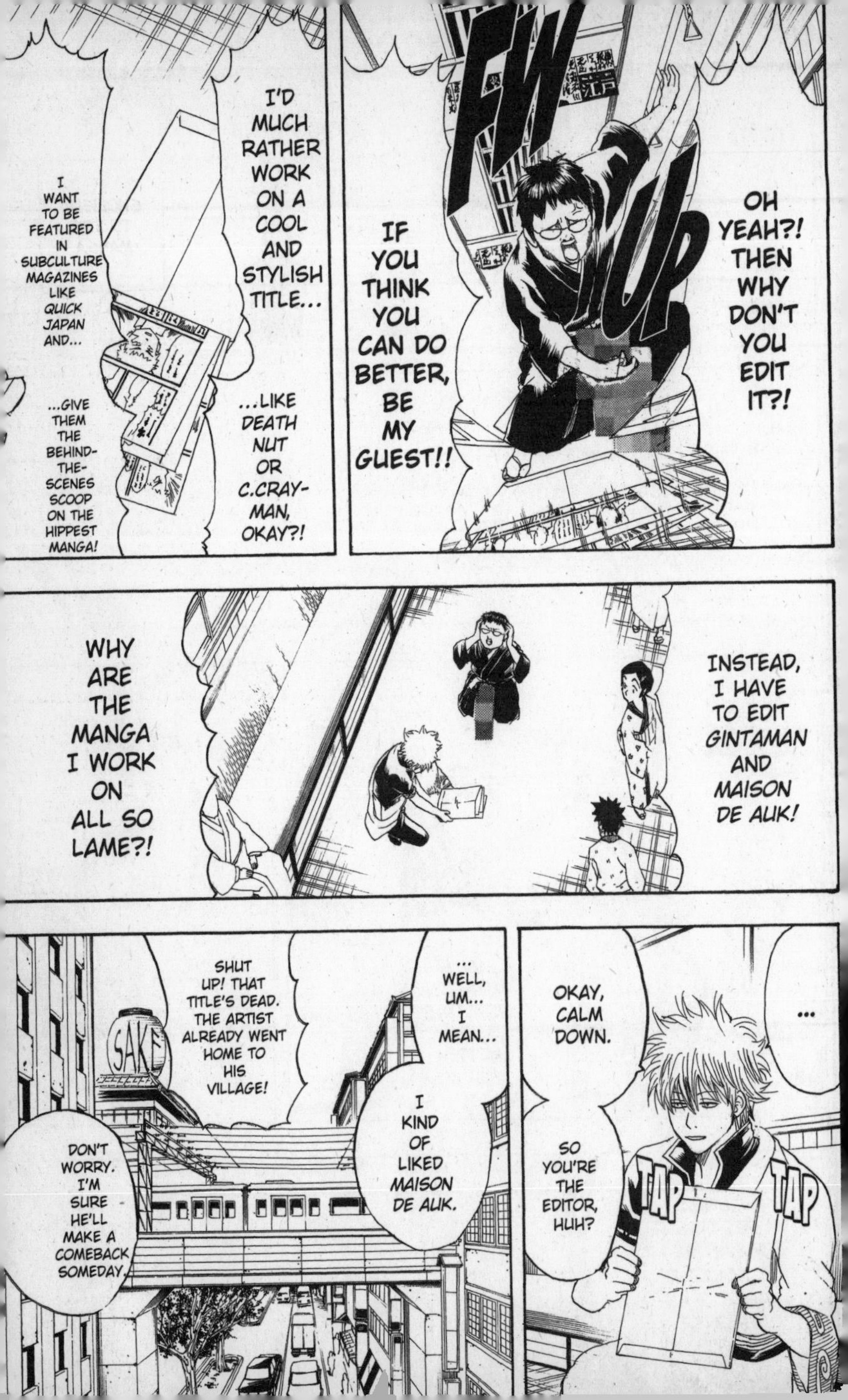
FWUP
OH YEAH?! THEN WHY DON'T YOU EDIT IT?!
IF YOU THINK YOU CAN DO BETTER, BE MY GUEST!!
I'D MUCH RATHER WORK ON A COOL AND STYLISH TITLE...
...LIKE DEATH NUT OR C.CRAY-MAN, OKAY?!
I WANT TO BE FEATURED IN SUBCULTURE MAGAZINES LIKE QUICK JAPAN AND...
...GIVE THEM THE BEHIND-THE-SCENES SCOOP ON THE HIPPEST MANGA!
INSTEAD, I HAVE TO EDIT GINTAMAN AND MAISON DE AUK!
WHY ARE THE MANGA I WORK ON ALL SO LAME?!
...
OKAY, CALM DOWN.
SO YOU'RE THE EDITOR, HUH?
TAP TAP
... WELL, UM... I MEAN...
I KIND OF LIKED MAISON DE AUK.
SHUT UP! THAT TITLE'S DEAD. THE ARTIST ALREADY WENT HOME TO HIS VILLAGE!
SAKE
DON'T WORRY. I'M SURE HE'LL MAKE A COMEBACK SOMEDAY.

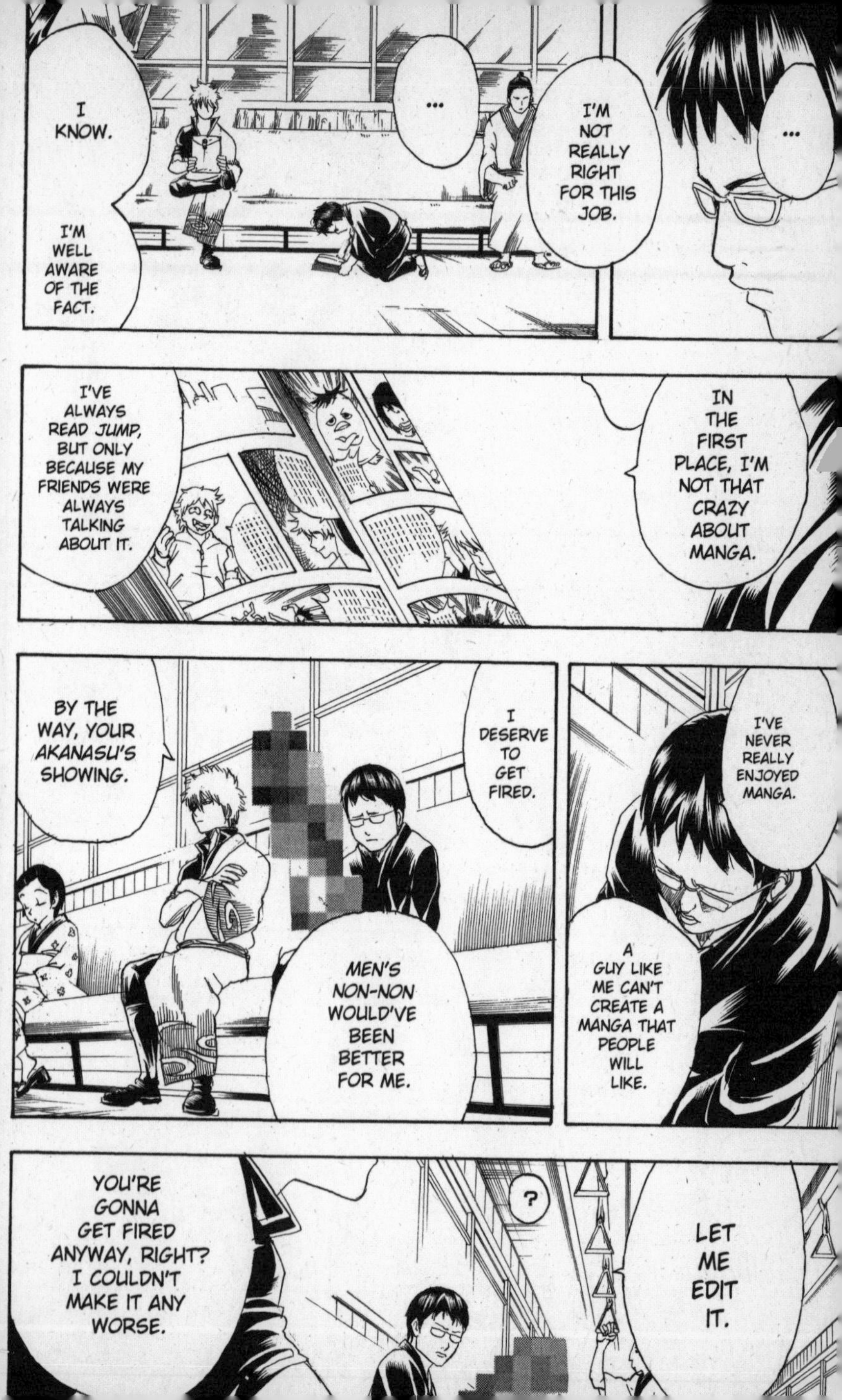
...
I'M NOT REALLY RIGHT FOR THIS JOB.
...
I KNOW.
I'M WELL AWARE OF THE FACT.
IN THE FIRST PLACE, I'M NOT THAT CRAZY ABOUT MANGA.
I'VE ALWAYS READ JUMP, BUT ONLY BECAUSE MY FRIENDS WERE ALWAYS TALKING ABOUT IT.
I'VE NEVER REALLY ENJOYED MANGA.
A GUY LIKE ME CAN'T CREATE A MANGA THAT PEOPLE WILL LIKE.
I DESERVE TO GET FIRED.
BY THE WAY, YOUR AKANASU'S SHOWING.
MEN'S NON-NON WOULD'VE BEEN BETTER FOR ME.
LET ME EDIT IT.
?
YOU'RE GONNA GET FIRED ANYWAY, RIGHT? I COULDN'T MAKE IT ANY WORSE.

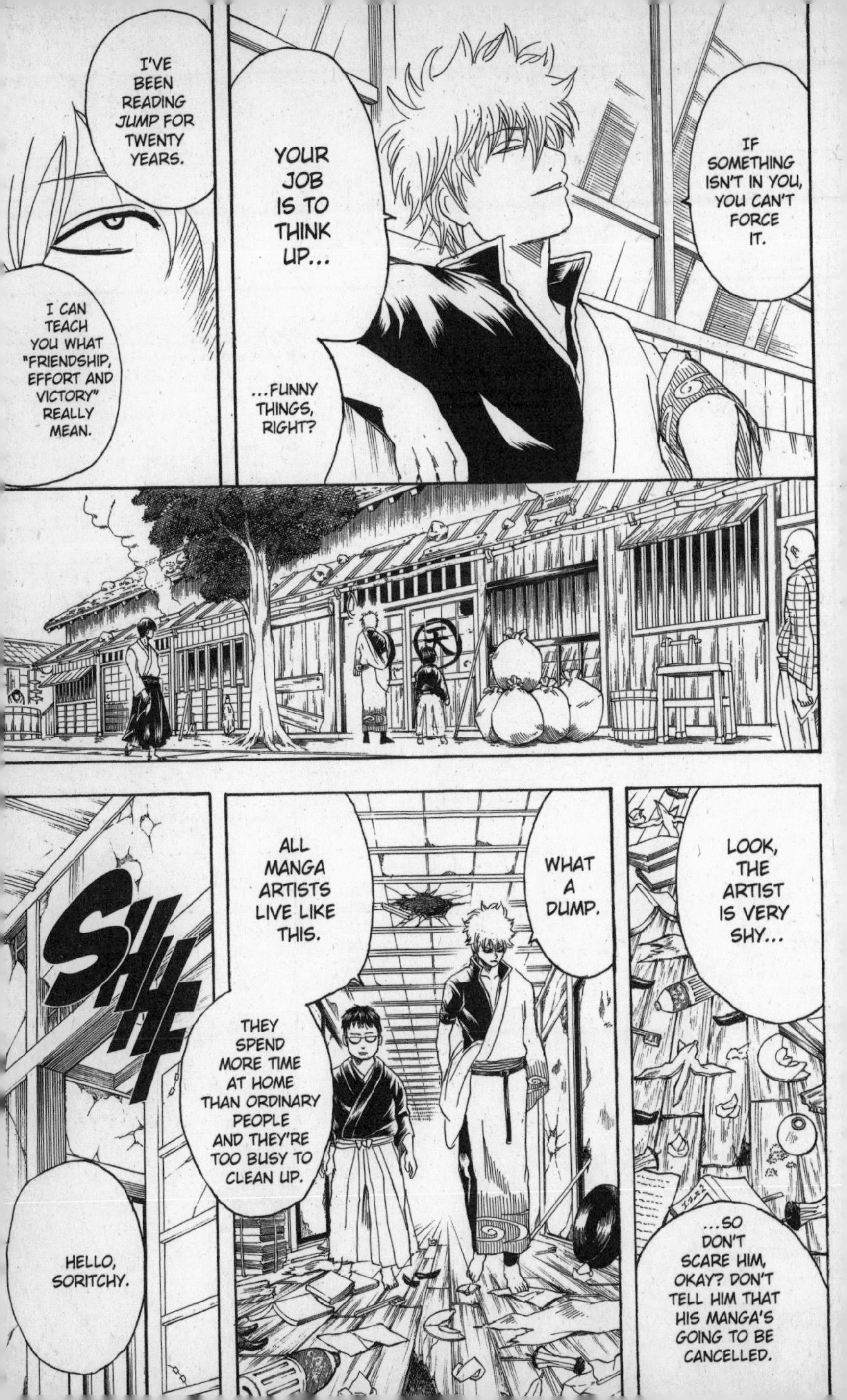
IF SOMETHING ISN'T IN YOU, YOU CAN'T FORCE IT.
YOUR JOB IS TO THINK UP...
...FUNNY THINGS, RIGHT?
I'VE BEEN READING JUMP FOR TWENTY YEARS.
I CAN TEACH YOU WHAT "FRIENDSHIP, EFFORT AND VICTORY" REALLY MEAN.
LOOK, THE ARTIST IS VERY SHY...
...SO DON'T SCARE HIM, OKAY? DON'T TELL HIM THAT HIS MANGA'S GOING TO BE CANCELLED.
WHAT A DUMP.
ALL MANGA ARTISTS LIVE LIKE THIS.
THEY SPEND MORE TIME AT HOME THAN ORDINARY PEOPLE AND THEY'RE TOO BUSY TO CLEAN UP.
SHH
HELLO, SORITCHY.

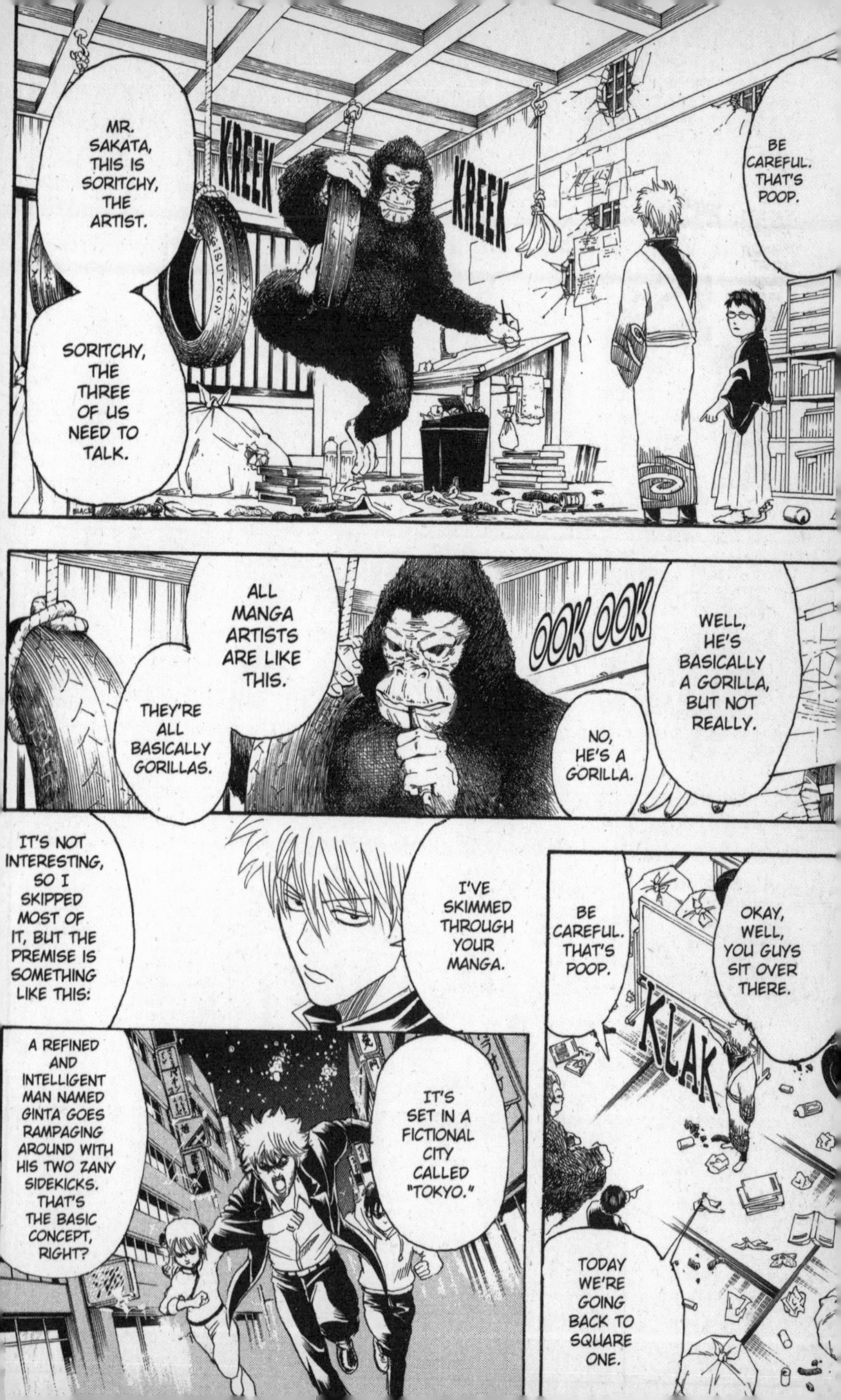
BE CAREFUL. THAT'S POOP.
KREEK
KREEK
MR. SAKATA, THIS IS SORITCHY, THE ARTIST.
SORITCHY, THE THREE OF US NEED TO TALK.
WELL, HE'S BASICALLY A GORILLA, BUT NOT REALLY.
NO, HE'S A GORILLA.
OOK OOK
ALL MANGA ARTISTS ARE LIKE THIS.
THEY'RE ALL BASICALLY GORILLAS.
OKAY, WELL, YOU GUYS SIT OVER THERE.
BE CAREFUL. THAT'S POOP.
KLAK
TODAY WE'RE GOING BACK TO SQUARE ONE.
I'VE SKIMMED THROUGH YOUR MANGA.
IT'S NOT INTERESTING, SO I SKIPPED MOST OF IT, BUT THE PREMISE IS SOMETHING LIKE THIS:
IT'S SET IN A FICTIONAL CITY CALLED "TOKYO."
A REFINED AND INTELLIGENT MAN NAMED GINTA GOES RAMPAGING AROUND WITH HIS TWO ZANY SIDEKICKS. THAT'S THE BASIC CONCEPT, RIGHT?

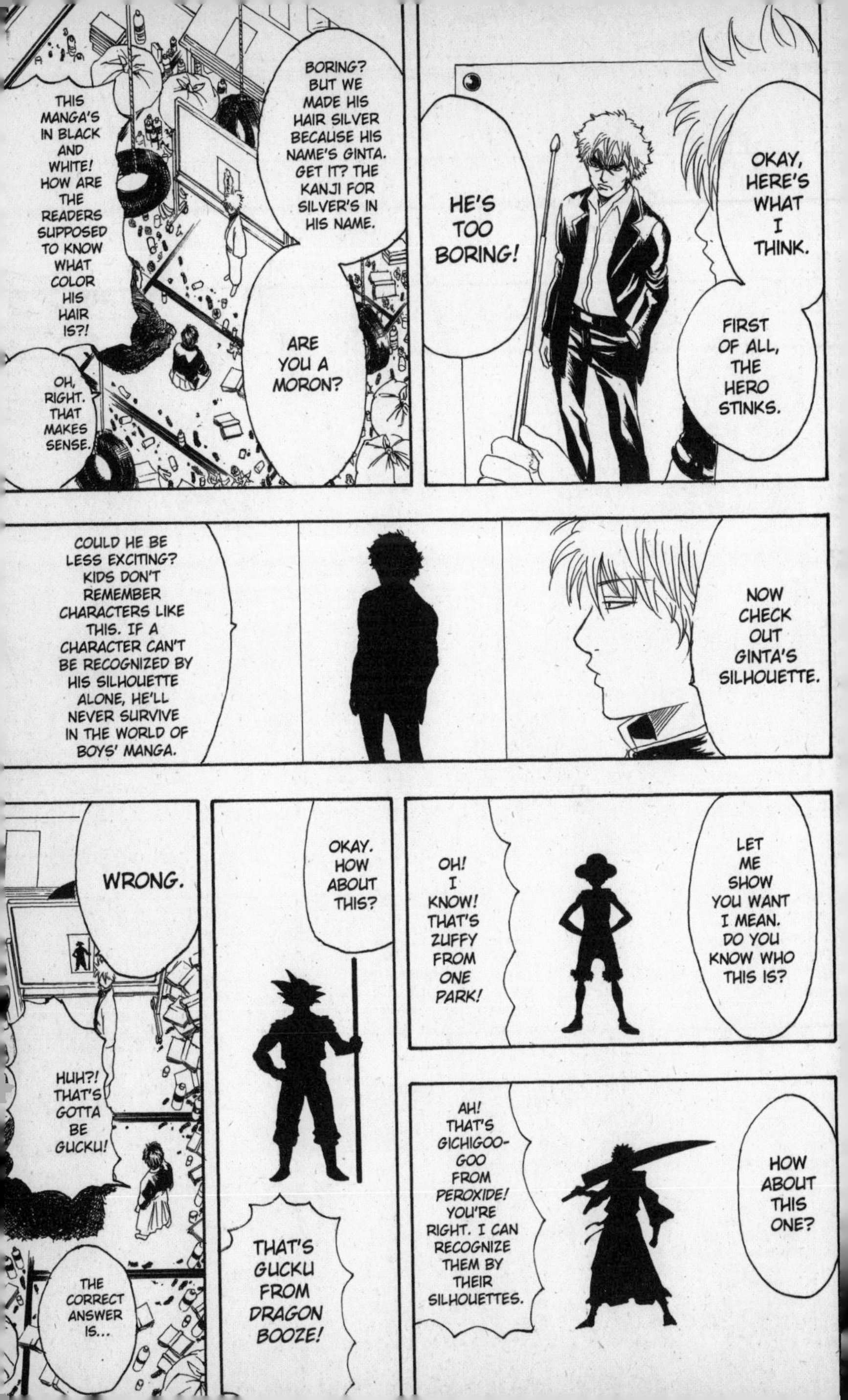
OKAY, HERE'S WHAT I THINK.
FIRST OF ALL, THE HERO STINKS.
HE'S TOO BORING!
BORING? BUT WE MADE HIS HAIR SILVER BECAUSE HIS NAME'S GINTA. GET IT? THE KANJI FOR SILVER'S IN HIS NAME.
ARE YOU A MORON?
THIS MANGA'S IN BLACK AND WHITE! HOW ARE THE READERS SUPPOSED TO KNOW WHAT COLOR HIS HAIR IS?!
OH, RIGHT. THAT MAKES SENSE.
NOW CHECK OUT GINTA'S SILHOUETTE.
COULD HE BE LESS EXCITING? KIDS DON'T REMEMBER CHARACTERS LIKE THIS. IF A CHARACTER CAN'T BE RECOGNIZED BY HIS SILHOUETTE ALONE, HE'LL NEVER SURVIVE IN THE WORLD OF BOYS' MANGA.
LET ME SHOW YOU WANT I MEAN. DO YOU KNOW WHO THIS IS?
OH! I KNOW! THAT'S ZUFFY FROM ONE PARK!
HOW ABOUT THIS ONE?
AH! THAT'S GICHIGOO-GOO FROM PEROXIDE! YOU'RE RIGHT. I CAN RECOGNIZE THEM BY THEIR SILHOUETTES.
OKAY. HOW ABOUT THIS?
THAT'S GUCKU FROM DRAGON BOOZE!
WRONG.
HUH?! THAT'S GOTTA BE GUCKU!
THE CORRECT ANSWER IS...

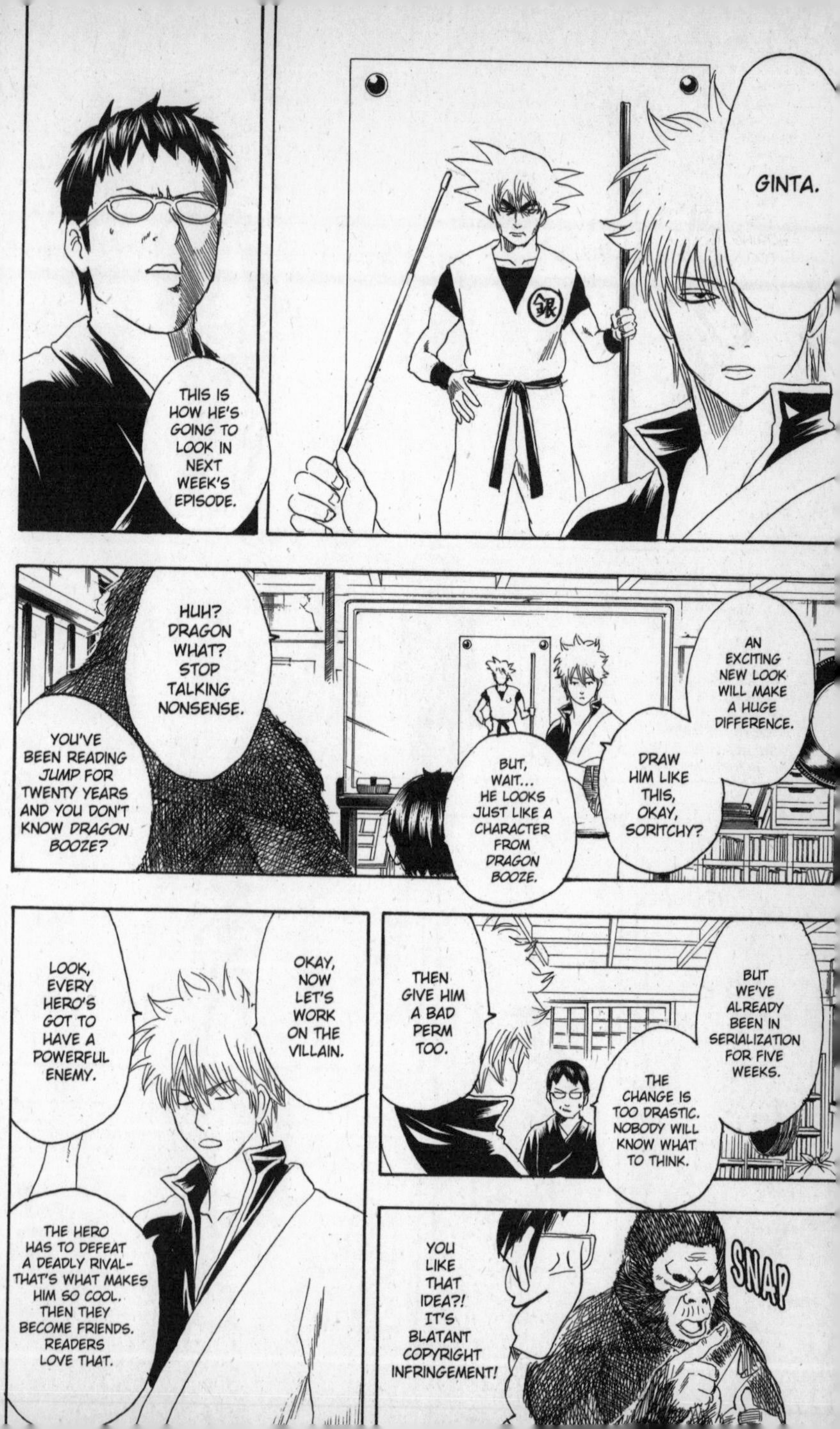
GINTA.
THIS IS HOW HE'S GOING TO LOOK IN NEXT WEEK'S EPISODE.
AN EXCITING NEW LOOK WILL MAKE A HUGE DIFFERENCE.
DRAW HIM LIKE THIS, OKAY, SORITCHY?
BUT, WAIT... HE LOOKS JUST LIKE A CHARACTER FROM DRAGON BOOZE.
HUH? DRAGON WHAT? STOP TALKING NONSENSE.
YOU'VE BEEN READING JUMP FOR TWENTY YEARS AND YOU DON'T KNOW DRAGON BOOZE?
BUT WE'VE ALREADY BEEN IN SERIALIZATION FOR FIVE WEEKS.
THE CHANGE IS TOO DRASTIC. NOBODY WILL KNOW WHAT TO THINK.
THEN GIVE HIM A BAD PERM TOO.
SNAP
YOU LIKE THAT IDEA?! IT'S BLATANT COPYRIGHT INFRINGEMENT!
OKAY, NOW LET'S WORK ON THE VILLAIN.
LOOK, EVERY HERO'S GOT TO HAVE A POWERFUL ENEMY.
THE HERO HAS TO DEFEAT A DEADLY RIVAL-THAT'S WHAT MAKES HIM SO COOL. THEN THEY BECOME FRIENDS. READERS LOVE THAT.

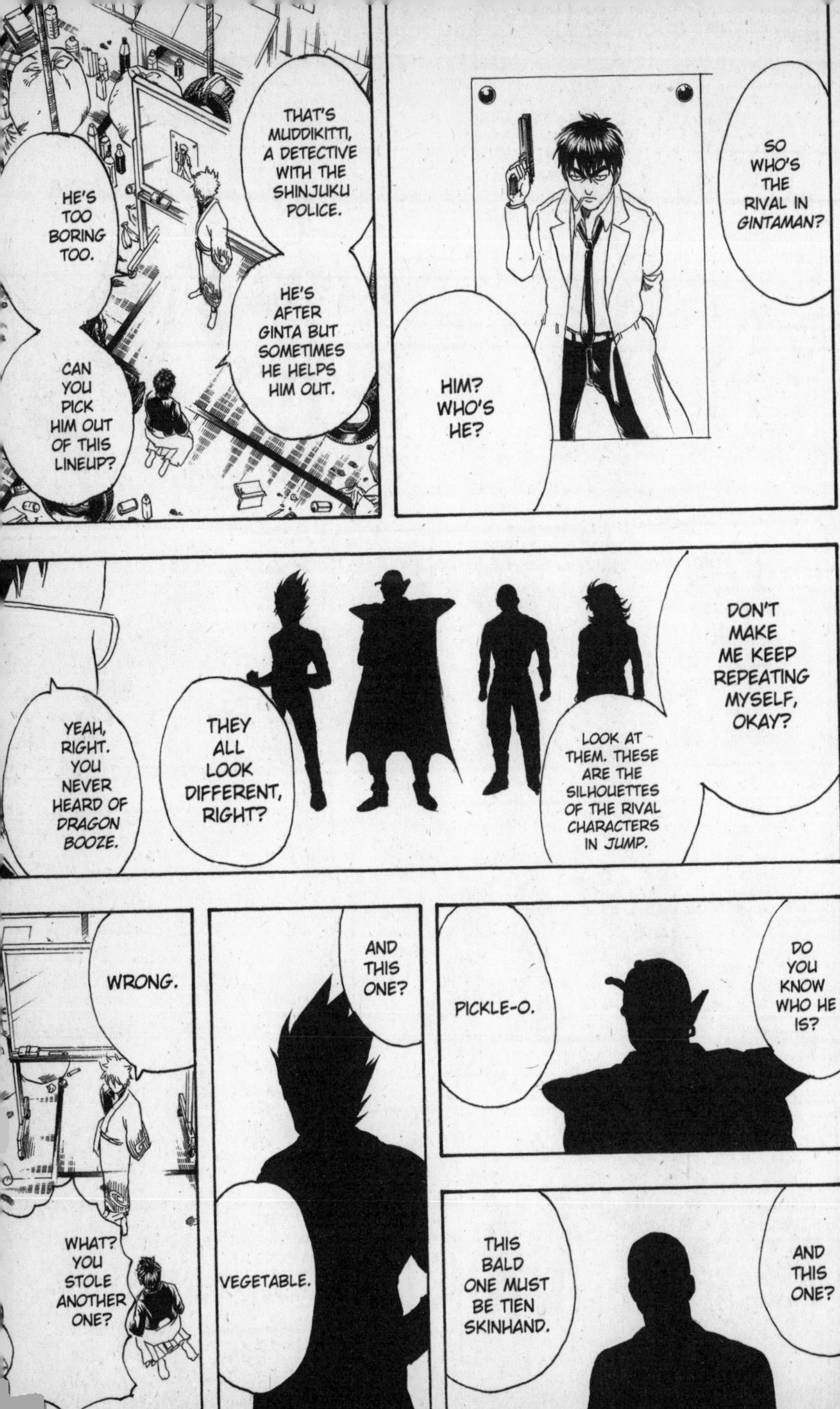

SO WHO'S THE RIVAL IN GINTAMAN?
HIM? WHO'S HE?
THAT'S MUDDIKITTI, A DETECTIVE WITH THE SHINJUKU POLICE.
HE'S AFTER GINTA BUT SOMETIMES HE HELPS HIM OUT.
HE'S TOO BORING TOO.
CAN YOU PICK HIM OUT OF THIS LINEUP?
DON'T MAKE ME KEEP REPEATING MYSELF, OKAY?
LOOK AT THEM. THESE ARE THE SILHOUETTES OF THE RIVAL CHARACTERS IN JUMP.
THEY ALL LOOK DIFFERENT, RIGHT?
YEAH, RIGHT. YOU NEVER HEARD OF DRAGON BOOZE.
DO YOU KNOW WHO HE IS?
PICKLE-O.
AND THIS ONE?
THIS BALD ONE MUST BE TIEN SKINHAND.
AND THIS ONE?
VEGETABLE.
WRONG.
WHAT? YOU STOLE ANOTHER ONE?

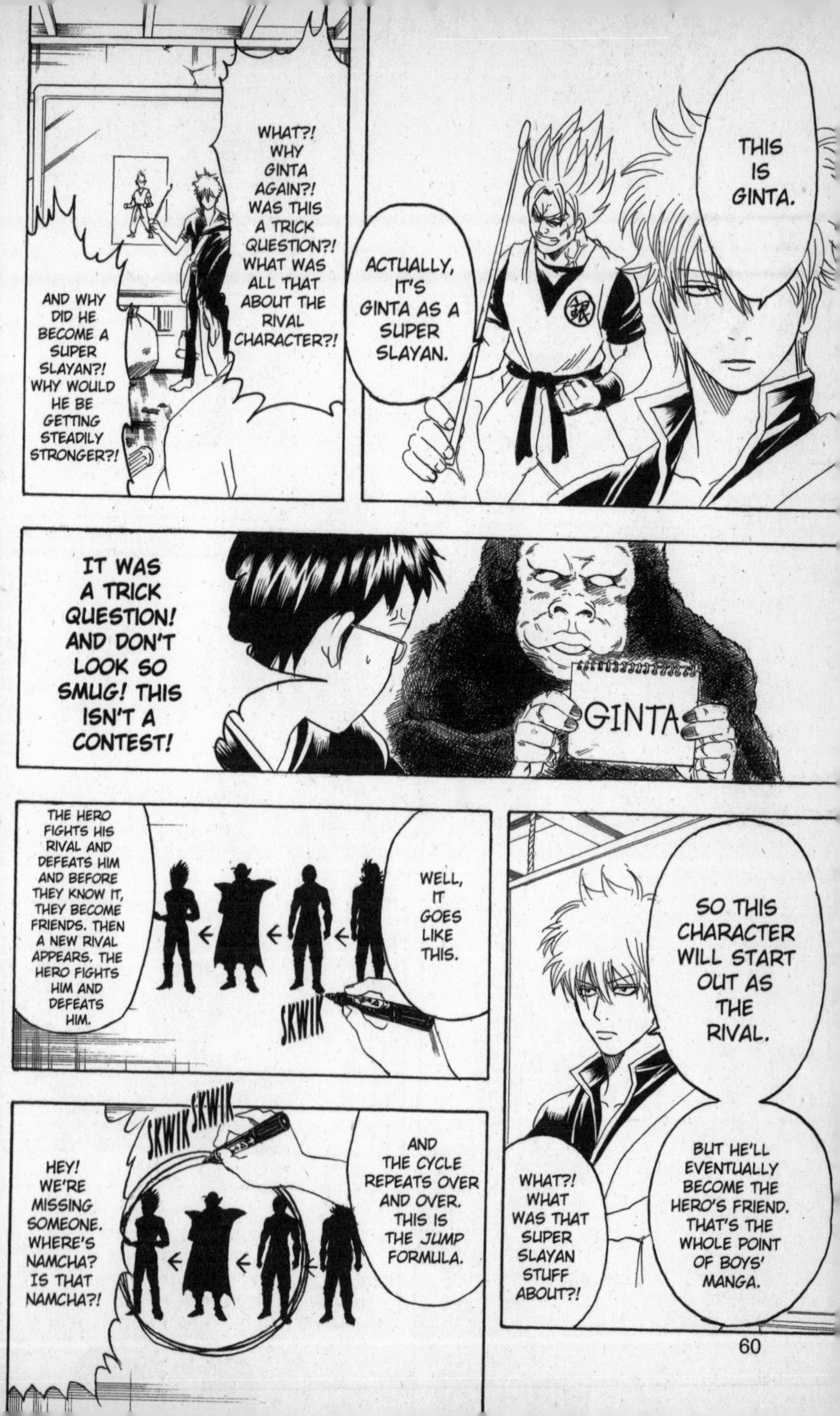
THIS IS GINTA.
ACTUALLY, IT'S GINTA AS A SUPER SLAYAN.
WHAT?! WHY GINTA AGAIN?! WAS THIS A TRICK QUESTION?! WHAT WAS ALL THAT ABOUT THE RIVAL CHARACTER?!
AND WHY DID HE BECOME A SUPER SLAYAN?! WHY WOULD HE BE GETTING STEADILY STRONGER?!
IT WAS A TRICK QUESTION! AND DON'T LOOK SO SMUG! THIS ISN'T A CONTEST!
GINTA
SO THIS CHARACTER WILL START OUT AS THE RIVAL.
BUT HE'LL EVENTUALLY BECOME THE HERO'S FRIEND. THAT'S THE WHOLE POINT OF BOYS' MANGA.
WHAT?! WHAT WAS THAT SUPER SLAYAN STUFF ABOUT?!
WELL, IT GOES LIKE THIS.
THE HERO FIGHTS HIS RIVAL AND DEFEATS HIM AND BEFORE THEY KNOW IT, THEY BECOME FRIENDS. THEN A NEW RIVAL APPEARS. THE HERO FIGHTS HIM AND DEFEATS HIM.
SKWIK
AND THE CYCLE REPEATS OVER AND OVER. THIS IS THE JUMP FORMULA.
SKWIK SKWIK
HEY! WE'RE MISSING SOMEONE. WHERE'S NAMCHA? IS THAT NAMCHA?!

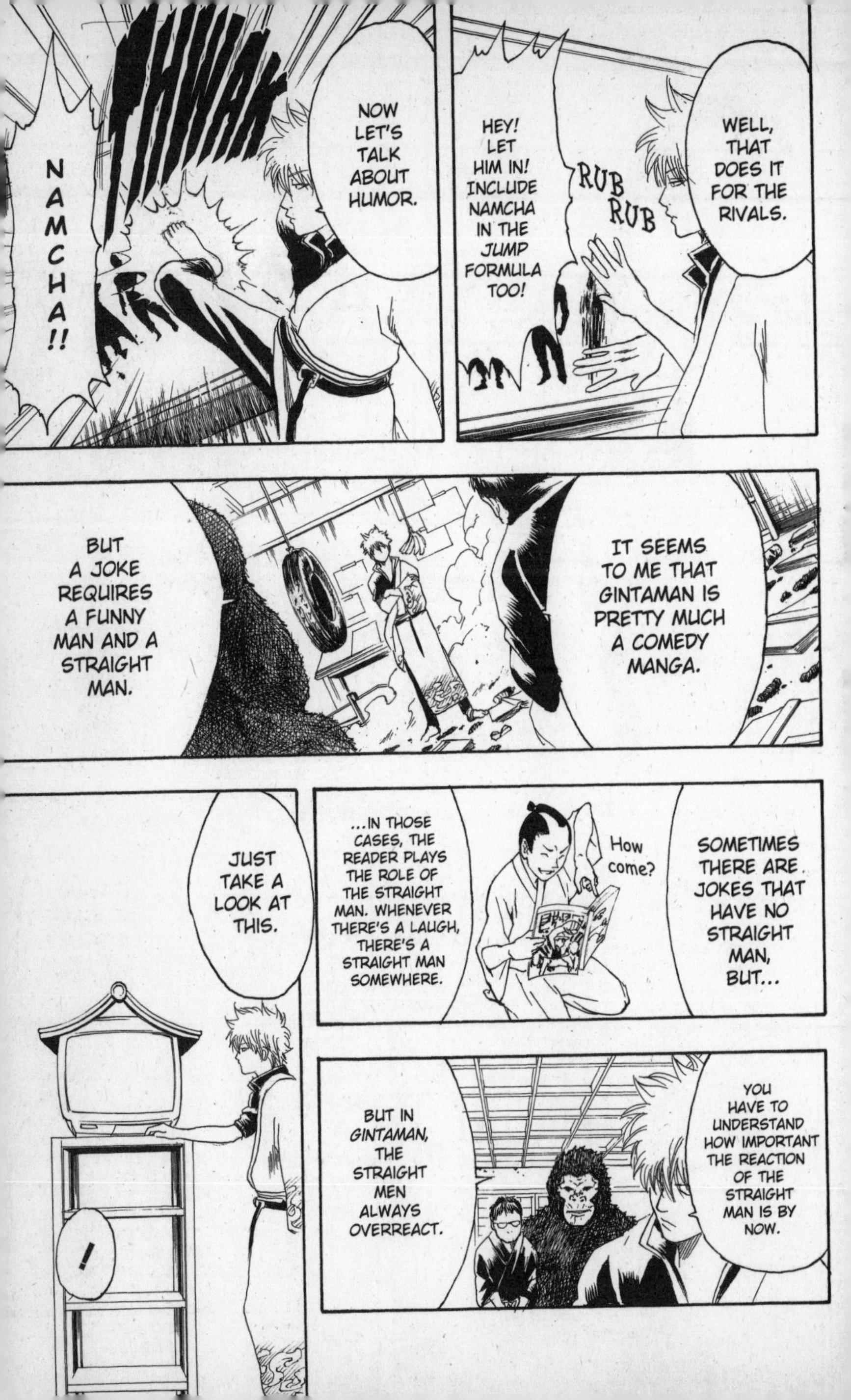
WELL, THAT DOES IT FOR THE RIVALS.
RUB RUB
HEY! LET HIM IN! INCLUDE NAMCHA IN THE JUMP FORMULA TOO!
NOW LET'S TALK ABOUT HUMOR.
THWAK
NAMCHA!!
IT SEEMS TO ME THAT GINTAMAN IS PRETTY MUCH A COMEDY MANGA.
BUT A JOKE REQUIRES A FUNNY MAN AND A STRAIGHT MAN.
SOMETIMES THERE ARE JOKES THAT HAVE NO STRAIGHT MAN, BUT...
How come?
...IN THOSE CASES, THE READER PLAYS THE ROLE OF THE STRAIGHT MAN. WHENEVER THERE'S A LAUGH, THERE'S A STRAIGHT MAN SOMEWHERE.
YOU HAVE TO UNDERSTAND HOW IMPORTANT THE REACTION OF THE STRAIGHT MAN IS BY NOW.
BUT IN GINTAMAN, THE STRAIGHT MEN ALWAYS OVERREACT.
JUST TAKE A LOOK AT THIS.
!

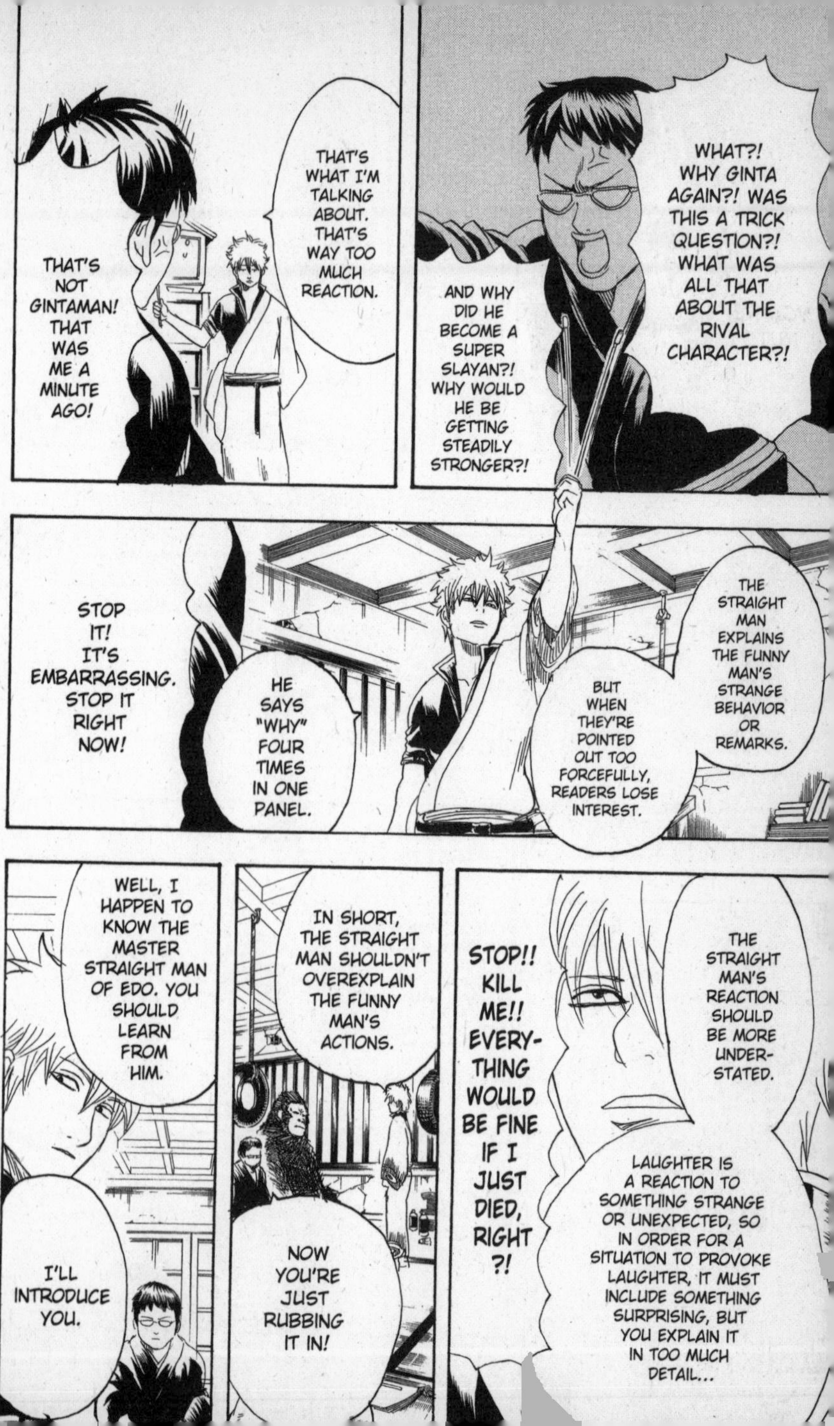
WHAT?! WHY GINTA AGAIN?! WAS THIS A TRICK QUESTION?! WHAT WAS ALL THAT ABOUT THE RIVAL CHARACTER?!
AND WHY DID HE BECOME A SUPER SLAYAN?! WHY WOULD HE BE GETTING STEADILY STRONGER?!
THAT'S WHAT I'M TALKING ABOUT. THAT'S WAY TOO MUCH REACTION.
THAT'S NOT GINTAMAN! THAT WAS ME A MINUTE AGO!
THE STRAIGHT MAN EXPLAINS THE FUNNY MAN'S STRANGE BEHAVIOR OR REMARKS.
BUT WHEN THEY'RE POINTED OUT TOO FORCEFULLY, READERS LOSE INTEREST.
HE SAYS "WHY" FOUR TIMES IN ONE PANEL.
STOP IT! IT'S EMBARRASSING. STOP IT RIGHT NOW!
THE STRAIGHT MAN'S REACTION SHOULD BE MORE UNDER-STATED.
LAUGHTER IS A REACTION TO SOMETHING STRANGE OR UNEXPECTED, SO IN ORDER FOR A SITUATION TO PROVOKE LAUGHTER, IT MUST INCLUDE SOMETHING SURPRISING, BUT YOU EXPLAIN IT IN TOO MUCH DETAIL...
STOP!! KILL ME!! EVERY-THING WOULD BE FINE IF I JUST DIED, RIGHT?!
IN SHORT, THE STRAIGHT MAN SHOULDN'T OVEREXPLAIN THE FUNNY MAN'S ACTIONS.
NOW YOU'RE JUST RUBBING IT IN!
WELL, I HAPPEN TO KNOW THE MASTER STRAIGHT MAN OF EDO. YOU SHOULD LEARN FROM HIM.
I'LL INTRODUCE YOU.

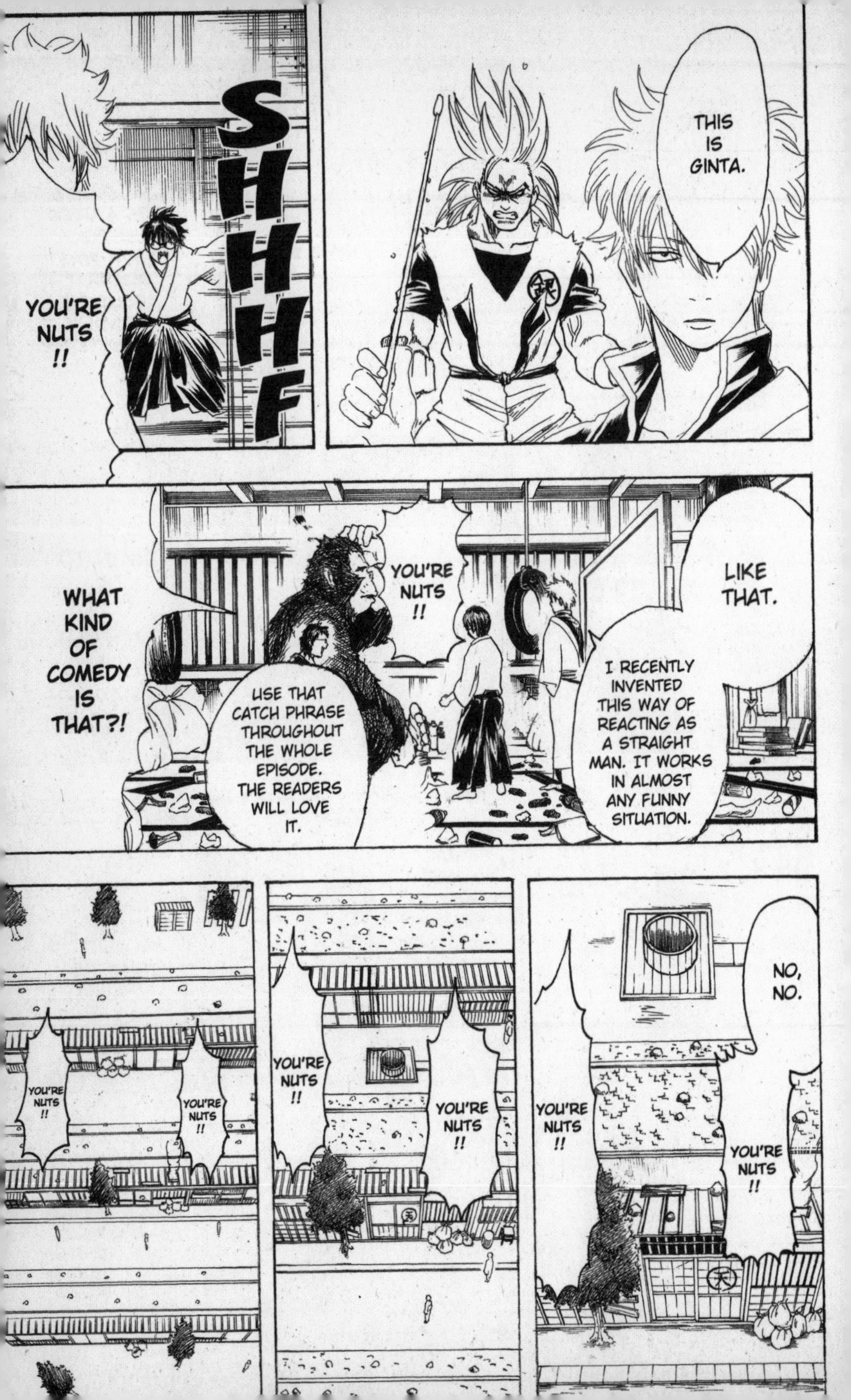
THIS IS GINTA.
SHHHF
YOU'RE NUTS !!
LIKE THAT.
I RECENTLY INVENTED THIS WAY OF REACTING AS A STRAIGHT MAN. IT WORKS IN ALMOST ANY FUNNY SITUATION.
YOU'RE NUTS !!
USE THAT CATCH PHRASE THROUGHOUT THE WHOLE EPISODE. THE READERS WILL LOVE IT.
WHAT KIND OF COMEDY IS THAT?!
NO, NO.
YOU'RE NUTS !!
YOU'RE NUTS !!
YOU'RE NUTS !!
YOU'RE NUTS !!
YOU'RE NUTS !!
YOU'RE NUTS !!

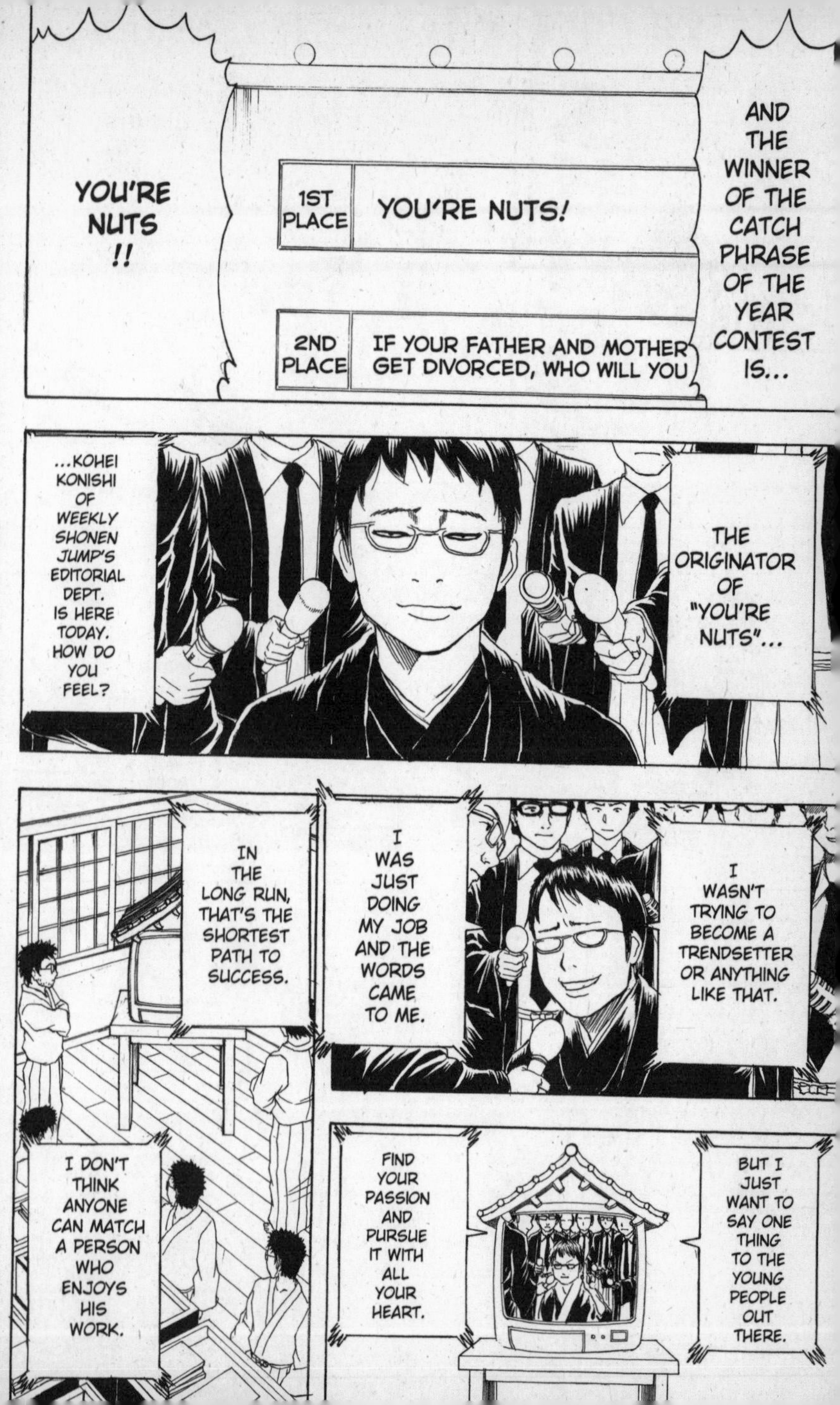
AND THE WINNER OF THE CATCH PHRASE OF THE YEAR CONTEST IS...
1ST PLACE
YOU'RE NUTS!
2ND PLACE
IF YOUR FATHER AND MOTHER GET DIVORCED, WHO WILL YOU
YOU'RE NUTS !!
THE ORIGINATOR OF "YOU'RE NUTS"...
...KOHEI KONISHI OF WEEKLY SHONEN JUMP'S EDITORIAL DEPT. IS HERE TODAY. HOW DO YOU FEEL?
I WASN'T TRYING TO BECOME A TRENDSETTER OR ANYTHING LIKE THAT.
I WAS JUST DOING MY JOB AND THE WORDS CAME TO ME.
BUT I JUST WANT TO SAY ONE THING TO THE YOUNG PEOPLE OUT THERE.
FIND YOUR PASSION AND PURSUE IT WITH ALL YOUR HEART.
IN THE LONG RUN, THAT'S THE SHORTEST PATH TO SUCCESS.
I DON'T THINK ANYONE CAN MATCH A PERSON WHO ENJOYS HIS WORK.

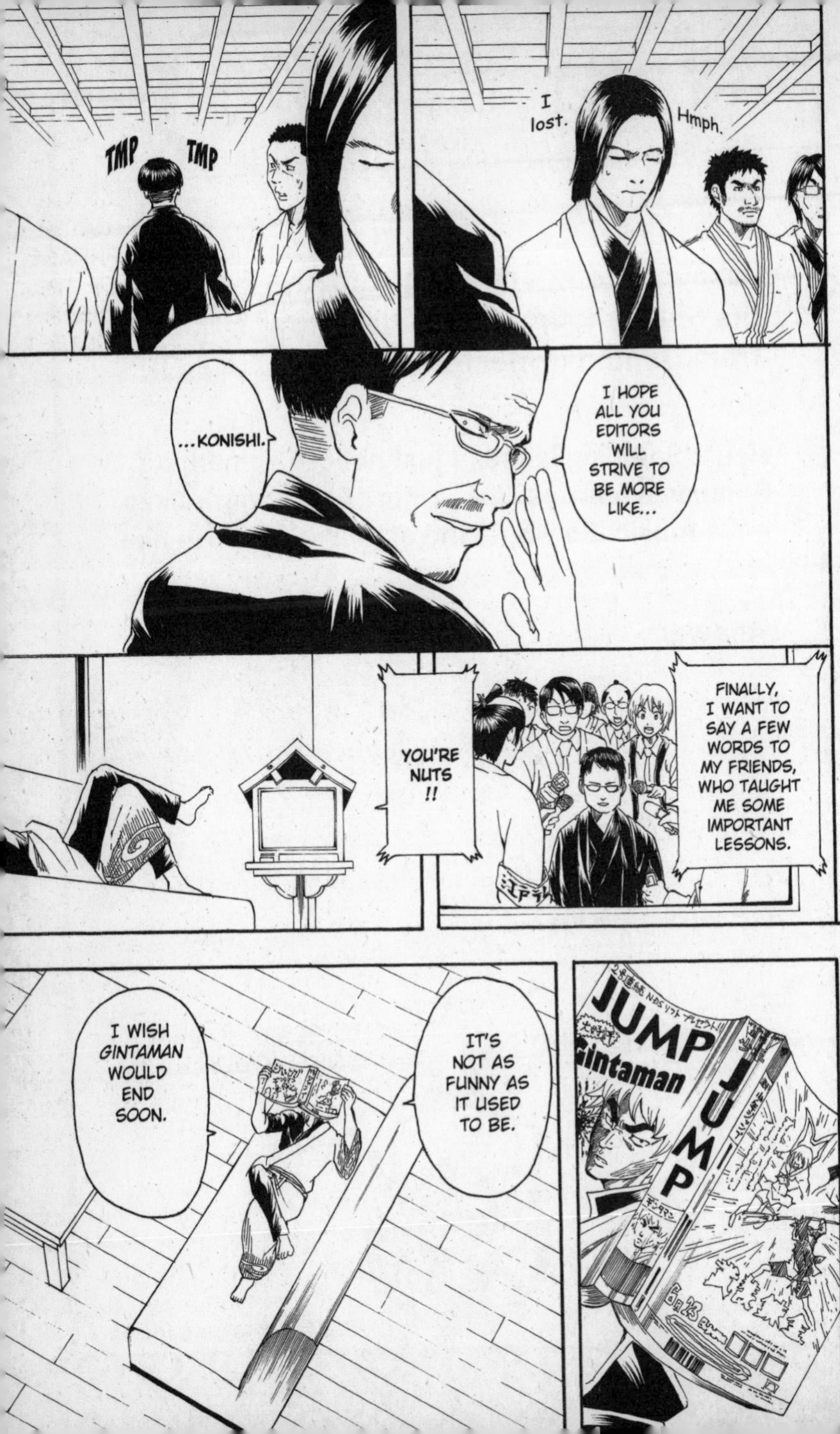
I lost.
Hmph.
TMP TMP
I HOPE ALL YOU EDITORS WILL STRIVE TO BE MORE LIKE...
...KONISHI.
FINALLY, I WANT TO SAY A FEW WORDS TO MY FRIENDS, WHO TAUGHT ME SOME IMPORTANT LESSONS.
YOU'RE NUTS!!
JUMP
Gintaman
JUMP
IT'S NOT AS FUNNY AS IT USED TO BE.
I WISH GINTAMAN WOULD END SOON.

Sorachi's Q&A
Hanging with the Readers #57

<Question from "I'm A Big Yorozuya Fan, but the Shinsengumi Are...Just Okay," from Gunma Prefecture>

Hello, Sorachi-Sensei. I just noticed something. Shinpachi idolizes Otsu, right? And Kagura likes enka music. So what kind of music does Gin like?

<Answer>

Gin doesn't really listen to music. He sings country music songs to himself sometimes. For your information, Okita likes *rakugo* storytelling. He looks like the kind of person who likes *rakugo*, doesn't he?

...KAIJARISUIGYO-NO SUIGYOMATSU...

JUGEMU-JUGEMU GOKONOSURIKIRE...

*PART OF AN ABSURDLY LONG NAME REPEATED IN A FAMOUS *RAKUGO* TALE.

(Q&A #58 is on page 106)

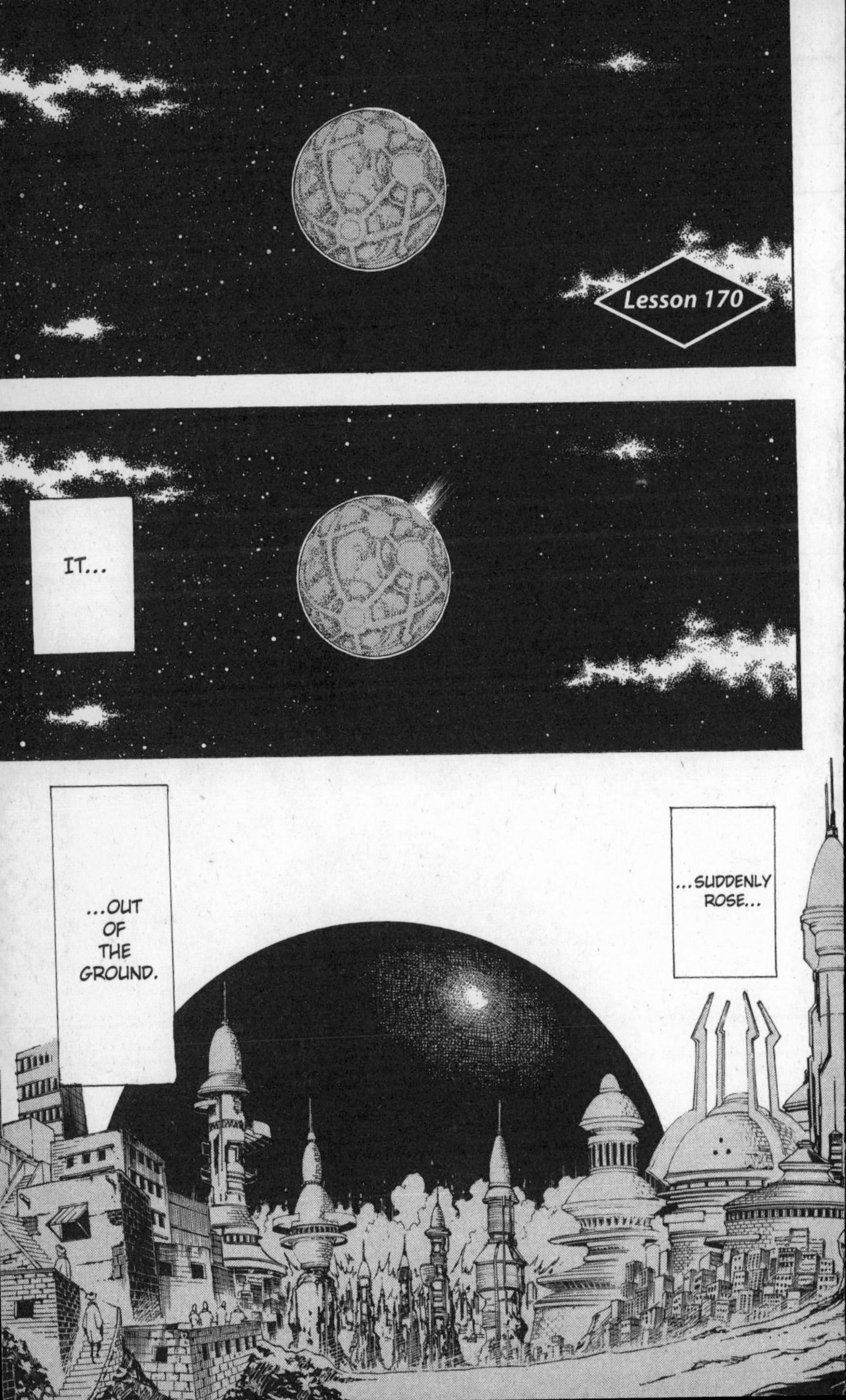
Lesson 170
IT...
...SUDDENLY ROSE...
...OUT OF THE GROUND.

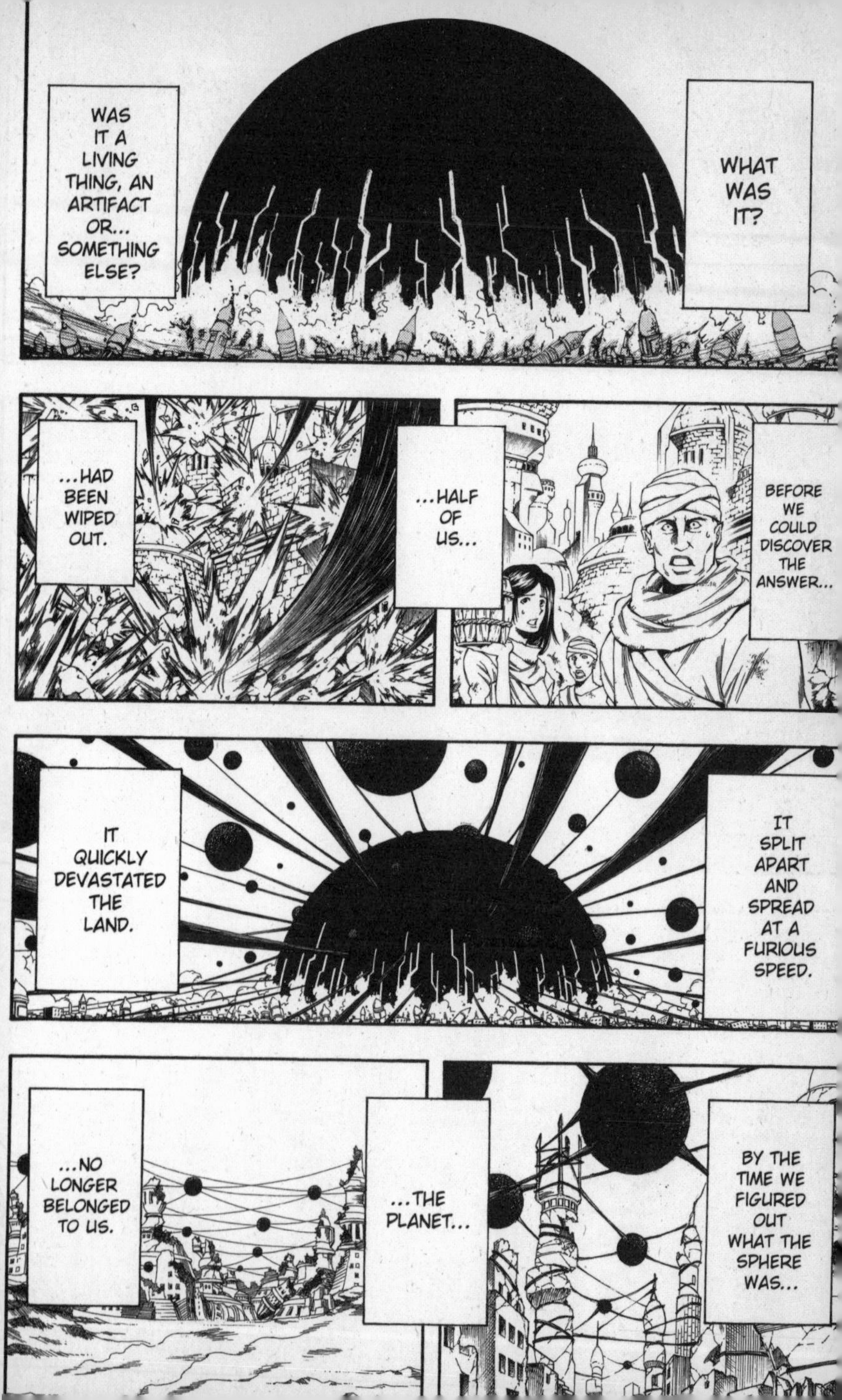

WHAT WAS IT?
WAS IT A LIVING THING, AN ARTIFACT OR... SOMETHING ELSE?
BEFORE WE COULD DISCOVER THE ANSWER...
...HALF OF US...
...HAD BEEN WIPED OUT.
IT SPLIT APART AND SPREAD AT A FURIOUS SPEED.
IT QUICKLY DEVASTATED THE LAND.
BY THE TIME WE FIGURED OUT WHAT THE SPHERE WAS...
...THE PLANET...
...NO LONGER BELONGED TO US.

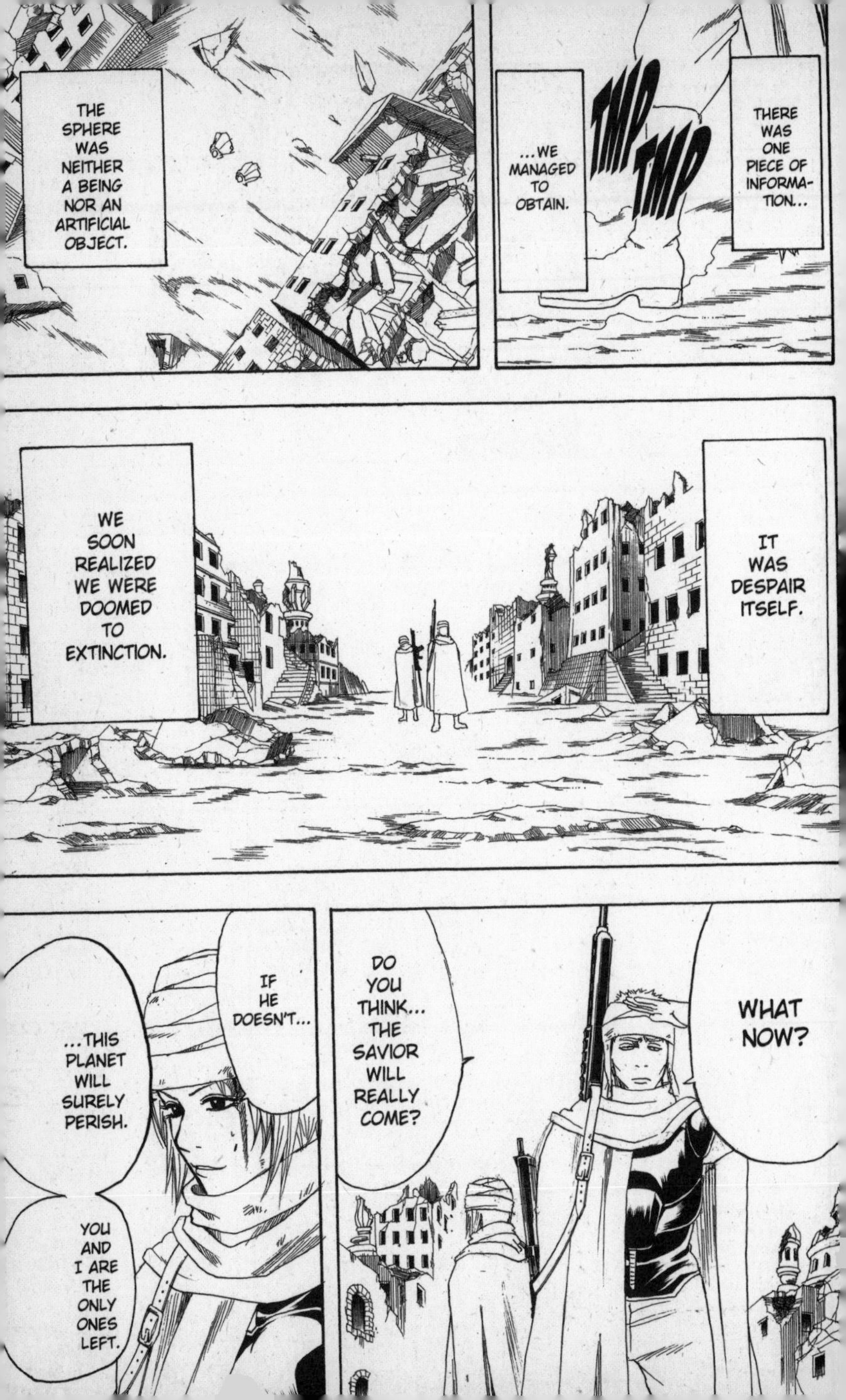

THERE WAS ONE PIECE OF INFORMATION...
...WE MANAGED TO OBTAIN.
TMP TMP
THE SPHERE WAS NEITHER A BEING NOR AN ARTIFICIAL OBJECT.
IT WAS DESPAIR ITSELF.
WE SOON REALIZED WE WERE DOOMED TO EXTINCTION.
WHAT NOW?
DO YOU THINK... THE SAVIOR WILL REALLY COME?
IF HE DOESN'T...
...THIS PLANET WILL SURELY PERISH.
YOU AND I ARE THE ONLY ONES LEFT.

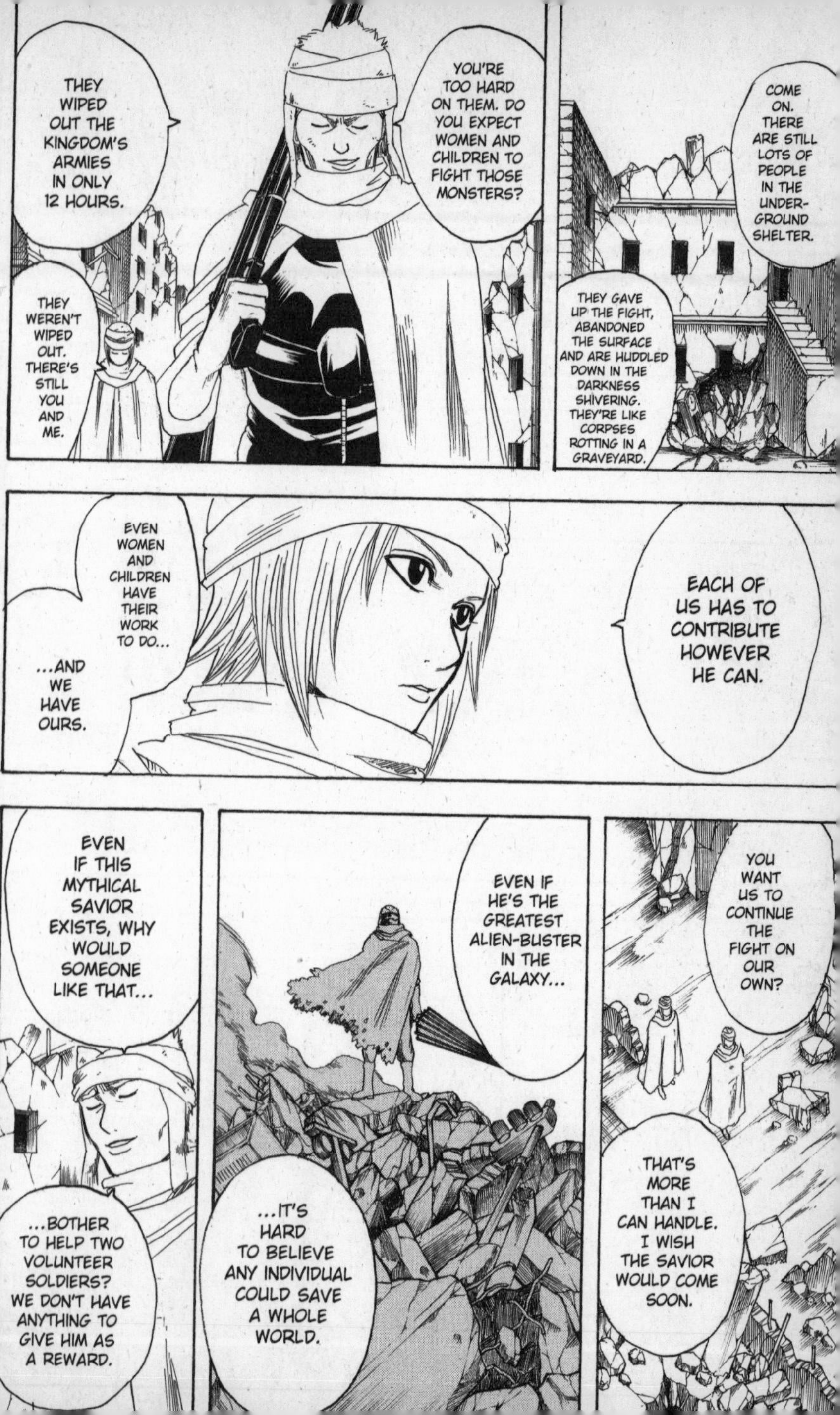
COME ON. THERE ARE STILL LOTS OF PEOPLE IN THE UNDER-GROUND SHELTER.
THEY GAVE UP THE FIGHT, ABANDONED THE SURFACE AND ARE HUDDLED DOWN IN THE DARKNESS SHIVERING. THEY'RE LIKE CORPSES ROTTING IN A GRAVEYARD.
YOU'RE TOO HARD ON THEM. DO YOU EXPECT WOMEN AND CHILDREN TO FIGHT THOSE MONSTERS?
THEY WIPED OUT THE KINGDOM'S ARMIES IN ONLY 12 HOURS.
THEY WEREN'T WIPED OUT. THERE'S STILL YOU AND ME.
EACH OF US HAS TO CONTRIBUTE HOWEVER HE CAN.
EVEN WOMEN AND CHILDREN HAVE THEIR WORK TO DO...
...AND WE HAVE OURS.
YOU WANT US TO CONTINUE THE FIGHT ON OUR OWN?
THAT'S MORE THAN I CAN HANDLE. I WISH THE SAVIOR WOULD COME SOON.
EVEN IF HE'S THE GREATEST ALIEN-BUSTER IN THE GALAXY...
...IT'S HARD TO BELIEVE ANY INDIVIDUAL COULD SAVE A WHOLE WORLD.
EVEN IF THIS MYTHICAL SAVIOR EXISTS, WHY WOULD SOMEONE LIKE THAT...
...BOTHER TO HELP TWO VOLUNTEER SOLDIERS? WE DON'T HAVE ANYTHING TO GIVE HIM AS A REWARD.

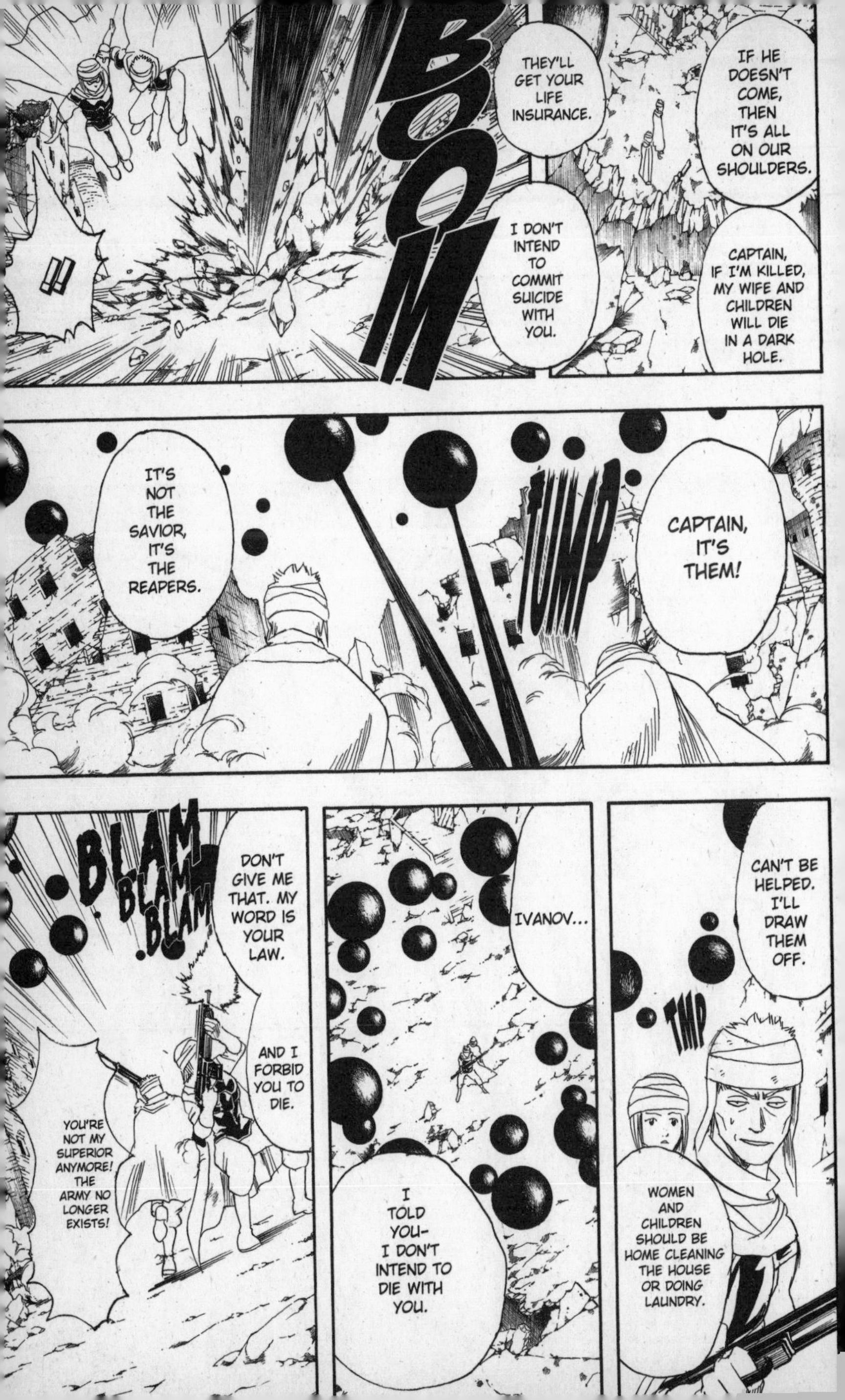
IF HE DOESN'T COME, THEN IT'S ALL ON OUR SHOULDERS.
CAPTAIN, IF I'M KILLED, MY WIFE AND CHILDREN WILL DIE IN A DARK HOLE.
THEY'LL GET YOUR LIFE INSURANCE.
I DON'T INTEND TO COMMIT SUICIDE WITH YOU.
BOOM
!!
CAPTAIN, IT'S THEM!
TUMP
IT'S NOT THE SAVIOR, IT'S THE REAPERS.
CAN'T BE HELPED. I'LL DRAW THEM OFF.
TMP
WOMEN AND CHILDREN SHOULD BE HOME CLEANING THE HOUSE OR DOING LAUNDRY.
IVANOV...
I TOLD YOU- I DON'T INTEND TO DIE WITH YOU.
DON'T GIVE ME THAT. MY WORD IS YOUR LAW.
BLAM BLAM BLAM
AND I FORBID YOU TO DIE.
YOU'RE NOT MY SUPERIOR ANYMORE! THE ARMY NO LONGER EXISTS!

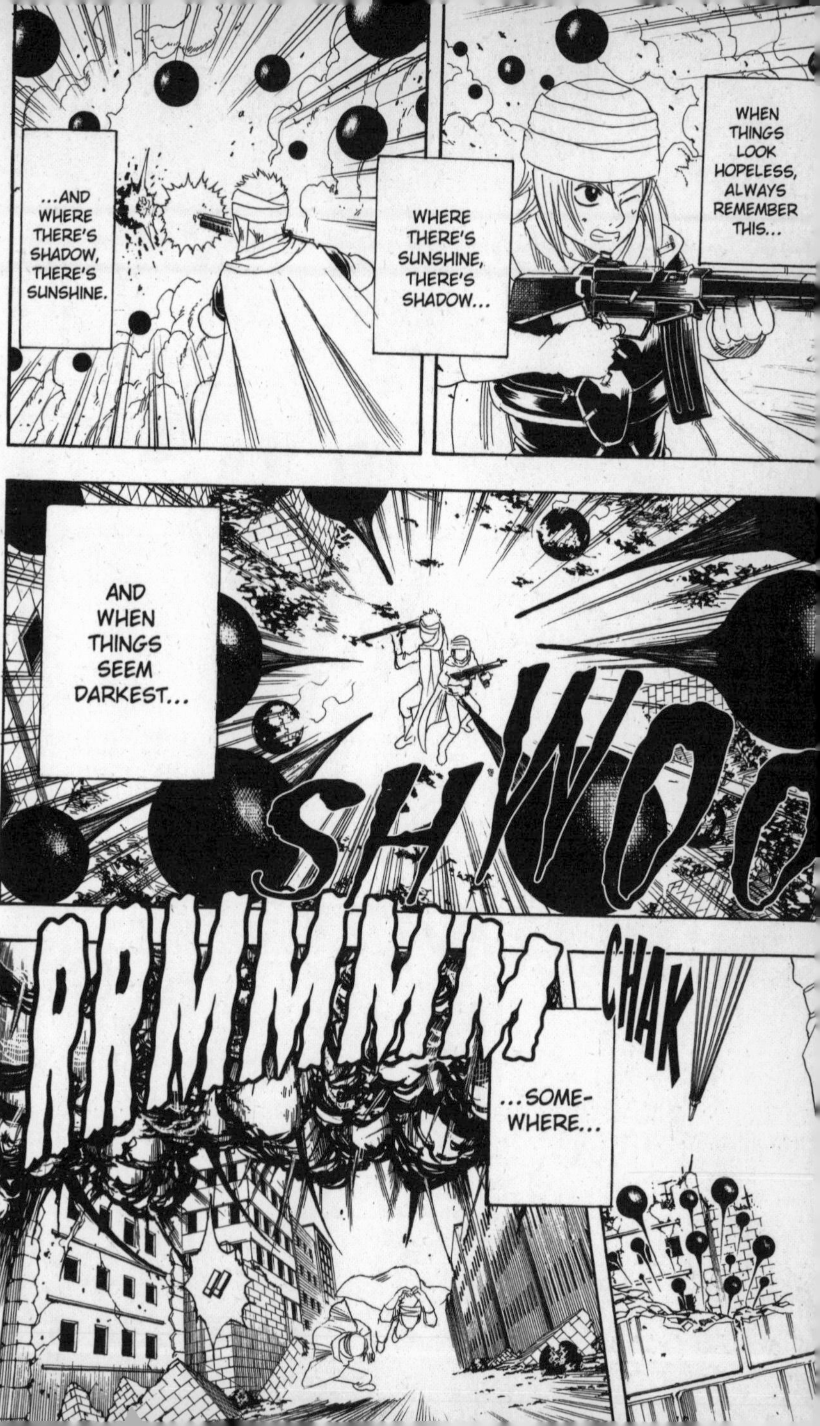
WHEN THINGS LOOK HOPELESS, ALWAYS REMEMBER THIS...
WHERE THERE'S SUNSHINE, THERE'S SHADOW...
...AND WHERE THERE'S SHADOW, THERE'S SUNSHINE.
AND WHEN THINGS SEEM DARKEST...
SHWOO
RRMMMM
CHAK
...SOME-WHERE...

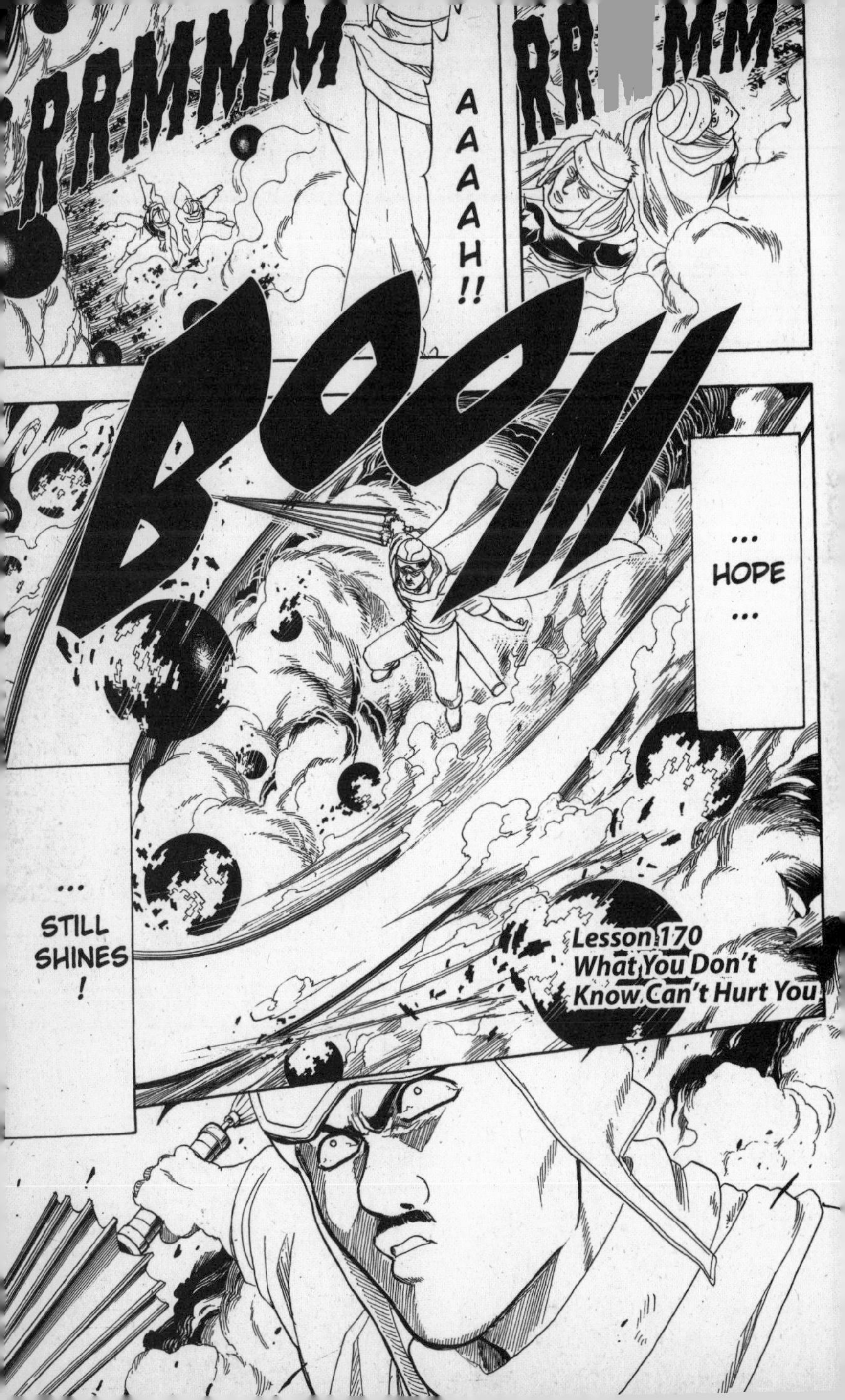

RR MM
AAAAAH!!
RRMMM
BOOM
... HOPE ...
Lesson 170
What You Don't Know Can't Hurt You
... STILL SHINES!

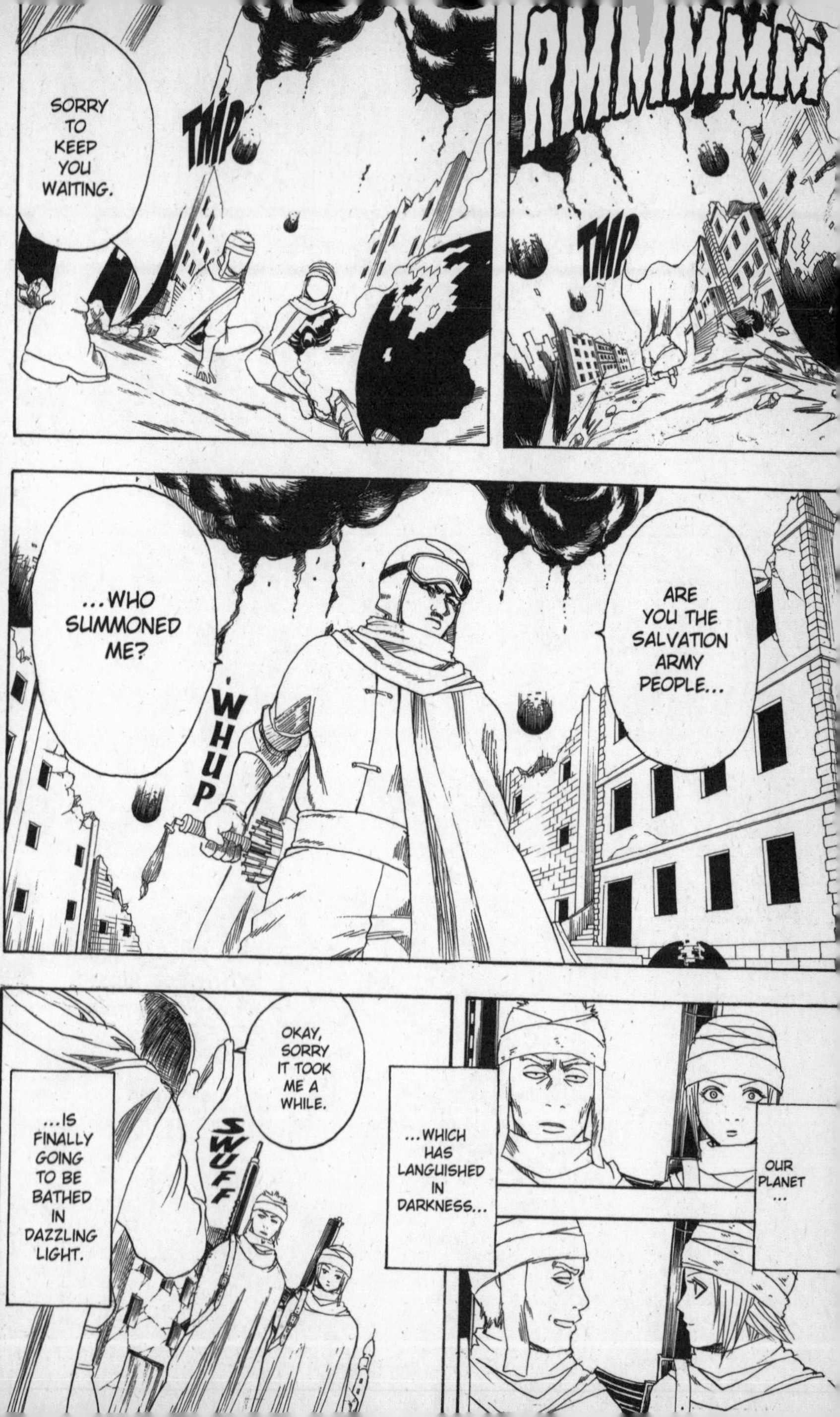
RMMMMMM
TMP
TMP
SORRY TO KEEP YOU WAITING.
ARE YOU THE SALVATION ARMY PEOPLE...
...WHO SUMMONED ME?
WHUP
OUR PLANET...
...WHICH HAS LANGUISHED IN DARKNESS...
OKAY, SORRY IT TOOK ME A WHILE.
SWUFF
...IS FINALLY GOING TO BE BATHED IN DAZZLING LIGHT.

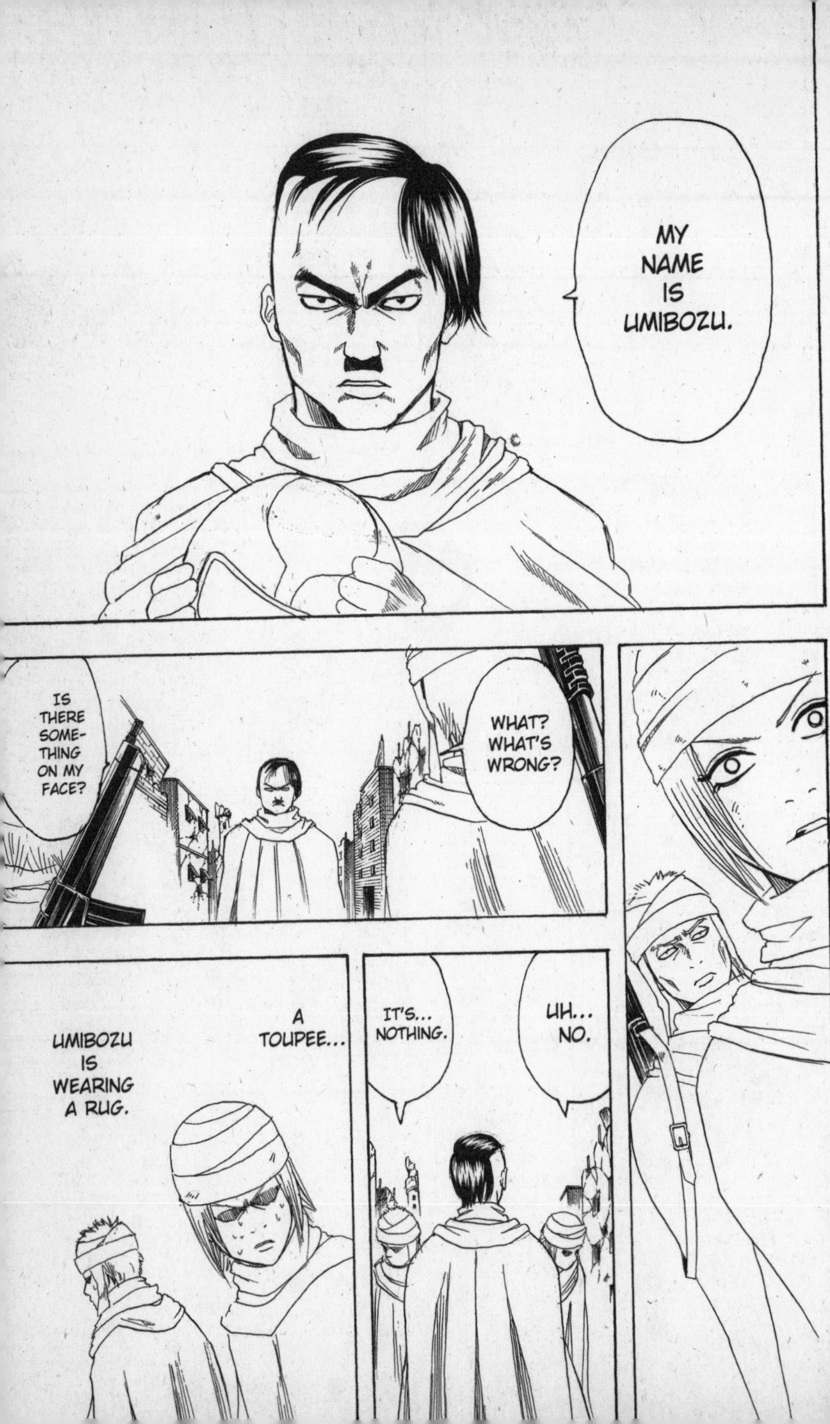
MY NAME IS UMIBOZU.
WHAT? WHAT'S WRONG?
IS THERE SOME-THING ON MY FACE?
UH... NO.
IT'S... NOTHING.
A TOUPEE...
UMIBOZU IS WEARING A RUG.

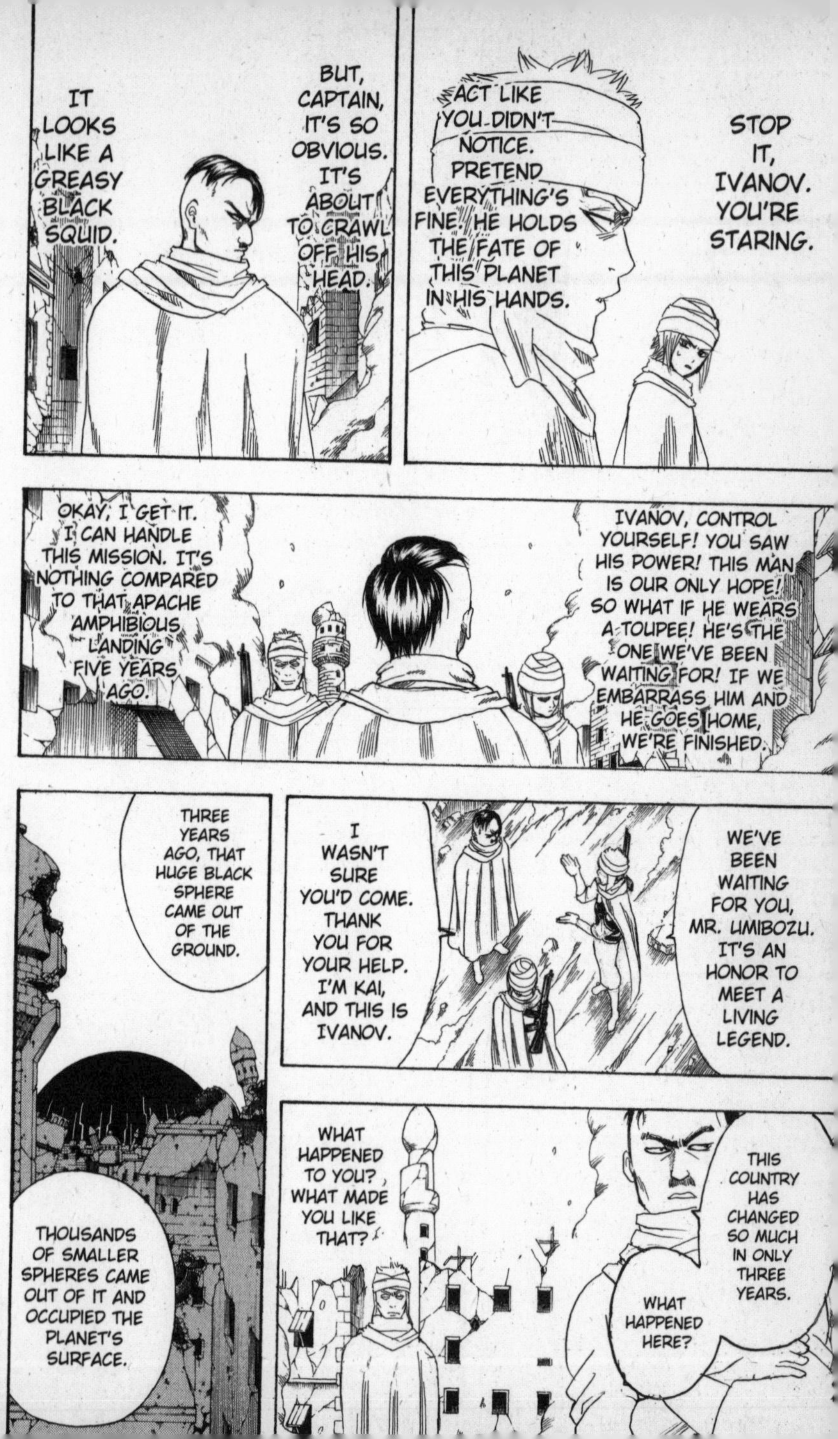
STOP IT, IVANOV. YOU'RE STARING.
ACT LIKE YOU DIDN'T NOTICE. PRETEND EVERYTHING'S FINE. HE HOLDS THE FATE OF THIS PLANET IN HIS HANDS.
BUT, CAPTAIN, IT'S SO OBVIOUS. IT'S ABOUT TO CRAWL OFF HIS HEAD.
IT LOOKS LIKE A GREASY BLACK SQUID.
IVANOV, CONTROL YOURSELF! YOU SAW HIS POWER! THIS MAN IS OUR ONLY HOPE! SO WHAT IF HE WEARS A TOUPEE! HE'S THE ONE WE'VE BEEN WAITING FOR! IF WE EMBARRASS HIM AND HE GOES HOME, WE'RE FINISHED.
OKAY, I GET IT. I CAN HANDLE THIS MISSION. IT'S NOTHING COMPARED TO THAT APACHE AMPHIBIOUS LANDING FIVE YEARS AGO.
WE'VE BEEN WAITING FOR YOU, MR. UMIBOZU. IT'S AN HONOR TO MEET A LIVING LEGEND.
I WASN'T SURE YOU'D COME. THANK YOU FOR YOUR HELP. I'M KAI, AND THIS IS IVANOV.
THIS COUNTRY HAS CHANGED SO MUCH IN ONLY THREE YEARS.
WHAT HAPPENED HERE?
WHAT HAPPENED TO YOU? WHAT MADE YOU LIKE THAT?
THREE YEARS AGO, THAT HUGE BLACK SPHERE CAME OUT OF THE GROUND.
THOUSANDS OF SMALLER SPHERES CAME OUT OF IT AND OCCUPIED THE PLANET'S SURFACE.

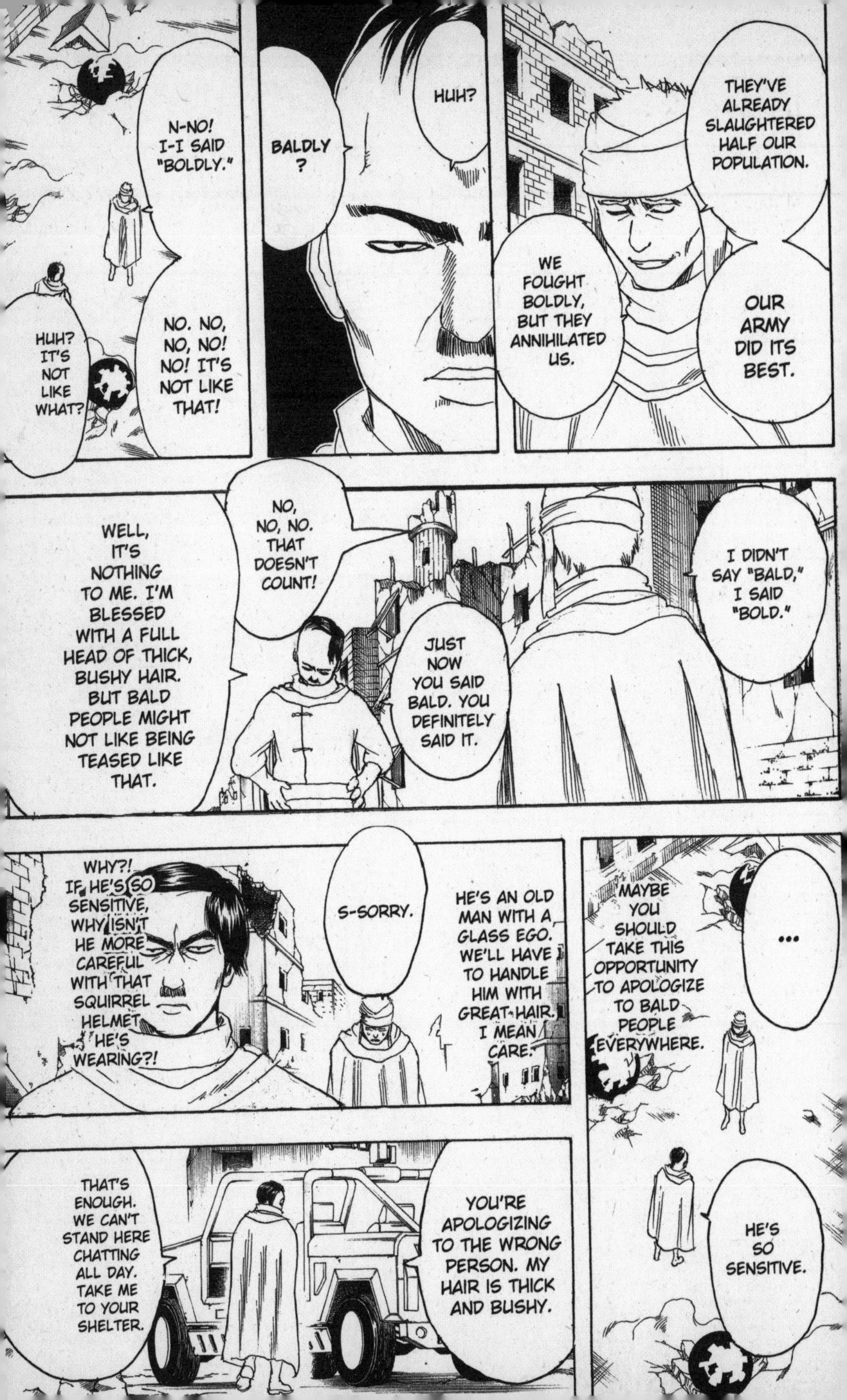
THEY'VE ALREADY SLAUGHTERED HALF OUR POPULATION.
OUR ARMY DID ITS BEST.
WE FOUGHT BOLDLY, BUT THEY ANNIHILATED US.
HUH?
BALDLY?
N-NO! I-I SAID "BOLDLY."
NO. NO, NO, NO! NO! IT'S NOT LIKE THAT!
HUH? IT'S NOT LIKE WHAT?
I DIDN'T SAY "BALD," I SAID "BOLD."
JUST NOW YOU SAID BALD. YOU DEFINITELY SAID IT.
NO, NO, NO. THAT DOESN'T COUNT!
WELL, IT'S NOTHING TO ME. I'M BLESSED WITH A FULL HEAD OF THICK, BUSHY HAIR. BUT BALD PEOPLE MIGHT NOT LIKE BEING TEASED LIKE THAT.
...
MAYBE YOU SHOULD TAKE THIS OPPORTUNITY TO APOLOGIZE TO BALD PEOPLE EVERYWHERE.
HE'S SO SENSITIVE.
S-SORRY.
HE'S AN OLD MAN WITH A GLASS EGO. WE'LL HAVE TO HANDLE HIM WITH GREAT HAIR. I MEAN CARE.
WHY?! IF HE'S SO SENSITIVE, WHY ISN'T HE MORE CAREFUL WITH THAT SQUIRREL HELMET HE'S WEARING?!
YOU'RE APOLOGIZING TO THE WRONG PERSON. MY HAIR IS THICK AND BUSHY.
THAT'S ENOUGH. WE CAN'T STAND HERE CHATTING ALL DAY. TAKE ME TO YOUR SHELTER.

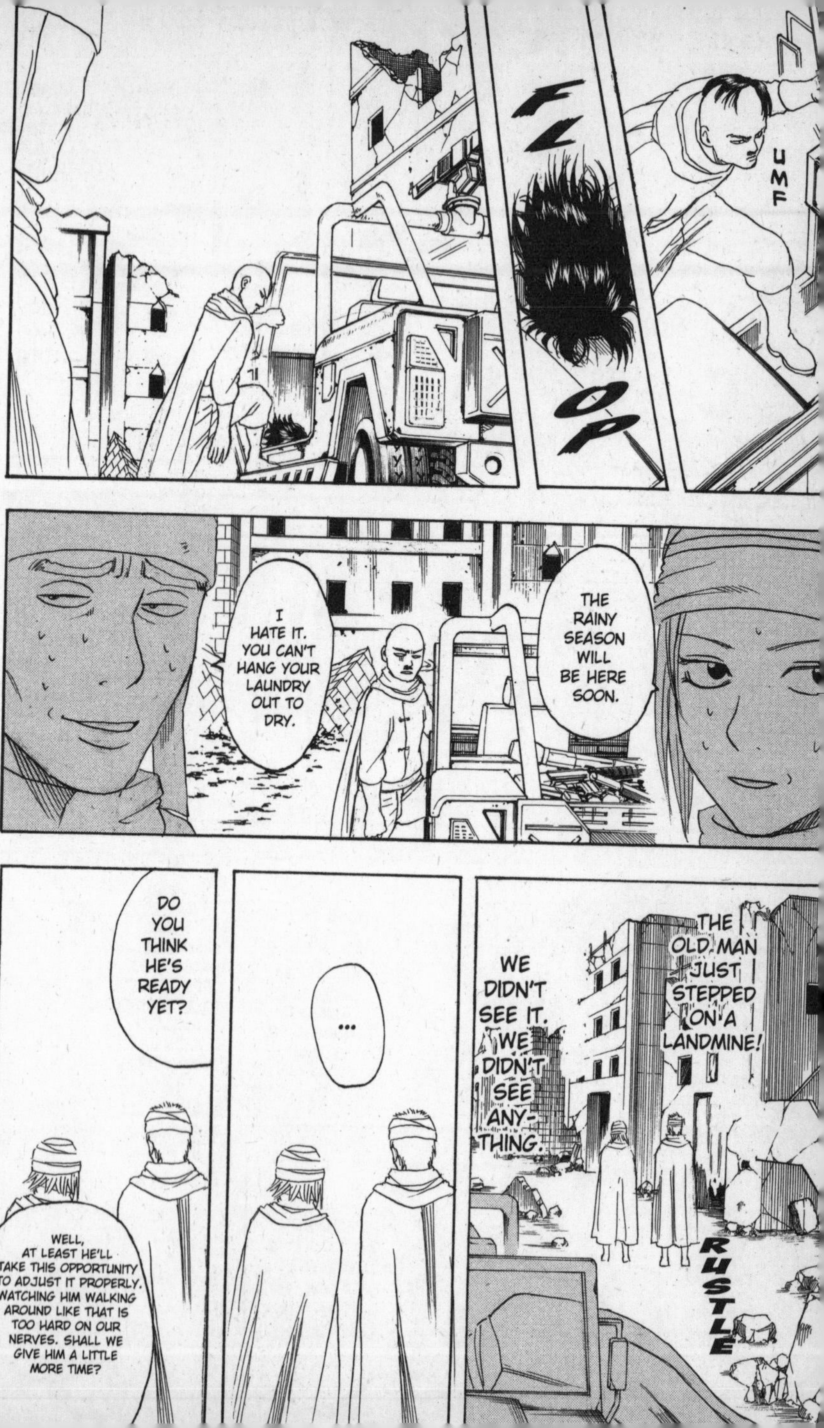
UMF
FLOP
THE RAINY SEASON WILL BE HERE SOON.
I HATE IT. YOU CAN'T HANG YOUR LAUNDRY OUT TO DRY.
THE OLD MAN JUST STEPPED ON A LANDMINE!
WE DIDN'T SEE IT. WE DIDN'T SEE ANYTHING.
RUSTLE
...
DO YOU THINK HE'S READY YET?
WELL, AT LEAST HE'LL TAKE THIS OPPORTUNITY TO ADJUST IT PROPERLY. WATCHING HIM WALKING AROUND LIKE THAT IS TOO HARD ON OUR NERVES. SHALL WE GIVE HIM A LITTLE MORE TIME?

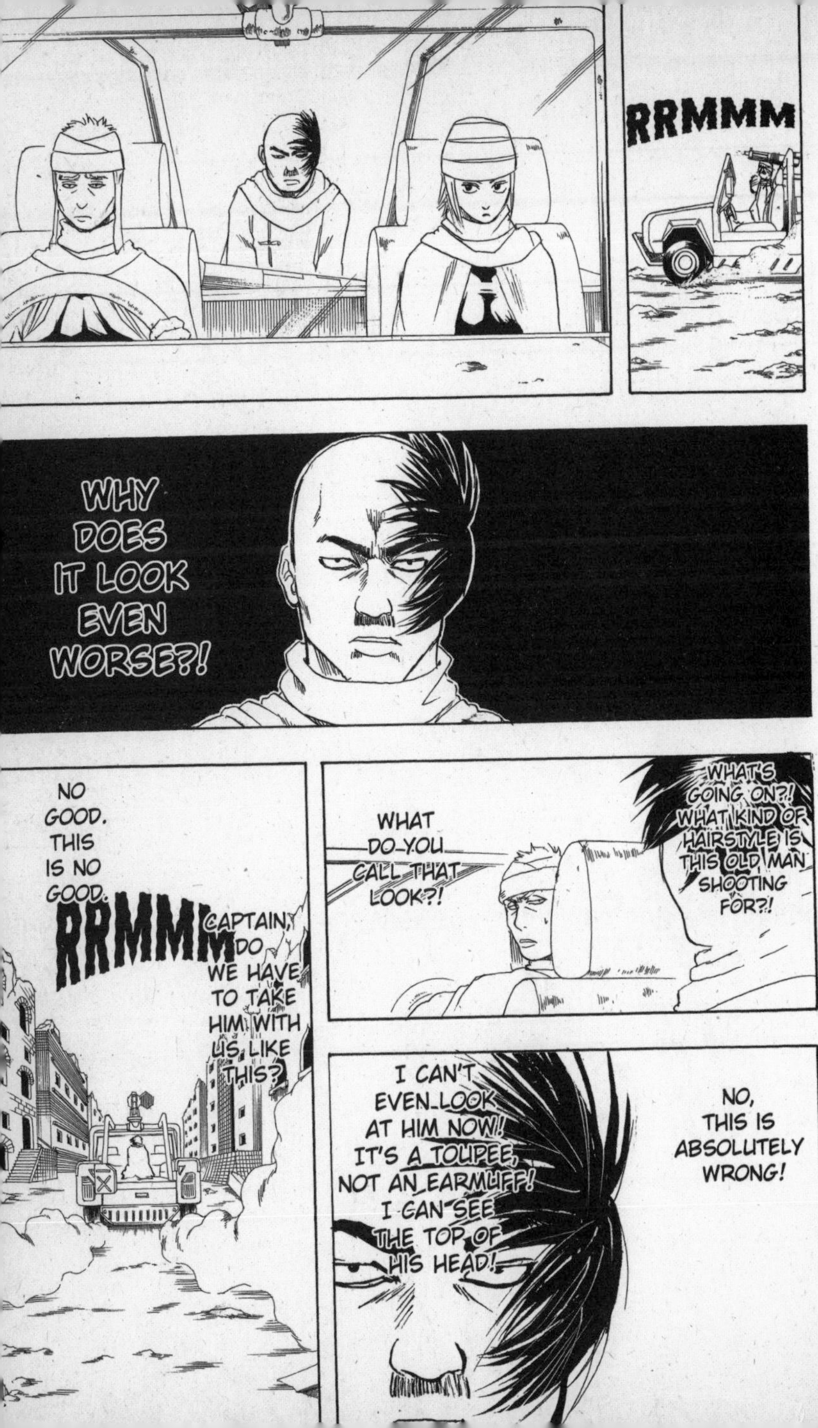
RRMMM
WHY DOES IT LOOK EVEN WORSE?!
WHAT'S GOING ON?! WHAT KIND OF HAIRSTYLE IS THIS OLD MAN SHOOTING FOR?!
WHAT DO YOU CALL THAT LOOK?!
NO, THIS IS ABSOLUTELY WRONG!
I CAN'T EVEN LOOK AT HIM NOW! IT'S A TOUPEE, NOT AN EARMUFF! I CAN SEE THE TOP OF HIS HEAD!
NO GOOD. THIS IS NO GOOD.
RRMMM
CAPTAIN, DO WE HAVE TO TAKE HIM WITH US, LIKE THIS?

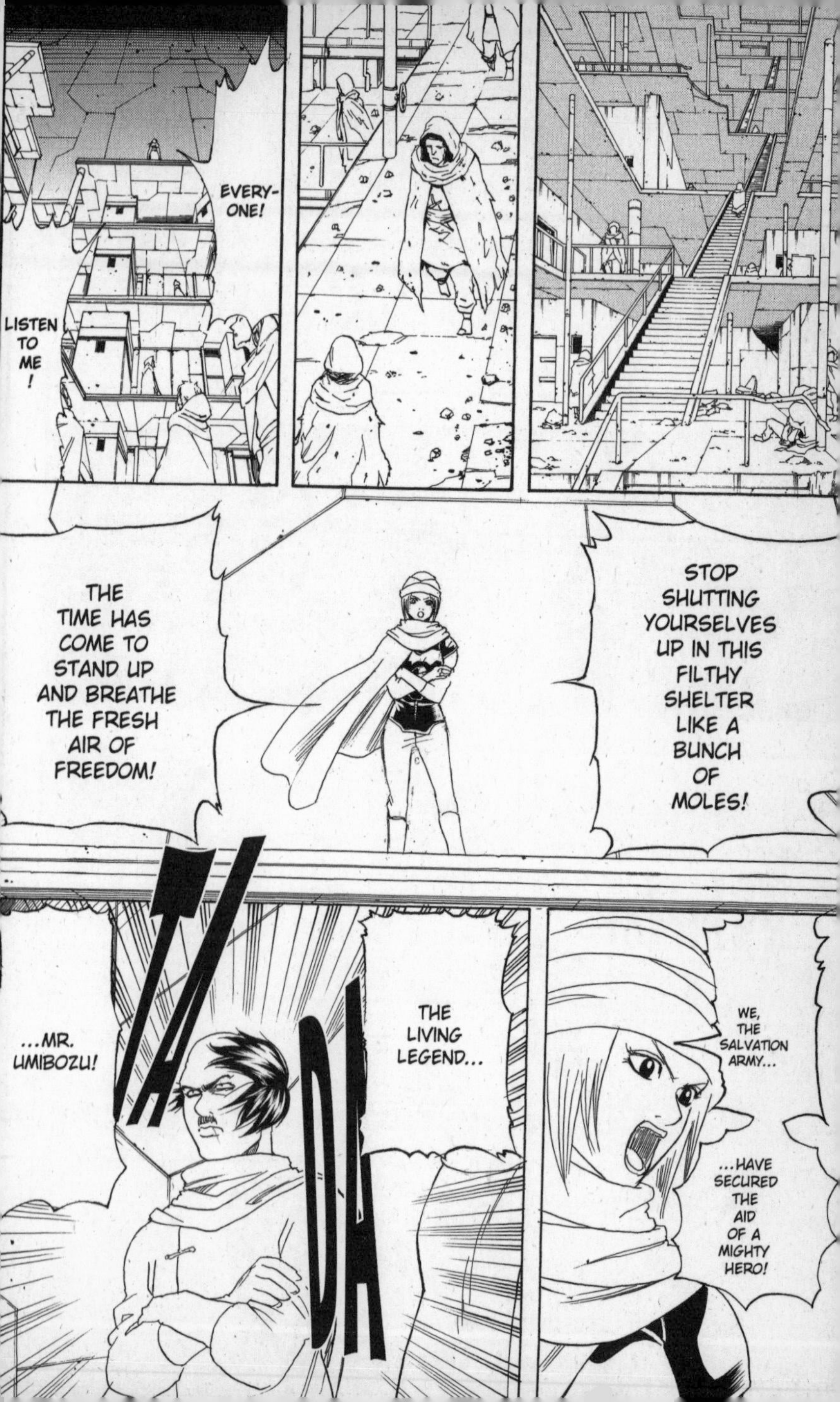
EVERY-ONE!
LISTEN TO ME!
STOP SHUTTING YOURSELVES UP IN THIS FILTHY SHELTER LIKE A BUNCH OF MOLES!
THE TIME HAS COME TO STAND UP AND BREATHE THE FRESH AIR OF FREEDOM!
WE, THE SALVATION ARMY...
...HAVE SECURED THE AID OF A MIGHTY HERO!
THE LIVING LEGEND...
TA
DA
...MR. UMIBOZU!

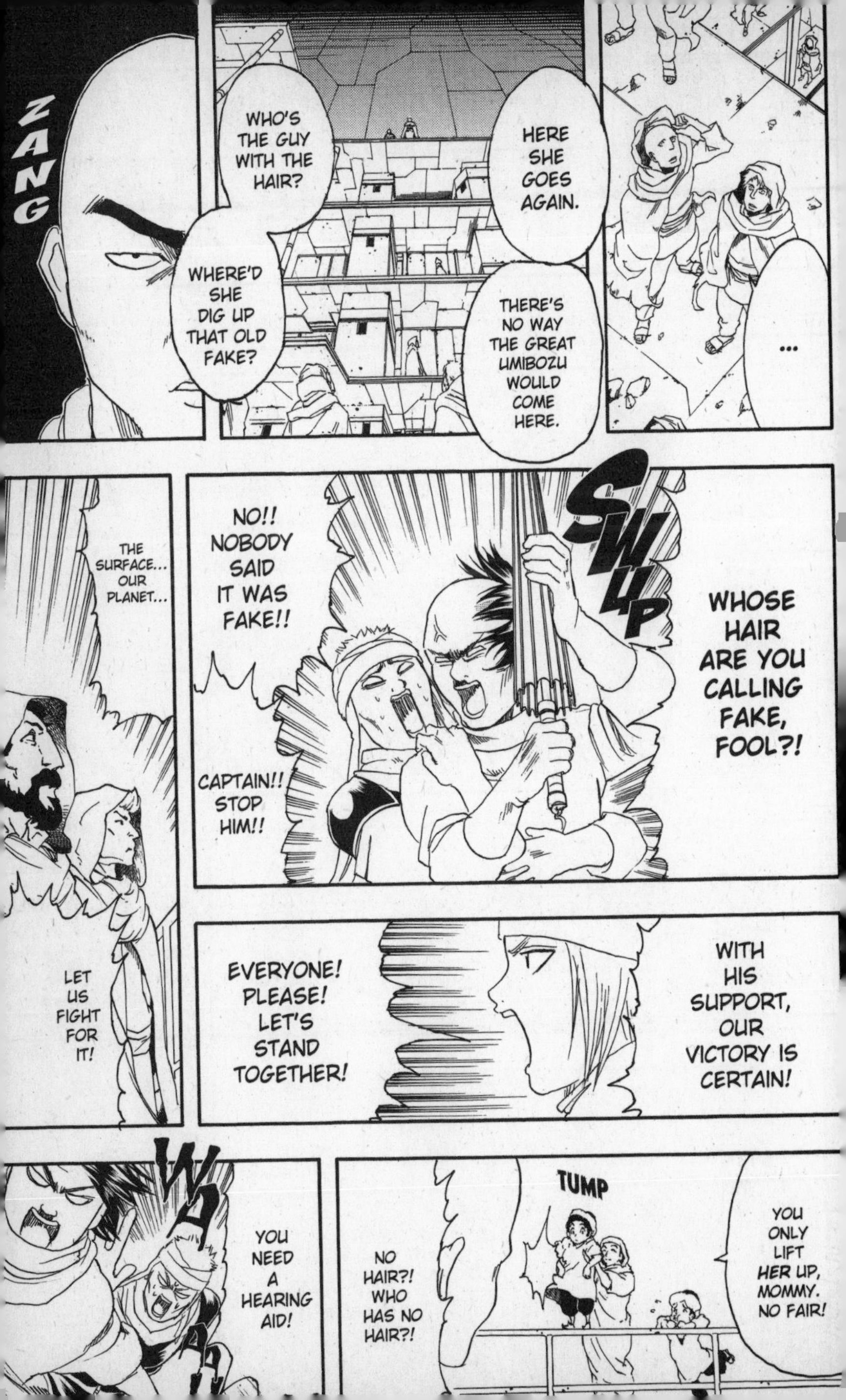
...
HERE SHE GOES AGAIN.
WHO'S THE GUY WITH THE HAIR?
THERE'S NO WAY THE GREAT UMIBOZU WOULD COME HERE.
WHERE'D SHE DIG UP THAT OLD FAKE?
ZANG
SWUP
WHOSE HAIR ARE YOU CALLING FAKE, FOOL?!
NO!! NOBODY SAID IT WAS FAKE!!
CAPTAIN!! STOP HIM!!
WITH HIS SUPPORT, OUR VICTORY IS CERTAIN!
EVERYONE! PLEASE! LET'S STAND TOGETHER!
THE SURFACE... OUR PLANET...
LET US FIGHT FOR IT!
YOU ONLY LIFT HER UP, MOMMY. NO FAIR!
TUMP
NO HAIR?! WHO HAS NO HAIR?!
YOU NEED A HEARING AID!
WA

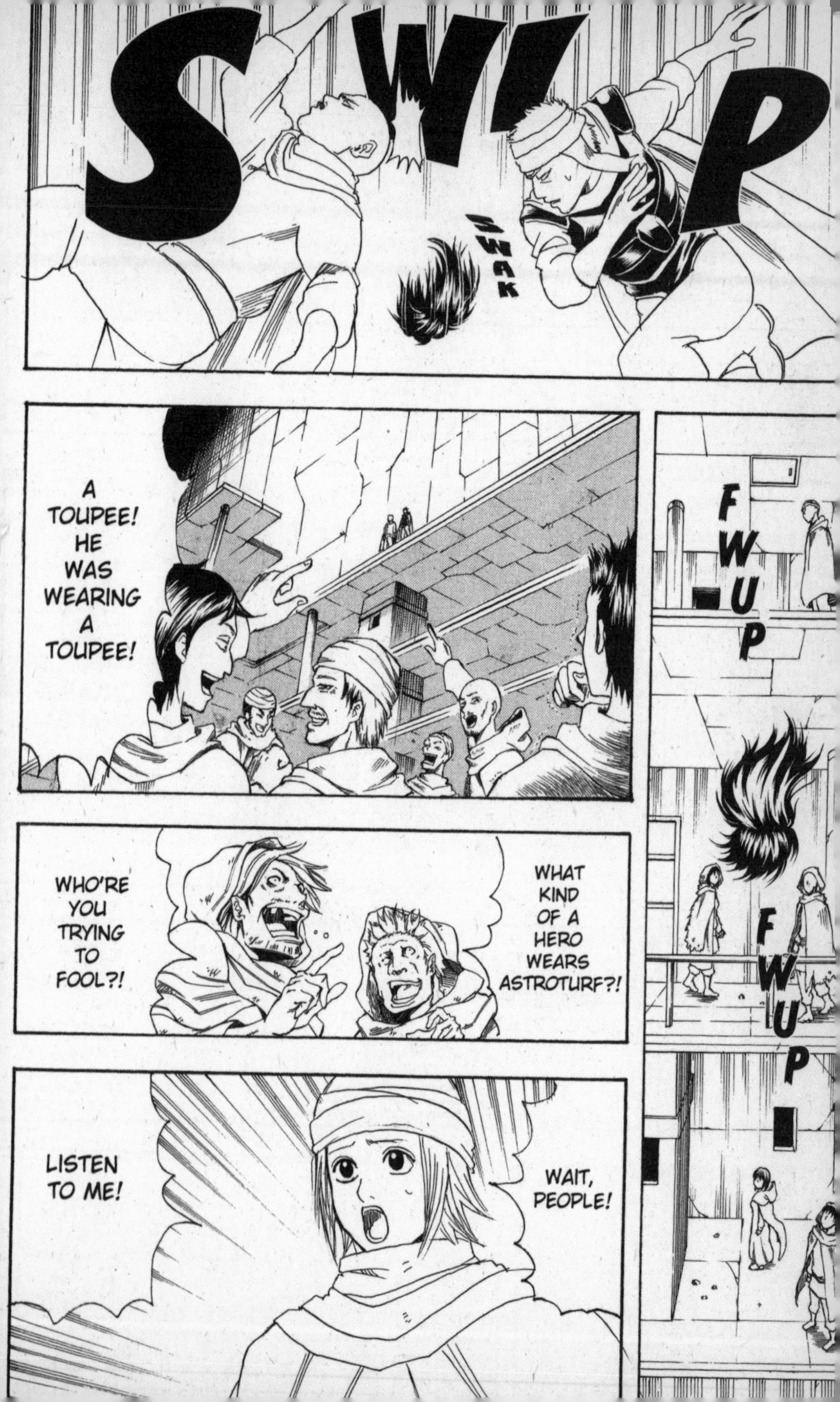
SWIP
SWAK
FWUP
FWUP
A TOUPEE! HE WAS WEARING A TOUPEE!
WHAT KIND OF A HERO WEARS ASTROTURF?!
WHO'RE YOU TRYING TO FOOL?!
WAIT, PEOPLE!
LISTEN TO ME!

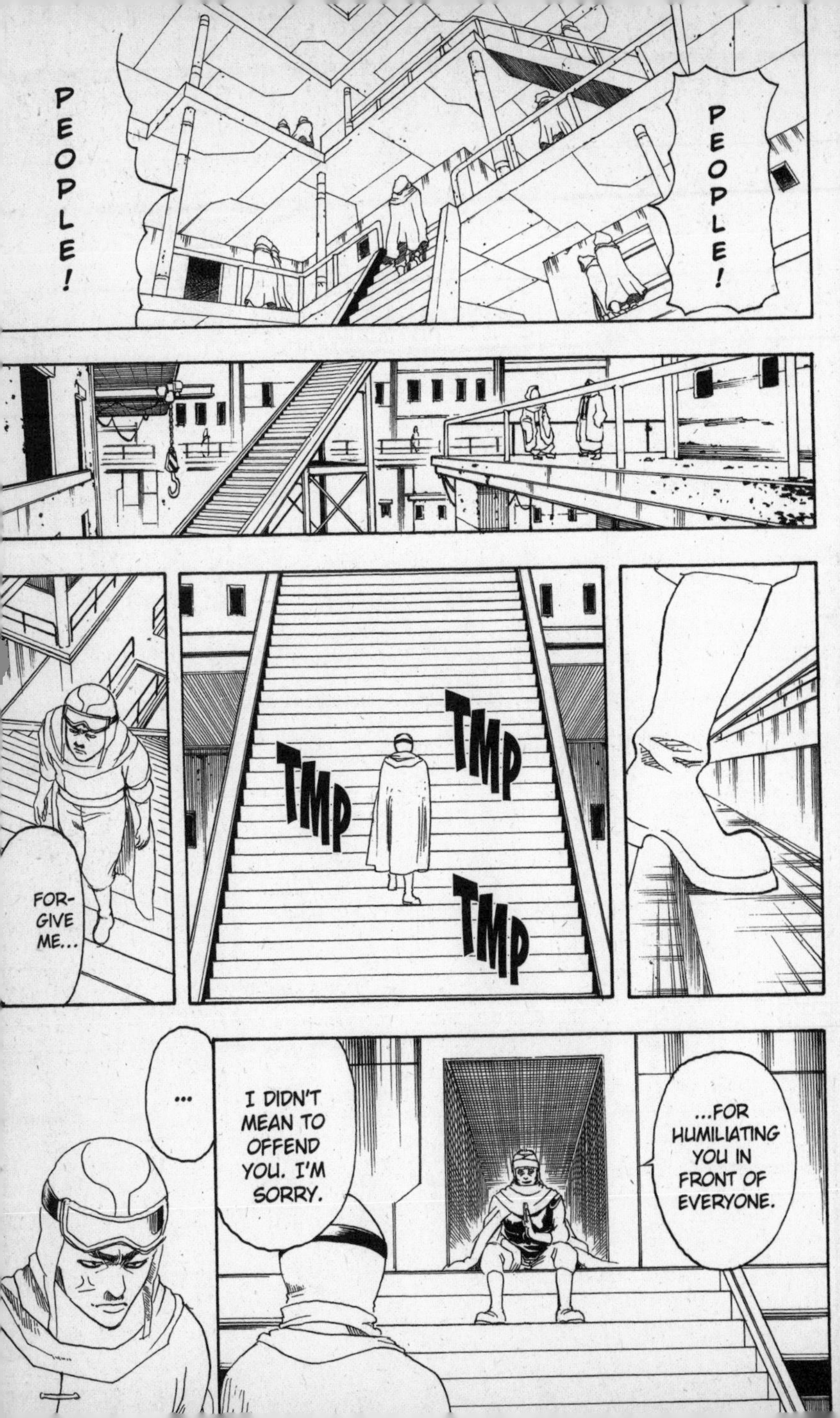
PEOPLE!
PEOPLE!
TMP
TMP
TMP
FOR-GIVE ME...
...FOR HUMILIATING YOU IN FRONT OF EVERYONE.
I DIDN'T MEAN TO OFFEND YOU. I'M SORRY.
...

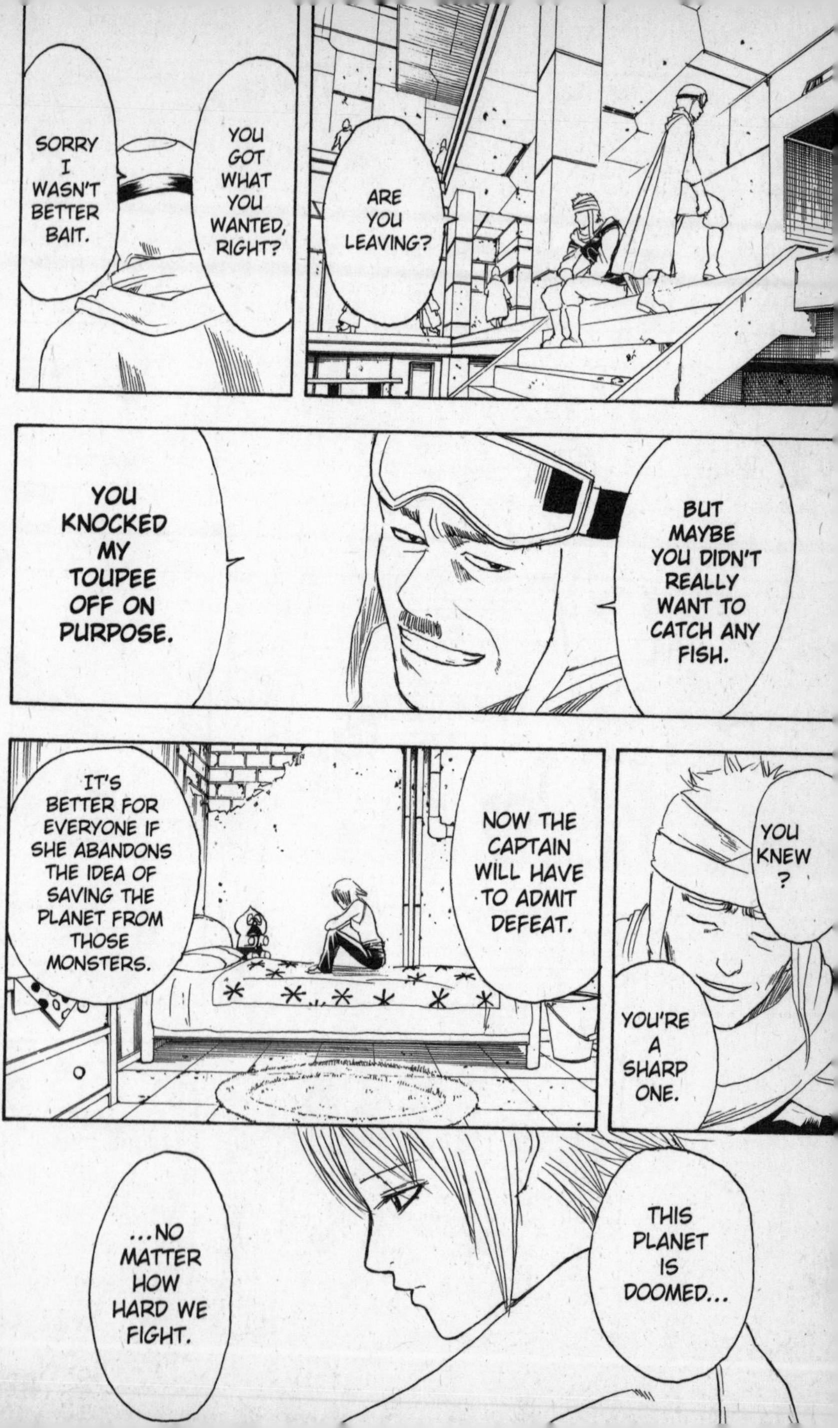
ARE YOU LEAVING?
YOU GOT WHAT YOU WANTED, RIGHT?
SORRY I WASN'T BETTER BAIT.
BUT MAYBE YOU DIDN'T REALLY WANT TO CATCH ANY FISH.
YOU KNOCKED MY TOUPEE OFF ON PURPOSE.
YOU KNEW?
YOU'RE A SHARP ONE.
NOW THE CAPTAIN WILL HAVE TO ADMIT DEFEAT.
IT'S BETTER FOR EVERYONE IF SHE ABANDONS THE IDEA OF SAVING THE PLANET FROM THOSE MONSTERS.
THIS PLANET IS DOOMED...
...NO MATTER HOW HARD WE FIGHT.

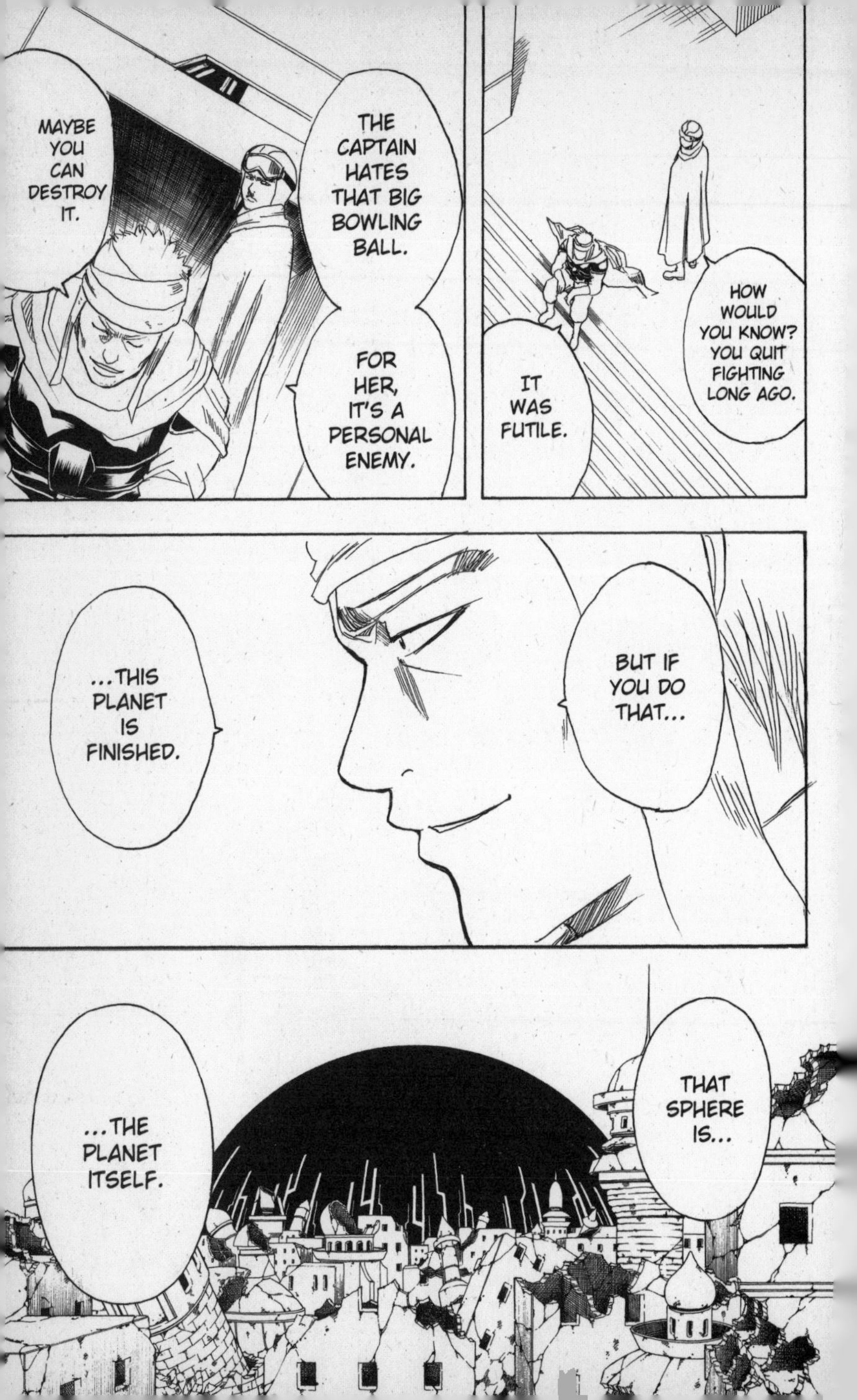
HOW WOULD YOU KNOW? YOU QUIT FIGHTING LONG AGO.
IT WAS FUTILE.
THE CAPTAIN HATES THAT BIG BOWLING BALL.
FOR HER, IT'S A PERSONAL ENEMY.
MAYBE YOU CAN DESTROY IT.
BUT IF YOU DO THAT...
...THIS PLANET IS FINISHED.
THAT SPHERE IS...
...THE PLANET ITSELF.

● Published in *Akamaru JUMP*, 2007 as the cover illustration for the September 25th extra issue

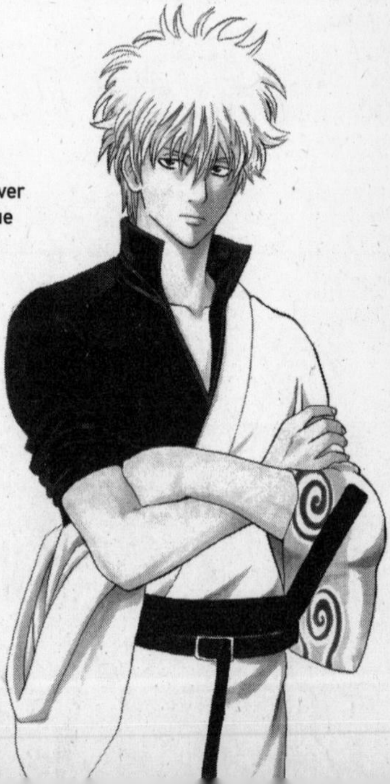

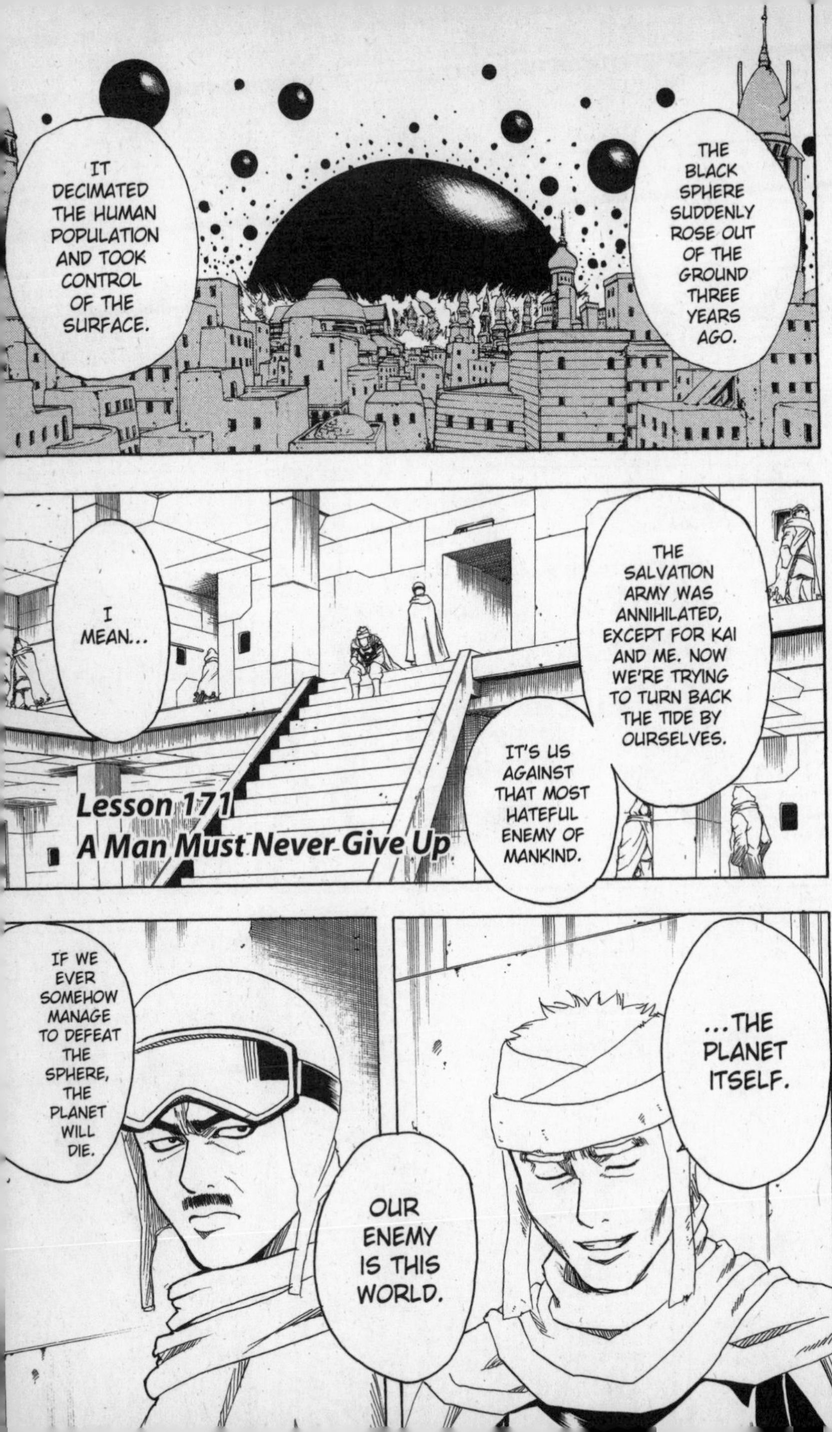
THE BLACK SPHERE SUDDENLY ROSE OUT OF THE GROUND THREE YEARS AGO.
IT DECIMATED THE HUMAN POPULATION AND TOOK CONTROL OF THE SURFACE.
THE SALVATION ARMY WAS ANNIHILATED, EXCEPT FOR KAI AND ME. NOW WE'RE TRYING TO TURN BACK THE TIDE BY OURSELVES.
IT'S US AGAINST THAT MOST HATEFUL ENEMY OF MANKIND.
I MEAN...
Lesson 171
A Man Must Never Give Up
OUR ENEMY IS THIS WORLD.
...THE PLANET ITSELF.
IF WE EVER SOMEHOW MANAGE TO DEFEAT THE SPHERE, THE PLANET WILL DIE.

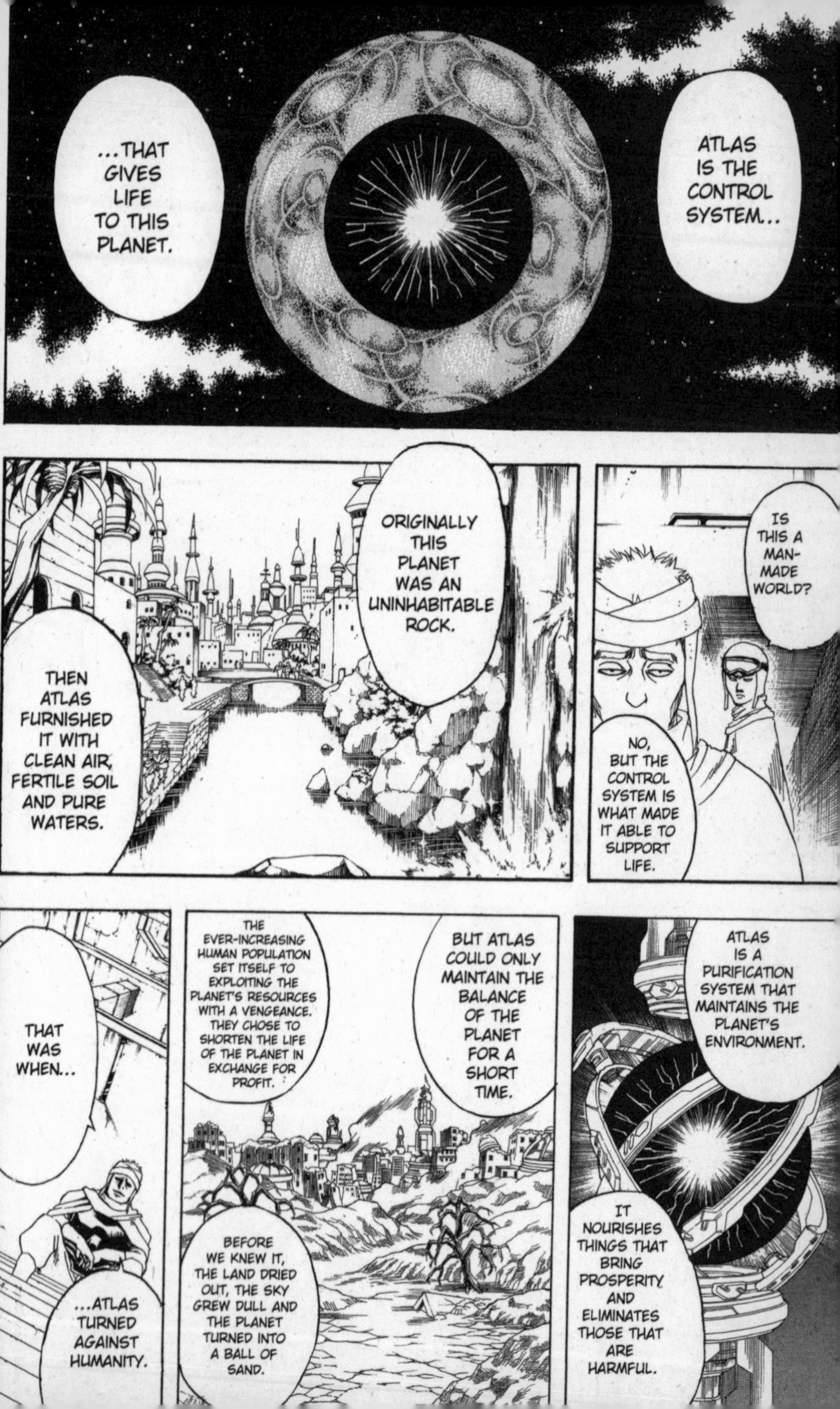
ATLAS IS THE CONTROL SYSTEM...
...THAT GIVES LIFE TO THIS PLANET.
IS THIS A MAN-MADE WORLD?
NO, BUT THE CONTROL SYSTEM IS WHAT MADE IT ABLE TO SUPPORT LIFE.
ORIGINALLY THIS PLANET WAS AN UNINHABITABLE ROCK.
THEN ATLAS FURNISHED IT WITH CLEAN AIR, FERTILE SOIL AND PURE WATERS.
ATLAS IS A PURIFICATION SYSTEM THAT MAINTAINS THE PLANET'S ENVIRONMENT.
IT NOURISHES THINGS THAT BRING PROSPERITY AND ELIMINATES THOSE THAT ARE HARMFUL.
BUT ATLAS COULD ONLY MAINTAIN THE BALANCE OF THE PLANET FOR A SHORT TIME.
THE EVER-INCREASING HUMAN POPULATION SET ITSELF TO EXPLOITING THE PLANET'S RESOURCES WITH A VENGEANCE. THEY CHOSE TO SHORTEN THE LIFE OF THE PLANET IN EXCHANGE FOR PROFIT.
BEFORE WE KNEW IT, THE LAND DRIED OUT, THE SKY GREW DULL AND THE PLANET TURNED INTO A BALL OF SAND.
THAT WAS WHEN...
...ATLAS TURNED AGAINST HUMANITY.

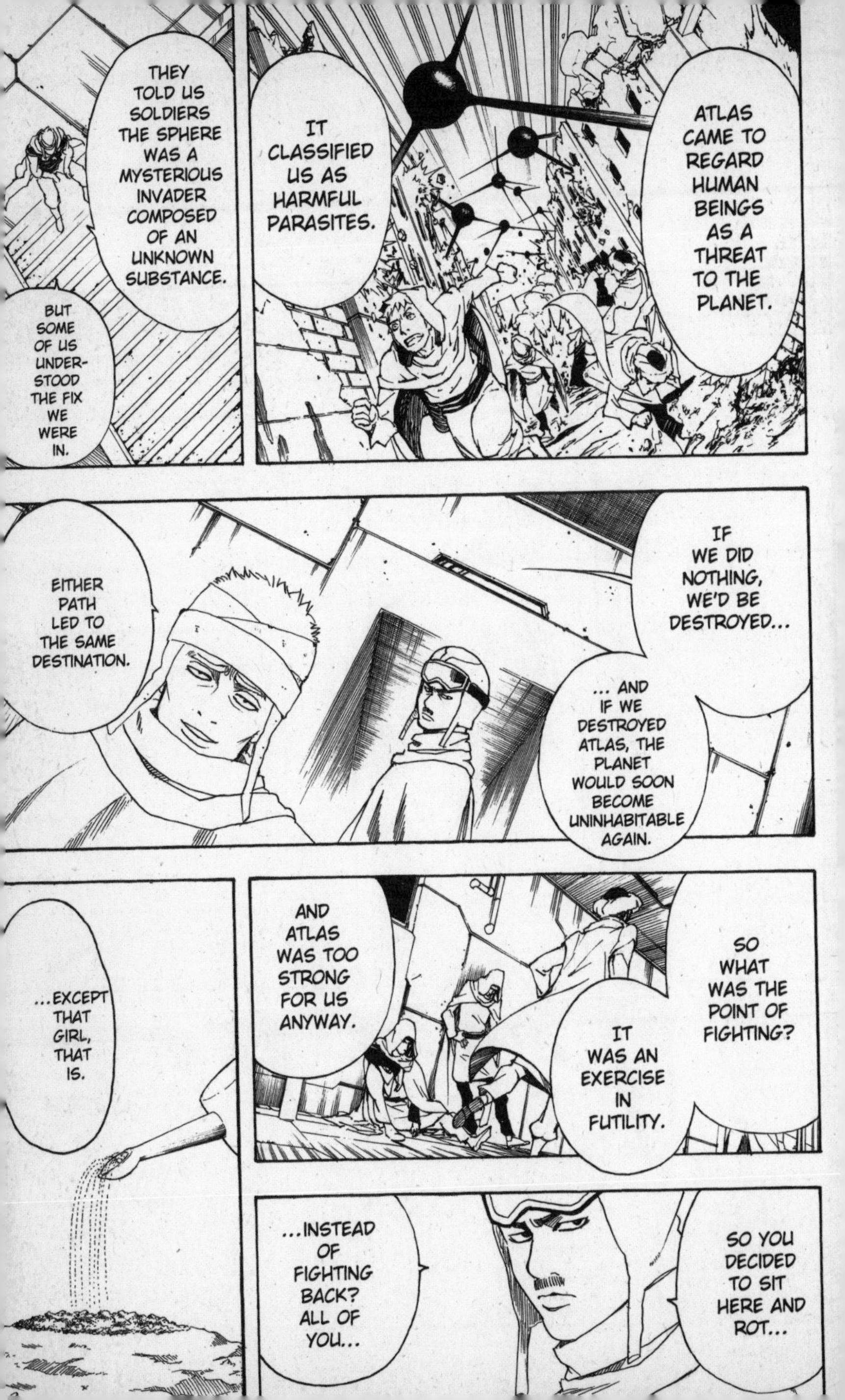

ATLAS CAME TO REGARD HUMAN BEINGS AS A THREAT TO THE PLANET.
IT CLASSIFIED US AS HARMFUL PARASITES.
THEY TOLD US SOLDIERS THE SPHERE WAS A MYSTERIOUS INVADER COMPOSED OF AN UNKNOWN SUBSTANCE.
BUT SOME OF US UNDER-STOOD THE FIX WE WERE IN.
IF WE DID NOTHING, WE'D BE DESTROYED...
... AND IF WE DESTROYED ATLAS, THE PLANET WOULD SOON BECOME UNINHABITABLE AGAIN.
EITHER PATH LED TO THE SAME DESTINATION.
SO WHAT WAS THE POINT OF FIGHTING?
IT WAS AN EXERCISE IN FUTILITY.
AND ATLAS WAS TOO STRONG FOR US ANYWAY.
SO YOU DECIDED TO SIT HERE AND ROT...
...INSTEAD OF FIGHTING BACK? ALL OF YOU...
...EXCEPT THAT GIRL, THAT IS.

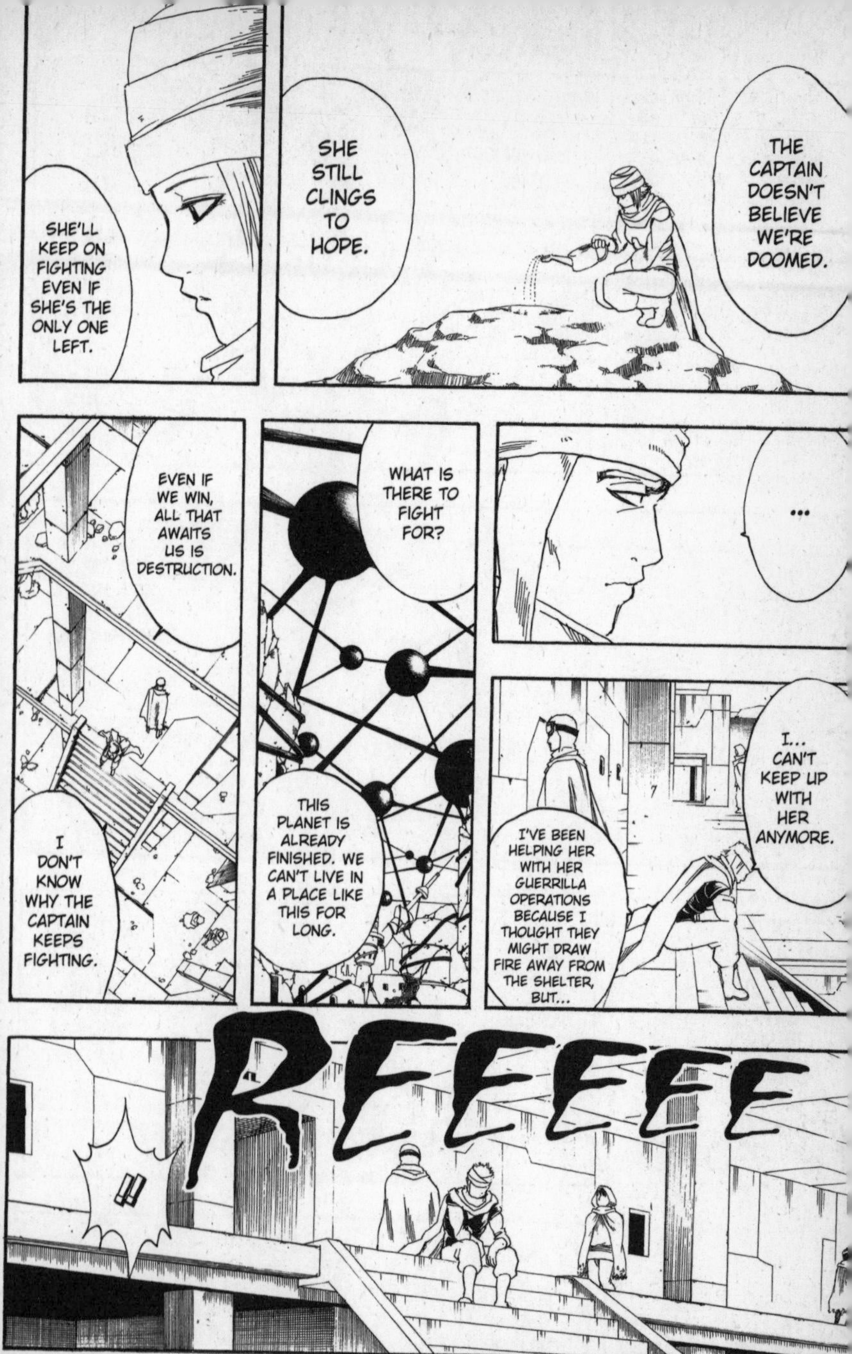
THE CAPTAIN DOESN'T BELIEVE WE'RE DOOMED.
SHE STILL CLINGS TO HOPE.
SHE'LL KEEP ON FIGHTING EVEN IF SHE'S THE ONLY ONE LEFT.
...
I... CAN'T KEEP UP WITH HER ANYMORE.
I'VE BEEN HELPING HER WITH HER GUERRILLA OPERATIONS BECAUSE I THOUGHT THEY MIGHT DRAW FIRE AWAY FROM THE SHELTER, BUT...
WHAT IS THERE TO FIGHT FOR?
THIS PLANET IS ALREADY FINISHED. WE CAN'T LIVE IN A PLACE LIKE THIS FOR LONG.
EVEN IF WE WIN, ALL THAT AWAITS US IS DESTRUCTION.
I DON'T KNOW WHY THE CAPTAIN KEEPS FIGHTING.
REEEEE
!!

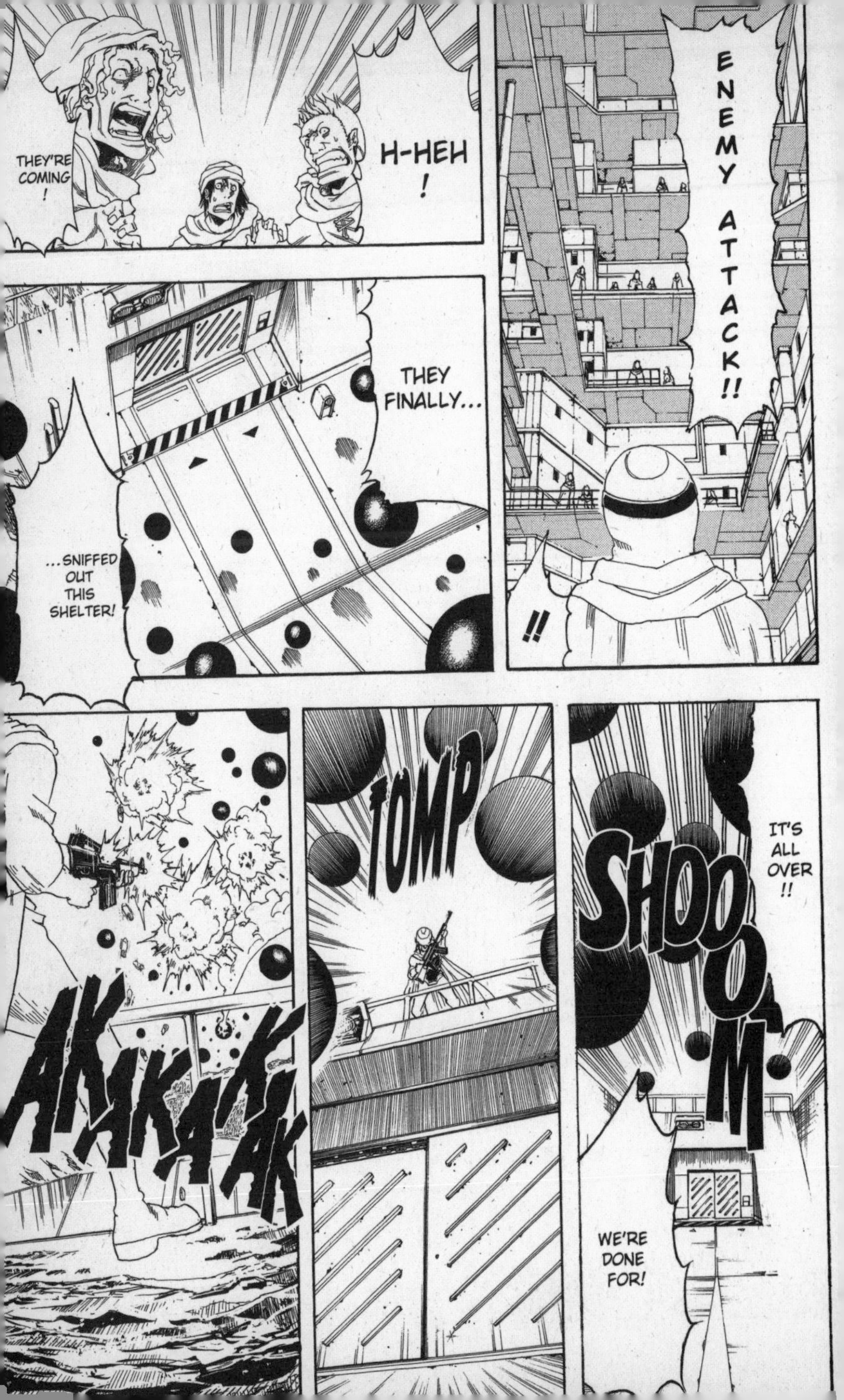
ENEMY ATTACK!!
!!
H-HEH!
THEY'RE COMING!
THEY FINALLY...
...SNIFFED OUT THIS SHELTER!
IT'S ALL OVER!!
SHOOOOM
WE'RE DONE FOR!
TOMP
AKKAKAK

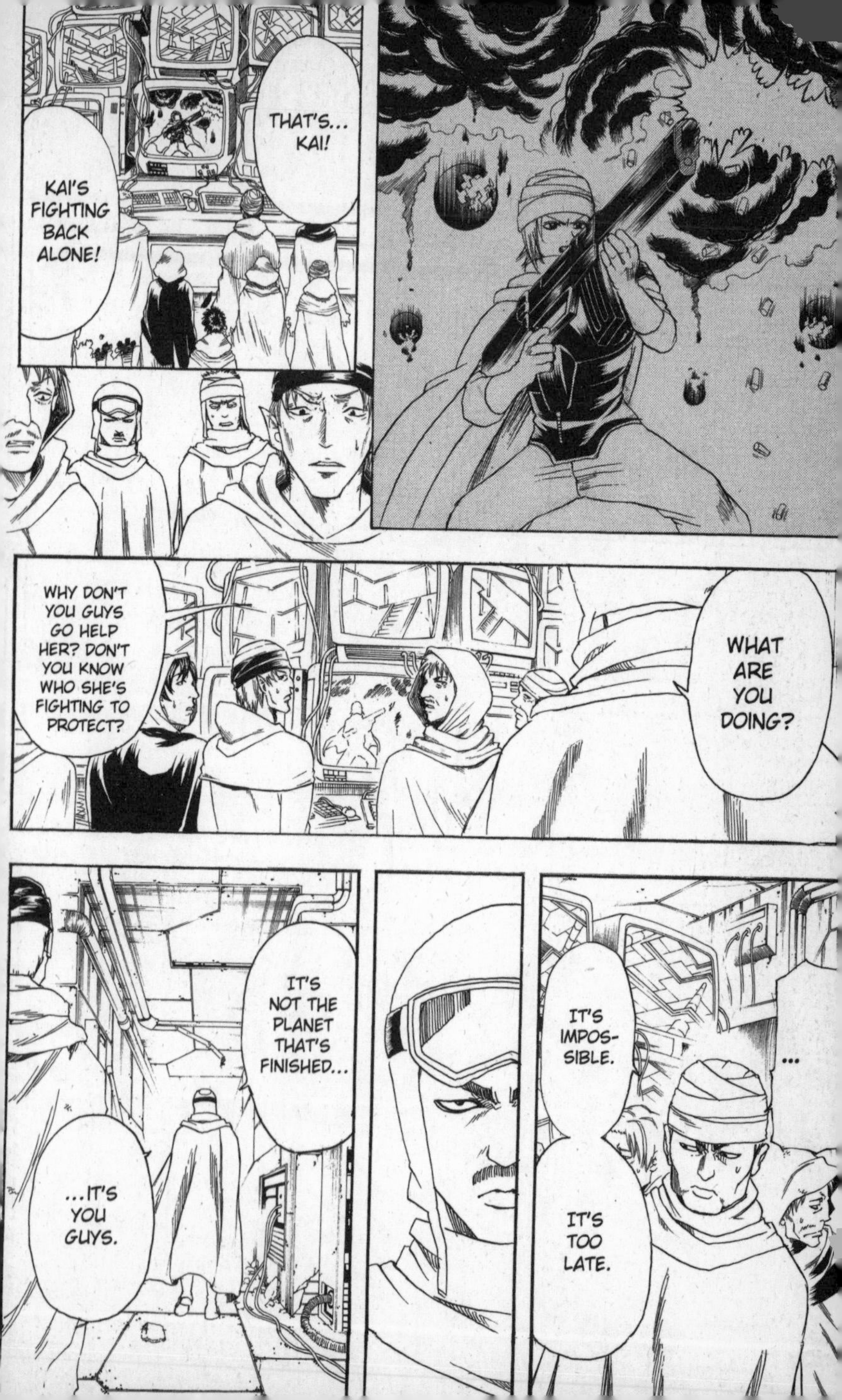
THAT'S... KAI!
KAI'S FIGHTING BACK ALONE!
WHAT ARE YOU DOING?
WHY DON'T YOU GUYS GO HELP HER? DON'T YOU KNOW WHO SHE'S FIGHTING TO PROTECT?
...
IT'S IMPOSSIBLE.
IT'S TOO LATE.
IT'S NOT THE PLANET THAT'S FINISHED...
...IT'S YOU GUYS.

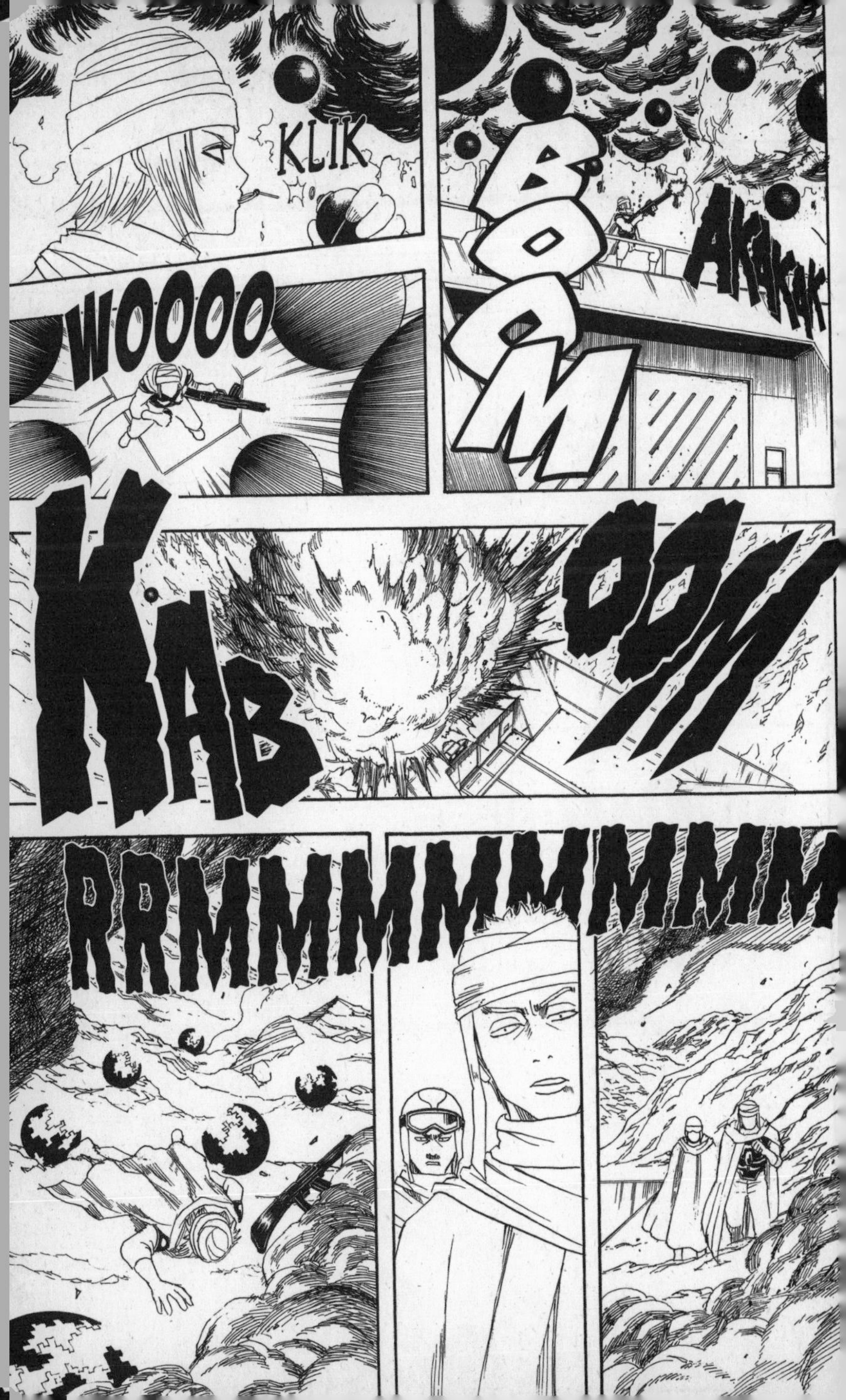
BOOM
AKAKAK
KLIK
WOOOO
KABOOM
RRMMMMMMMMMMM

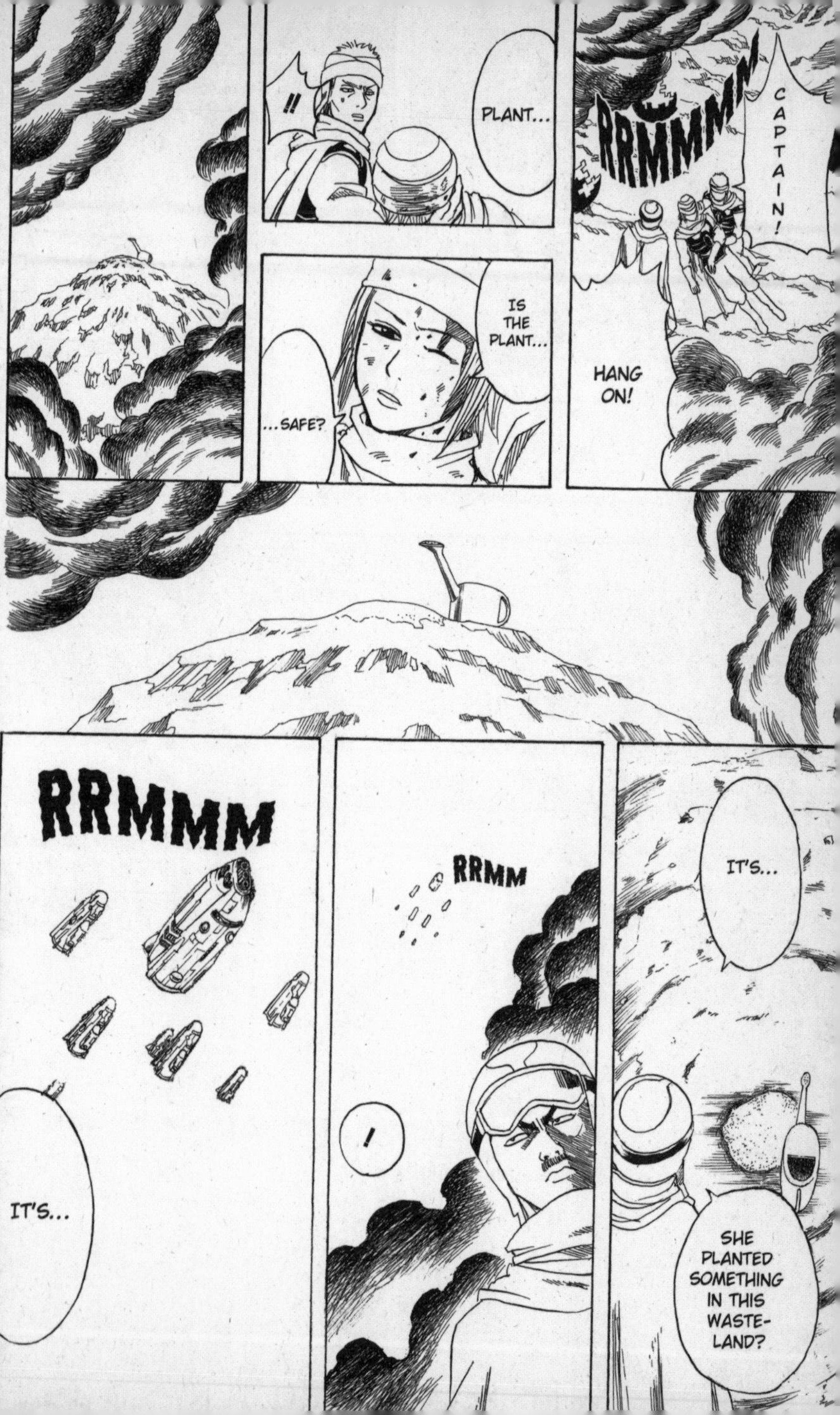

CAPTAIN!
RRMMMM
HANG ON!
!!
PLANT...
IS THE PLANT...
...SAFE?
IT'S...
SHE PLANTED SOMETHING IN THIS WASTE-LAND?
RRMM
!
RRMMMM
IT'S...

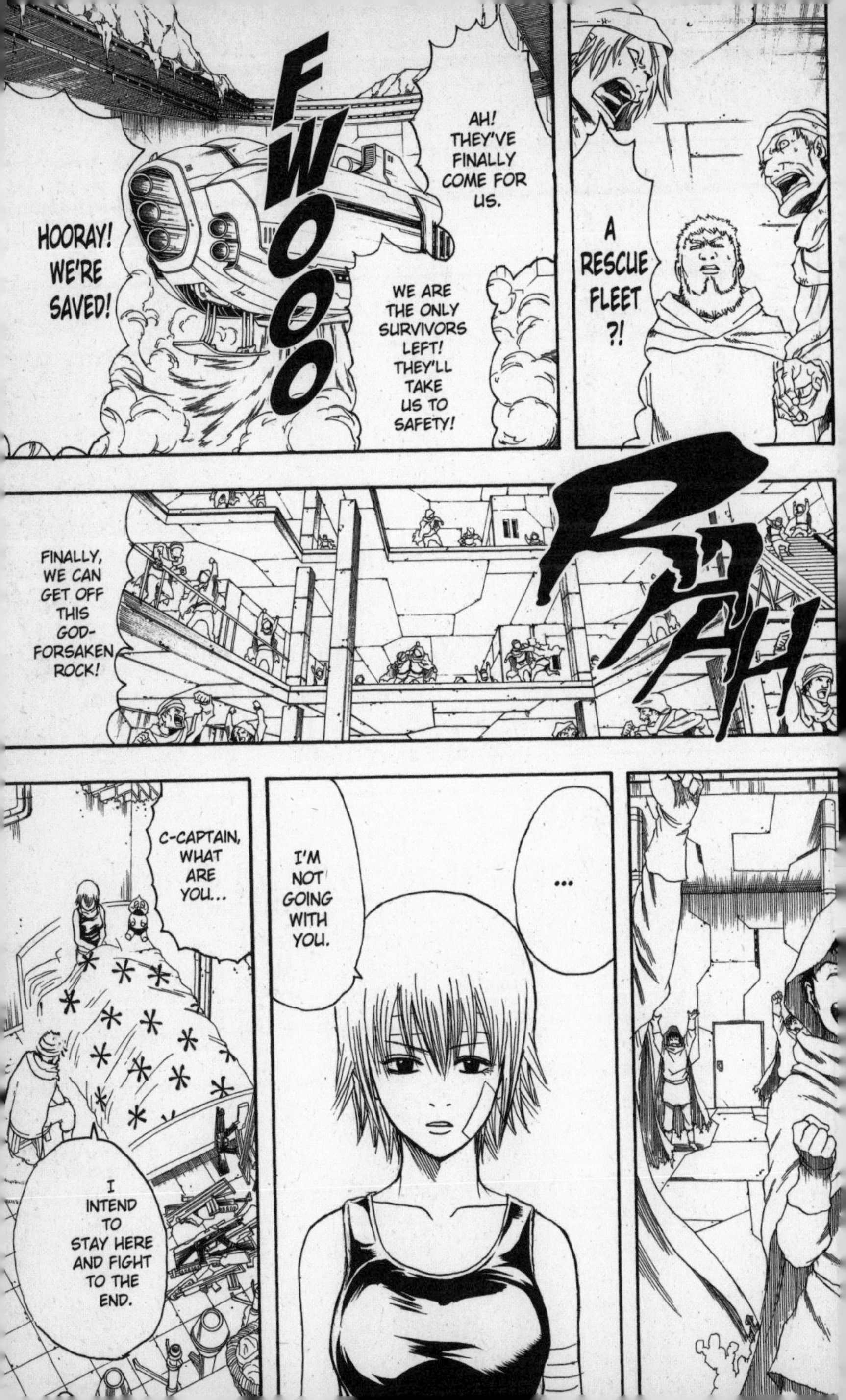
A RESCUE FLEET ?!
AH! THEY'VE FINALLY COME FOR US.
FWOOOO
WE ARE THE ONLY SURVIVORS LEFT! THEY'LL TAKE US TO SAFETY!
HOORAY! WE'RE SAVED!
RAAH
FINALLY, WE CAN GET OFF THIS GOD-FORSAKEN ROCK!
...
I'M NOT GOING WITH YOU.
C-CAPTAIN, WHAT ARE YOU...
I INTEND TO STAY HERE AND FIGHT TO THE END.

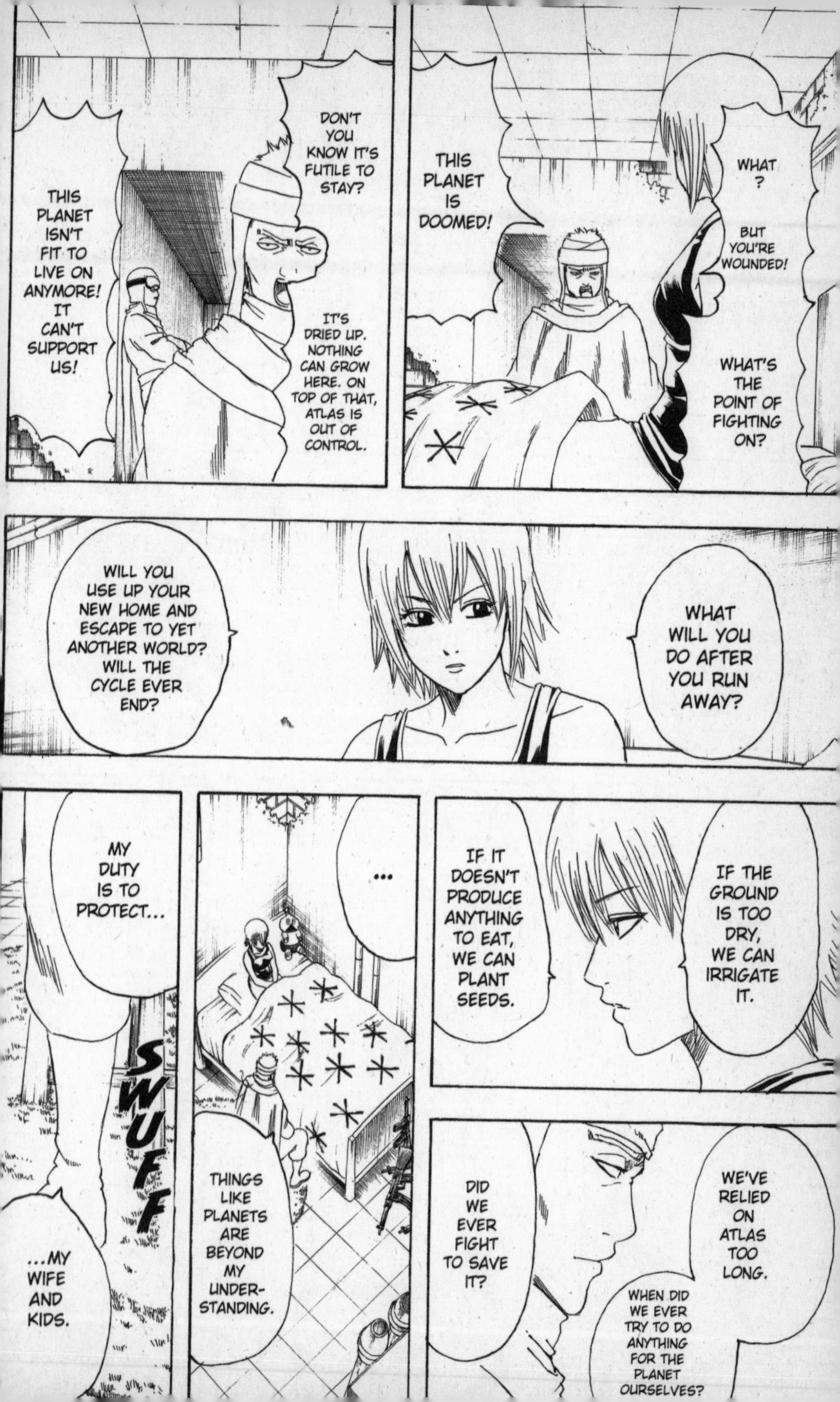
WHAT? BUT YOU'RE WOUNDED!
THIS PLANET IS DOOMED!
WHAT'S THE POINT OF FIGHTING ON?
DON'T YOU KNOW IT'S FUTILE TO STAY?
THIS PLANET ISN'T FIT TO LIVE ON ANYMORE! IT CAN'T SUPPORT US!
IT'S DRIED UP. NOTHING CAN GROW HERE. ON TOP OF THAT, ATLAS IS OUT OF CONTROL.
WHAT WILL YOU DO AFTER YOU RUN AWAY?
WILL YOU USE UP YOUR NEW HOME AND ESCAPE TO YET ANOTHER WORLD? WILL THE CYCLE EVER END?
IF THE GROUND IS TOO DRY, WE CAN IRRIGATE IT.
IF IT DOESN'T PRODUCE ANYTHING TO EAT, WE CAN PLANT SEEDS.
WE'VE RELIED ON ATLAS TOO LONG.
DID WE EVER FIGHT TO SAVE IT?
WHEN DID WE EVER TRY TO DO ANYTHING FOR THE PLANET OURSELVES?
...
THINGS LIKE PLANETS ARE BEYOND MY UNDER-STANDING.
MY DUTY IS TO PROTECT...
SWUFF
...MY WIFE AND KIDS.

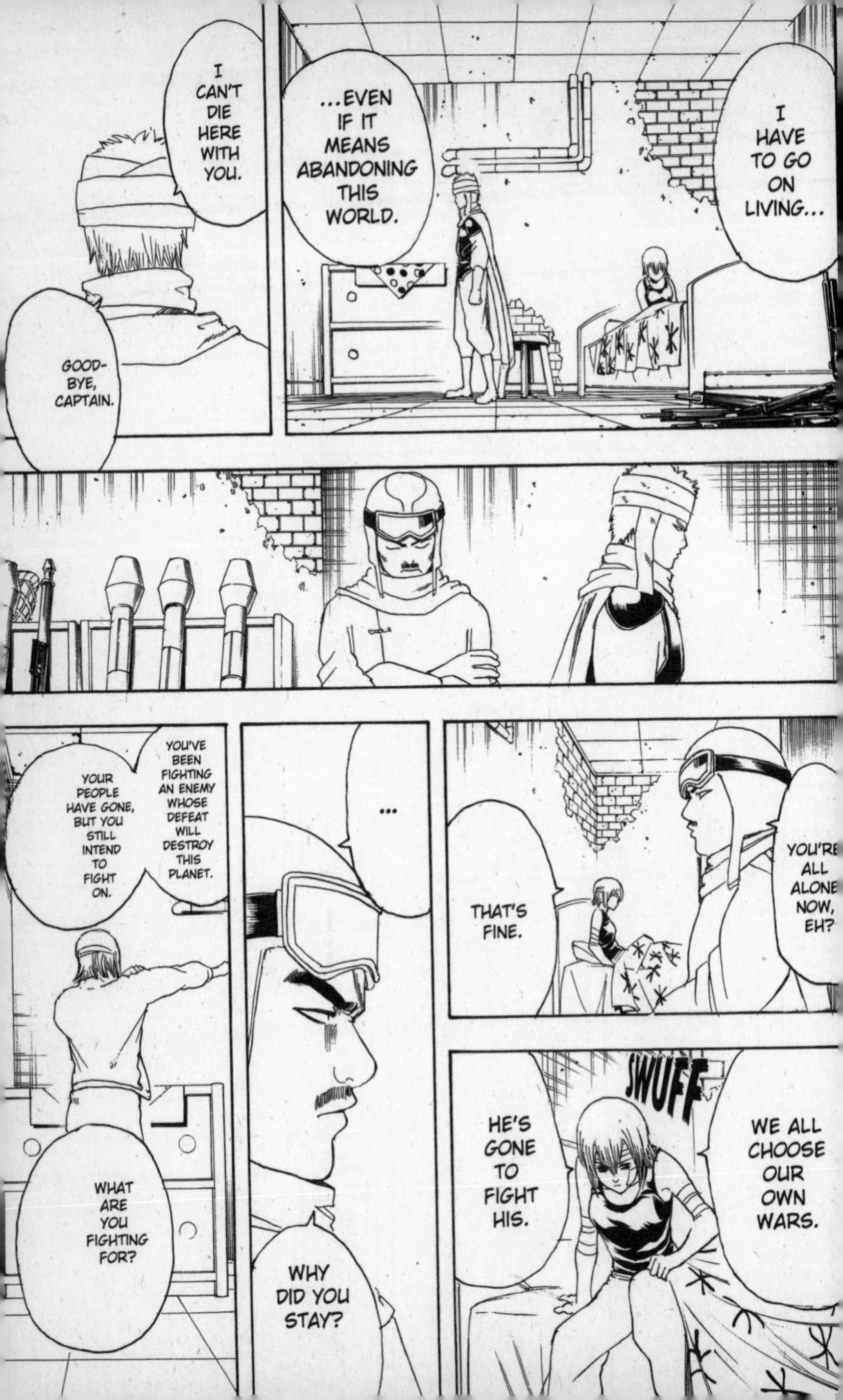
I HAVE TO GO ON LIVING...
...EVEN IF IT MEANS ABANDONING THIS WORLD.
I CAN'T DIE HERE WITH YOU.
GOOD-BYE, CAPTAIN.
YOU'RE ALL ALONE NOW, EH?
THAT'S FINE.
SWUFF
WE ALL CHOOSE OUR OWN WARS.
HE'S GONE TO FIGHT HIS.
...
WHY DID YOU STAY?
YOU'VE BEEN FIGHTING AN ENEMY WHOSE DEFEAT WILL DESTROY THIS PLANET.
YOUR PEOPLE HAVE GONE, BUT YOU STILL INTEND TO FIGHT ON.
WHAT ARE YOU FIGHTING FOR?

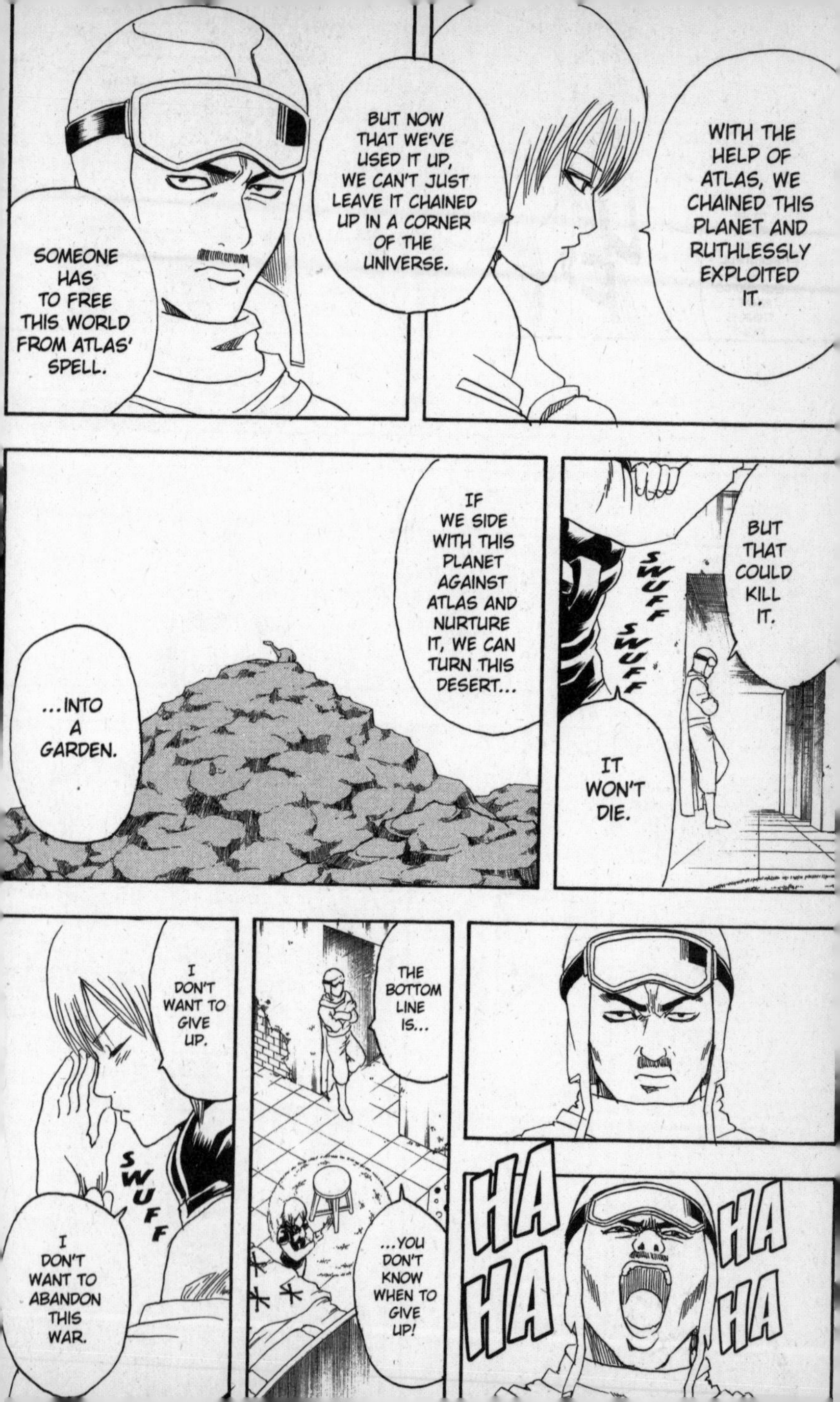
WITH THE HELP OF ATLAS, WE CHAINED THIS PLANET AND RUTHLESSLY EXPLOITED IT.
BUT NOW THAT WE'VE USED IT UP, WE CAN'T JUST LEAVE IT CHAINED UP IN A CORNER OF THE UNIVERSE.
SOMEONE HAS TO FREE THIS WORLD FROM ATLAS' SPELL.
BUT THAT COULD KILL IT.
SWUFF SWUFF
IT WON'T DIE.
IF WE SIDE WITH THIS PLANET AGAINST ATLAS AND NURTURE IT, WE CAN TURN THIS DESERT...
...INTO A GARDEN.
HA HA
HA HA
THE BOTTOM LINE IS...
...YOU DON'T KNOW WHEN TO GIVE UP!
I DON'T WANT TO GIVE UP.
SWUFF
I DON'T WANT TO ABANDON THIS WAR.

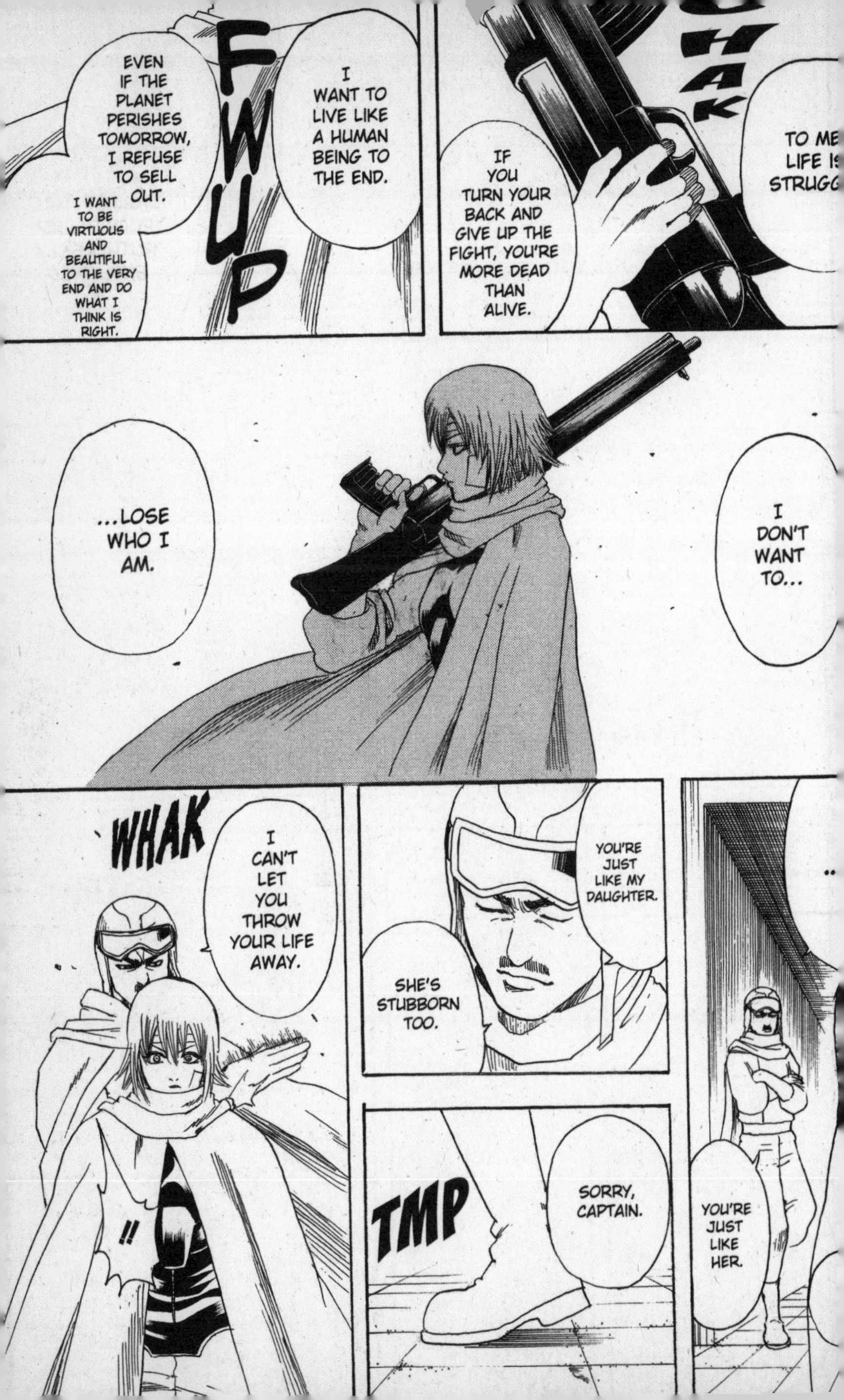
HAK
TO ME LIFE IS STRUGG
IF YOU TURN YOUR BACK AND GIVE UP THE FIGHT, YOU'RE MORE DEAD THAN ALIVE.
I WANT TO LIVE LIKE A HUMAN BEING TO THE END.
FWUP
EVEN IF THE PLANET PERISHES TOMORROW, I REFUSE TO SELL OUT.
I WANT TO BE VIRTUOUS AND BEAUTIFUL TO THE VERY END AND DO WHAT I THINK IS RIGHT.
I DON'T WANT TO...
...LOSE WHO I AM.
..
YOU'RE JUST LIKE HER.
YOU'RE JUST LIKE MY DAUGHTER.
SHE'S STUBBORN TOO.
SORRY, CAPTAIN.
TMP
WHAK
I CAN'T LET YOU THROW YOUR LIFE AWAY.
!!

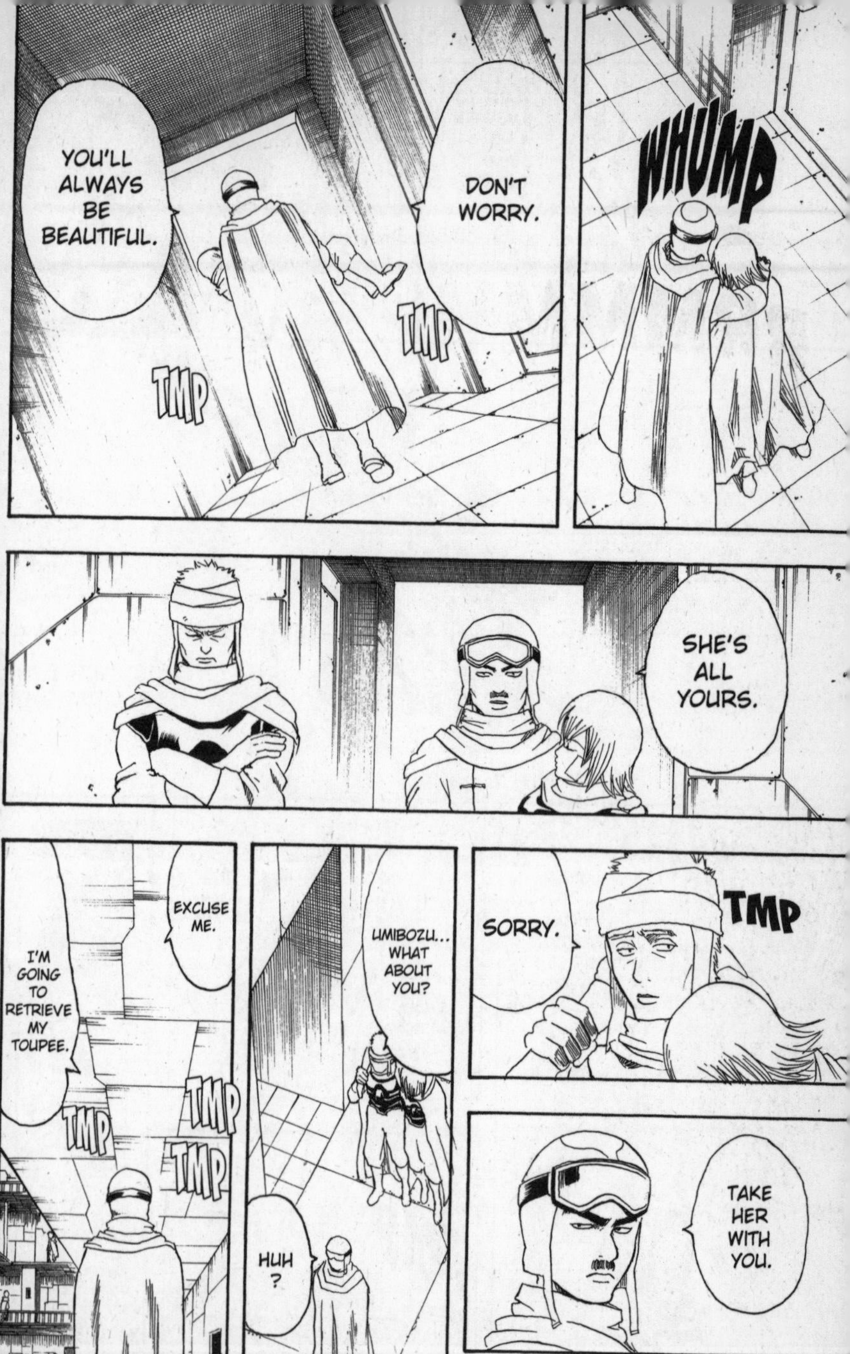
WHUMP
DON'T WORRY.
TMP
YOU'LL ALWAYS BE BEAUTIFUL.
TMP
SHE'S ALL YOURS.
TMP
SORRY.
TAKE HER WITH YOU.
UMIBOZU... WHAT ABOUT YOU?
HUH?
EXCUSE ME.
TMP
I'M GOING TO RETRIEVE MY TOUPEE.
TMP
TMP

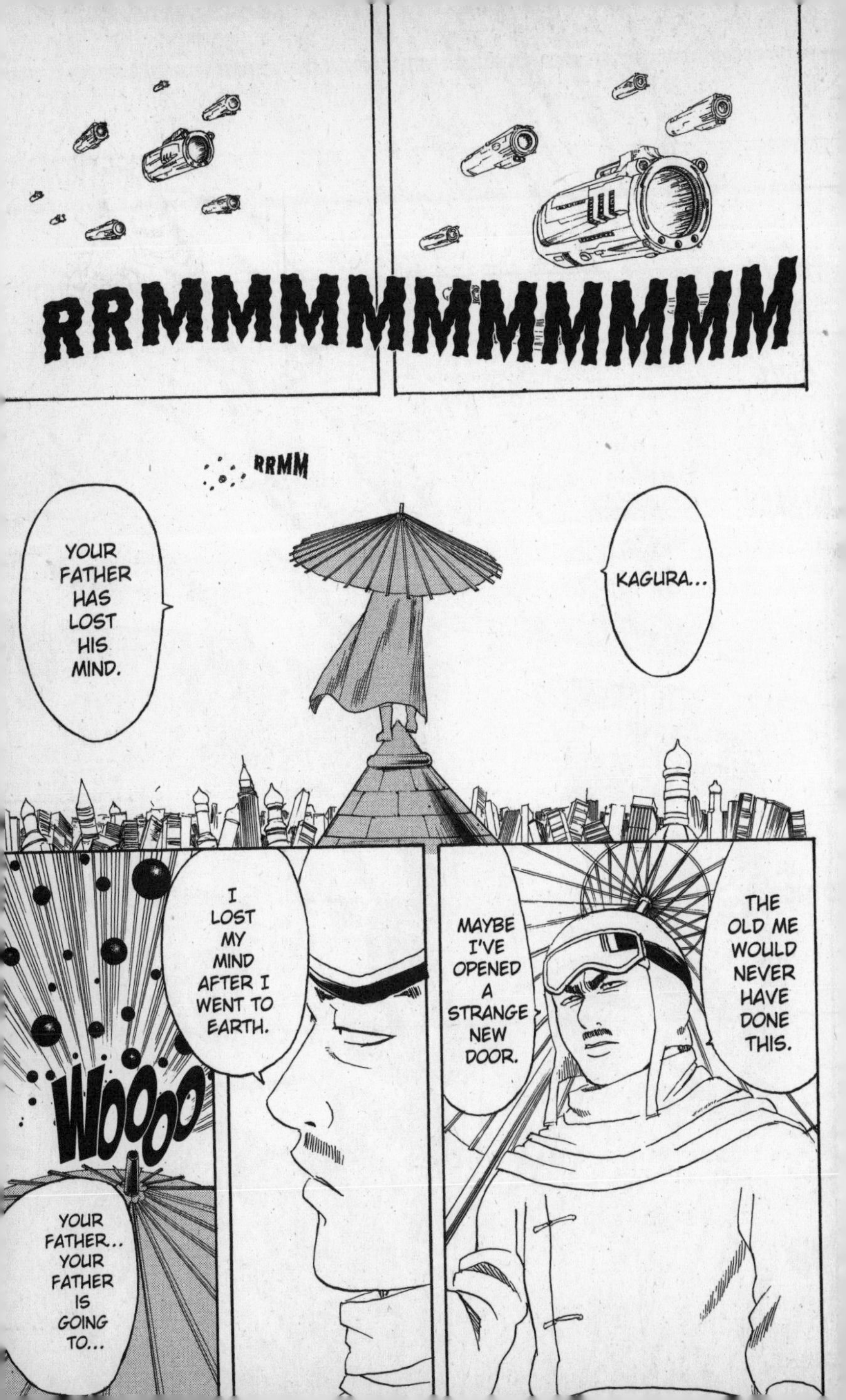
RRMMMMMMMMMMMM
RRMM
KAGURA...
YOUR FATHER HAS LOST HIS MIND.
THE OLD ME WOULD NEVER HAVE DONE THIS.
MAYBE I'VE OPENED A STRANGE NEW DOOR.
I LOST MY MIND AFTER I WENT TO EARTH.
WOOOO
YOUR FATHER... YOUR FATHER IS GOING TO...

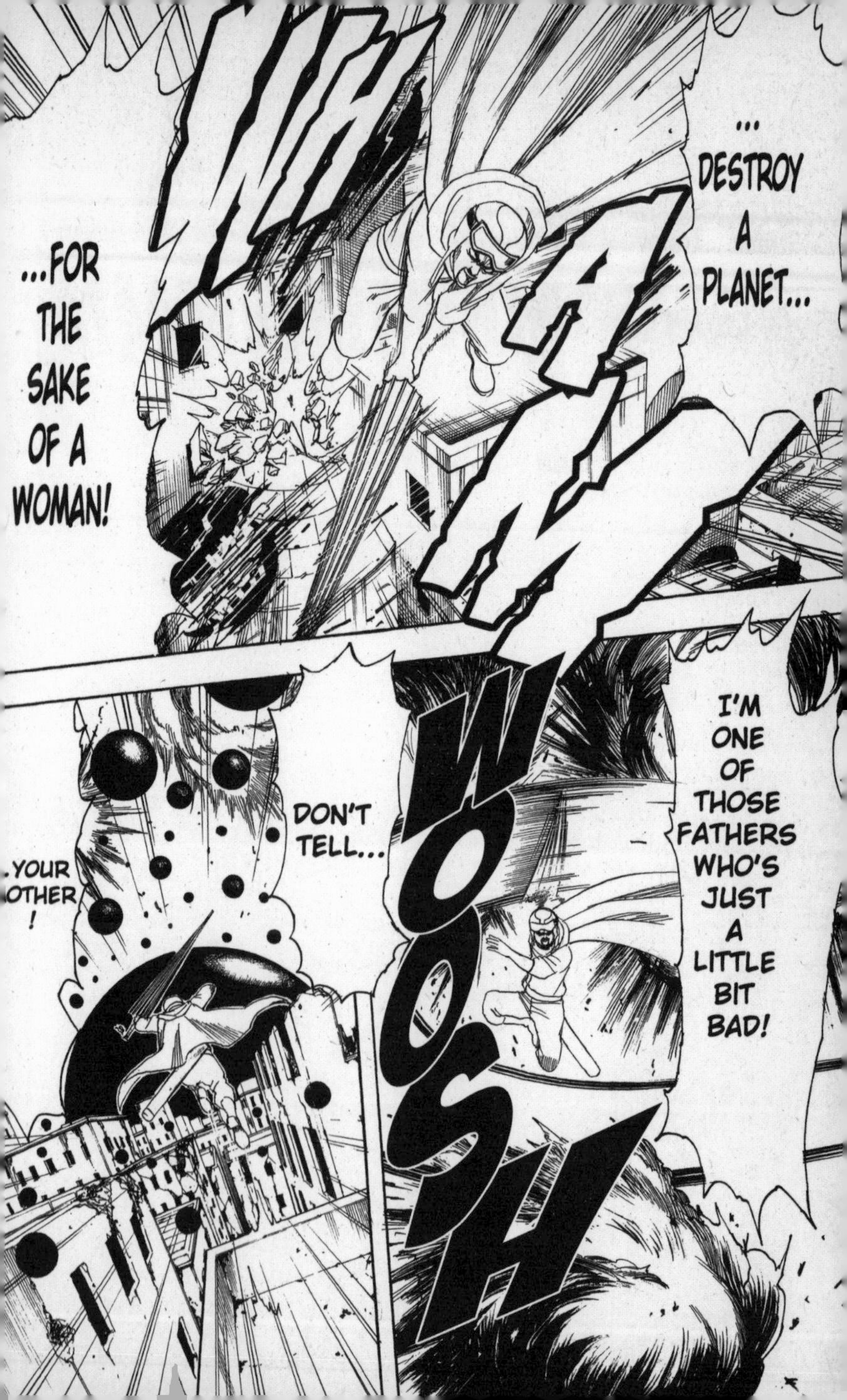

... DESTROY A PLANET...
...FOR THE SAKE OF A WOMAN!
WHAAM
I'M ONE OF THOSE FATHERS WHO'S JUST A LITTLE BIT BAD!
WHOOSH
DON'T TELL...
.YOUR OTHER!

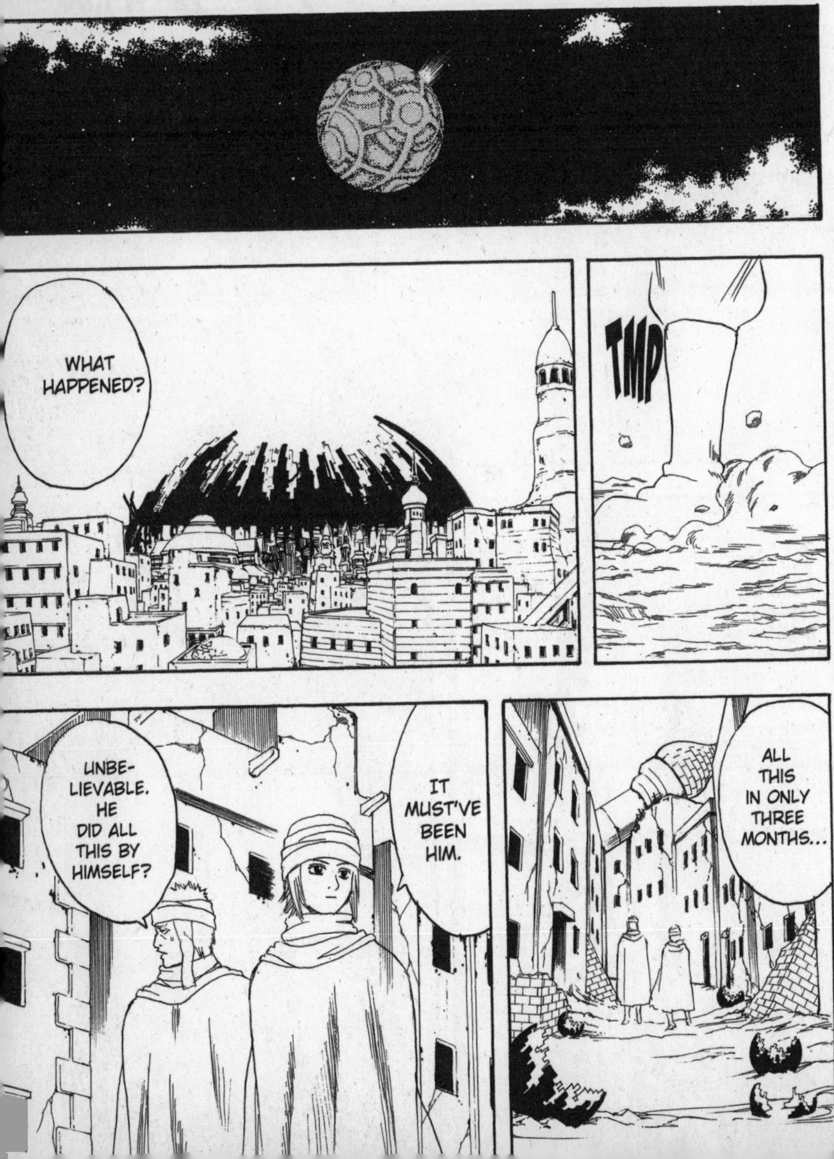
TMP
WHAT HAPPENED?
ALL THIS IN ONLY THREE MONTHS...
IT MUST'VE BEEN HIM.
UNBE-LIEVABLE. HE DID ALL THIS BY HIMSELF?

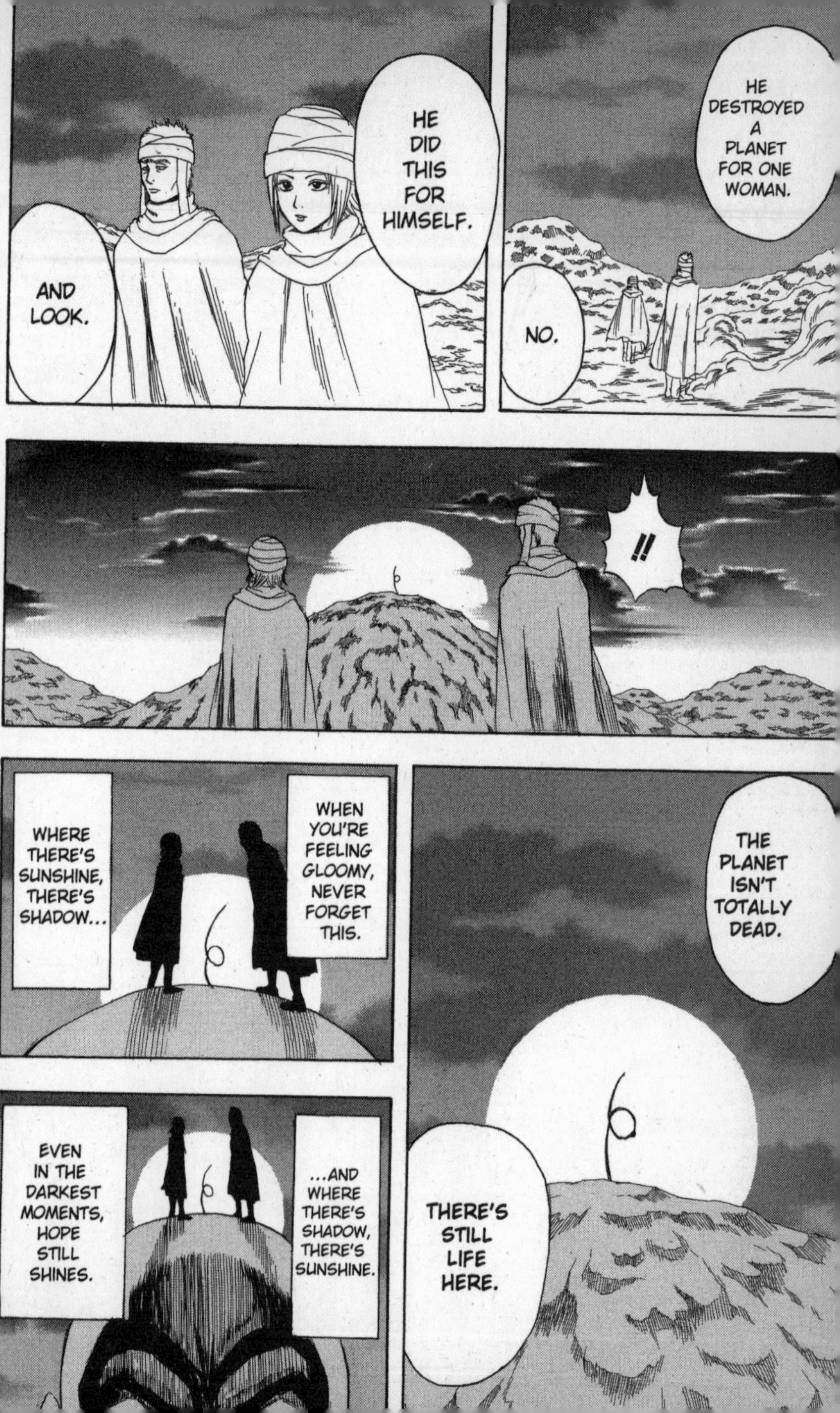
HE DESTROYED A PLANET FOR ONE WOMAN.
NO.
HE DID THIS FOR HIMSELF.
AND LOOK.
!!
THE PLANET ISN'T TOTALLY DEAD.
THERE'S STILL LIFE HERE.
WHEN YOU'RE FEELING GLOOMY, NEVER FORGET THIS.
WHERE THERE'S SUNSHINE, THERE'S SHADOW...
...AND WHERE THERE'S SHADOW, THERE'S SUNSHINE.
EVEN IN THE DARKEST MOMENTS, HOPE STILL SHINES.

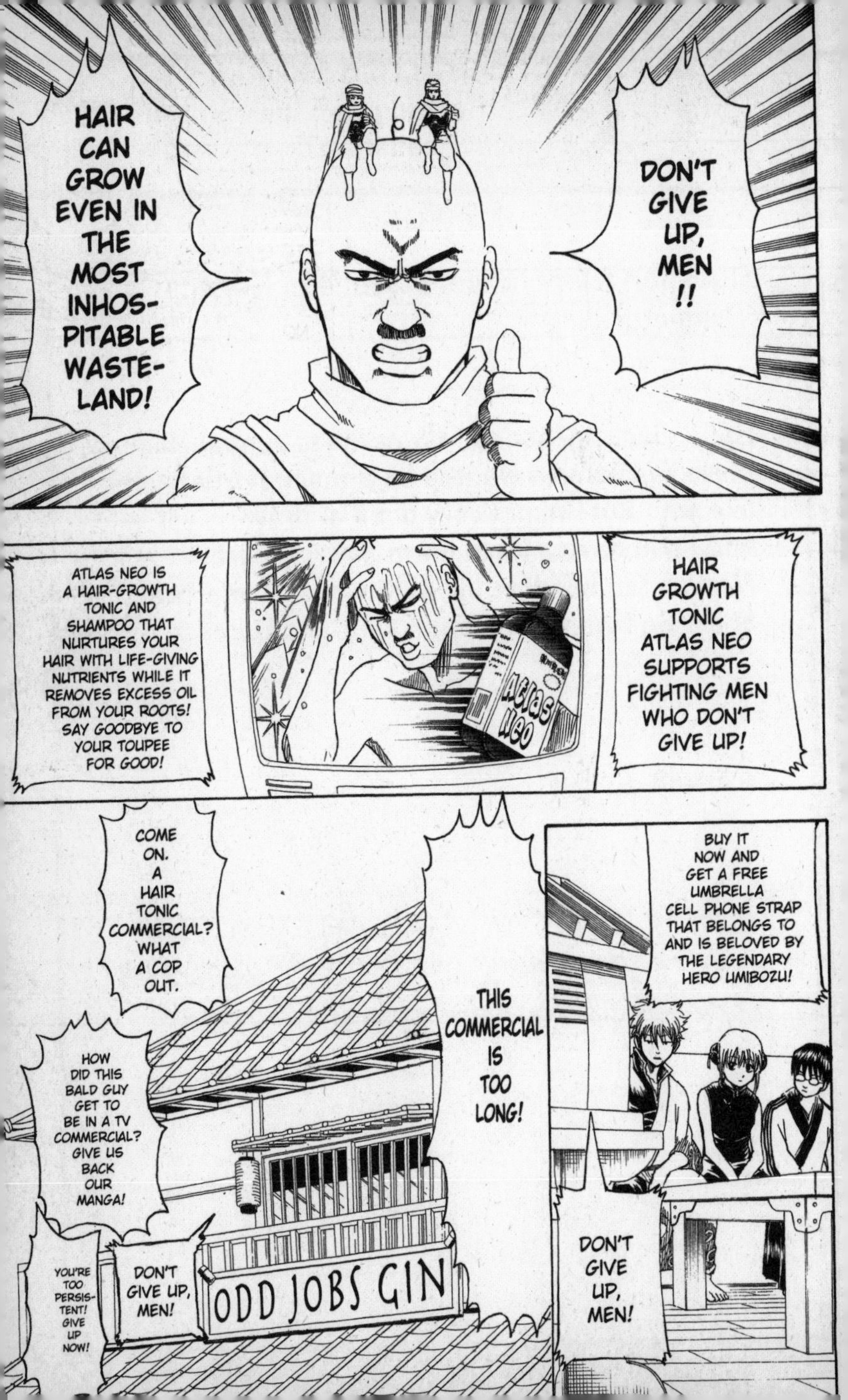
DON'T GIVE UP, MEN!!
HAIR CAN GROW EVEN IN THE MOST INHOS-PITABLE WASTE-LAND!
Atlas neo
HAIR GROWTH TONIC ATLAS NEO SUPPORTS FIGHTING MEN WHO DON'T GIVE UP!
ATLAS NEO IS A HAIR-GROWTH TONIC AND SHAMPOO THAT NURTURES YOUR HAIR WITH LIFE-GIVING NUTRIENTS WHILE IT REMOVES EXCESS OIL FROM YOUR ROOTS! SAY GOODBYE TO YOUR TOUPEE FOR GOOD!
BUY IT NOW AND GET A FREE UMBRELLA CELL PHONE STRAP THAT BELONGS TO AND IS BELOVED BY THE LEGENDARY HERO UMIBOZU!
DON'T GIVE UP, MEN!
THIS COMMERCIAL IS TOO LONG!
COME ON. A HAIR TONIC COMMERCIAL? WHAT A COP OUT.
HOW DID THIS BALD GUY GET TO BE IN A TV COMMERCIAL? GIVE US BACK OUR MANGA!
DON'T GIVE UP, MEN!
YOU'RE TOO PERSIS-TENT! GIVE UP NOW!
ODD JOBS GIN

Sorachi's Q&A
Hanging with the Readers #58

<Question from Junpei Masuda of Kanagawa Prefecture>

Hello, Sorachi-Sensei. My name is Junpei Masuda. I love *Gin Tama*. I want to be a manga artist just like you. But I'm not very good at drawing yet and I still have a lot to learn. I always draw *Naruto*, but my drawing ability hasn't improved at all. So I want to become your pupil.

<Answer>

I hate to break this to you, but you're probably better off learning from Kishimoto-Sensei, Junpei.

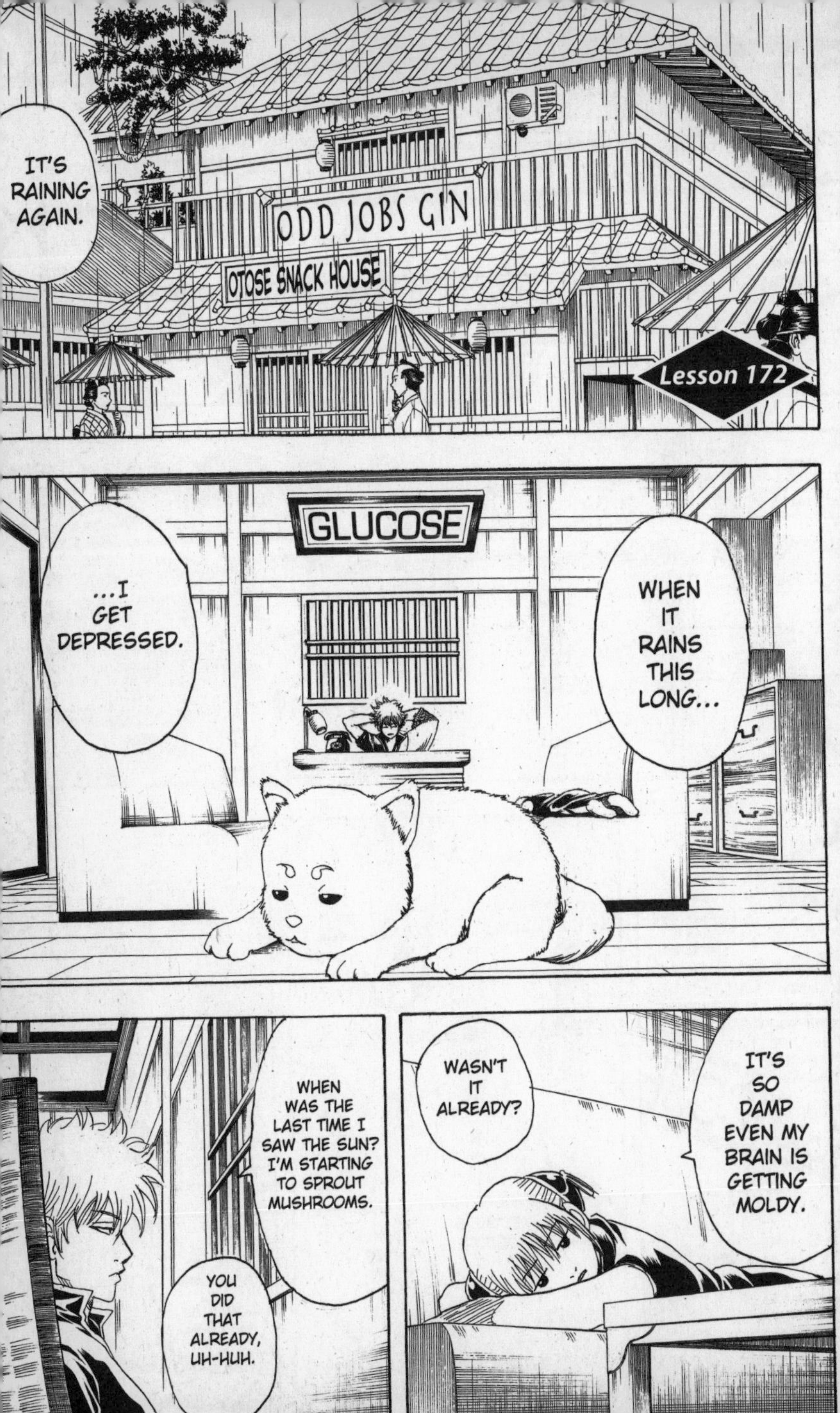
IT'S RAINING AGAIN.
ODD JOBS GIN
OTOSE SNACK HOUSE
Lesson 172
GLUCOSE
WHEN IT RAINS THIS LONG...
...I GET DEPRESSED.
IT'S SO DAMP EVEN MY BRAIN IS GETTING MOLDY.
WASN'T IT ALREADY?
WHEN WAS THE LAST TIME I SAW THE SUN? I'M STARTING TO SPROUT MUSHROOMS.
YOU DID THAT ALREADY, UH-HUH.

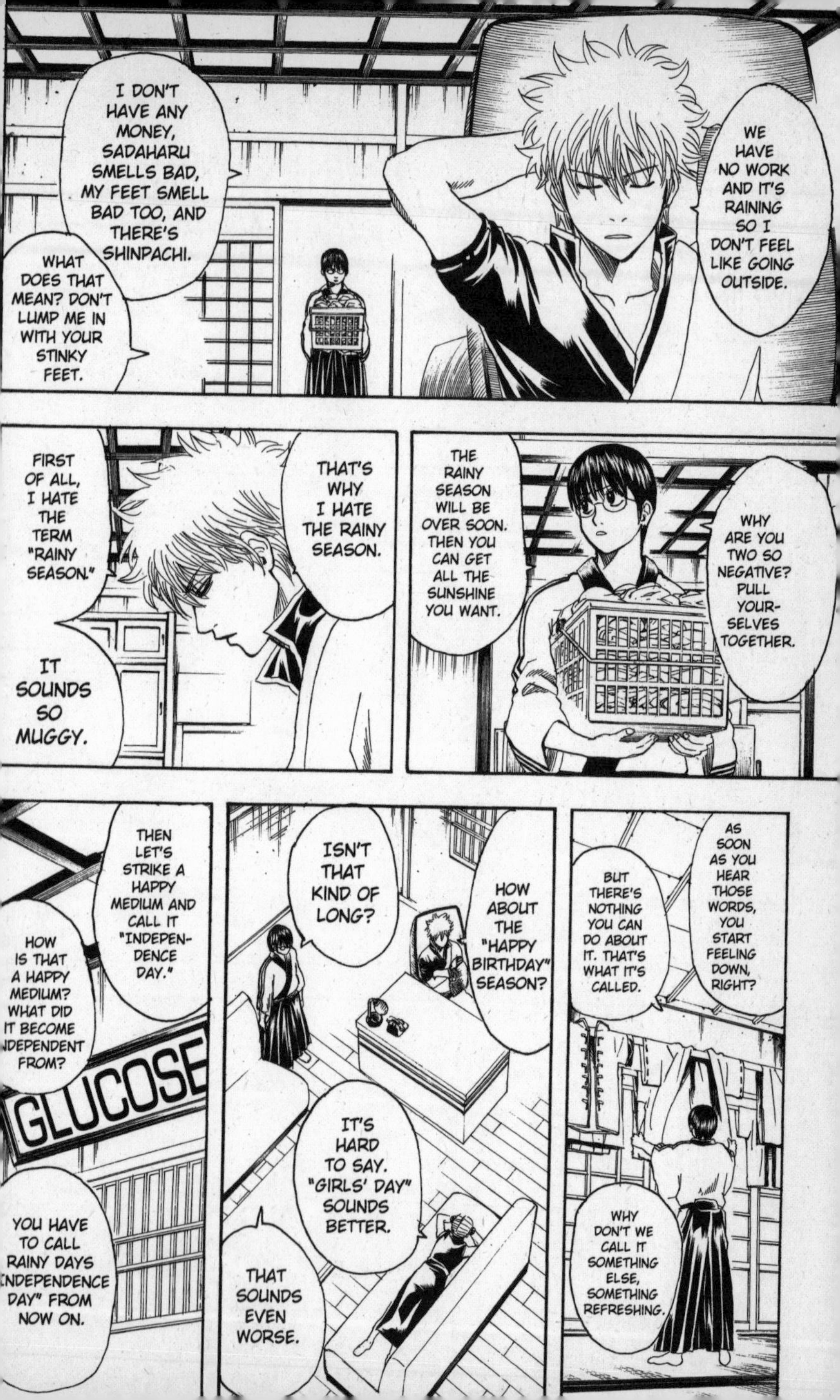
WE HAVE NO WORK AND IT'S RAINING SO I DON'T FEEL LIKE GOING OUTSIDE.
I DON'T HAVE ANY MONEY, SADAHARU SMELLS BAD, MY FEET SMELL BAD TOO, AND THERE'S SHINPACHI.
WHAT DOES THAT MEAN? DON'T LUMP ME IN WITH YOUR STINKY FEET.
WHY ARE YOU TWO SO NEGATIVE? PULL YOURSELVES TOGETHER.
THE RAINY SEASON WILL BE OVER SOON. THEN YOU CAN GET ALL THE SUNSHINE YOU WANT.
THAT'S WHY I HATE THE RAINY SEASON.
FIRST OF ALL, I HATE THE TERM "RAINY SEASON."
IT SOUNDS SO MUGGY.
AS SOON AS YOU HEAR THOSE WORDS, YOU START FEELING DOWN, RIGHT?
BUT THERE'S NOTHING YOU CAN DO ABOUT IT. THAT'S WHAT IT'S CALLED.
WHY DON'T WE CALL IT SOMETHING ELSE, SOMETHING REFRESHING.
HOW ABOUT THE "HAPPY BIRTHDAY" SEASON?
ISN'T THAT KIND OF LONG?
IT'S HARD TO SAY. "GIRLS' DAY" SOUNDS BETTER.
THAT SOUNDS EVEN WORSE.
THEN LET'S STRIKE A HAPPY MEDIUM AND CALL IT "INDEPENDENCE DAY."
HOW IS THAT A HAPPY MEDIUM? WHAT DID IT BECOME INDEPENDENT FROM?
GLUCOSE
YOU HAVE TO CALL RAINY DAYS "INDEPENDENCE DAY" FROM NOW ON.

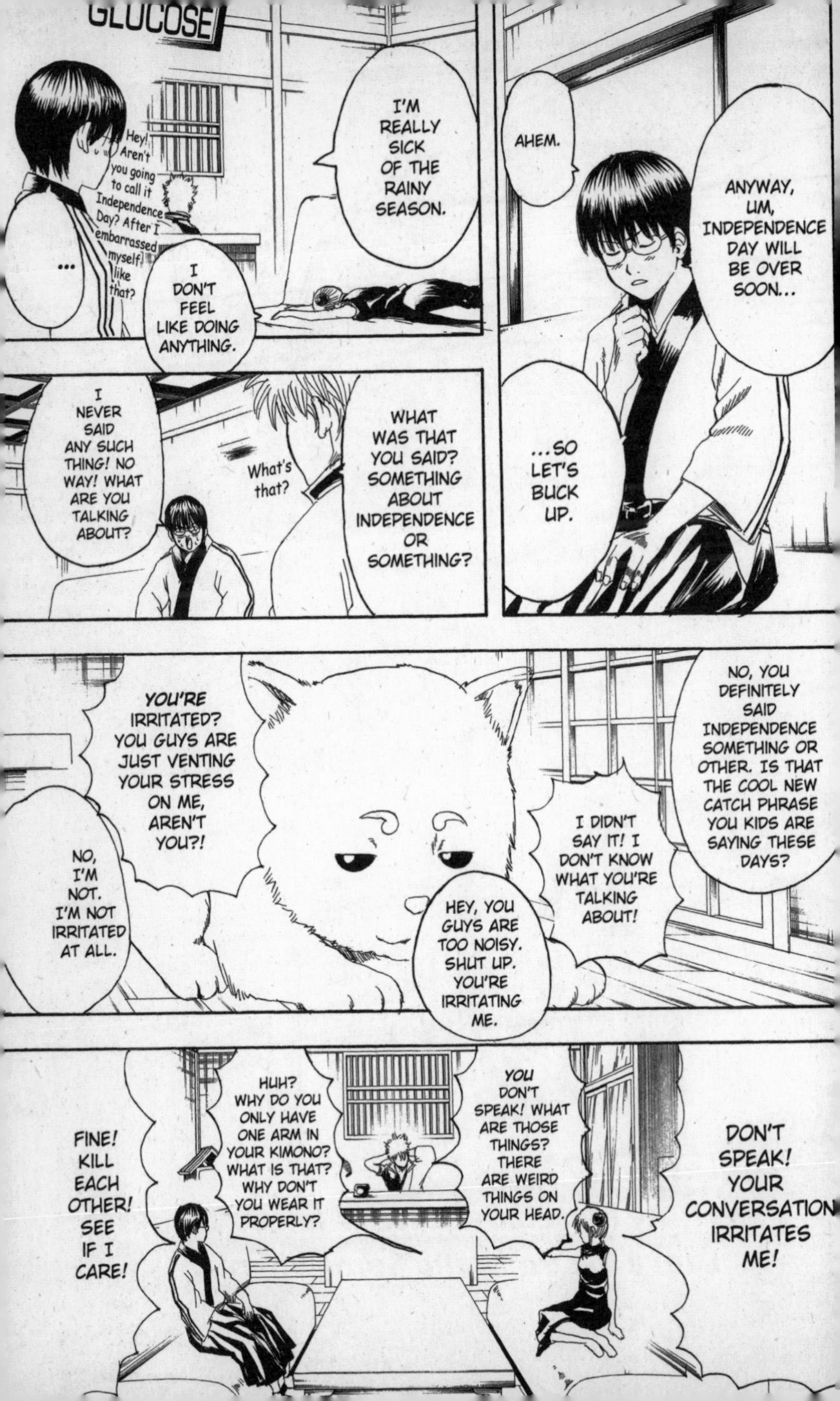
AHEM.
ANYWAY, UM, INDEPENDENCE DAY WILL BE OVER SOON...
...SO LET'S BUCK UP.
GLUCOSE
I'M REALLY SICK OF THE RAINY SEASON.
I DON'T FEEL LIKE DOING ANYTHING.
Hey! Aren't you going to call it Independence Day? After I embarrassed myself like that?
...
WHAT WAS THAT YOU SAID? SOMETHING ABOUT INDEPENDENCE OR SOMETHING?
What's that?
I NEVER SAID ANY SUCH THING! NO WAY! WHAT ARE YOU TALKING ABOUT?
NO, YOU DEFINITELY SAID INDEPENDENCE SOMETHING OR OTHER. IS THAT THE COOL NEW CATCH PHRASE YOU KIDS ARE SAYING THESE DAYS?
I DIDN'T SAY IT! I DON'T KNOW WHAT YOU'RE TALKING ABOUT!
HEY, YOU GUYS ARE TOO NOISY. SHUT UP. YOU'RE IRRITATING ME.
YOU'RE IRRITATED? YOU GUYS ARE JUST VENTING YOUR STRESS ON ME, AREN'T YOU?!
NO, I'M NOT. I'M NOT IRRITATED AT ALL.
DON'T SPEAK! YOUR CONVERSATION IRRITATES ME!
YOU DON'T SPEAK! WHAT ARE THOSE THINGS? THERE ARE WEIRD THINGS ON YOUR HEAD.
HUH? WHY DO YOU ONLY HAVE ONE ARM IN YOUR KIMONO? WHAT IS THAT? WHY DON'T YOU WEAR IT PROPERLY?
FINE! KILL EACH OTHER! SEE IF I CARE!

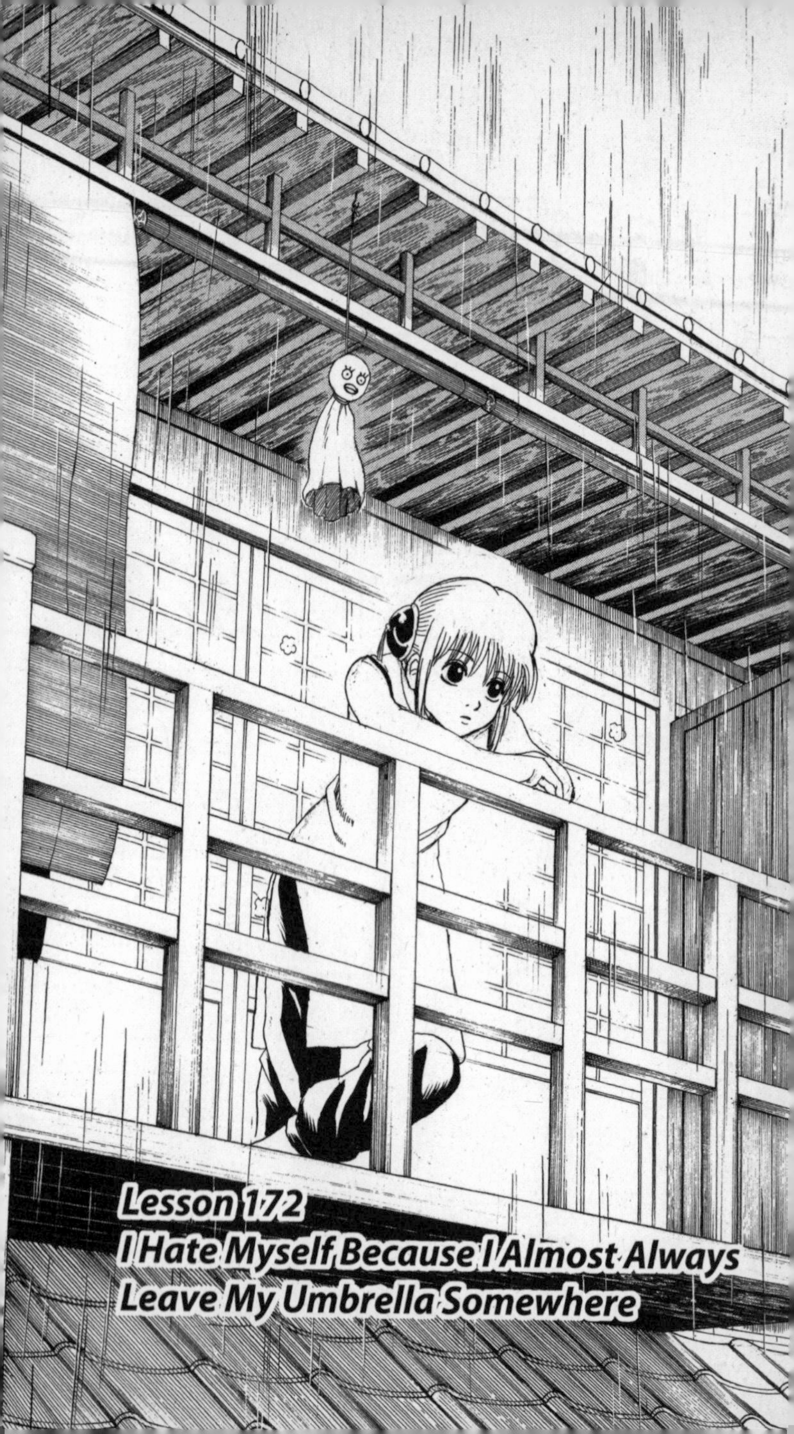
Lesson 172
I Hate Myself Because I Almost Always
Leave My Umbrella Somewhere

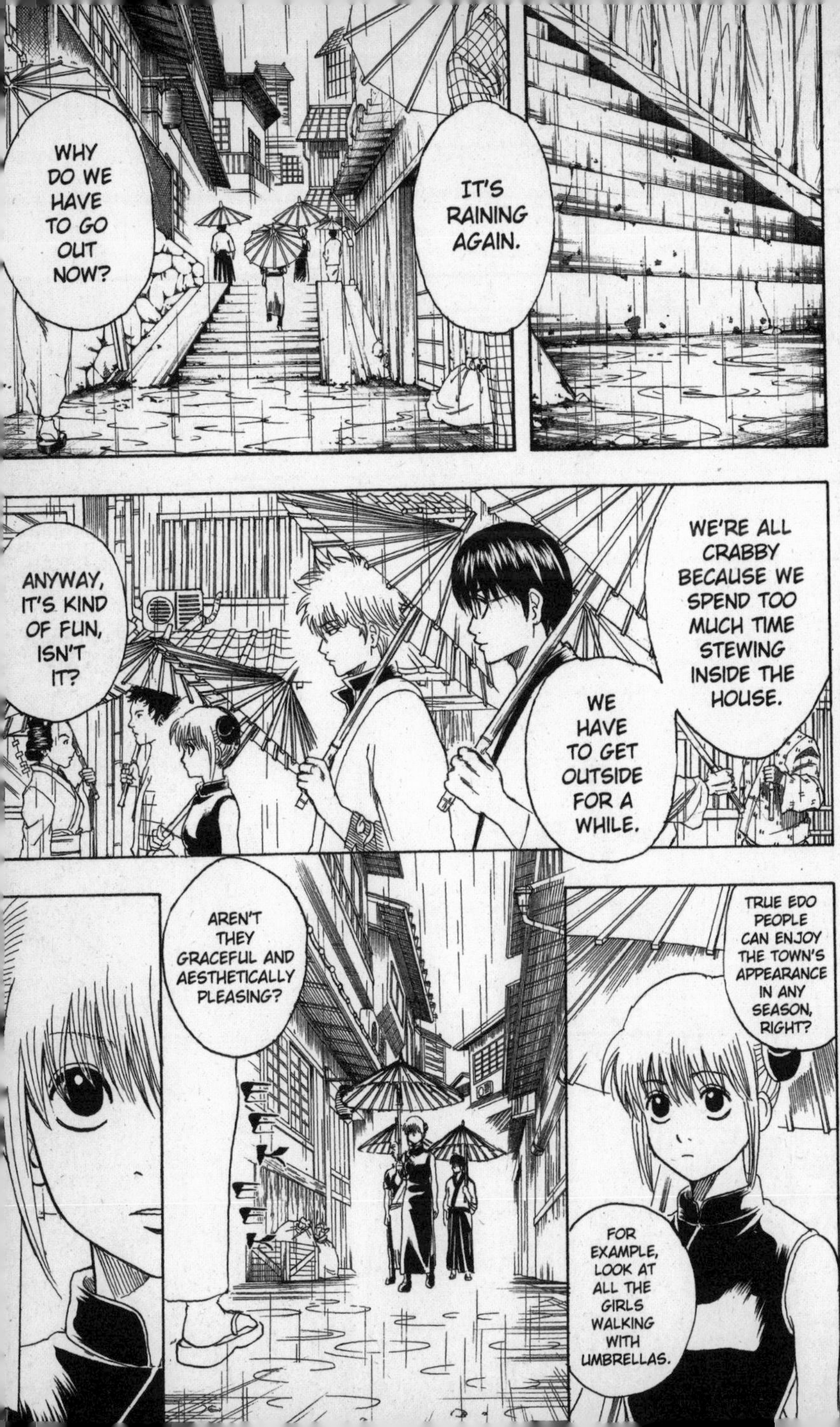
IT'S RAINING AGAIN.
WHY DO WE HAVE TO GO OUT NOW?
WE'RE ALL CRABBY BECAUSE WE SPEND TOO MUCH TIME STEWING INSIDE THE HOUSE.
WE HAVE TO GET OUTSIDE FOR A WHILE.
ANYWAY, IT'S KIND OF FUN, ISN'T IT?
TRUE EDO PEOPLE CAN ENJOY THE TOWN'S APPEARANCE IN ANY SEASON, RIGHT?
FOR EXAMPLE, LOOK AT ALL THE GIRLS WALKING WITH UMBRELLAS.
AREN'T THEY GRACEFUL AND AESTHETICALLY PLEASING?

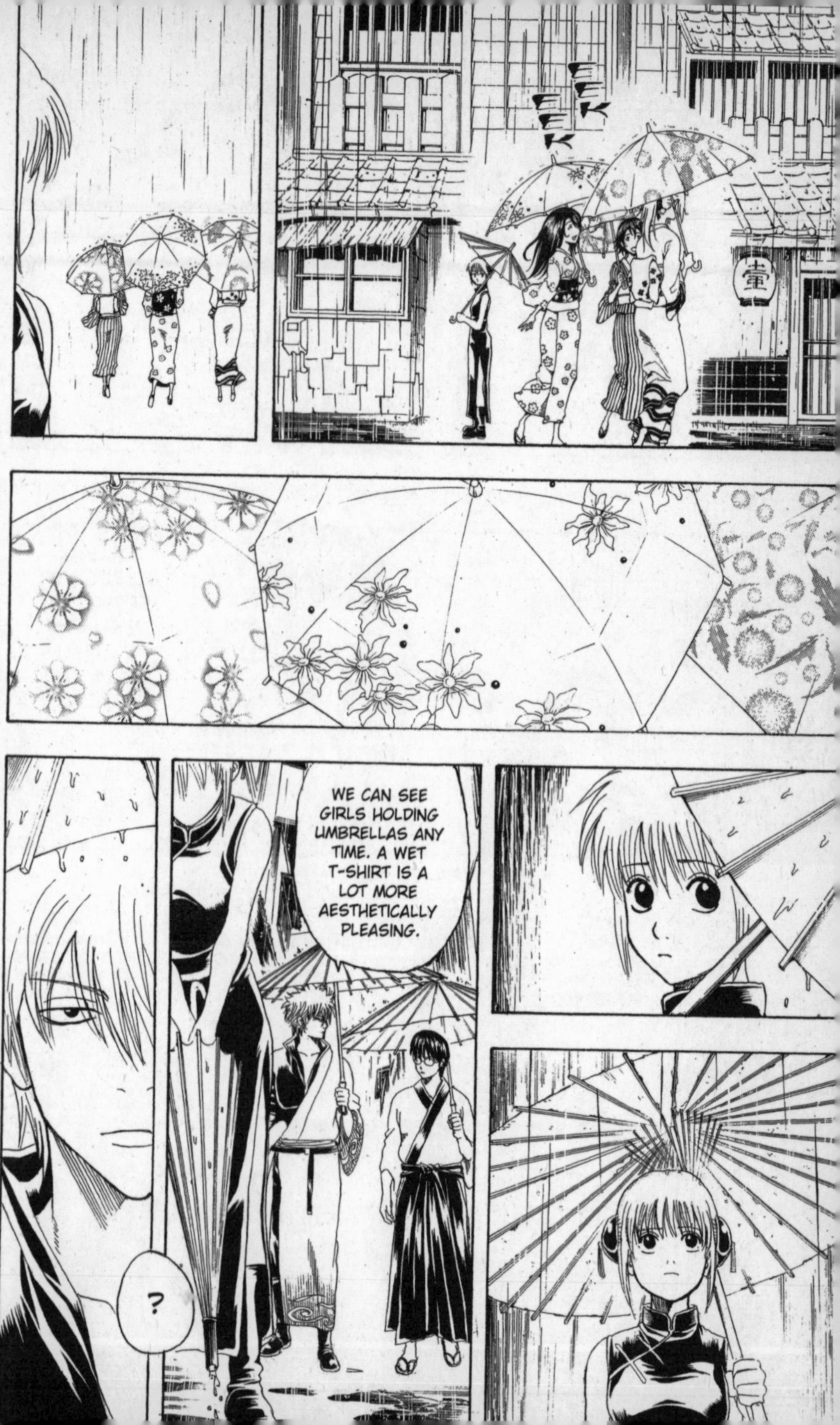
EEK
EEK
EEK
WE CAN SEE GIRLS HOLDING UMBRELLAS ANY TIME. A WET T-SHIRT IS A LOT MORE AESTHETICALLY PLEASING.
?

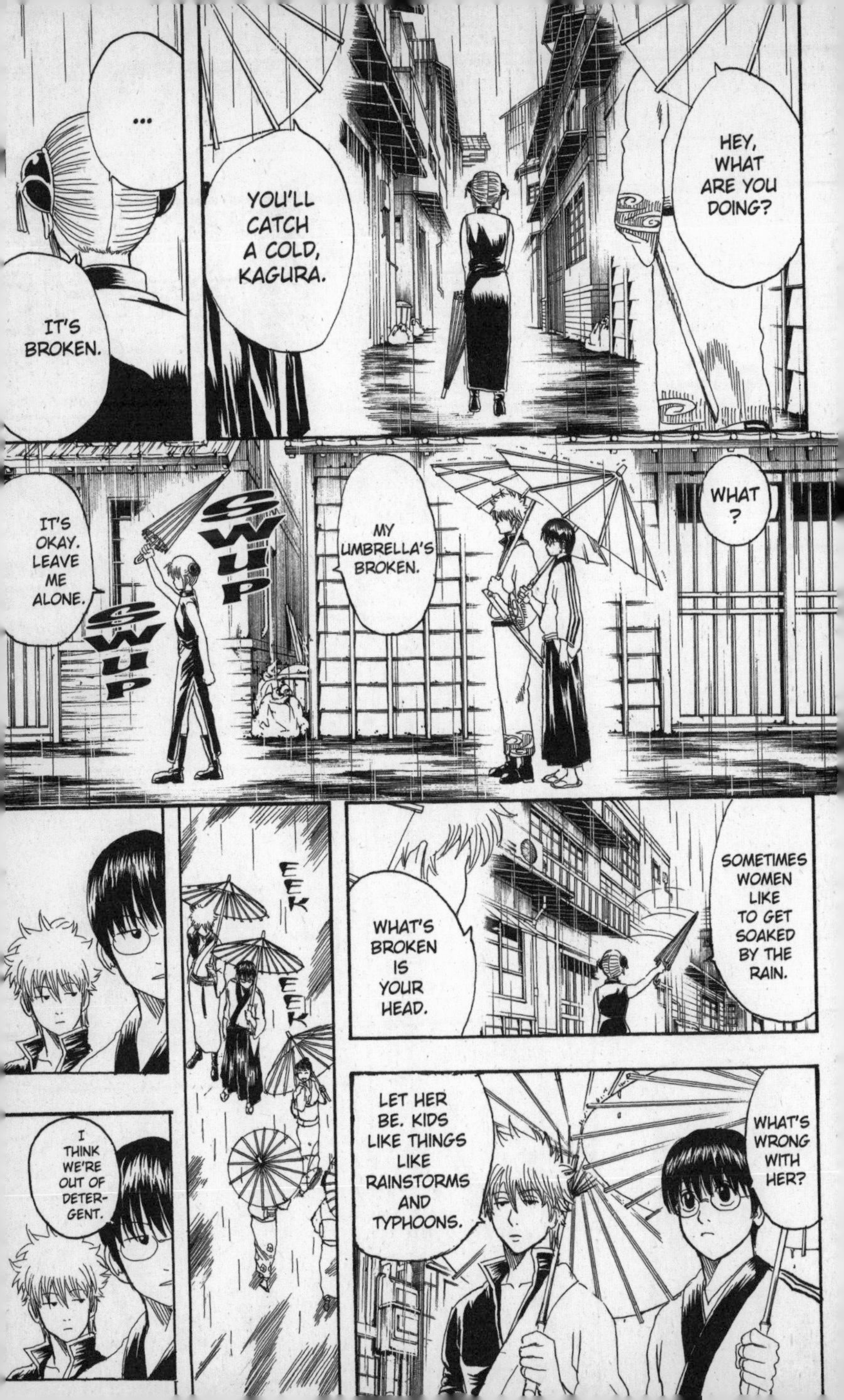
HEY, WHAT ARE YOU DOING?
YOU'LL CATCH A COLD, KAGURA.
...
IT'S BROKEN.
WHAT?
MY UMBRELLA'S BROKEN.
IT'S OKAY. LEAVE ME ALONE.
SWUP
SWUP
SOMETIMES WOMEN LIKE TO GET SOAKED BY THE RAIN.
WHAT'S BROKEN IS YOUR HEAD.
WHAT'S WRONG WITH HER?
LET HER BE. KIDS LIKE THINGS LIKE RAINSTORMS AND TYPHOONS.
EEK
EEK
I THINK WE'RE OUT OF DETER-GENT.

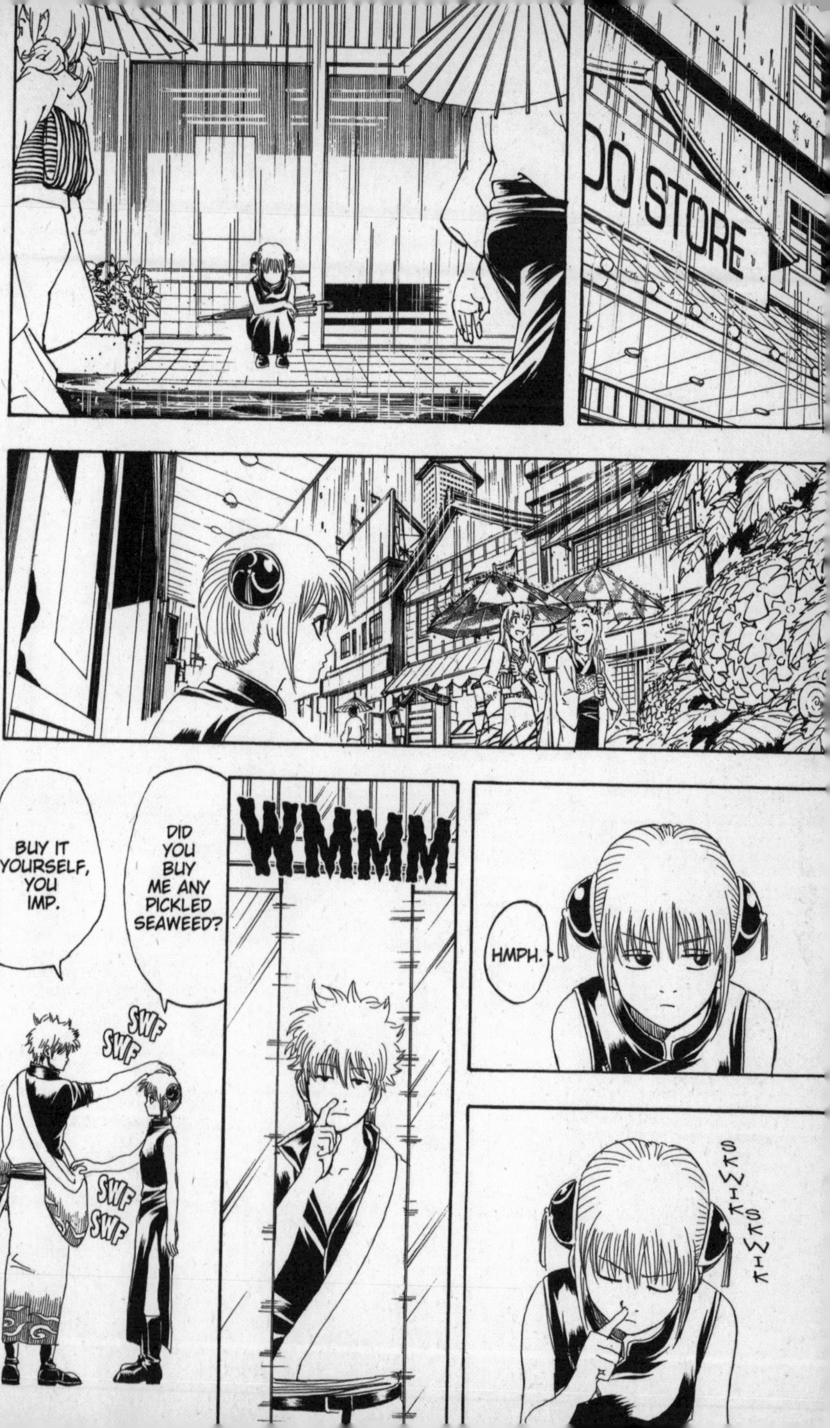
DO STORE
HMPH.
SKWIK SKWIK
WMMM
DID YOU BUY ME ANY PICKLED SEAWEED?
BUY IT YOURSELF, YOU IMP.
SWF SWF
SWF SWF

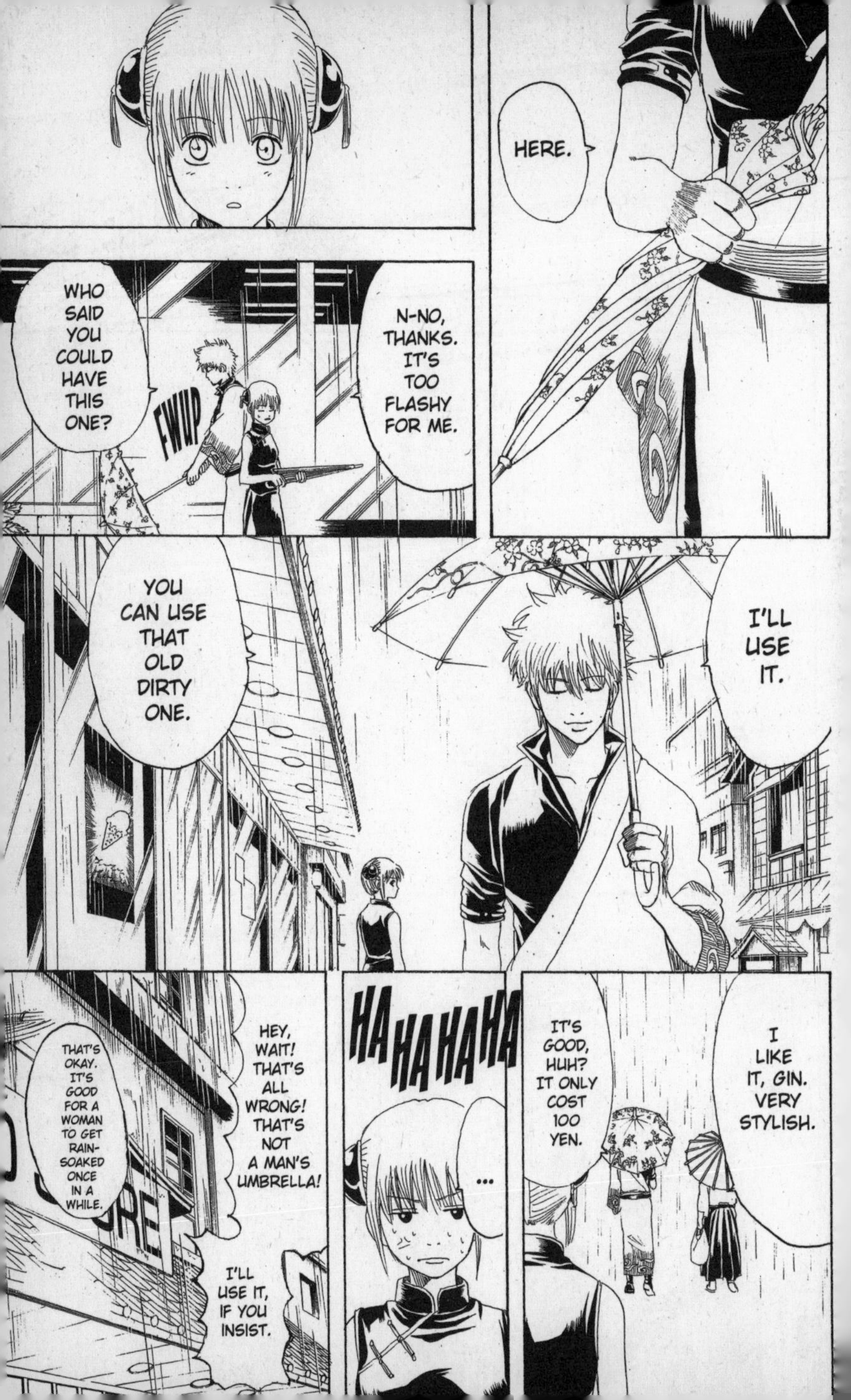
HERE.
N-NO, THANKS. IT'S TOO FLASHY FOR ME.
FWUP
WHO SAID YOU COULD HAVE THIS ONE?
I'LL USE IT.
YOU CAN USE THAT OLD DIRTY ONE.
I LIKE IT, GIN. VERY STYLISH.
IT'S GOOD, HUH? IT ONLY COST 100 YEN.
HAHAHAHA
...
HEY, WAIT! THAT'S ALL WRONG! THAT'S NOT A MAN'S UMBRELLA!
THAT'S OKAY. IT'S GOOD FOR A WOMAN TO GET RAIN-SOAKED ONCE IN A WHILE.
I'LL USE IT, IF YOU INSIST.

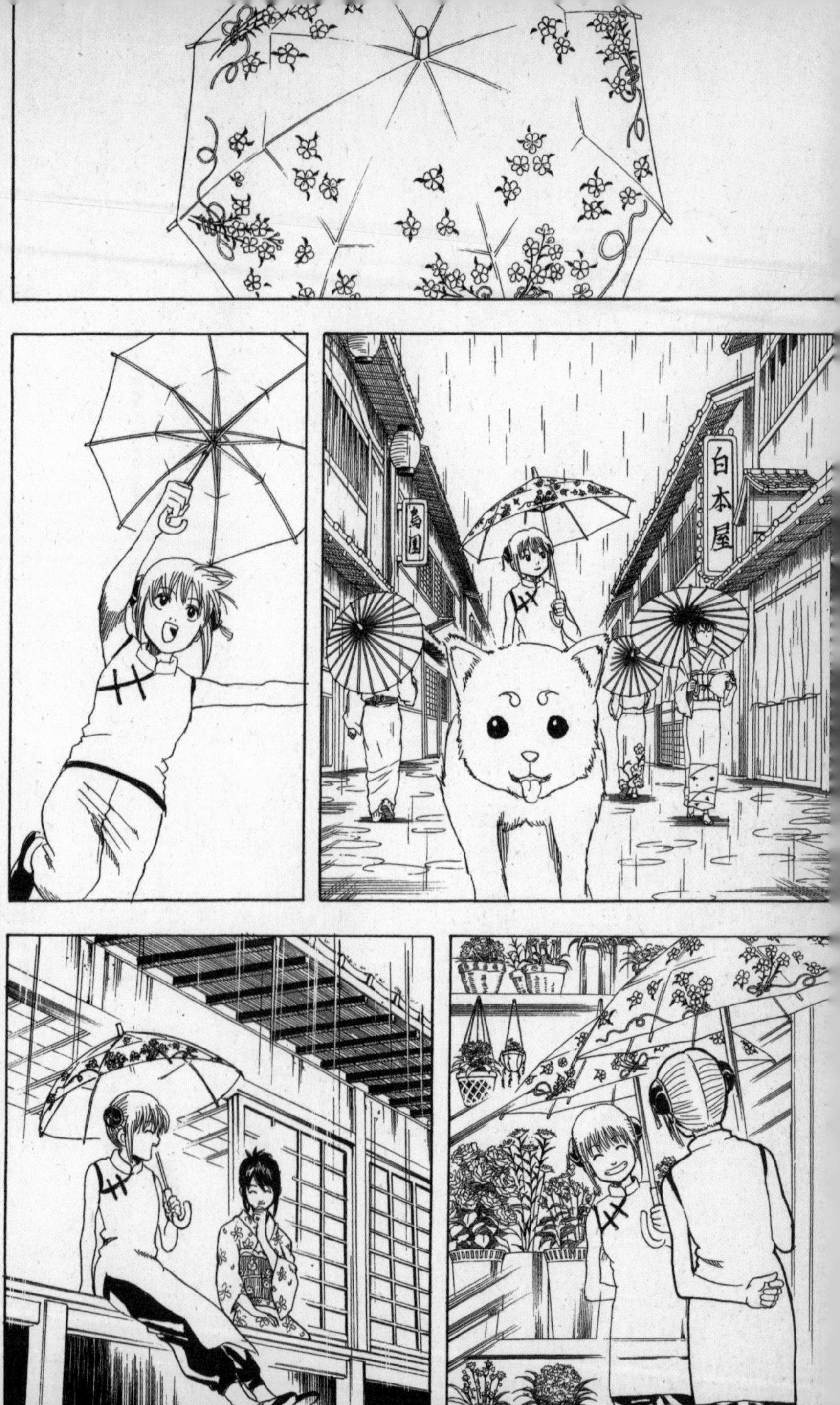
白本屋

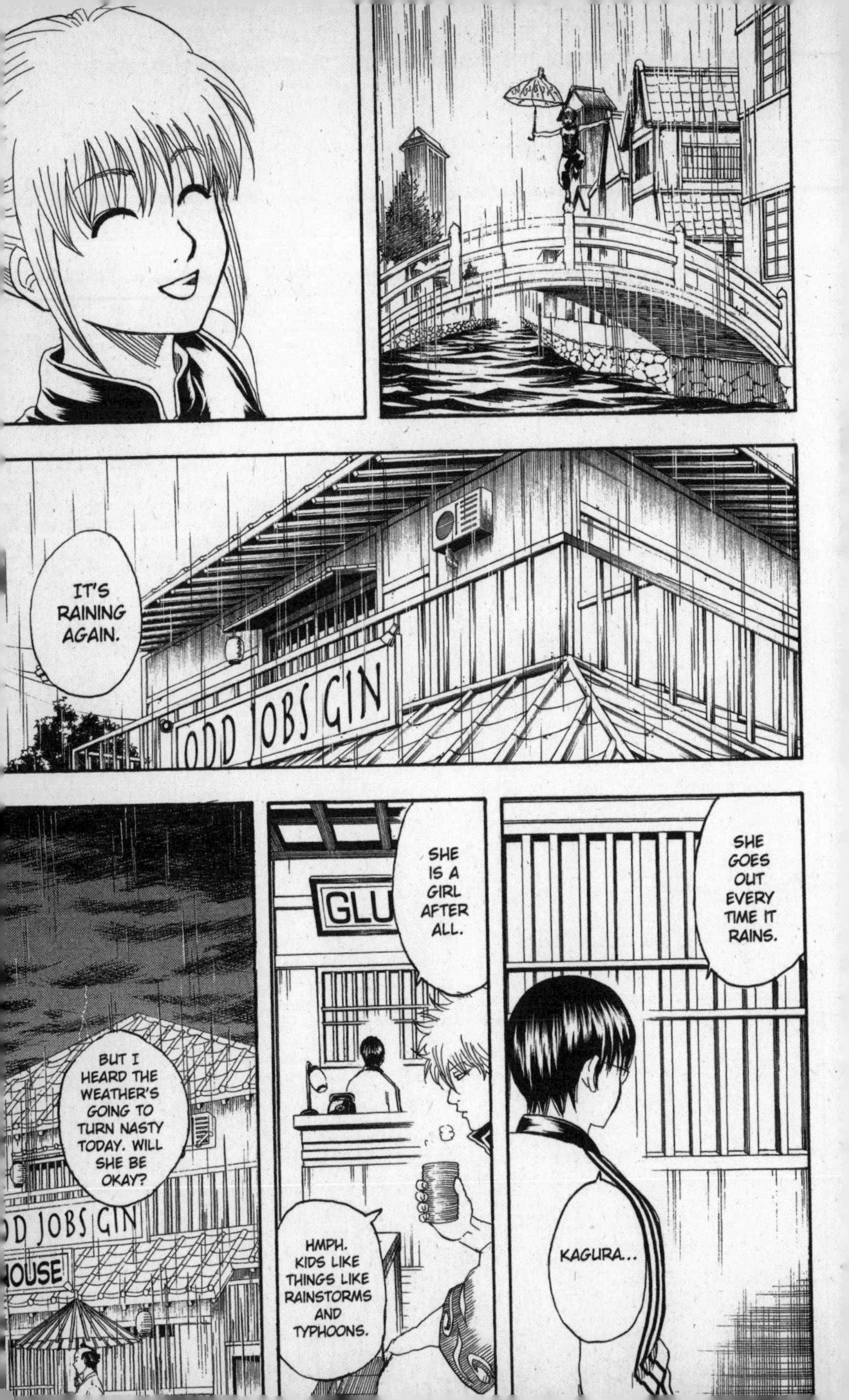
IT'S RAINING AGAIN.
ODD JOBS GIN
SHE GOES OUT EVERY TIME IT RAINS.
KAGURA...
SHE IS A GIRL AFTER ALL.
HMPH. KIDS LIKE THINGS LIKE RAINSTORMS AND TYPHOONS.
BUT I HEARD THE WEATHER'S GOING TO TURN NASTY TODAY. WILL SHE BE OKAY?

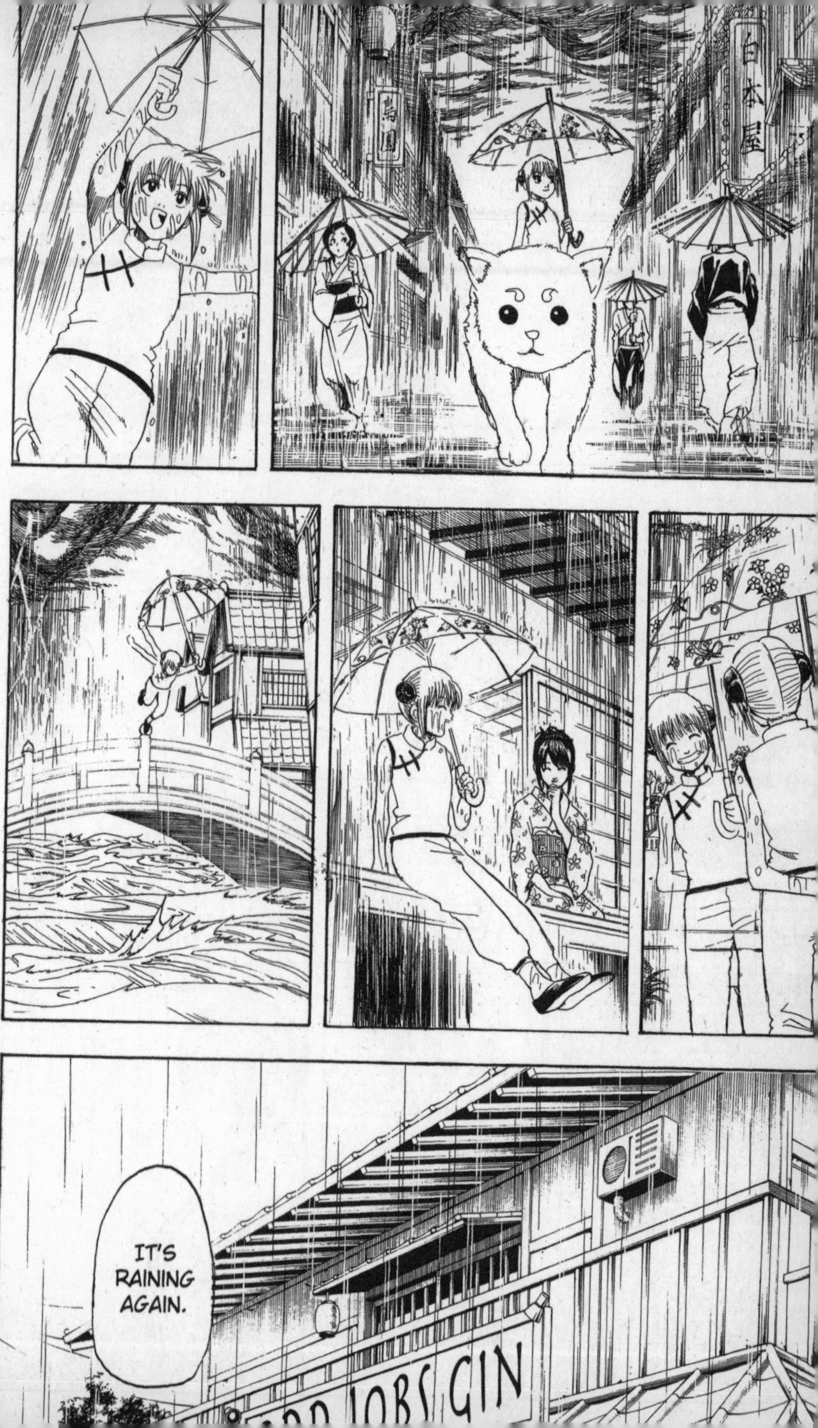
IT'S RAINING AGAIN.
JOBS GIN

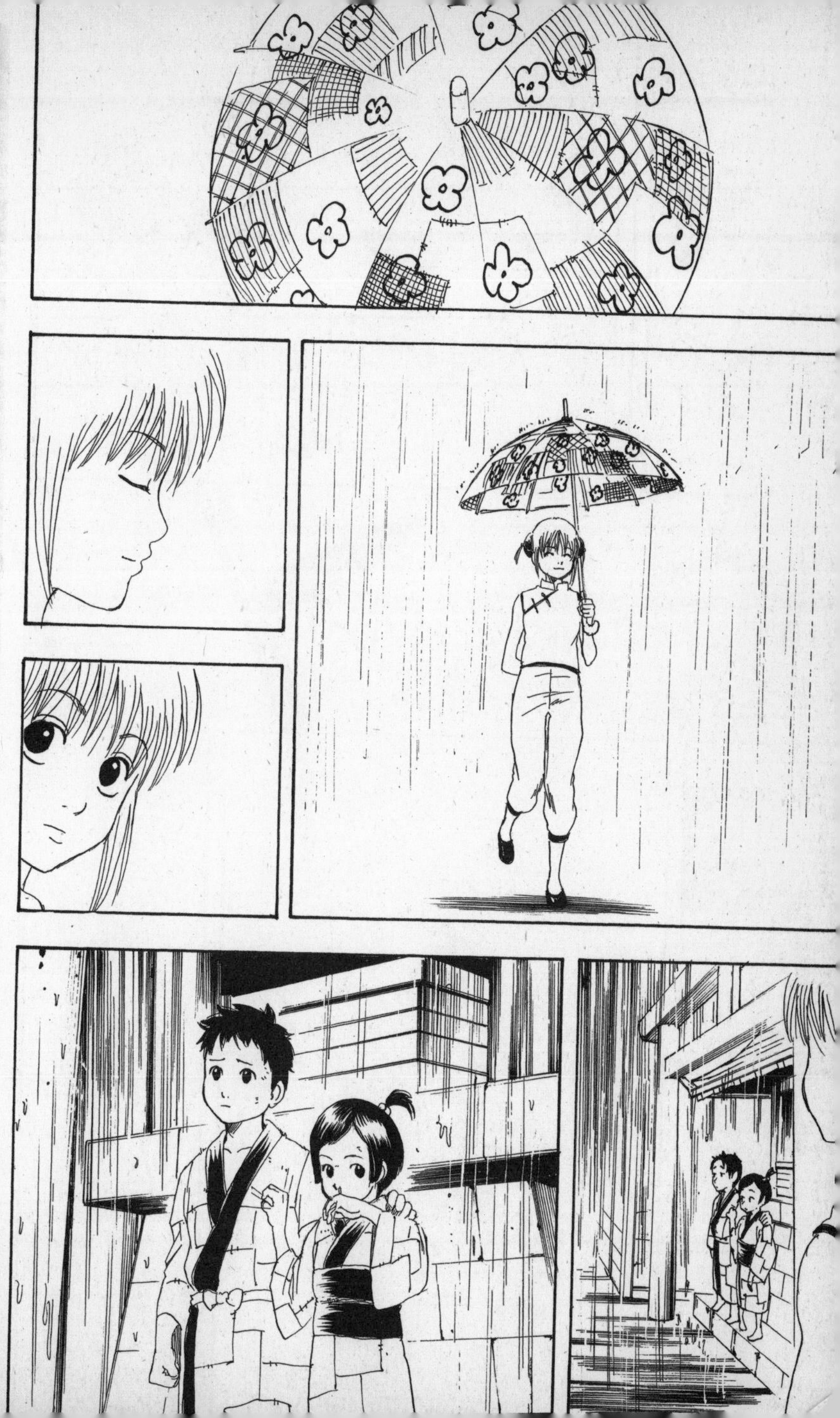

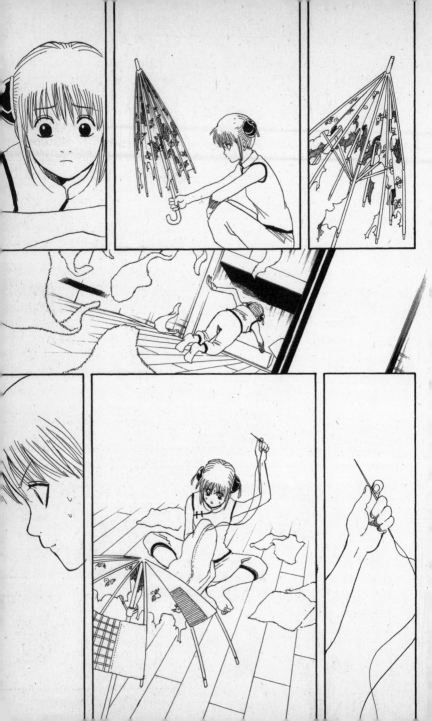

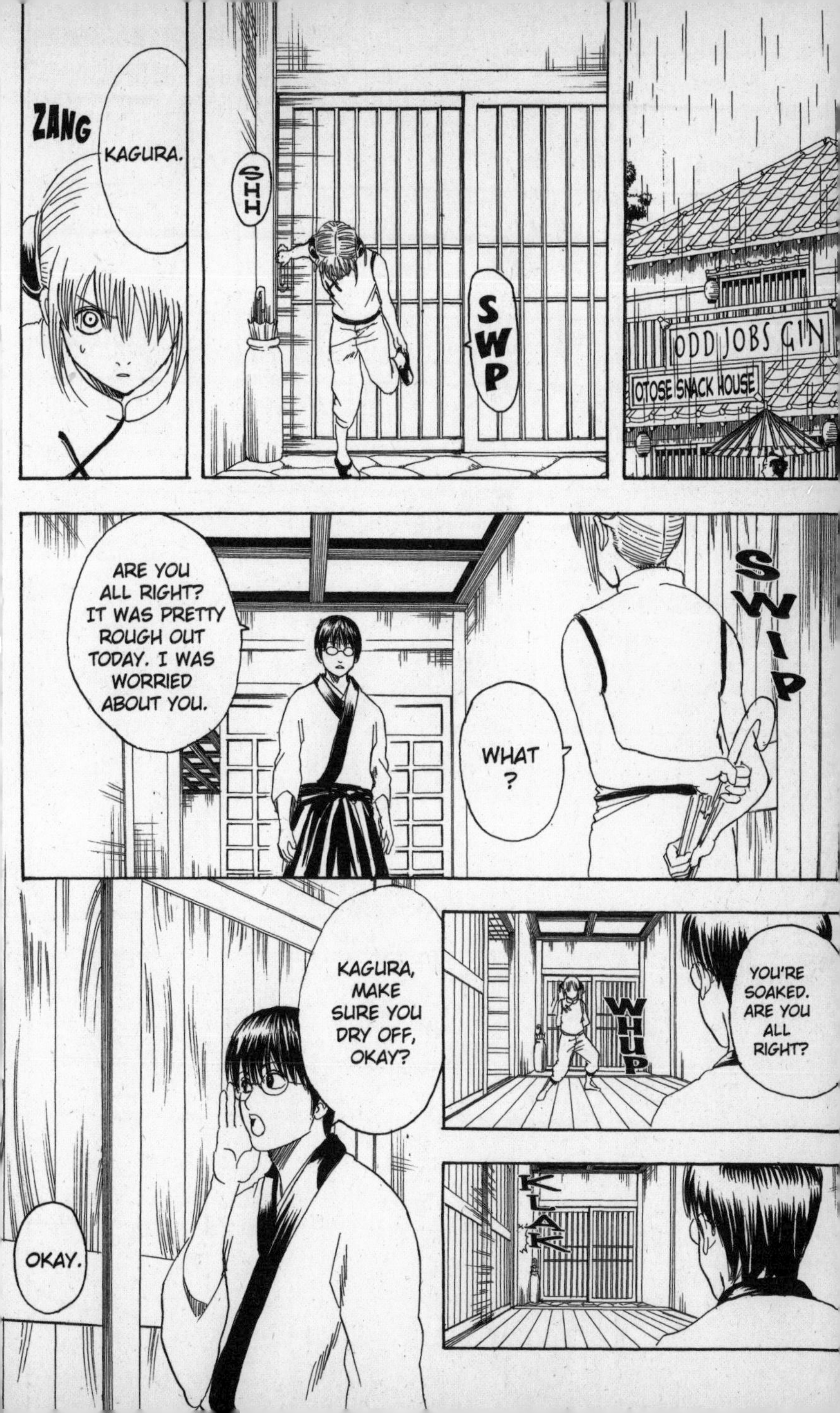
ODD JOBS GIN
OTOSE SNACK HOUSE
SHH
SWP
ZANG
KAGURA.
SWIP
WHAT ?
ARE YOU ALL RIGHT? IT WAS PRETTY ROUGH OUT TODAY. I WAS WORRIED ABOUT YOU.
YOU'RE SOAKED. ARE YOU ALL RIGHT?
WHUP
KLAK
KAGURA, MAKE SURE YOU DRY OFF, OKAY?
OKAY.

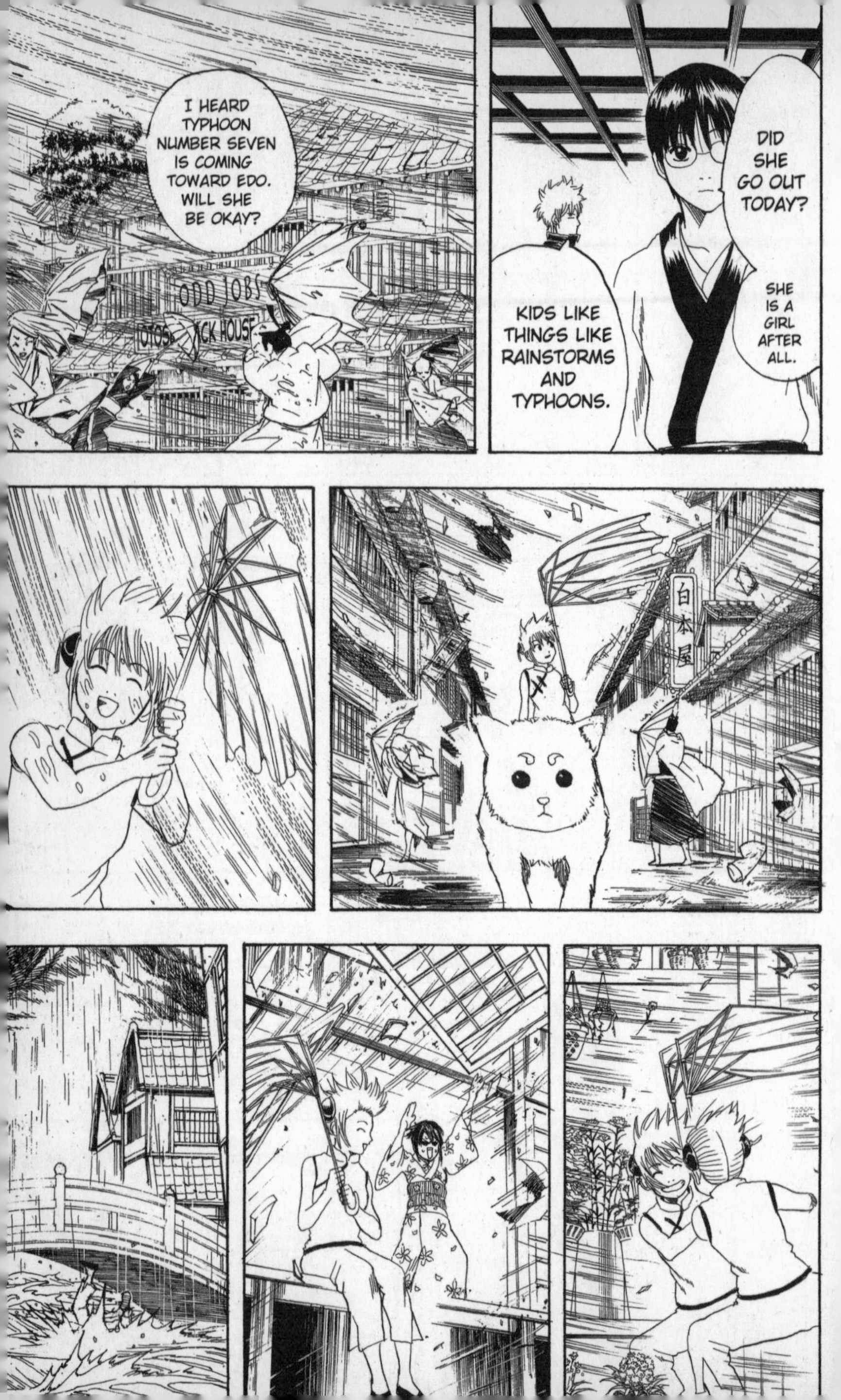
DID SHE GO OUT TODAY?
SHE IS A GIRL AFTER ALL.
KIDS LIKE THINGS LIKE RAINSTORMS AND TYPHOONS.
I HEARD TYPHOON NUMBER SEVEN IS COMING TOWARD EDO. WILL SHE BE OKAY?
ODD JOBS

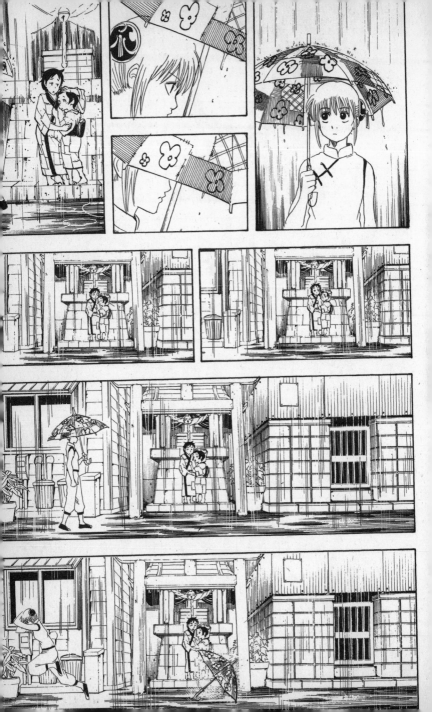

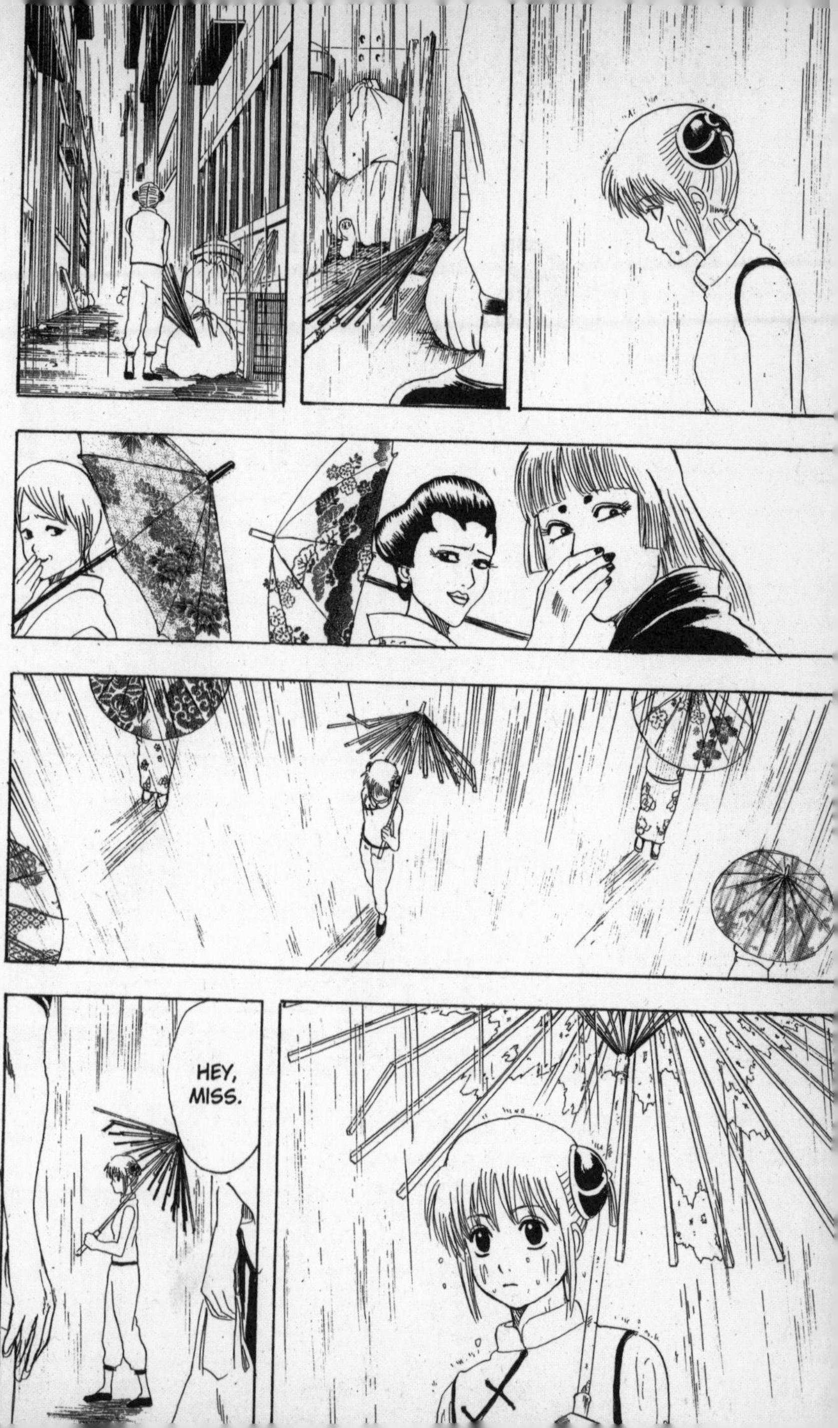
HEY, MISS.

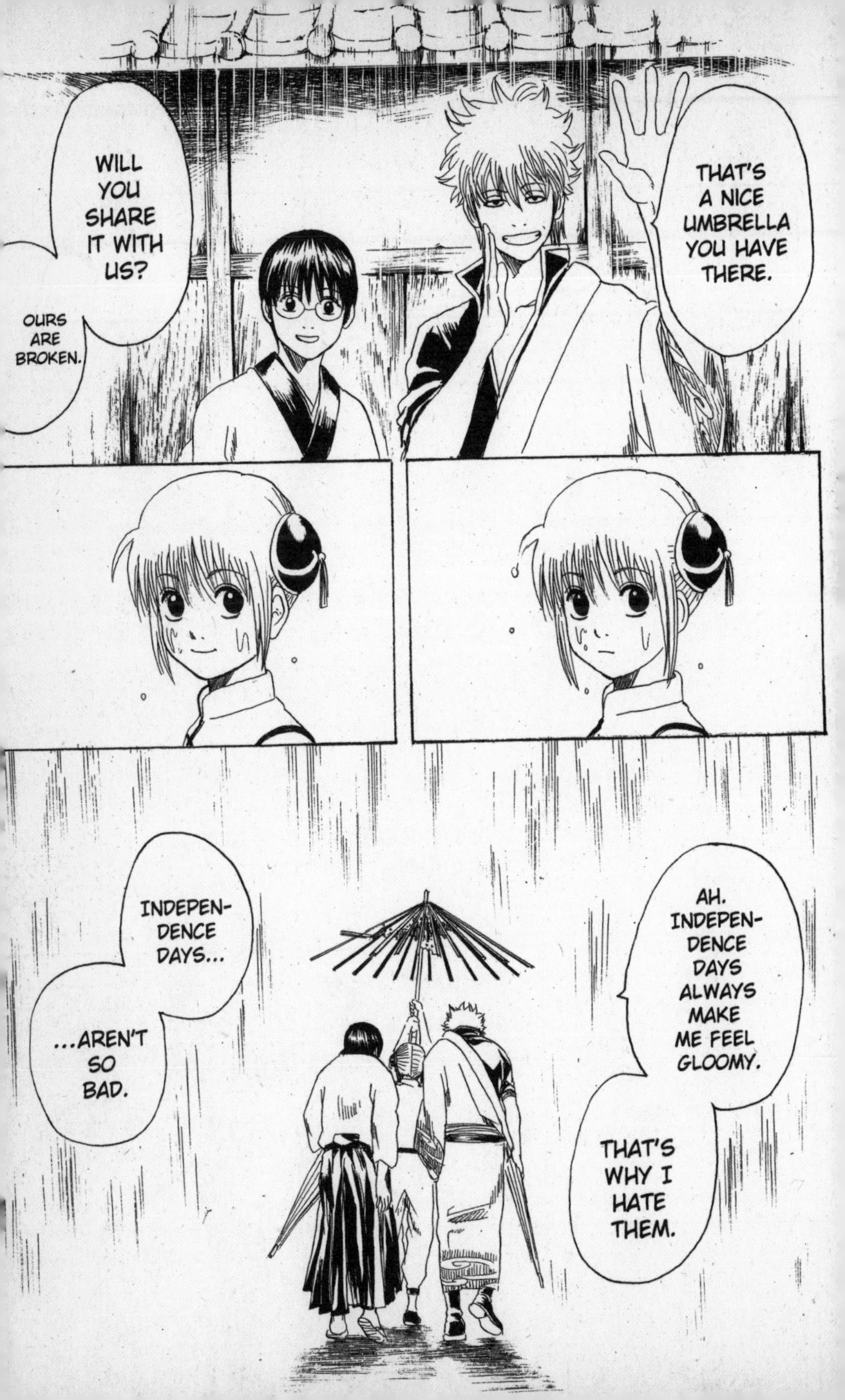
THAT'S A NICE UMBRELLA YOU HAVE THERE.
WILL YOU SHARE IT WITH US?
OURS ARE BROKEN.
AH. INDEPENDENCE DAYS ALWAYS MAKE ME FEEL GLOOMY.
THAT'S WHY I HATE THEM.
INDEPENDENCE DAYS...
...AREN'T SO BAD.

● An illustration from *Akamaru Jump* 2007.
  the September 25 extra issue bonus postcard

DON'T SIT AROUND WATCHING CARTOONS ALL SUMMER. DO YOUR HOMEWORK.

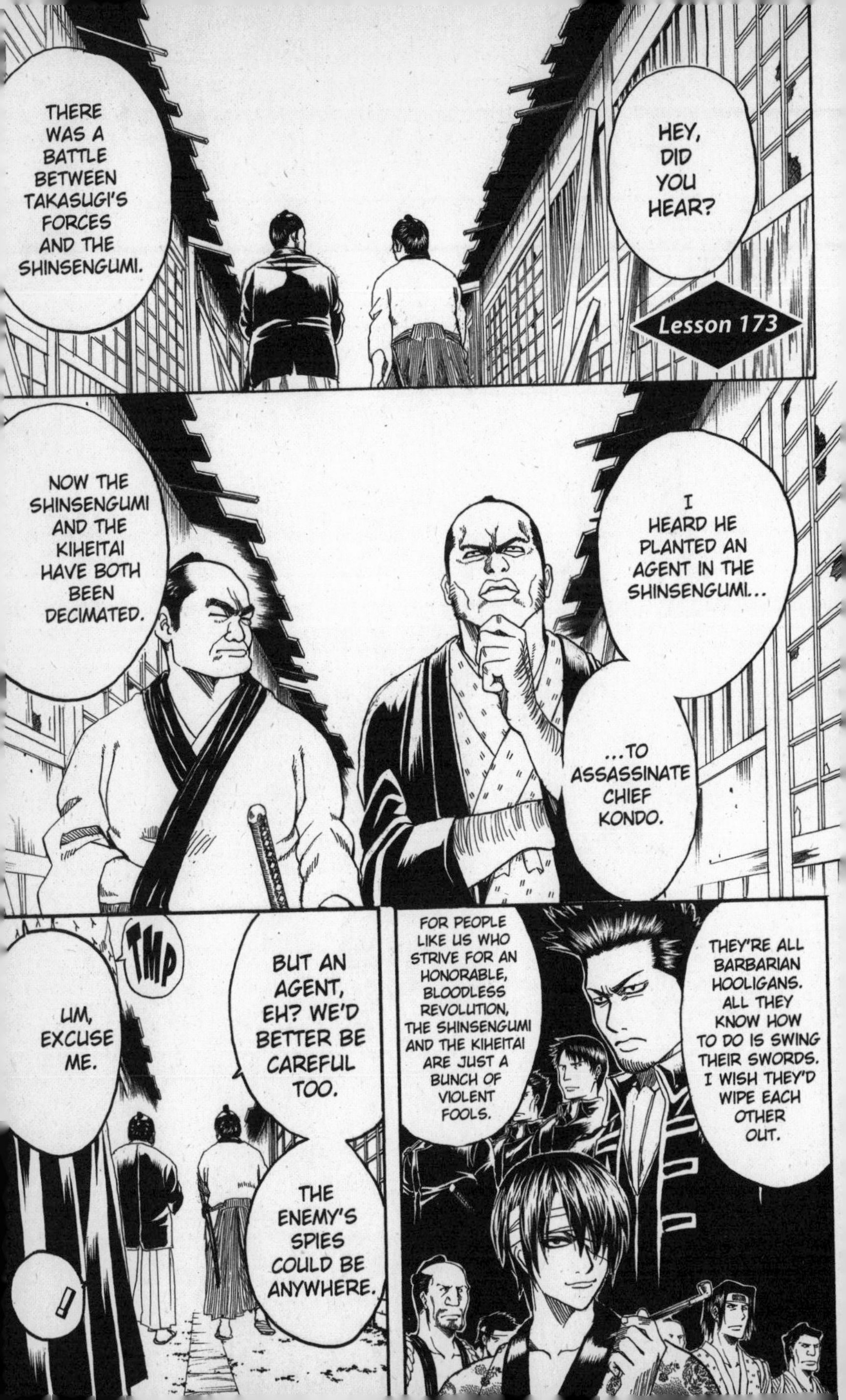
HEY, DID YOU HEAR?
Lesson 173
THERE WAS A BATTLE BETWEEN TAKASUGI'S FORCES AND THE SHINSENGUMI.
I HEARD HE PLANTED AN AGENT IN THE SHINSENGUMI...
...TO ASSASSINATE CHIEF KONDO.
NOW THE SHINSENGUMI AND THE KIHEITAI HAVE BOTH BEEN DECIMATED.
THEY'RE ALL BARBARIAN HOOLIGANS. ALL THEY KNOW HOW TO DO IS SWING THEIR SWORDS. I WISH THEY'D WIPE EACH OTHER OUT.
FOR PEOPLE LIKE US WHO STRIVE FOR AN HONORABLE, BLOODLESS REVOLUTION, THE SHINSENGUMI AND THE KIHEITAI ARE JUST A BUNCH OF VIOLENT FOOLS.
BUT AN AGENT, EH? WE'D BETTER BE CAREFUL TOO.
THE ENEMY'S SPIES COULD BE ANYWHERE.
TMP
UM, EXCUSE ME.
!

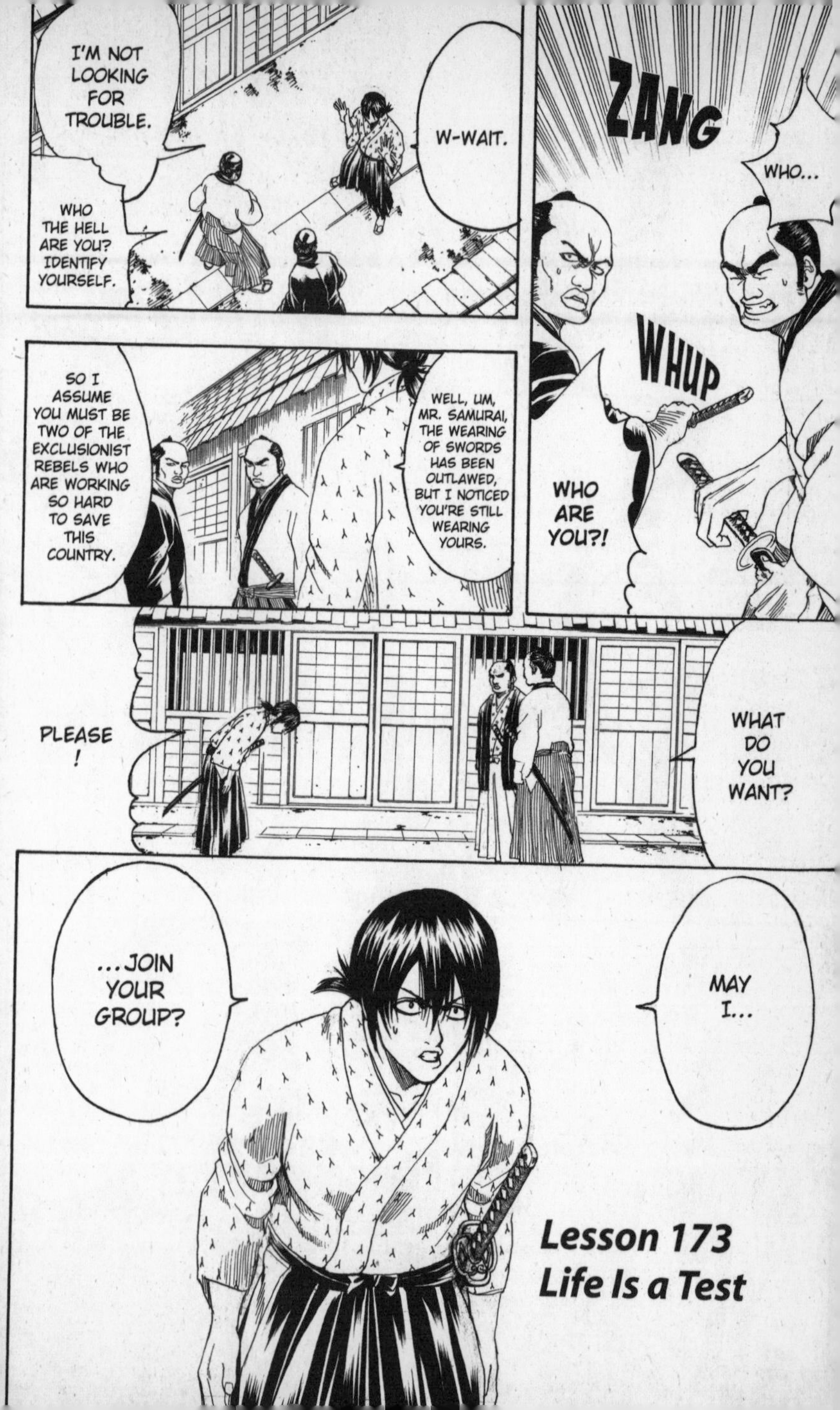
ZANG
WHO...
WHUP
WHO ARE YOU?!
W-WAIT.
I'M NOT LOOKING FOR TROUBLE.
WHO THE HELL ARE YOU? IDENTIFY YOURSELF.
WELL, UM, MR. SAMURAI, THE WEARING OF SWORDS HAS BEEN OUTLAWED, BUT I NOTICED YOU'RE STILL WEARING YOURS.
SO I ASSUME YOU MUST BE TWO OF THE EXCLUSIONIST REBELS WHO ARE WORKING SO HARD TO SAVE THIS COUNTRY.
WHAT DO YOU WANT?
PLEASE!
MAY I...
...JOIN YOUR GROUP?

Lesson 173
Life Is a Test

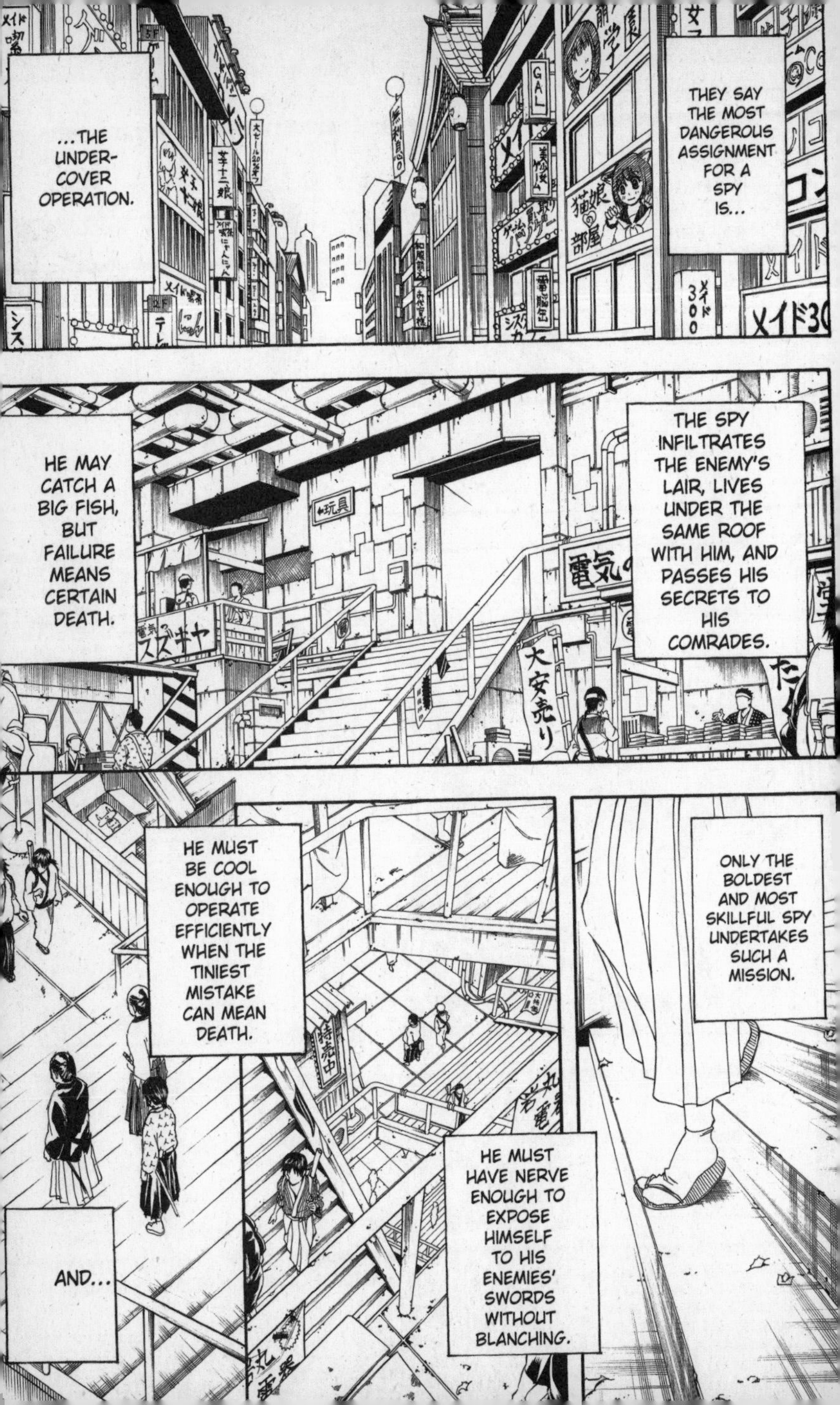

THEY SAY THE MOST DANGEROUS ASSIGNMENT FOR A SPY IS...
...THE UNDER-COVER OPERATION.
THE SPY INFILTRATES THE ENEMY'S LAIR, LIVES UNDER THE SAME ROOF WITH HIM, AND PASSES HIS SECRETS TO HIS COMRADES.
HE MAY CATCH A BIG FISH, BUT FAILURE MEANS CERTAIN DEATH.
ONLY THE BOLDEST AND MOST SKILLFUL SPY UNDERTAKES SUCH A MISSION.
HE MUST BE COOL ENOUGH TO OPERATE EFFICIENTLY WHEN THE TINIEST MISTAKE CAN MEAN DEATH.
HE MUST HAVE NERVE ENOUGH TO EXPOSE HIMSELF TO HIS ENEMIES' SWORDS WITHOUT BLANCHING.
AND...

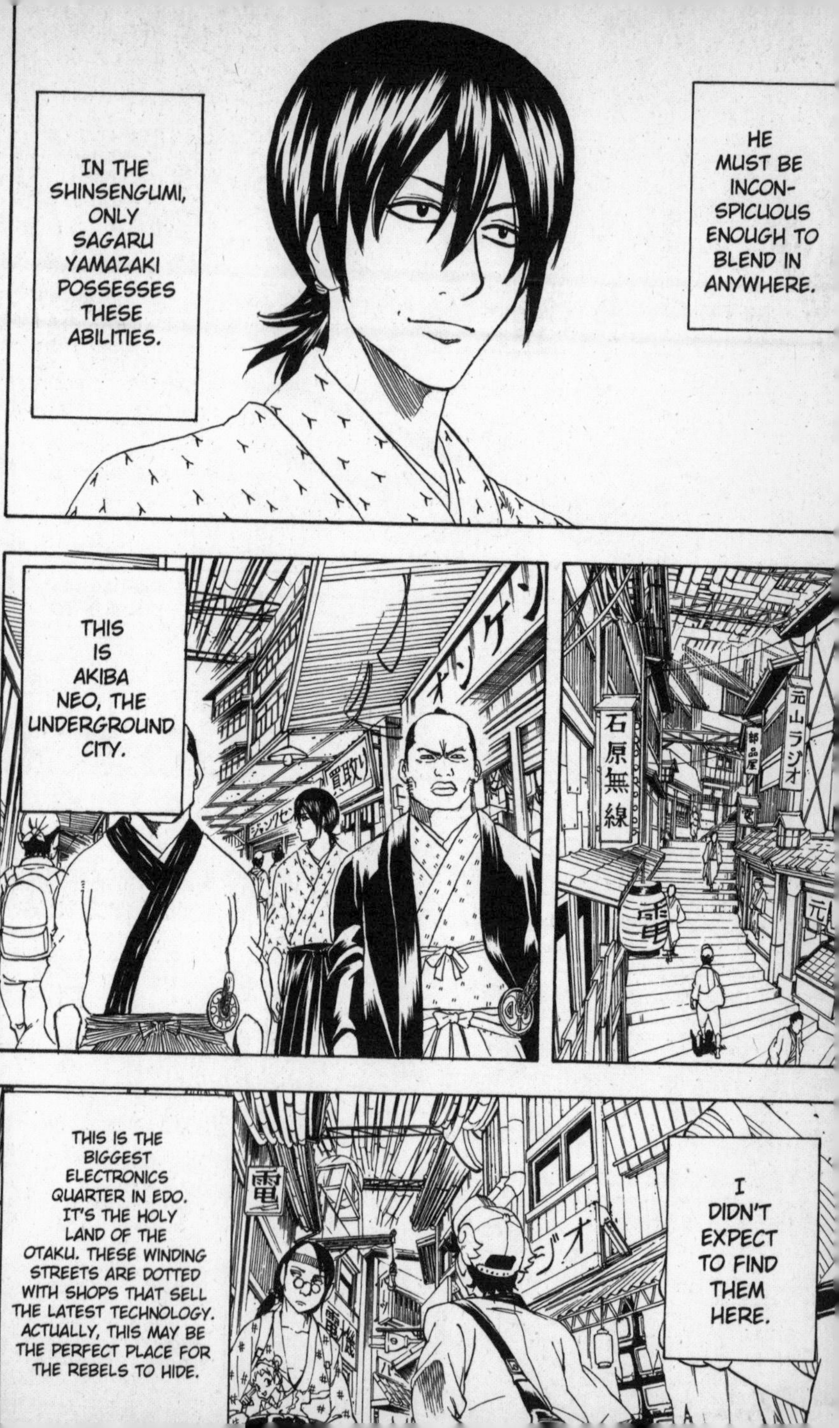
HE MUST BE INCONSPICUOUS ENOUGH TO BLEND IN ANYWHERE.
IN THE SHINSENGUMI, ONLY SAGARU YAMAZAKI POSSESSES THESE ABILITIES.
元山ラジオ
部品屋
石原無線
THIS IS AKIBA NEO, THE UNDERGROUND CITY.
オンケン
買取り
I DIDN'T EXPECT TO FIND THEM HERE.
THIS IS THE BIGGEST ELECTRONICS QUARTER IN EDO. IT'S THE HOLY LAND OF THE OTAKU. THESE WINDING STREETS ARE DOTTED WITH SHOPS THAT SELL THE LATEST TECHNOLOGY. ACTUALLY, THIS MAY BE THE PERFECT PLACE FOR THE REBELS TO HIDE.

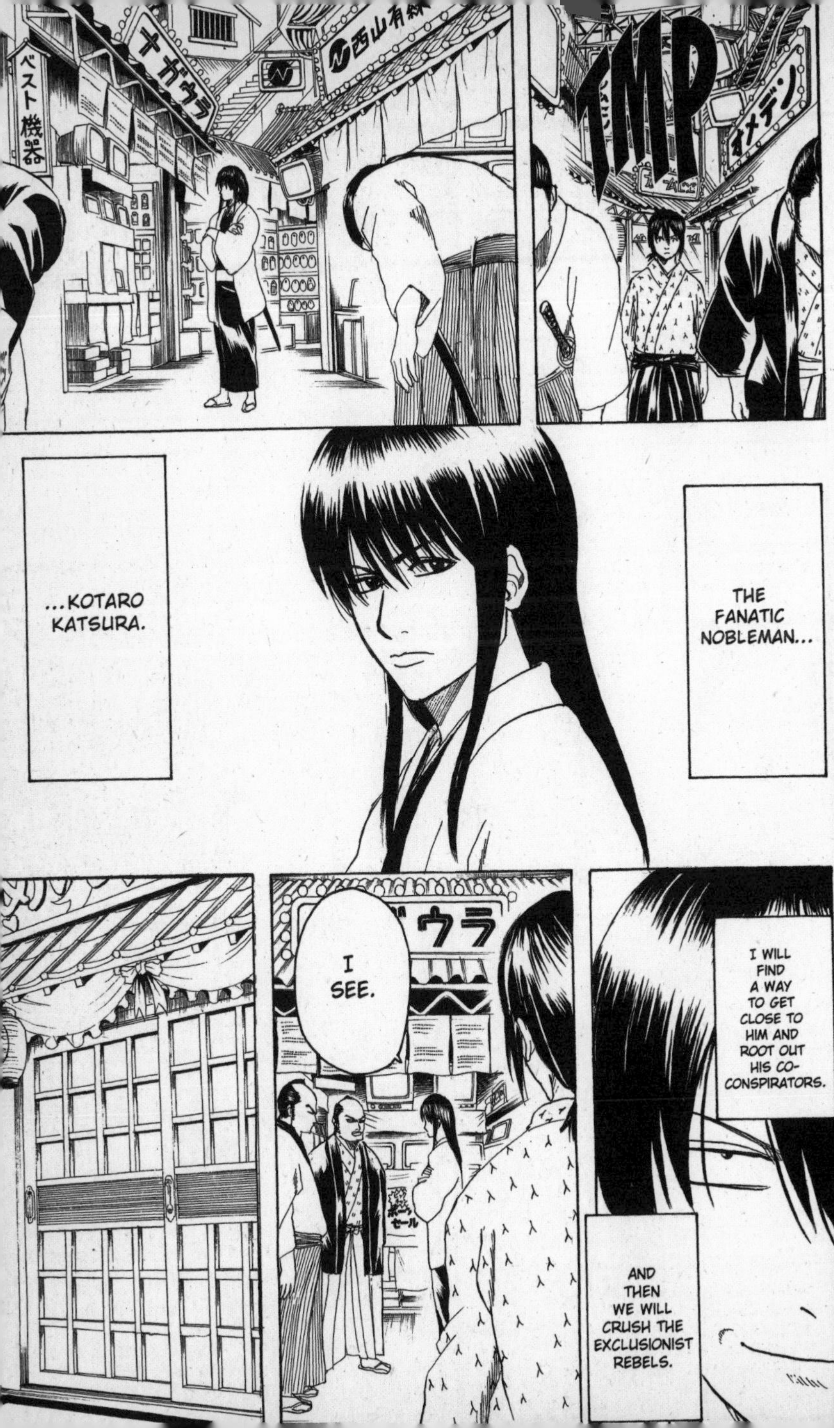
TMP
オメデン
ナガウラ
ベスト機器
THE FANATIC NOBLEMAN...
...KOTARO KATSURA.
I WILL FIND A WAY TO GET CLOSE TO HIM AND ROOT OUT HIS CO-CONSPIRATORS.
AND THEN WE WILL CRUSH THE EXCLUSIONIST REBELS.
I SEE.

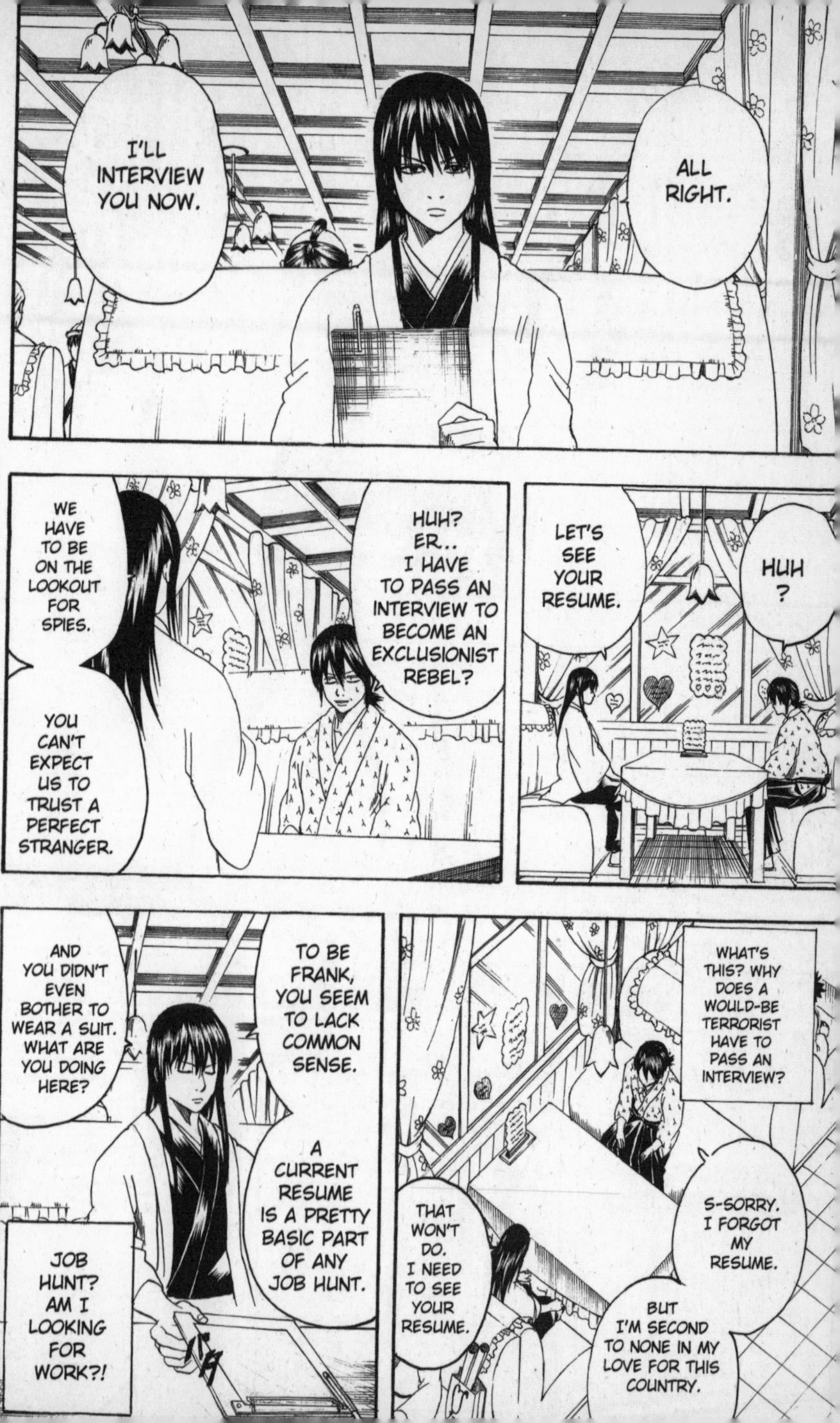
I'LL INTERVIEW YOU NOW.
ALL RIGHT.
LET'S SEE YOUR RESUME.
HUH ?
HUH? ER.. I HAVE TO PASS AN INTERVIEW TO BECOME AN EXCLUSIONIST REBEL?
WE HAVE TO BE ON THE LOOKOUT FOR SPIES.
YOU CAN'T EXPECT US TO TRUST A PERFECT STRANGER.
WHAT'S THIS? WHY DOES A WOULD-BE TERRORIST HAVE TO PASS AN INTERVIEW?
S-SORRY. I FORGOT MY RESUME.
THAT WON'T DO. I NEED TO SEE YOUR RESUME.
BUT I'M SECOND TO NONE IN MY LOVE FOR THIS COUNTRY.
TO BE FRANK, YOU SEEM TO LACK COMMON SENSE.
AND YOU DIDN'T EVEN BOTHER TO WEAR A SUIT. WHAT ARE YOU DOING HERE?
A CURRENT RESUME IS A PRETTY BASIC PART OF ANY JOB HUNT.
JOB HUNT? AM I LOOKING FOR WORK?!

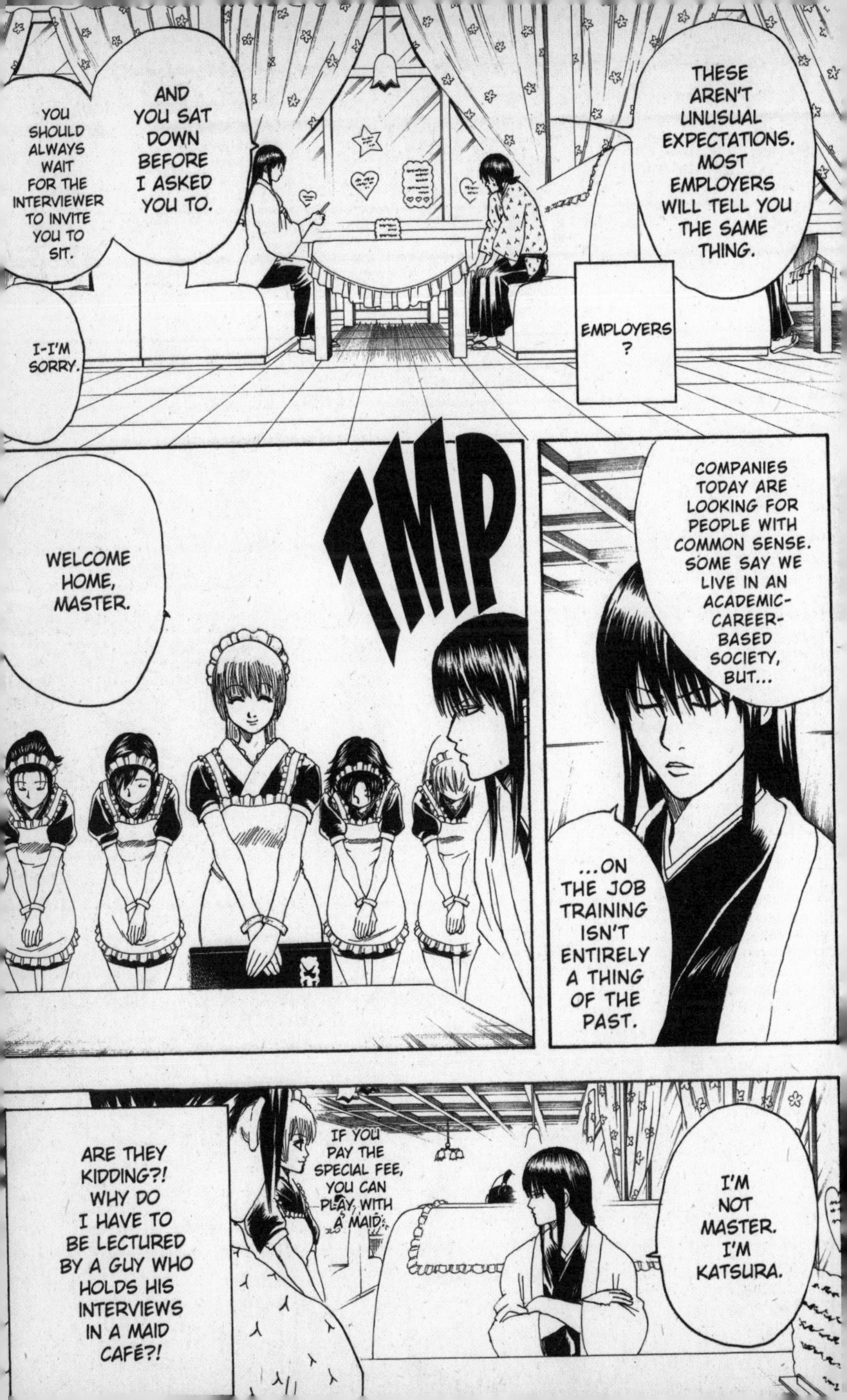
THESE AREN'T UNUSUAL EXPECTATIONS. MOST EMPLOYERS WILL TELL YOU THE SAME THING.
AND YOU SAT DOWN BEFORE I ASKED YOU TO.
YOU SHOULD ALWAYS WAIT FOR THE INTERVIEWER TO INVITE YOU TO SIT.
EMPLOYERS ?
I-I'M SORRY.
COMPANIES TODAY ARE LOOKING FOR PEOPLE WITH COMMON SENSE. SOME SAY WE LIVE IN AN ACADEMIC-CAREER-BASED SOCIETY, BUT...
...ON THE JOB TRAINING ISN'T ENTIRELY A THING OF THE PAST.
TMP
WELCOME HOME, MASTER.
I'M NOT MASTER. I'M KATSURA.
IF YOU PAY THE SPECIAL FEE, YOU CAN PLAY WITH A MAID.
ARE THEY KIDDING?! WHY DO I HAVE TO BE LECTURED BY A GUY WHO HOLDS HIS INTERVIEWS IN A MAID CAFÉ?!

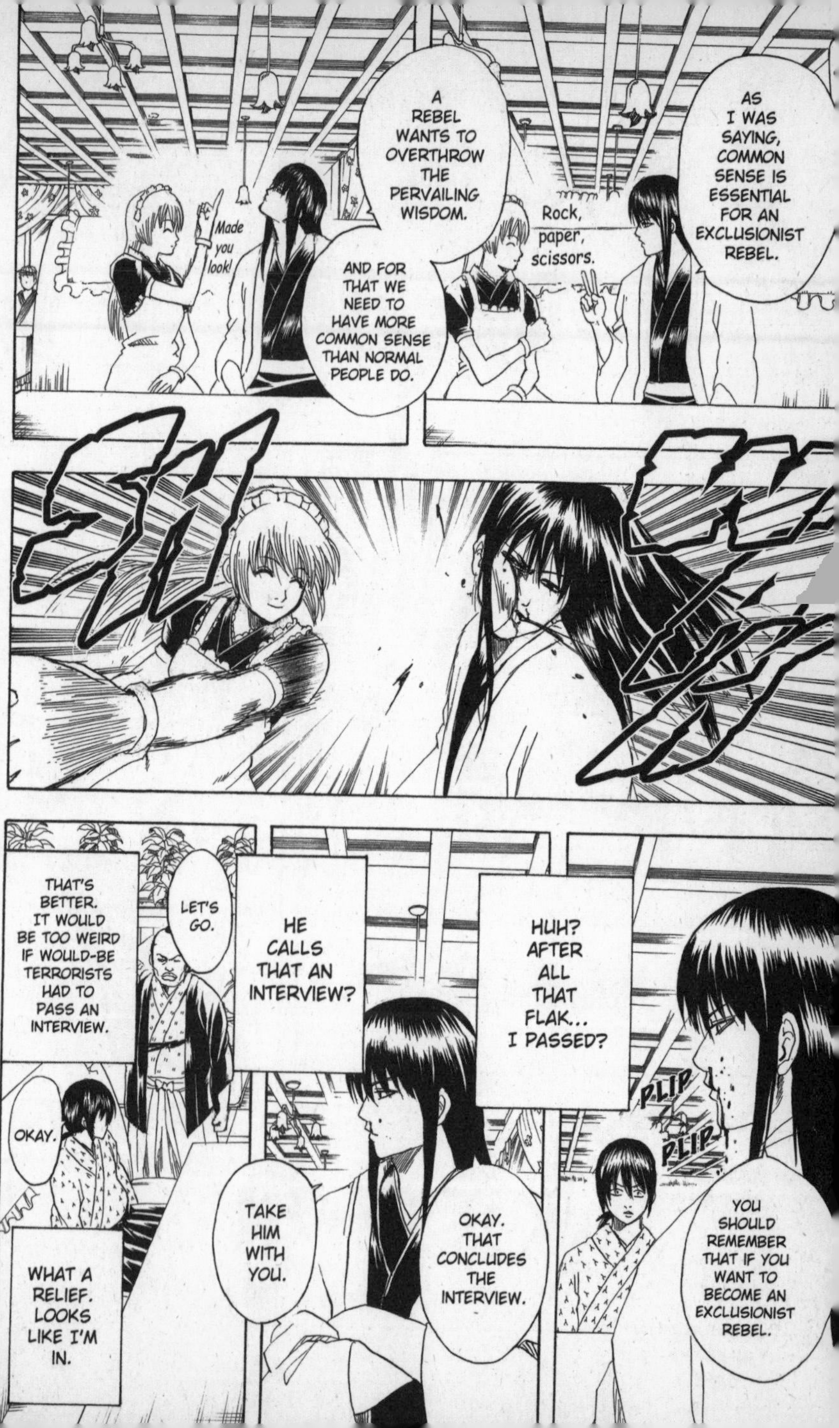
AS I WAS SAYING, COMMON SENSE IS ESSENTIAL FOR AN EXCLUSIONIST REBEL.
Rock, paper, scissors.
A REBEL WANTS TO OVERTHROW THE PERVAILING WISDOM.
AND FOR THAT WE NEED TO HAVE MORE COMMON SENSE THAN NORMAL PEOPLE DO.
Made you look!
YOU SHOULD REMEMBER THAT IF YOU WANT TO BECOME AN EXCLUSIONIST REBEL.
PLIP
PLIP
HUH? AFTER ALL THAT FLAK... I PASSED?
OKAY. THAT CONCLUDES THE INTERVIEW.
TAKE HIM WITH YOU.
HE CALLS THAT AN INTERVIEW?
LET'S GO.
THAT'S BETTER. IT WOULD BE TOO WEIRD IF WOULD-BE TERRORISTS HAD TO PASS AN INTERVIEW.
OKAY.
WHAT A RELIEF. LOOKS LIKE I'M IN.

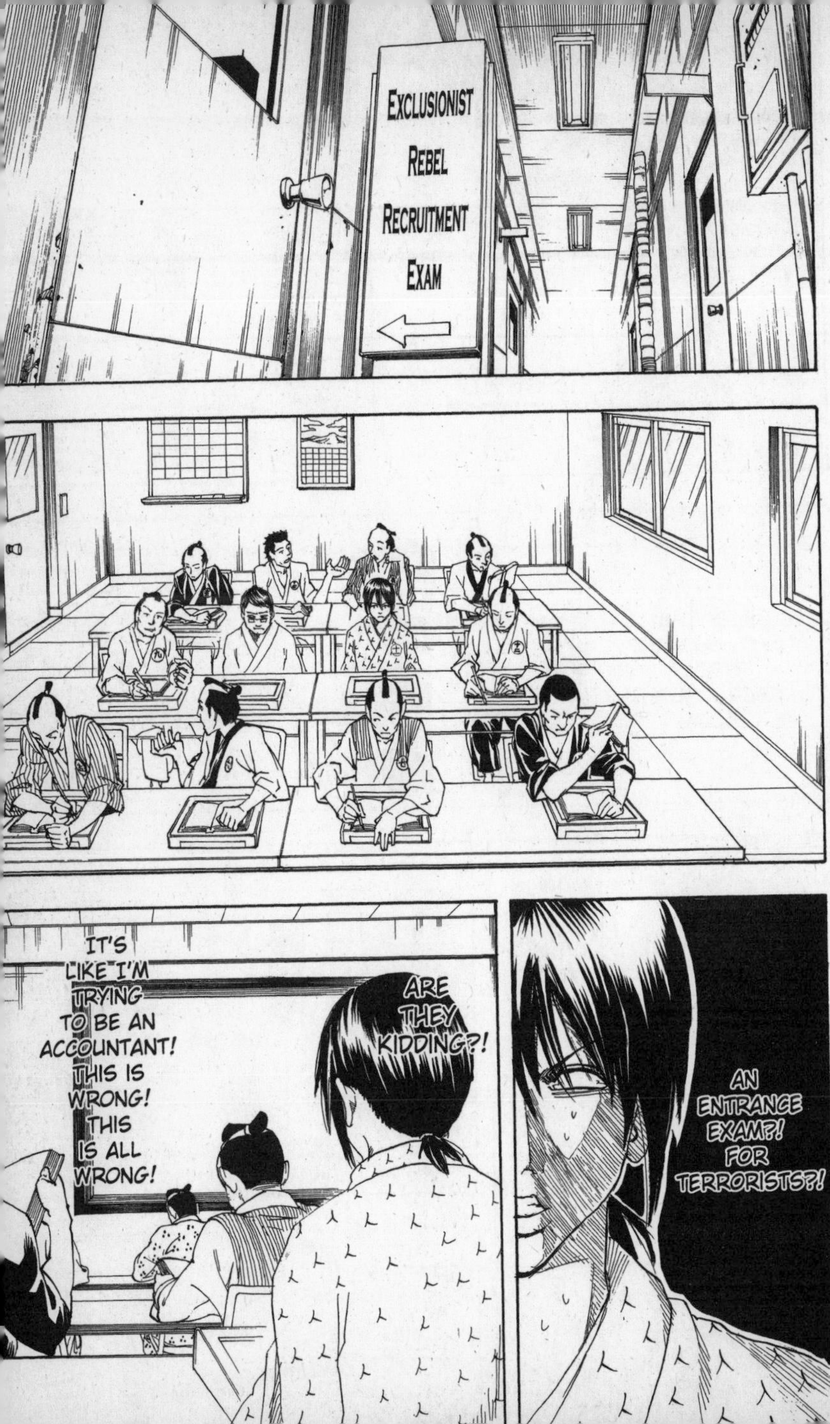
EXCLUSIONIST REBEL RECRUITMENT EXAM
AN ENTRANCE EXAM?! FOR TERRORISTS?!
ARE THEY KIDDING?!
IT'S LIKE I'M TRYING TO BE AN ACCOUNTANT! THIS IS WRONG! THIS IS ALL WRONG!

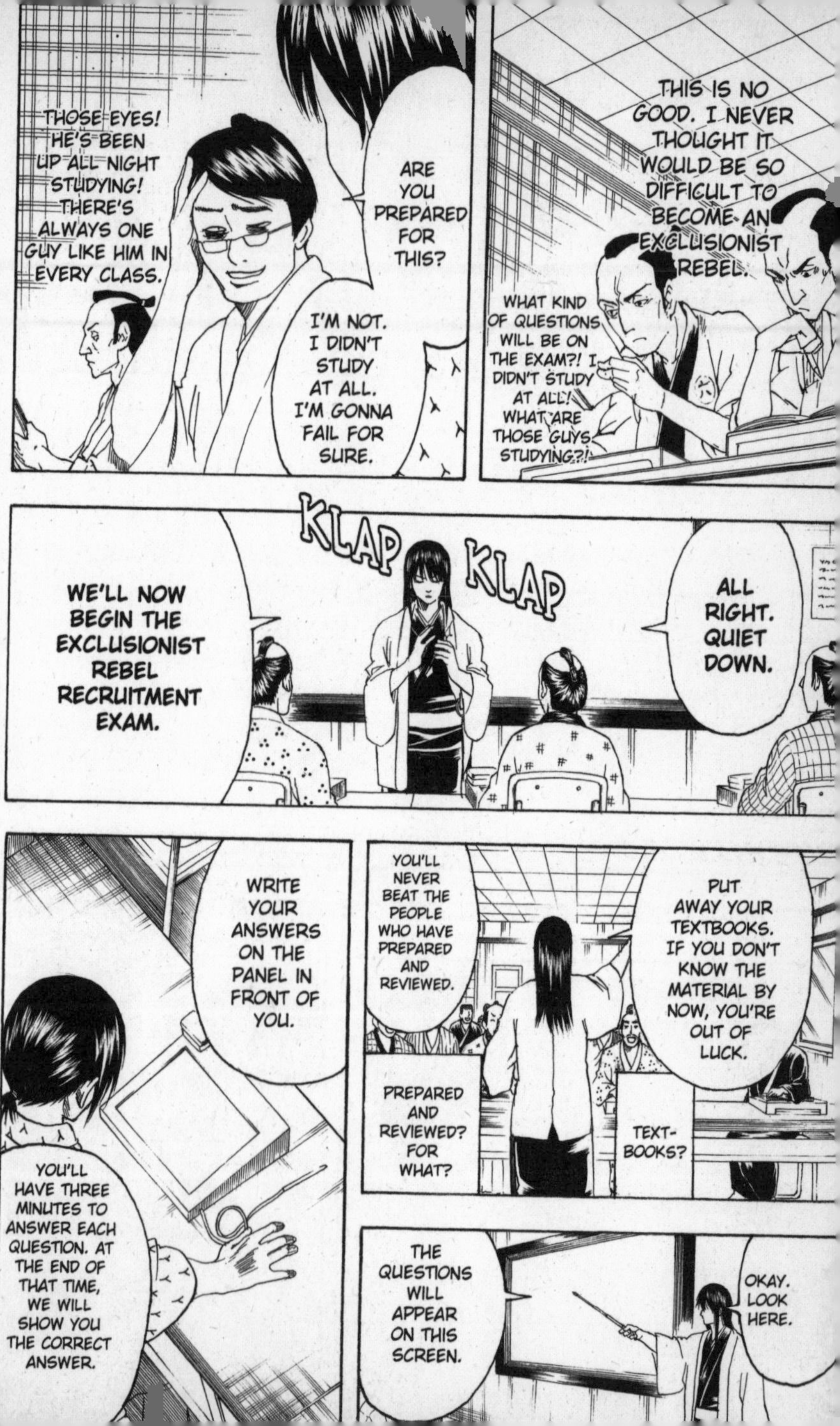
THIS IS NO GOOD. I NEVER THOUGHT IT WOULD BE SO DIFFICULT TO BECOME AN EXCLUSIONIST REBEL.
WHAT KIND OF QUESTIONS WILL BE ON THE EXAM?! I DIDN'T STUDY AT ALL! WHAT ARE THOSE GUYS STUDYING?!
ARE YOU PREPARED FOR THIS?
I'M NOT. I DIDN'T STUDY AT ALL. I'M GONNA FAIL FOR SURE.
THOSE EYES! HE'S BEEN UP ALL NIGHT STUDYING! THERE'S ALWAYS ONE GUY LIKE HIM IN EVERY CLASS.
ALL RIGHT. QUIET DOWN.
KLAP KLAP
WE'LL NOW BEGIN THE EXCLUSIONIST REBEL RECRUITMENT EXAM.
PUT AWAY YOUR TEXTBOOKS. IF YOU DON'T KNOW THE MATERIAL BY NOW, YOU'RE OUT OF LUCK.
TEXT-BOOKS?
YOU'LL NEVER BEAT THE PEOPLE WHO HAVE PREPARED AND REVIEWED.
PREPARED AND REVIEWED? FOR WHAT?
OKAY. LOOK HERE.
THE QUESTIONS WILL APPEAR ON THIS SCREEN.
WRITE YOUR ANSWERS ON THE PANEL IN FRONT OF YOU.
YOU'LL HAVE THREE MINUTES TO ANSWER EACH QUESTION. AT THE END OF THAT TIME, WE WILL SHOW YOU THE CORRECT ANSWER.

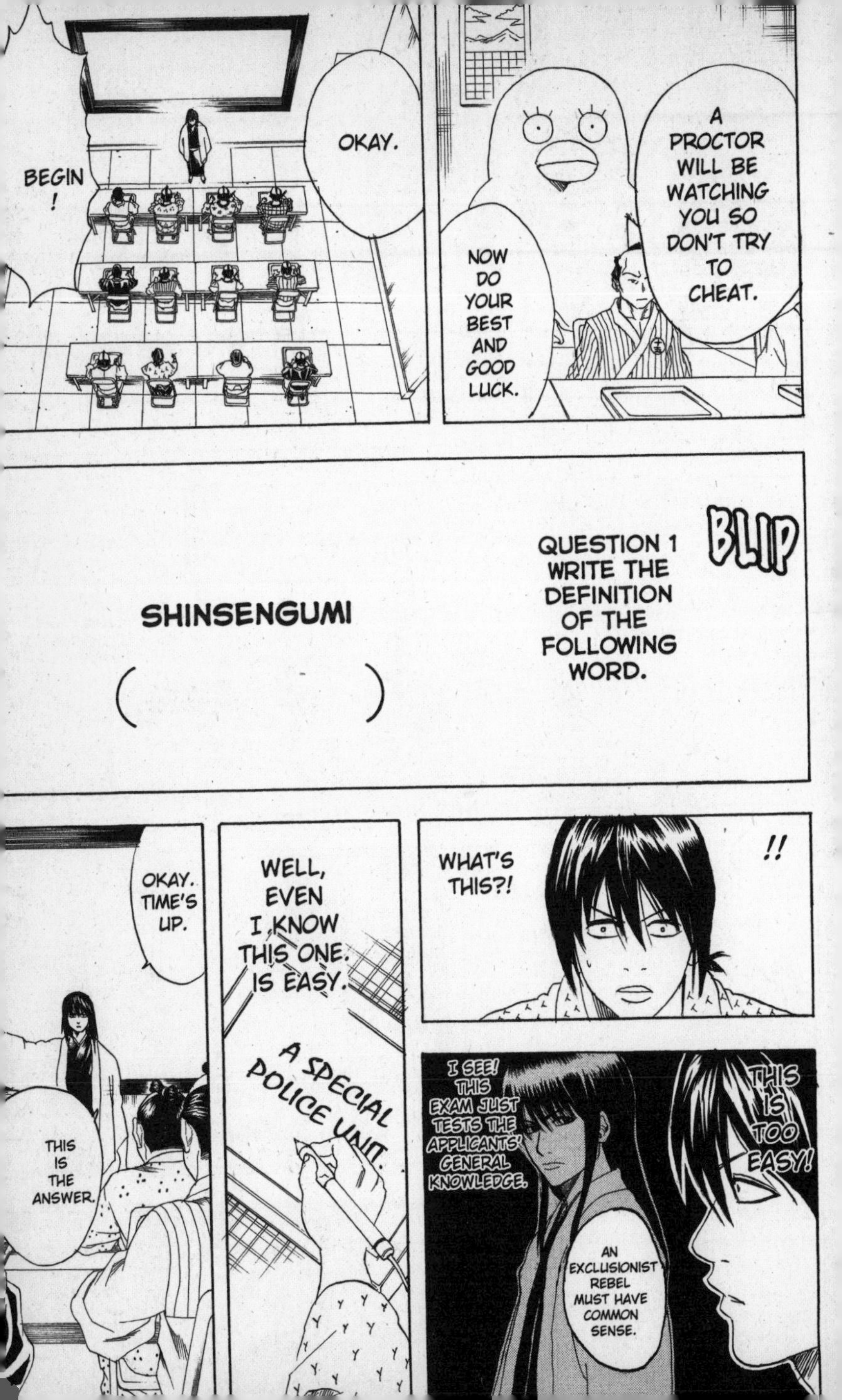
A PROCTOR WILL BE WATCHING YOU SO DON'T TRY TO CHEAT.
NOW DO YOUR BEST AND GOOD LUCK.
OKAY.
BEGIN!
BLIP
QUESTION 1 WRITE THE DEFINITION OF THE FOLLOWING WORD.
SHINSENGUMI
(-)
!!
WHAT'S THIS?!
THIS IS TOO EASY!
I SEE! THIS EXAM JUST TESTS THE APPLICANTS' GENERAL KNOWLEDGE.
AN EXCLUSIONIST REBEL MUST HAVE COMMON SENSE.
WELL, EVEN I KNOW THIS ONE. IS EASY.
A SPECIAL POLICE UNIT.
OKAY. TIME'S UP.
THIS IS THE ANSWER.

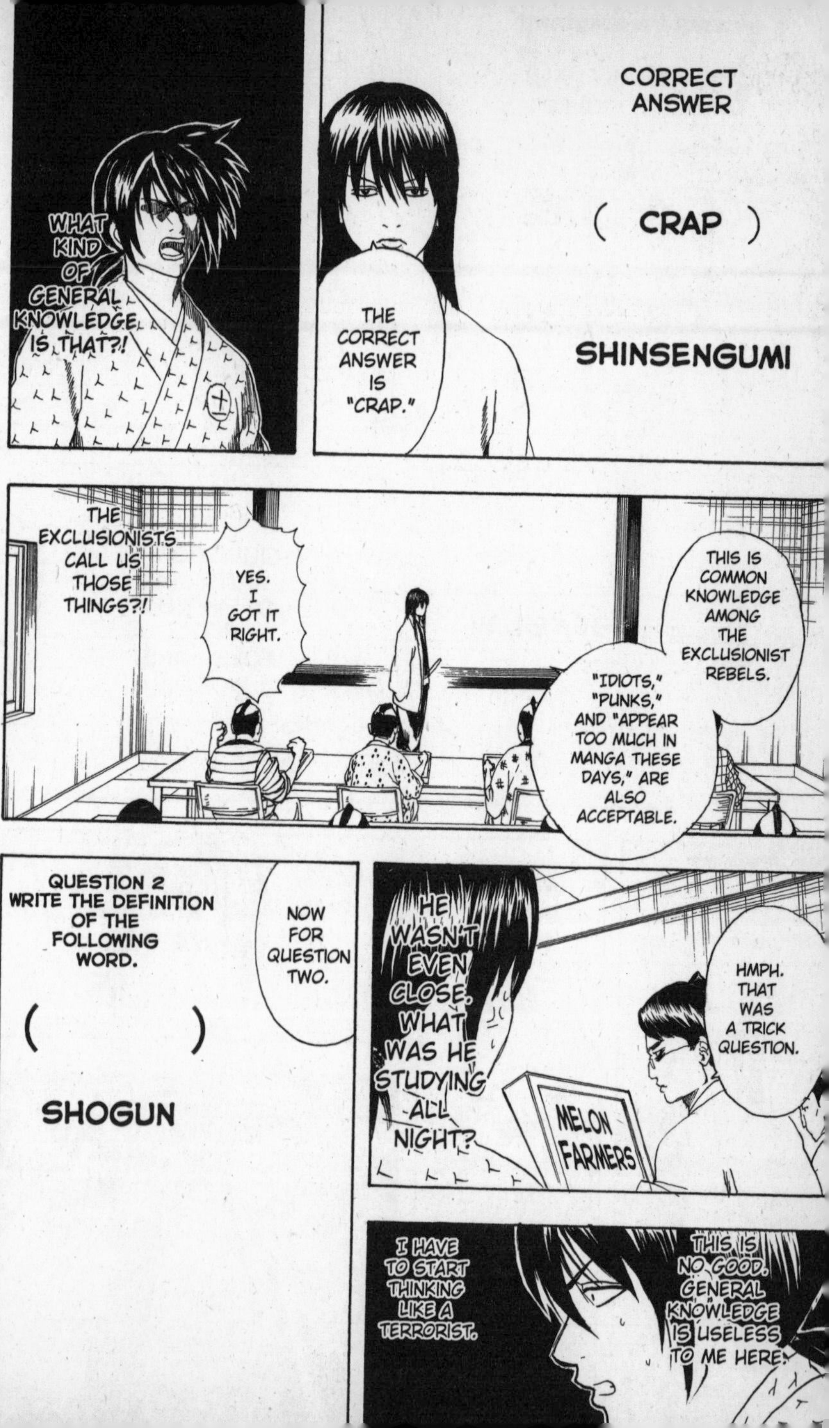

CORRECT ANSWER
(CRAP)
SHINSENGUMI
THE CORRECT ANSWER IS "CRAP."
WHAT KIND OF GENERAL KNOWLEDGE IS THAT?!
THIS IS COMMON KNOWLEDGE AMONG THE EXCLUSIONIST REBELS.
"IDIOTS," "PUNKS," AND "APPEAR TOO MUCH IN MANGA THESE DAYS," ARE ALSO ACCEPTABLE.
YES. I GOT IT RIGHT.
THE EXCLUSIONISTS CALL US THOSE THINGS?!
HMPH. THAT WAS A TRICK QUESTION.
HE WASN'T EVEN CLOSE. WHAT WAS HE STUDYING ALL NIGHT?
MELON FARMERS
THIS IS NO GOOD. GENERAL KNOWLEDGE IS USELESS TO ME HERE.
I HAVE TO START THINKING LIKE A TERRORIST.
NOW FOR QUESTION TWO.
QUESTION 2 WRITE THE DEFINITION OF THE FOLLOWING WORD.
( )
SHOGUN

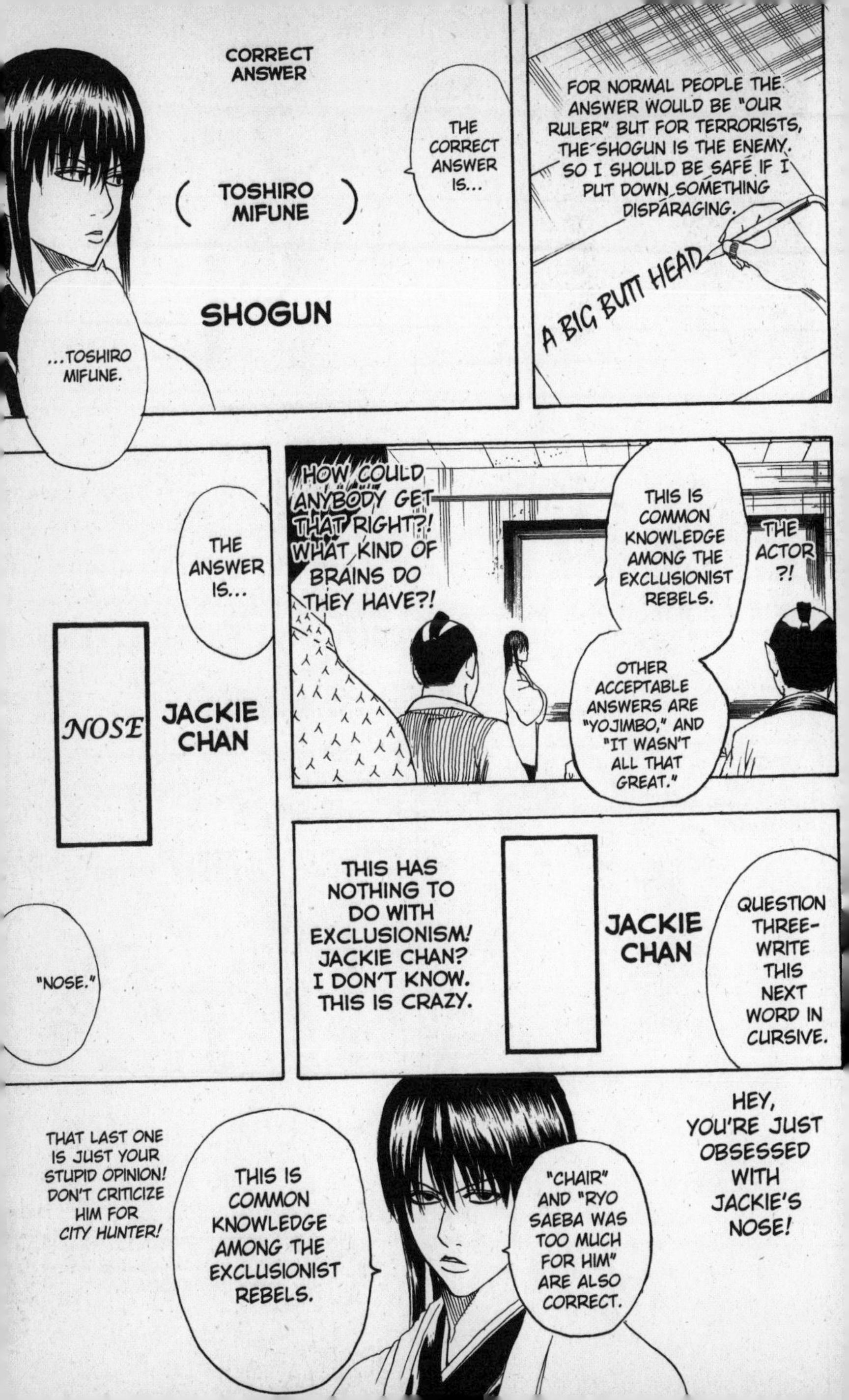
FOR NORMAL PEOPLE THE ANSWER WOULD BE "OUR RULER" BUT FOR TERRORISTS, THE SHOGUN IS THE ENEMY. SO I SHOULD BE SAFE IF I PUT DOWN SOMETHING DISPARAGING.
A BIG BUTT HEAD
THE CORRECT ANSWER IS...
CORRECT ANSWER
(TOSHIRO MIFUNE)
SHOGUN
...TOSHIRO MIFUNE.
THE ACTOR?!
THIS IS COMMON KNOWLEDGE AMONG THE EXCLUSIONIST REBELS.
OTHER ACCEPTABLE ANSWERS ARE "YOJIMBO," AND "IT WASN'T ALL THAT GREAT."
HOW COULD ANYBODY GET THAT RIGHT?! WHAT KIND OF BRAINS DO THEY HAVE?!
QUESTION THREE- WRITE THIS NEXT WORD IN CURSIVE.
JACKIE CHAN
THIS HAS NOTHING TO DO WITH EXCLUSIONISM! JACKIE CHAN? I DON'T KNOW. THIS IS CRAZY.
THE ANSWER IS...
JACKIE CHAN
NOSE
"NOSE."
HEY, YOU'RE JUST OBSESSED WITH JACKIE'S NOSE!
"CHAIR" AND "RYO SAEBA WAS TOO MUCH FOR HIM" ARE ALSO CORRECT.
THIS IS COMMON KNOWLEDGE AMONG THE EXCLUSIONIST REBELS.
THAT LAST ONE IS JUST YOUR STUPID OPINION! DON'T CRITICIZE HIM FOR CITY HUNTER!

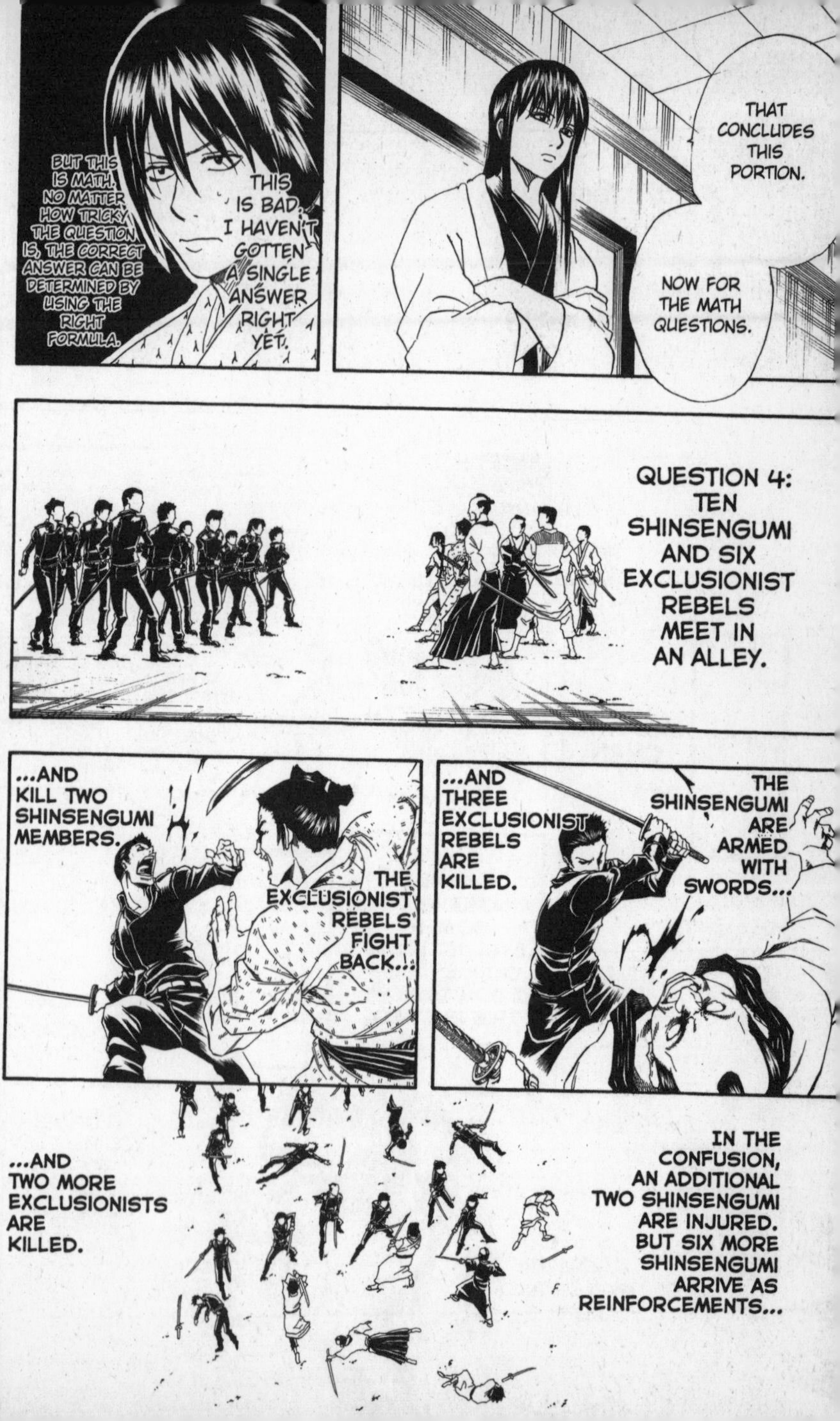
THAT CONCLUDES THIS PORTION.
NOW FOR THE MATH QUESTIONS.
THIS IS BAD. I HAVEN'T GOTTEN A SINGLE ANSWER RIGHT YET.
BUT THIS IS MATH. NO MATTER HOW TRICKY THE QUESTION IS, THE CORRECT ANSWER CAN BE DETERMINED BY USING THE RIGHT FORMULA.
QUESTION 4: TEN SHINSENGUMI AND SIX EXCLUSIONIST REBELS MEET IN AN ALLEY.
THE SHINSENGUMI ARE ARMED WITH SWORDS...
...AND THREE EXCLUSIONIST REBELS ARE KILLED.
THE EXCLUSIONIST REBELS FIGHT BACK...
...AND KILL TWO SHINSENGUMI MEMBERS.
IN THE CONFUSION, AN ADDITIONAL TWO SHINSENGUMI ARE INJURED. BUT SIX MORE SHINSENGUMI ARRIVE AS REINFORCEMENTS...
...AND TWO MORE EXCLUSIONISTS ARE KILLED.

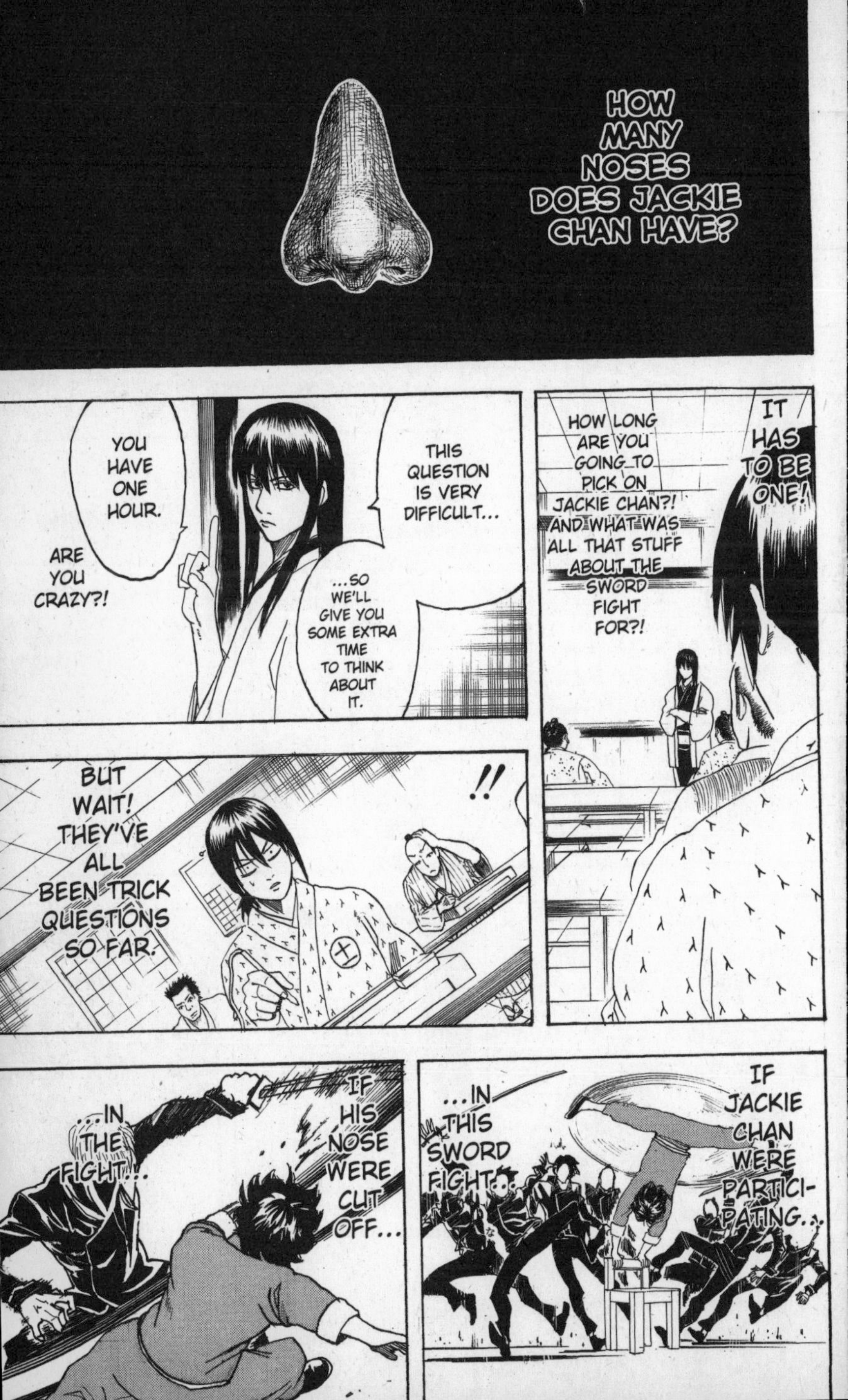
HOW MANY NOSES DOES JACKIE CHAN HAVE?
IT HAS TO BE ONE!
HOW LONG ARE YOU GOING TO PICK ON JACKIE CHAN?! AND WHAT WAS ALL THAT STUFF ABOUT THE SWORD FIGHT FOR?!
THIS QUESTION IS VERY DIFFICULT...
...SO WE'LL GIVE YOU SOME EXTRA TIME TO THINK ABOUT IT.
YOU HAVE ONE HOUR.
ARE YOU CRAZY?!
!!
BUT WAIT! THEY'VE ALL BEEN TRICK QUESTIONS SO FAR.
IF JACKIE CHAN WERE PARTICIPATING...
...IN THIS SWORD FIGHT...
IF HIS NOSE WERE CUT OFF...
...IN THE FIGHT...

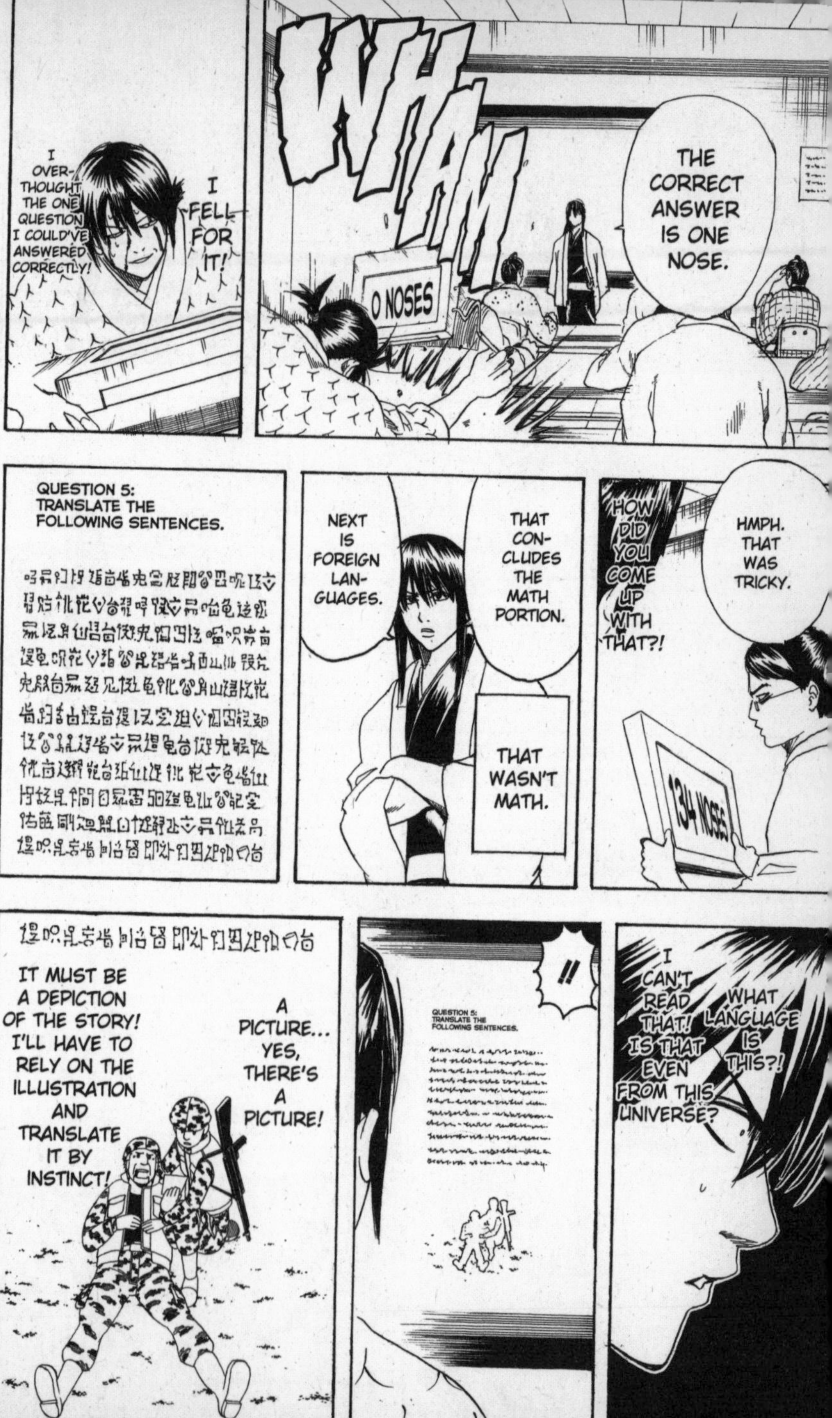
WHAM
THE CORRECT ANSWER IS ONE NOSE.
0 NOSES
I FELL FOR IT!
I OVER-THOUGHT THE ONE QUESTION I COULD'VE ANSWERED CORRECTLY!
HMPH. THAT WAS TRICKY.
134 NOSES
HOW DID YOU COME UP WITH THAT?!
THAT CONCLUDES THE MATH PORTION.
NEXT IS FOREIGN LANGUAGES.
THAT WASN'T MATH.
QUESTION 5: TRANSLATE THE FOLLOWING SENTENCES.
WHAT LANGUAGE IS THIS?!
I CAN'T READ THAT! IS THAT EVEN FROM THIS UNIVERSE?
!!
QUESTION 5: TRANSLATE THE FOLLOWING SENTENCES.
A PICTURE... YES, THERE'S A PICTURE!
IT MUST BE A DEPICTION OF THE STORY! I'LL HAVE TO RELY ON THE ILLUSTRATION AND TRANSLATE IT BY INSTINCT!

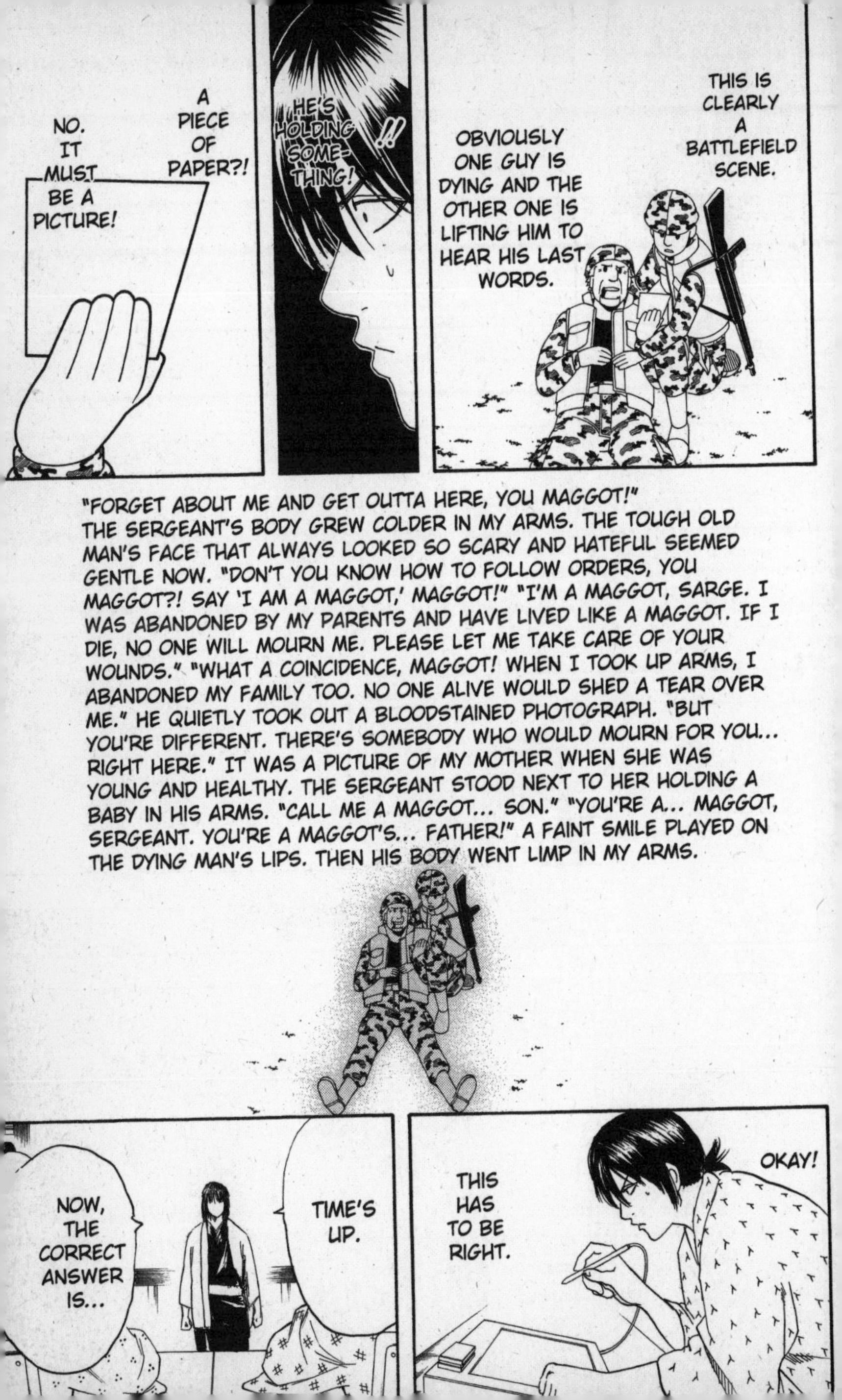
THIS IS CLEARLY A BATTLEFIELD SCENE.
OBVIOUSLY ONE GUY IS DYING AND THE OTHER ONE IS LIFTING HIM TO HEAR HIS LAST WORDS.
HE'S HOLDING SOME-THING!
!!
A PIECE OF PAPER?!
NO. IT MUST BE A PICTURE!
"FORGET ABOUT ME AND GET OUTTA HERE, YOU MAGGOT!" THE SERGEANT'S BODY GREW COLDER IN MY ARMS. THE TOUGH OLD MAN'S FACE THAT ALWAYS LOOKED SO SCARY AND HATEFUL SEEMED GENTLE NOW. "DON'T YOU KNOW HOW TO FOLLOW ORDERS, YOU MAGGOT?! SAY 'I AM A MAGGOT,' MAGGOT!" "I'M A MAGGOT, SARGE. I WAS ABANDONED BY MY PARENTS AND HAVE LIVED LIKE A MAGGOT. IF I DIE, NO ONE WILL MOURN ME. PLEASE LET ME TAKE CARE OF YOUR WOUNDS." "WHAT A COINCIDENCE, MAGGOT! WHEN I TOOK UP ARMS, I ABANDONED MY FAMILY TOO. NO ONE ALIVE WOULD SHED A TEAR OVER ME." HE QUIETLY TOOK OUT A BLOODSTAINED PHOTOGRAPH. "BUT YOU'RE DIFFERENT. THERE'S SOMEBODY WHO WOULD MOURN FOR YOU... RIGHT HERE." IT WAS A PICTURE OF MY MOTHER WHEN SHE WAS YOUNG AND HEALTHY. THE SERGEANT STOOD NEXT TO HER HOLDING A BABY IN HIS ARMS. "CALL ME A MAGGOT... SON." "YOU'RE A... MAGGOT, SERGEANT. YOU'RE A MAGGOT'S... FATHER!" A FAINT SMILE PLAYED ON THE DYING MAN'S LIPS. THEN HIS BODY WENT LIMP IN MY ARMS.
OKAY!
THIS HAS TO BE RIGHT.
TIME'S UP.
NOW, THE CORRECT ANSWER IS...

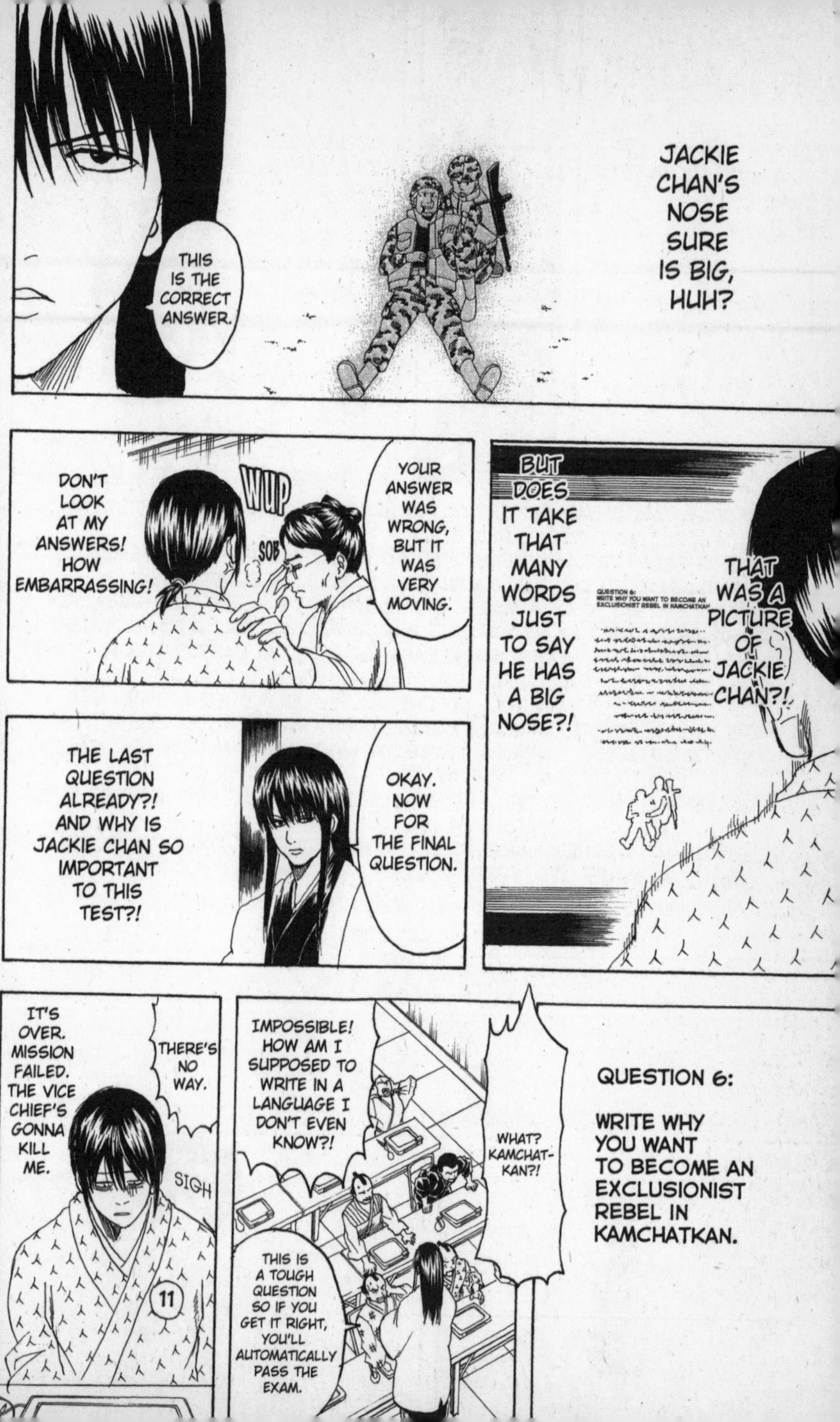
JACKIE CHAN'S NOSE SURE IS BIG, HUH?
THIS IS THE CORRECT ANSWER.
THAT WAS A PICTURE OF JACKIE CHAN?!
QUESTION 6: WRITE WHY YOU WANT TO BECOME AN EXCLUSIONIST REBEL IN KAMCHATKAN
BUT DOES IT TAKE THAT MANY WORDS JUST TO SAY HE HAS A BIG NOSE?!
YOUR ANSWER WAS WRONG, BUT IT WAS VERY MOVING.
WUP
SOB
DON'T LOOK AT MY ANSWERS! HOW EMBARRASSING!
OKAY. NOW FOR THE FINAL QUESTION.
THE LAST QUESTION ALREADY?! AND WHY IS JACKIE CHAN SO IMPORTANT TO THIS TEST?!
QUESTION 6:
WRITE WHY YOU WANT TO BECOME AN EXCLUSIONIST REBEL IN KAMCHATKAN.
WHAT? KAMCHAT-KAN?!
IMPOSSIBLE! HOW AM I SUPPOSED TO WRITE IN A LANGUAGE I DON'T EVEN KNOW?!
THIS IS A TOUGH QUESTION SO IF YOU GET IT RIGHT, YOU'LL AUTOMATICALLY PASS THE EXAM.
THERE'S NO WAY.
IT'S OVER. MISSION FAILED. THE VICE CHIEF'S GONNA KILL ME.
SIGH

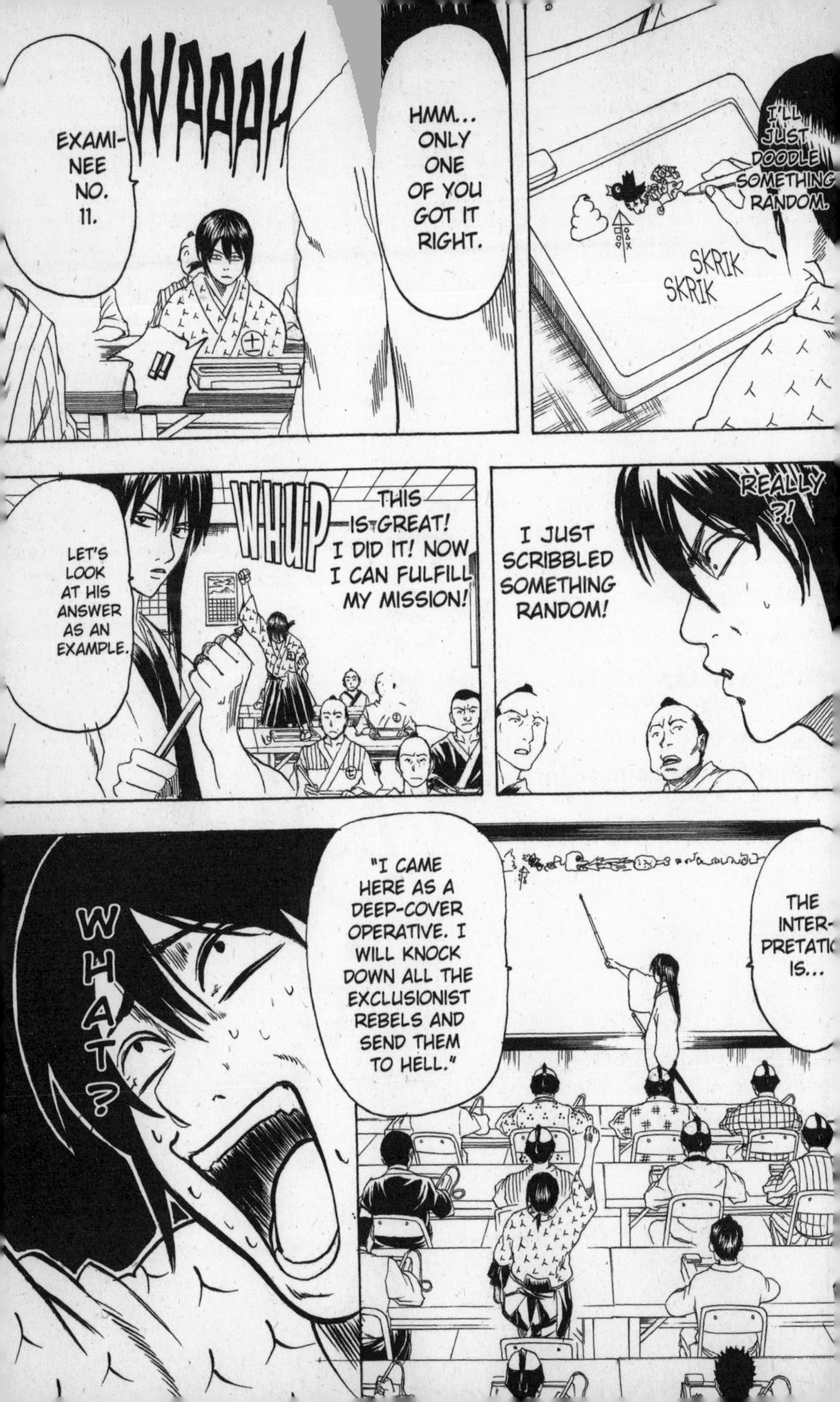
I'LL JUST DOODLE SOMETHING RANDOM.
SKRIK SKRIK
HMM... ONLY ONE OF YOU GOT IT RIGHT.
WAAAH
EXAMINEE NO. 11.
!!
REALLY?!
I JUST SCRIBBLED SOMETHING RANDOM!
THIS IS GREAT! I DID IT! NOW I CAN FULFILL MY MISSION!
WHUP
LET'S LOOK AT HIS ANSWER AS AN EXAMPLE.
THE INTER-PRETATI IS...
"I CAME HERE AS A DEEP-COVER OPERATIVE. I WILL KNOCK DOWN ALL THE EXCLUSIONIST REBELS AND SEND THEM TO HELL."
WHAT?

Send us your Fan Art!

We'd like to give you, our loyal *Gin Tama* readers, a chance to show off your artistic talents! Send us your drawings of the Yorozuya crew or your other favorite characters from *Gin Tama*! If they're good enough to impress Granny Otose (which ain't easy), you just might see them in the pages of future VIZ Media volumes of *Gin Tama*!

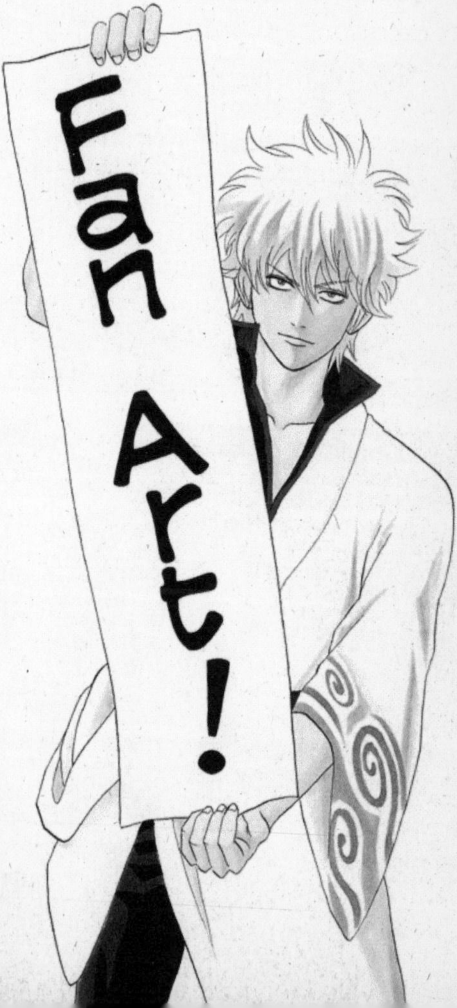
Fan Art!

;end your fan art to:

VIZ Media
Attn: Mike Montesa, Editor
295 Bay St.
San Francisco, CA 94133

e sure to include the signed
lease form available here:
tp://www.shonenjump.com/
nart/Fan_Art_Release.pdf
ıbmissions will not be returned.
ıbmissions without a signed
lease form will be fed to the
nanto sea lions at Fisherman's
'harf...

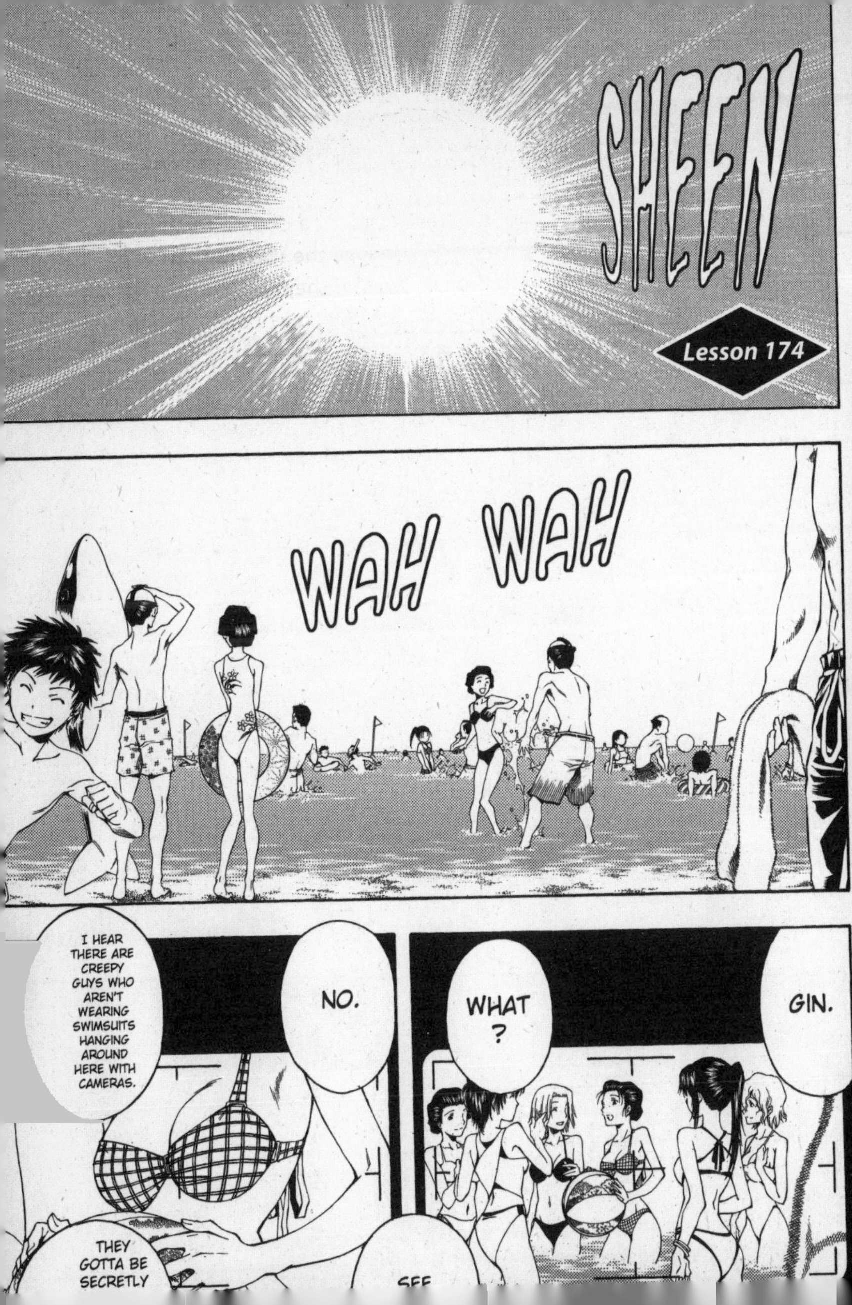
SHEEN
Lesson 174
WAH WAH
GIN.
WHAT ?
NO.
I HEAR THERE ARE CREEPY GUYS WHO AREN'T WEARING SWIMSUITS HANGING AROUND HERE WITH CAMERAS.
THEY GOTTA BE SECRETLY

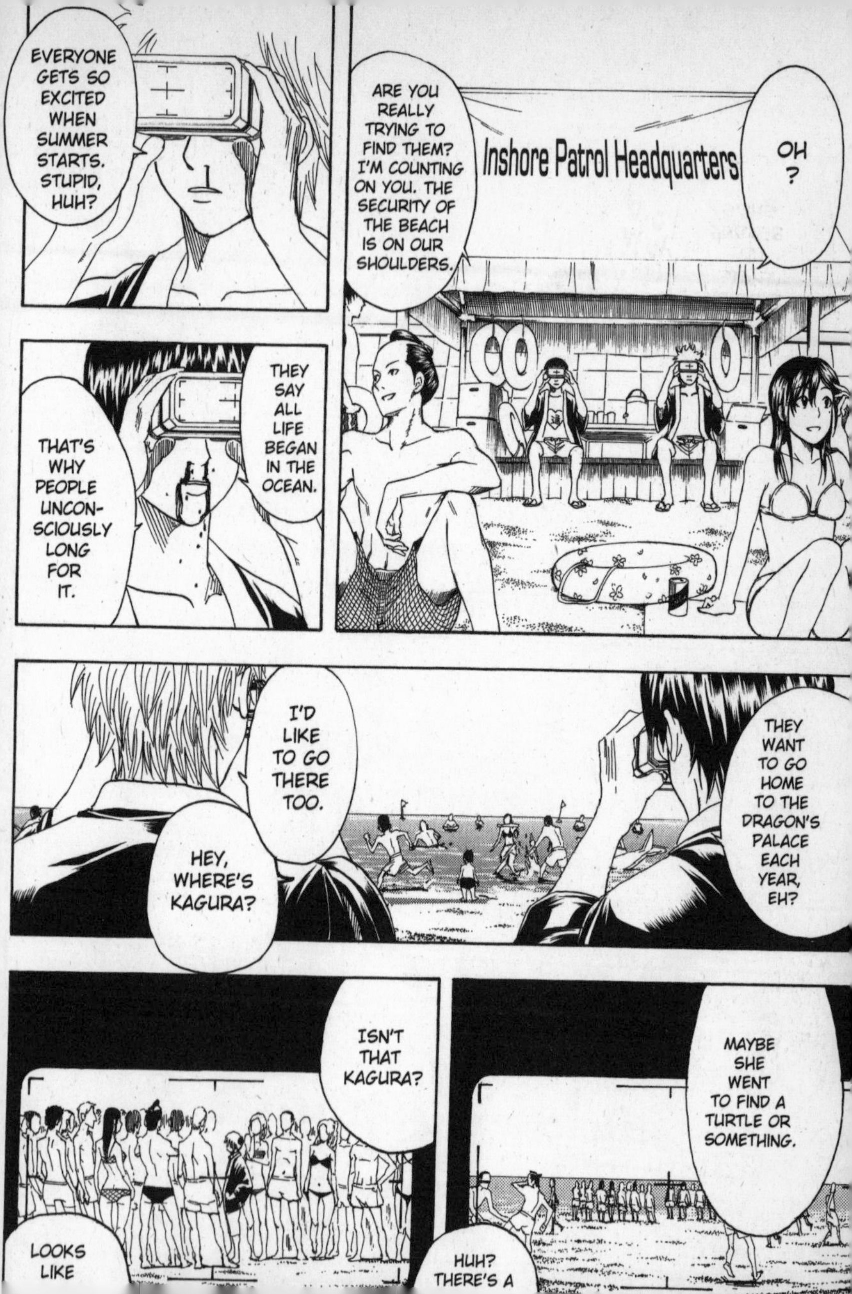
OH ?
Inshore Patrol Headquarters
ARE YOU REALLY TRYING TO FIND THEM? I'M COUNTING ON YOU. THE SECURITY OF THE BEACH IS ON OUR SHOULDERS.
EVERYONE GETS SO EXCITED WHEN SUMMER STARTS. STUPID, HUH?
THEY SAY ALL LIFE BEGAN IN THE OCEAN.
THAT'S WHY PEOPLE UNCON-SCIOUSLY LONG FOR IT.
THEY WANT TO GO HOME TO THE DRAGON'S PALACE EACH YEAR, EH?
I'D LIKE TO GO THERE TOO.
HEY, WHERE'S KAGURA?
MAYBE SHE WENT TO FIND A TURTLE OR SOMETHING.
HUH? THERE'S A
ISN'T THAT KAGURA?
LOOKS LIKE

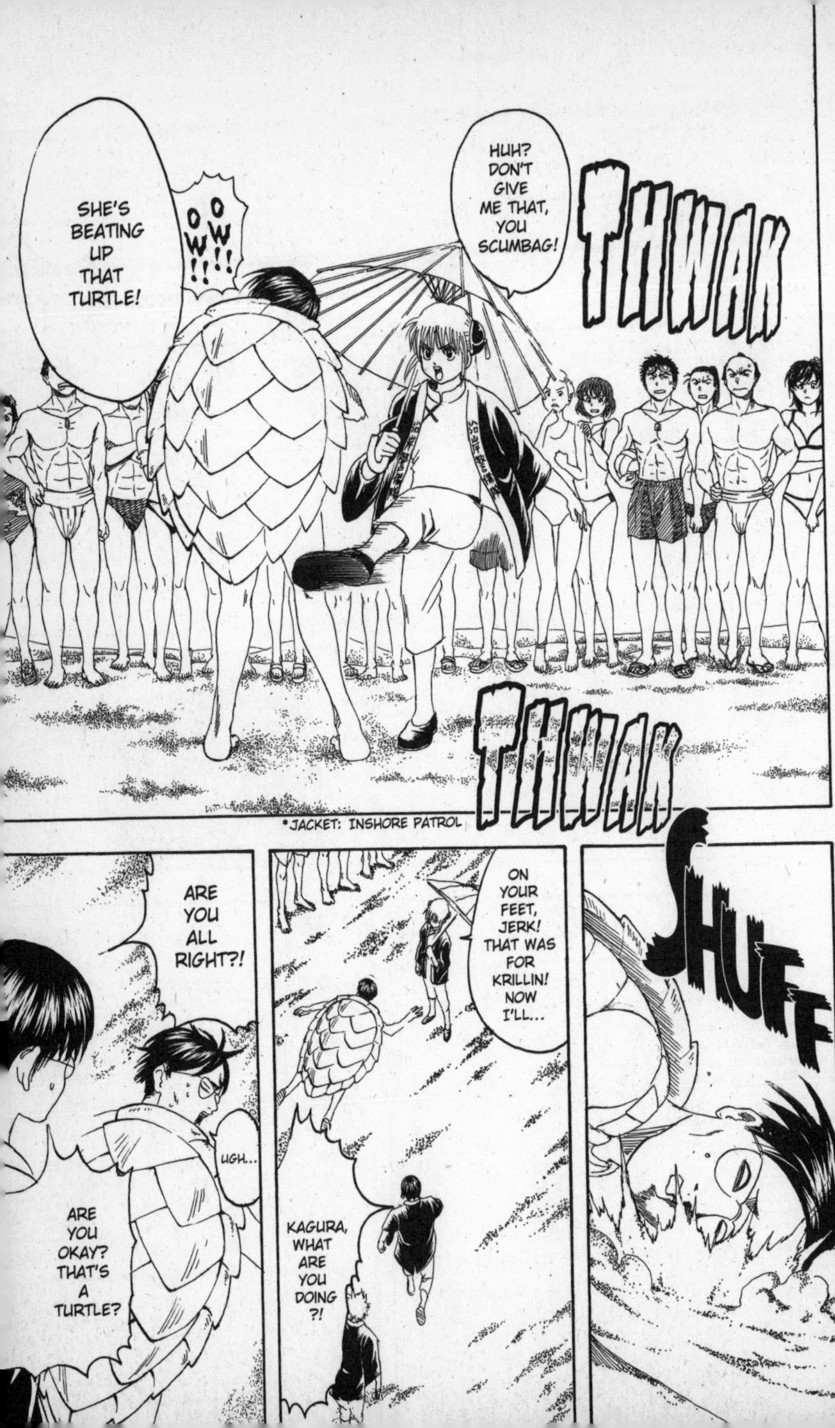
THWAK
HUH? DON'T GIVE ME THAT, YOU SCUMBAG!
OW!! OW!!
SHE'S BEATING UP THAT TURTLE!
THWAK
SHUFF
ON YOUR FEET, JERK! THAT WAS FOR KRILLIN! NOW I'LL...
KAGURA, WHAT ARE YOU DOING?!
ARE YOU ALL RIGHT?!
UGH...
ARE YOU OKAY? THAT'S A TURTLE?
*JACKET: INSHORE PATROL

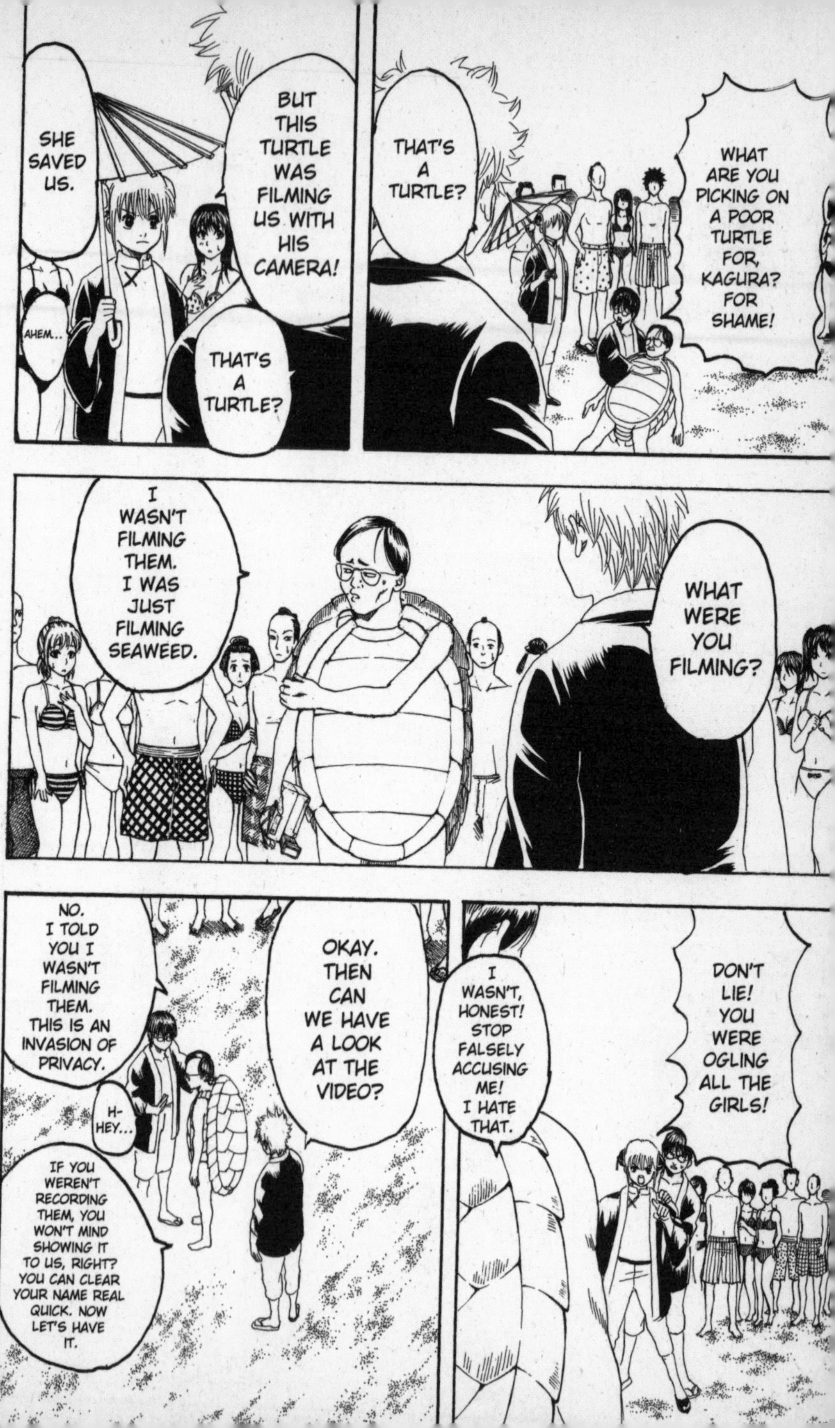

WHAT ARE YOU PICKING ON A POOR TURTLE FOR, KAGURA? FOR SHAME!
THAT'S A TURTLE?
BUT THIS TURTLE WAS FILMING US WITH HIS CAMERA!
SHE SAVED US.
THAT'S A TURTLE?
AHEM...
WHAT WERE YOU FILMING?
I WASN'T FILMING THEM. I WAS JUST FILMING SEAWEED.
DON'T LIE! YOU WERE OGLING ALL THE GIRLS!
I WASN'T, HONEST! STOP FALSELY ACCUSING ME! I HATE THAT.
OKAY. THEN CAN WE HAVE A LOOK AT THE VIDEO?
NO. I TOLD YOU I WASN'T FILMING THEM. THIS IS AN INVASION OF PRIVACY.
H-HEY...
IF YOU WEREN'T RECORDING THEM, YOU WON'T MIND SHOWING IT TO US, RIGHT? YOU CAN CLEAR YOUR NAME REAL QUICK. NOW LET'S HAVE IT.

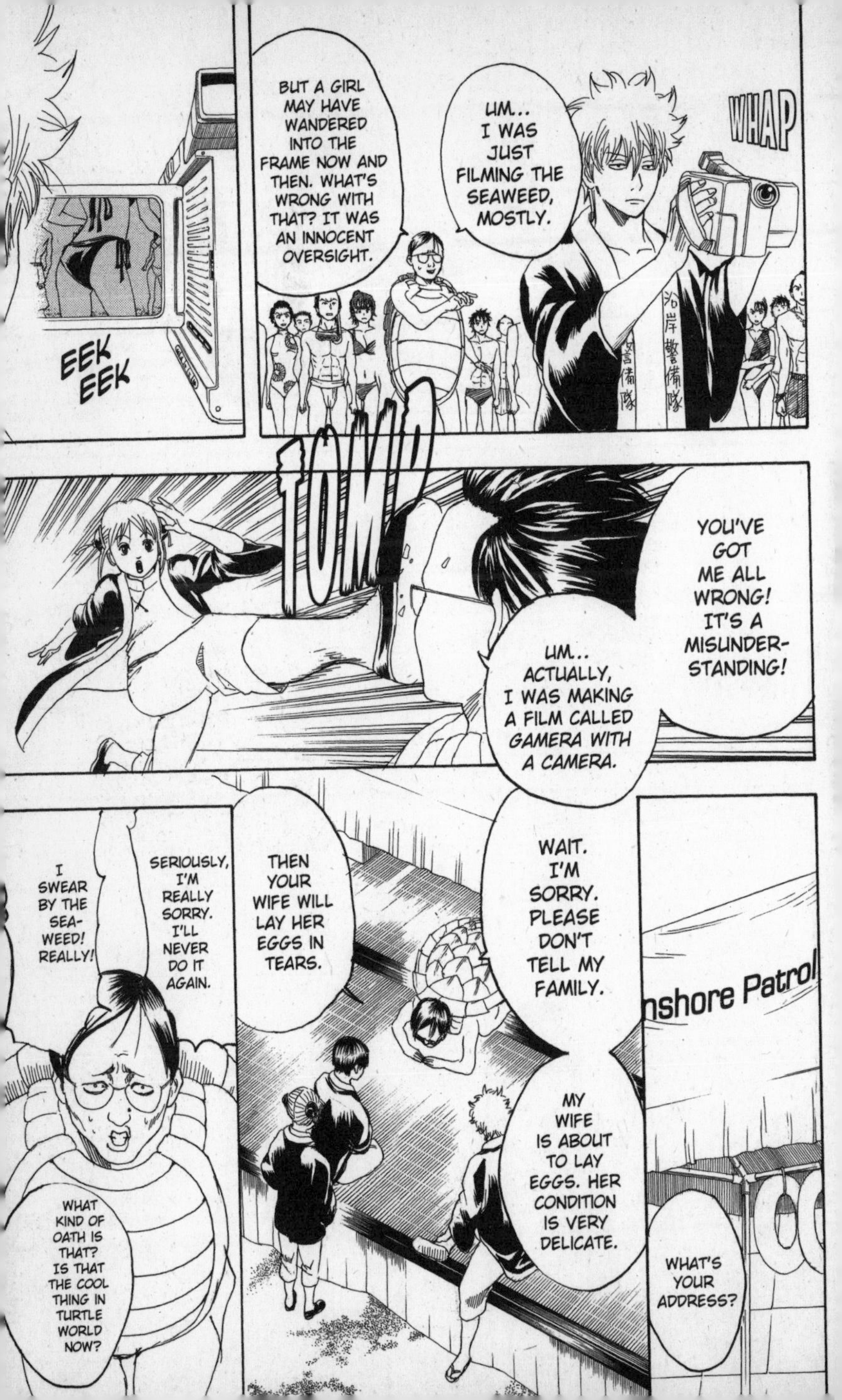
WHAP
UM... I WAS JUST FILMING THE SEAWEED, MOSTLY.
沿岸警備隊
BUT A GIRL MAY HAVE WANDERED INTO THE FRAME NOW AND THEN. WHAT'S WRONG WITH THAT? IT WAS AN INNOCENT OVERSIGHT.
EEK EEK
TOMP
YOU'VE GOT ME ALL WRONG! IT'S A MISUNDERSTANDING!
UM.. ACTUALLY, I WAS MAKING A FILM CALLED GAMERA WITH A CAMERA.
nshore Patrol
WHAT'S YOUR ADDRESS?
WAIT. I'M SORRY. PLEASE DON'T TELL MY FAMILY.
MY WIFE IS ABOUT TO LAY EGGS. HER CONDITION IS VERY DELICATE.
THEN YOUR WIFE WILL LAY HER EGGS IN TEARS.
SERIOUSLY, I'M REALLY SORRY. I'LL NEVER DO IT AGAIN.
I SWEAR BY THE SEA-WEED! REALLY!
WHAT KIND OF OATH IS THAT? IS THAT THE COOL THING IN TURTLE WORLD NOW?

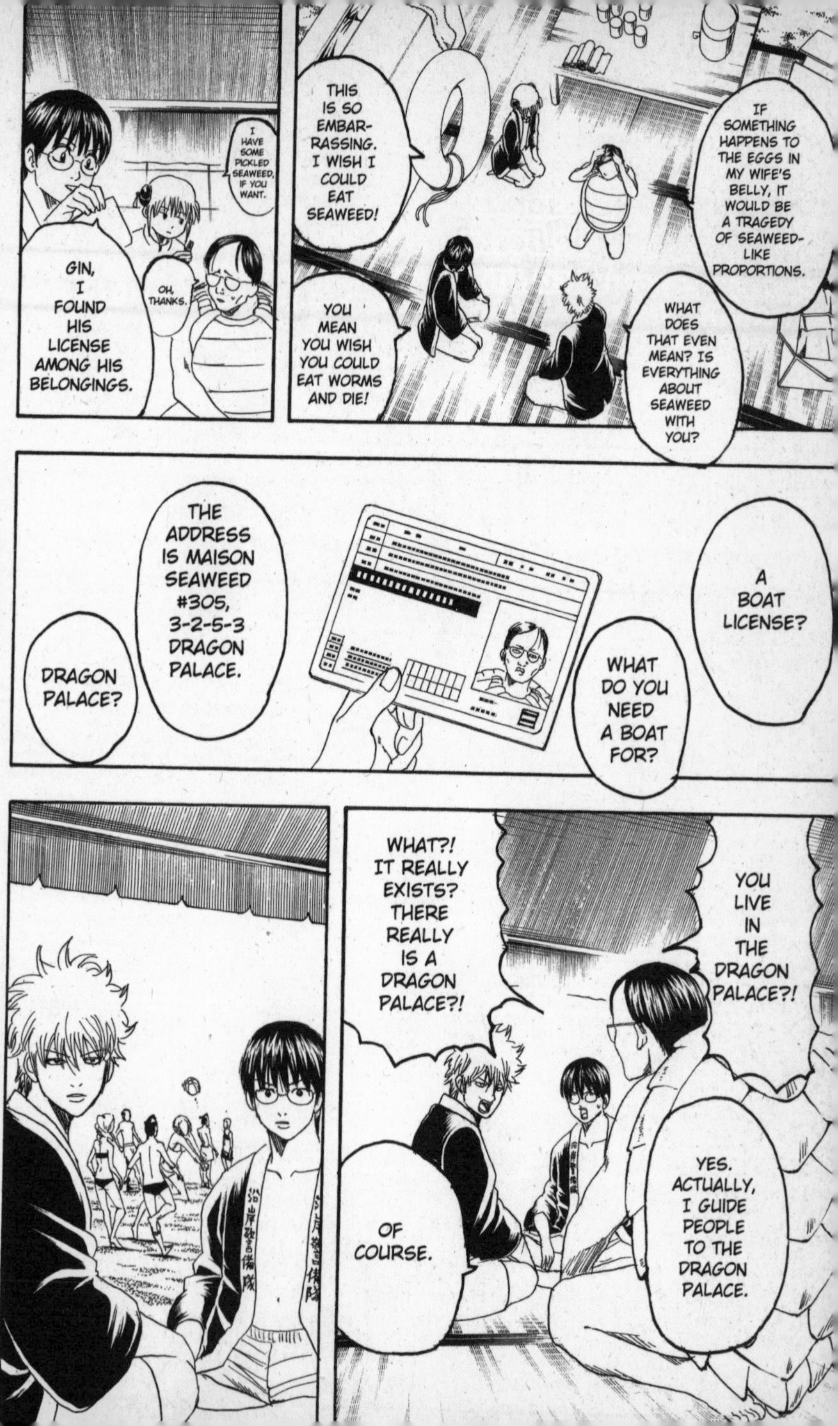
IF SOMETHING HAPPENS TO THE EGGS IN MY WIFE'S BELLY, IT WOULD BE A TRAGEDY OF SEAWEED-LIKE PROPORTIONS.
THIS IS SO EMBARRASSING. I WISH I COULD EAT SEAWEED!
WHAT DOES THAT EVEN MEAN? IS EVERYTHING ABOUT SEAWEED WITH YOU?
YOU MEAN YOU WISH YOU COULD EAT WORMS AND DIE!
I HAVE SOME PICKLED SEAWEED, IF YOU WANT.
OH, THANKS.
GIN, I FOUND HIS LICENSE AMONG HIS BELONGINGS.
A BOAT LICENSE?
WHAT DO YOU NEED A BOAT FOR?
THE ADDRESS IS MAISON SEAWEED #305, 3-2-5-3 DRAGON PALACE.
DRAGON PALACE?
YOU LIVE IN THE DRAGON PALACE?!
WHAT?! IT REALLY EXISTS? THERE REALLY IS A DRAGON PALACE?!
YES. ACTUALLY, I GUIDE PEOPLE TO THE DRAGON PALACE.
OF COURSE.

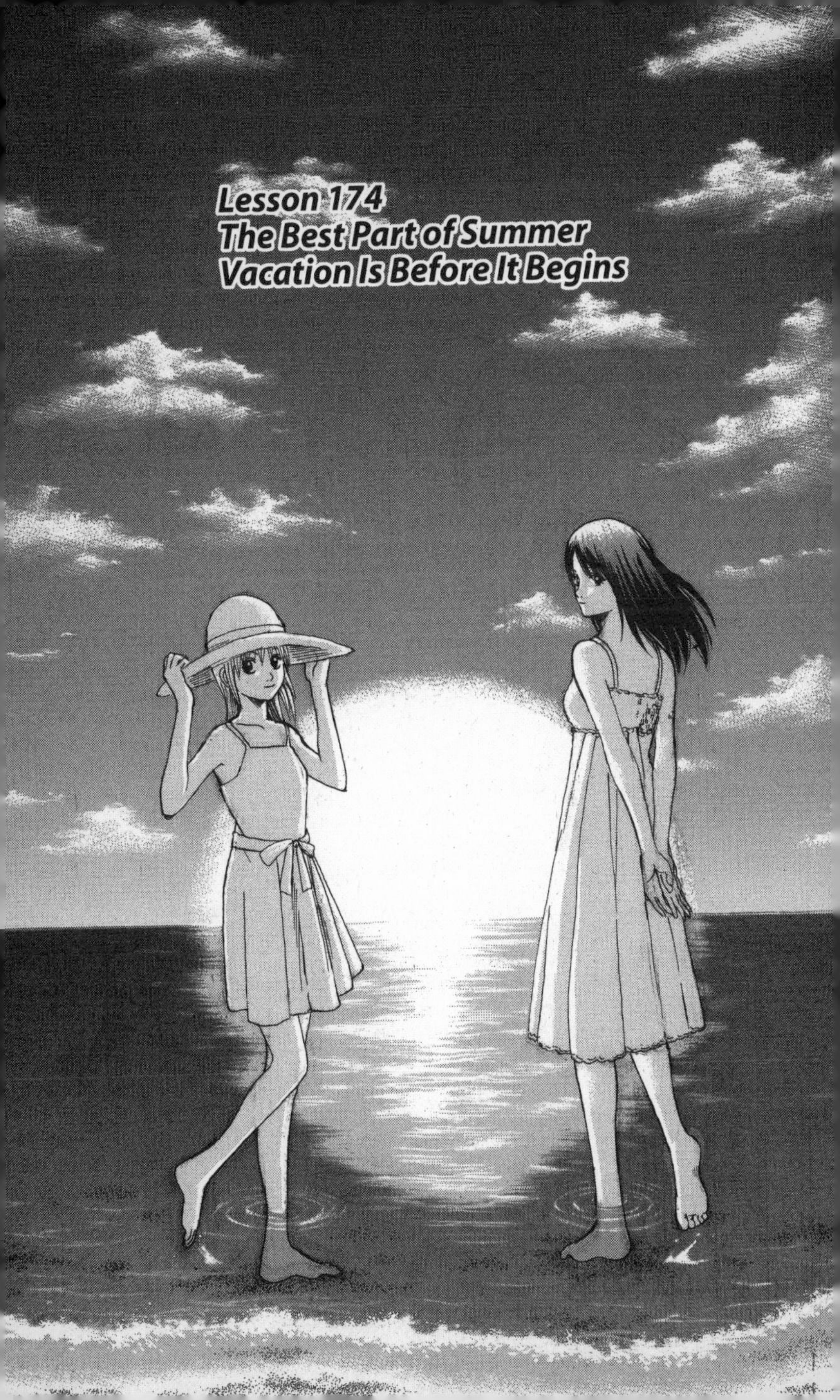
Lesson 174
The Best Part of Summer
Vacation Is Before It Begins

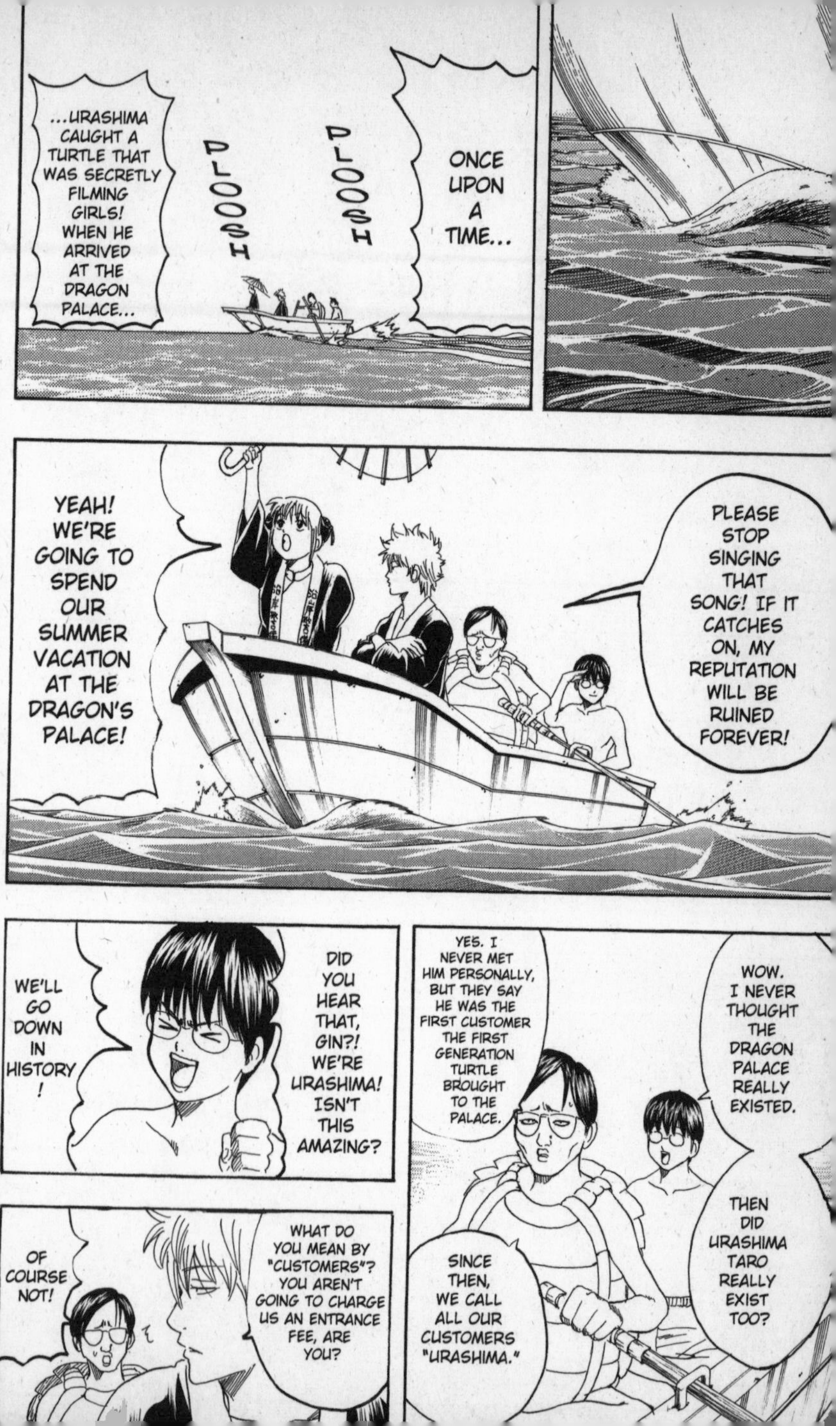
ONCE UPON A TIME...
PLOOSH
PLOOSH
...URASHIMA CAUGHT A TURTLE THAT WAS SECRETLY FILMING GIRLS! WHEN HE ARRIVED AT THE DRAGON PALACE...
YEAH! WE'RE GOING TO SPEND OUR SUMMER VACATION AT THE DRAGON'S PALACE!
PLEASE STOP SINGING THAT SONG! IF IT CATCHES ON, MY REPUTATION WILL BE RUINED FOREVER!
WOW. I NEVER THOUGHT THE DRAGON PALACE REALLY EXISTED.
THEN DID URASHIMA TARO REALLY EXIST TOO?
YES. I NEVER MET HIM PERSONALLY, BUT THEY SAY HE WAS THE FIRST CUSTOMER THE FIRST GENERATION TURTLE BROUGHT TO THE PALACE.
SINCE THEN, WE CALL ALL OUR CUSTOMERS "URASHIMA."
DID YOU HEAR THAT, GIN?! WE'RE URASHIMA! ISN'T THIS AMAZING?
WE'LL GO DOWN IN HISTORY!
WHAT DO YOU MEAN BY "CUSTOMERS"? YOU AREN'T GOING TO CHARGE US AN ENTRANCE FEE, ARE YOU?
OF COURSE NOT!

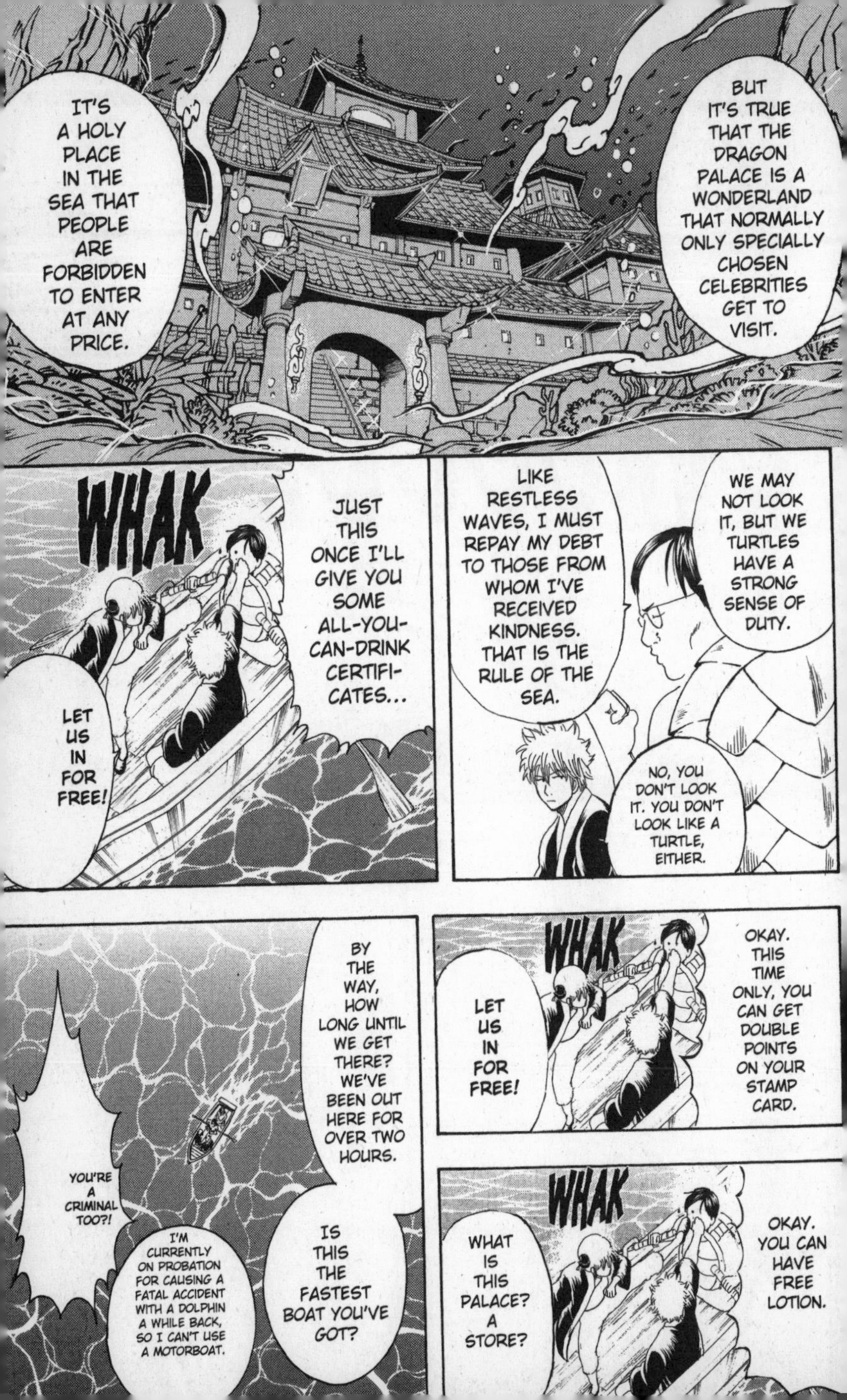
BUT IT'S TRUE THAT THE DRAGON PALACE IS A WONDERLAND THAT NORMALLY ONLY SPECIALLY CHOSEN CELEBRITIES GET TO VISIT.
IT'S A HOLY PLACE IN THE SEA THAT PEOPLE ARE FORBIDDEN TO ENTER AT ANY PRICE.
WE MAY NOT LOOK IT, BUT WE TURTLES HAVE A STRONG SENSE OF DUTY.
LIKE RESTLESS WAVES, I MUST REPAY MY DEBT TO THOSE FROM WHOM I'VE RECEIVED KINDNESS. THAT IS THE RULE OF THE SEA.
NO, YOU DON'T LOOK IT. YOU DON'T LOOK LIKE A TURTLE, EITHER.
WHAK
JUST THIS ONCE I'LL GIVE YOU SOME ALL-YOU-CAN-DRINK CERTIFICATES...
LET US IN FOR FREE!
OKAY. THIS TIME ONLY, YOU CAN GET DOUBLE POINTS ON YOUR STAMP CARD.
WHAK
LET US IN FOR FREE!
OKAY. YOU CAN HAVE FREE LOTION.
WHAK
WHAT IS THIS PALACE? A STORE?
BY THE WAY, HOW LONG UNTIL WE GET THERE? WE'VE BEEN OUT HERE FOR OVER TWO HOURS.
IS THIS THE FASTEST BOAT YOU'VE GOT?
YOU'RE A CRIMINAL TOO?!
I'M CURRENTLY ON PROBATION FOR CAUSING A FATAL ACCIDENT WITH A DOLPHIN A WHILE BACK, SO I CAN'T USE A MOTORBOAT.

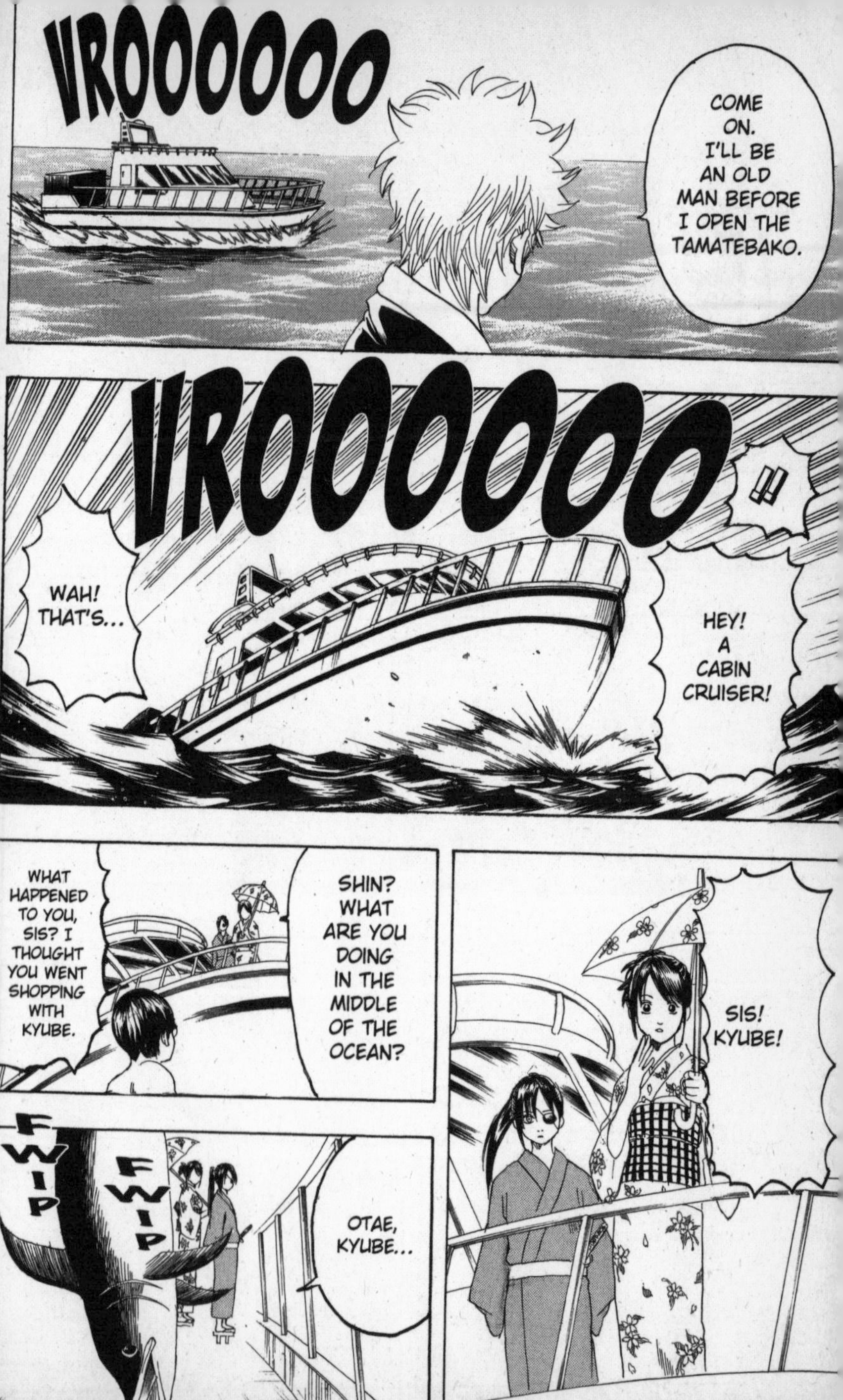
VROOOOOO
COME ON. I'LL BE AN OLD MAN BEFORE I OPEN THE TAMATEBAKO.
VROOOOOO!!
HEY! A CABIN CRUISER!
WAH! THAT'S...
SIS! KYUBE!
SHIN? WHAT ARE YOU DOING IN THE MIDDLE OF THE OCEAN?
WHAT HAPPENED TO YOU, SIS? I THOUGHT YOU WENT SHOPPING WITH KYUBE.
OTAE, KYUBE...
FWIP
FWIP

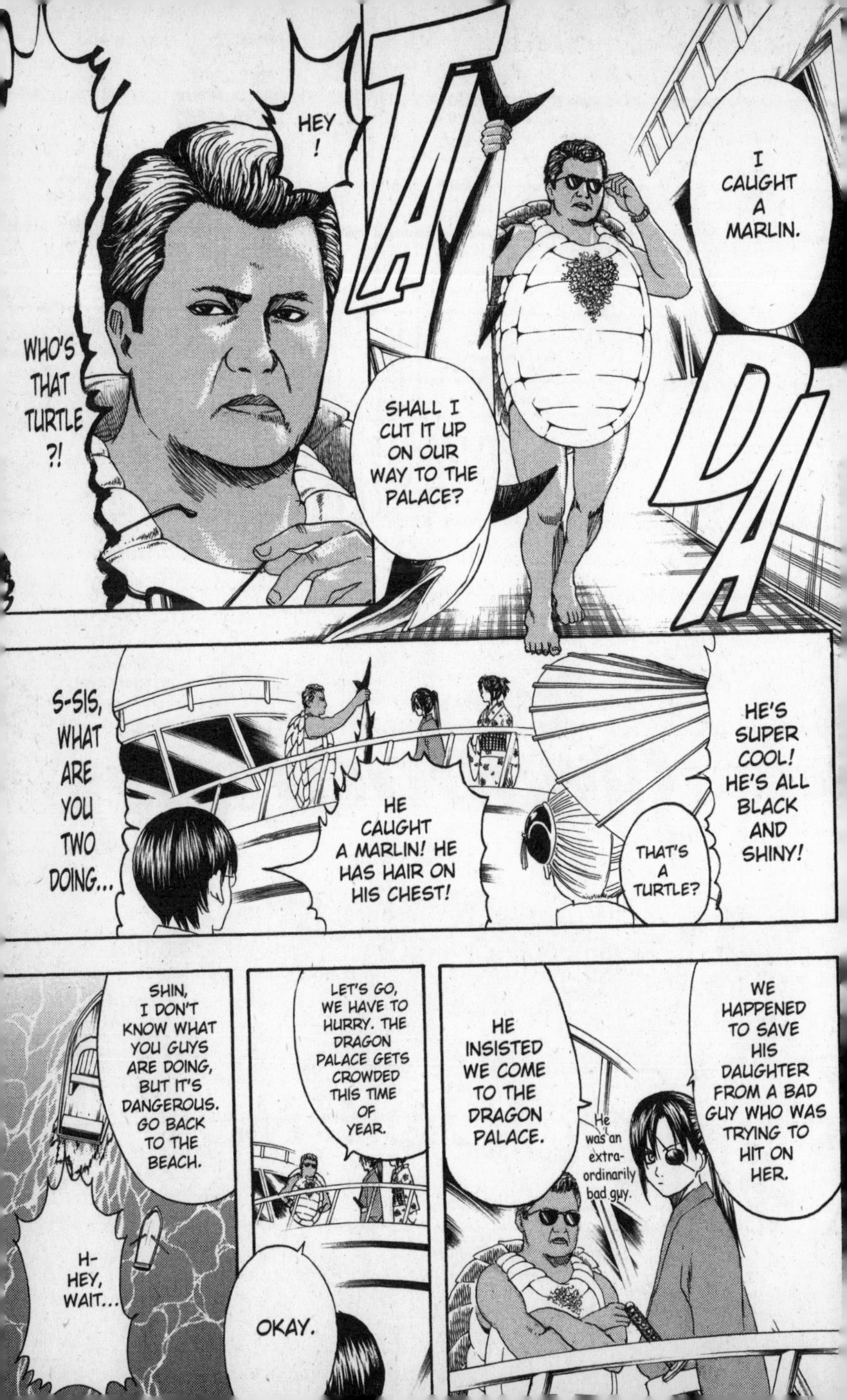
I CAUGHT A MARLIN.
TA
DA
SHALL I CUT IT UP ON OUR WAY TO THE PALACE?
HEY!
WHO'S THAT TURTLE?!
HE'S SUPER COOL! HE'S ALL BLACK AND SHINY!
THAT'S A TURTLE?
HE CAUGHT A MARLIN! HE HAS HAIR ON HIS CHEST!
S-SIS, WHAT ARE YOU TWO DOING...
WE HAPPENED TO SAVE HIS DAUGHTER FROM A BAD GUY WHO WAS TRYING TO HIT ON HER.
He was an extra-ordinarily bad guy.
HE INSISTED WE COME TO THE DRAGON PALACE.
LET'S GO, WE HAVE TO HURRY. THE DRAGON PALACE GETS CROWDED THIS TIME OF YEAR.
OKAY.
SHIN, I DON'T KNOW WHAT YOU GUYS ARE DOING, BUT IT'S DANGEROUS. GO BACK TO THE BEACH.
H-HEY, WAIT...

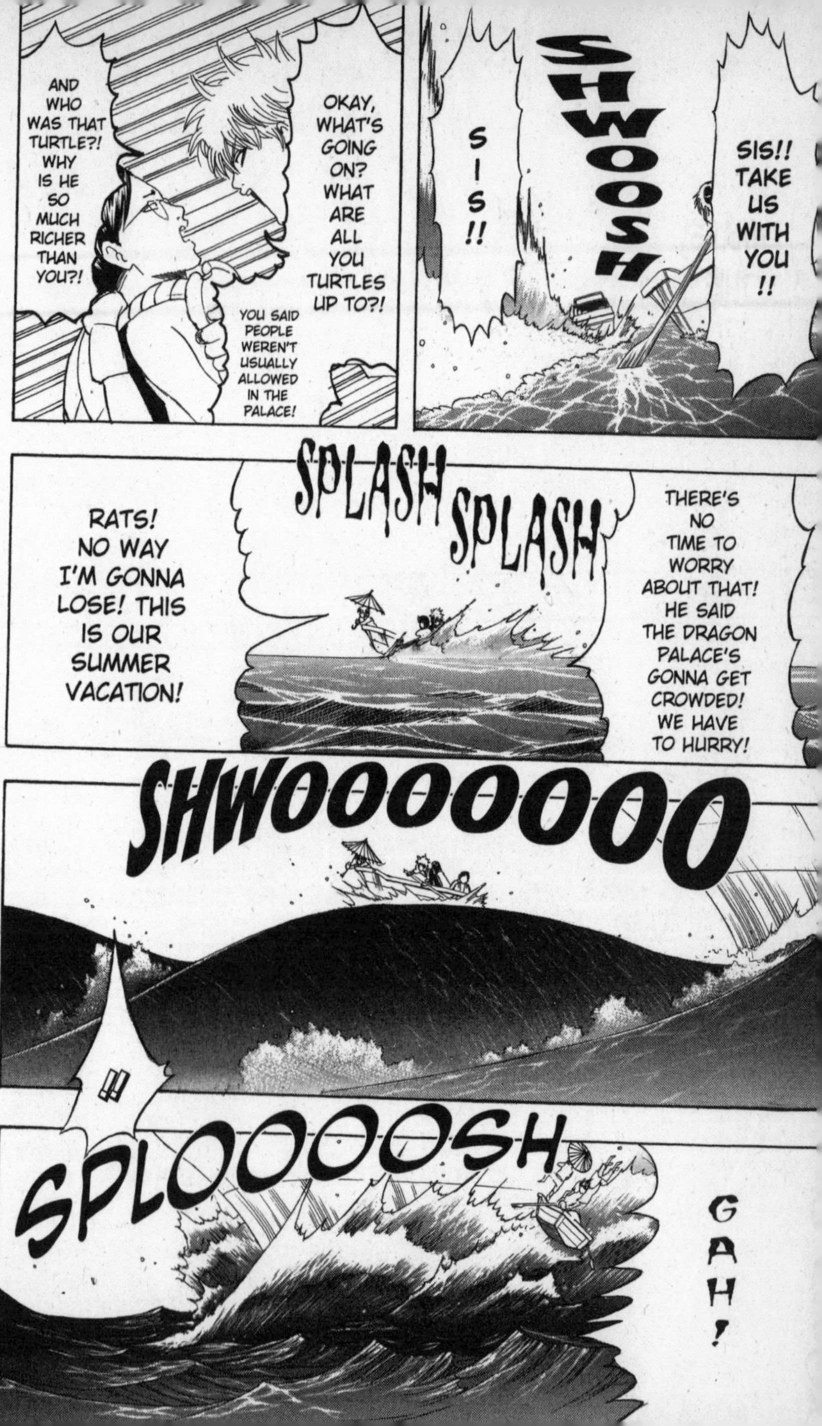
SIS!! TAKE US WITH YOU!!
SHWOOSH
SIS!!
OKAY, WHAT'S GOING ON? WHAT ARE ALL YOU TURTLES UP TO?!
AND WHO WAS THAT TURTLE?! WHY IS HE SO MUCH RICHER THAN YOU?!
YOU SAID PEOPLE WEREN'T USUALLY ALLOWED IN THE PALACE!
THERE'S NO TIME TO WORRY ABOUT THAT! HE SAID THE DRAGON PALACE'S GONNA GET CROWDED! WE HAVE TO HURRY!
SPLASH SPLASH
RATS! NO WAY I'M GONNA LOSE! THIS IS OUR SUMMER VACATION!
SHWOOOOOOOO
GAH!
SPLOOOOSH
!!

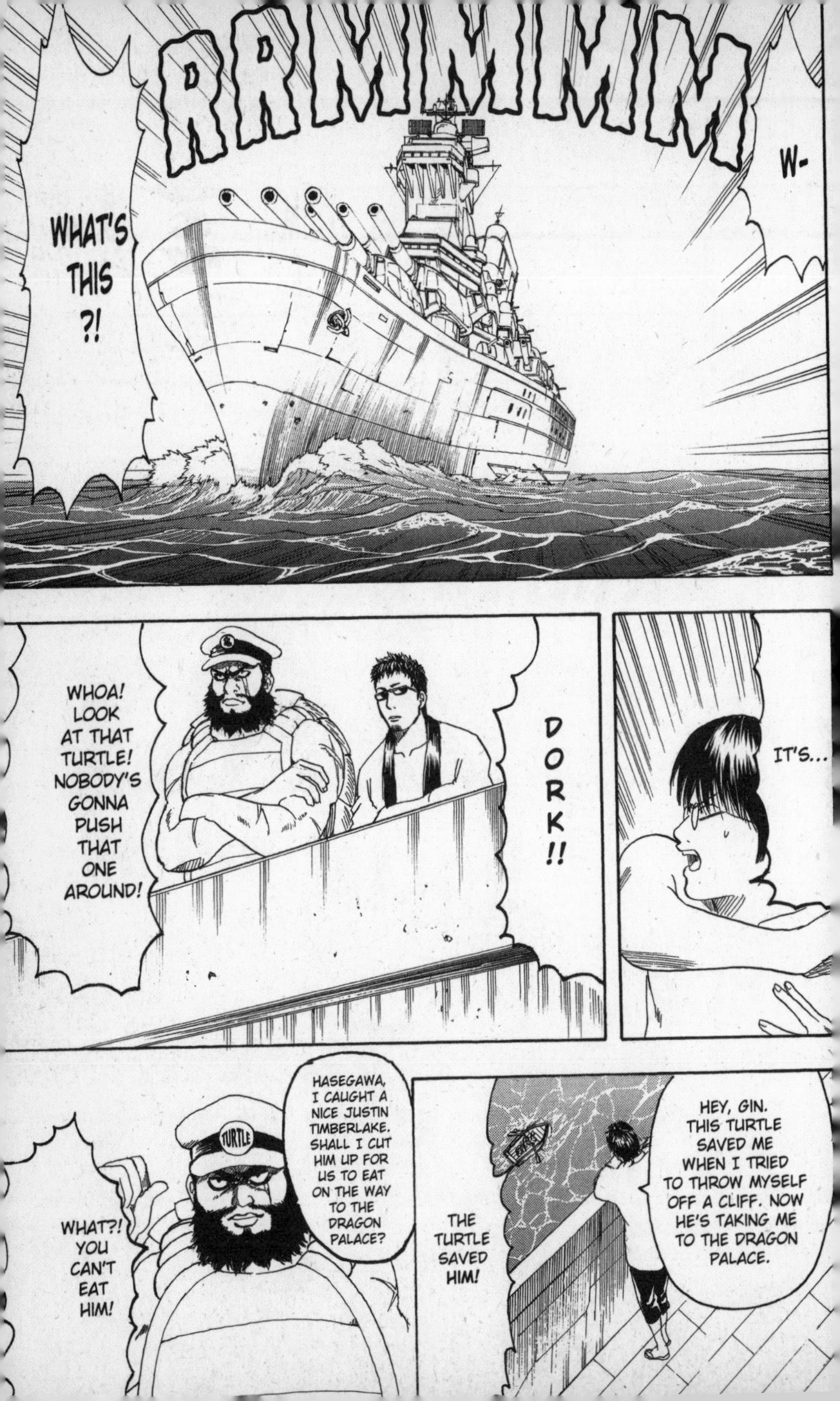
RRMMMM
W-
WHAT'S THIS ?!
IT'S...
DORK!!
WHOA! LOOK AT THAT TURTLE! NOBODY'S GONNA PUSH THAT ONE AROUND!
HEY, GIN. THIS TURTLE SAVED ME WHEN I TRIED TO THROW MYSELF OFF A CLIFF. NOW HE'S TAKING ME TO THE DRAGON PALACE.
THE TURTLE SAVED HIM!
HASEGAWA, I CAUGHT A NICE JUSTIN TIMBERLAKE. SHALL I CUT HIM UP FOR US TO EAT ON THE WAY TO THE DRAGON PALACE?
TURTLE
WHAT?! YOU CAN'T EAT HIM!

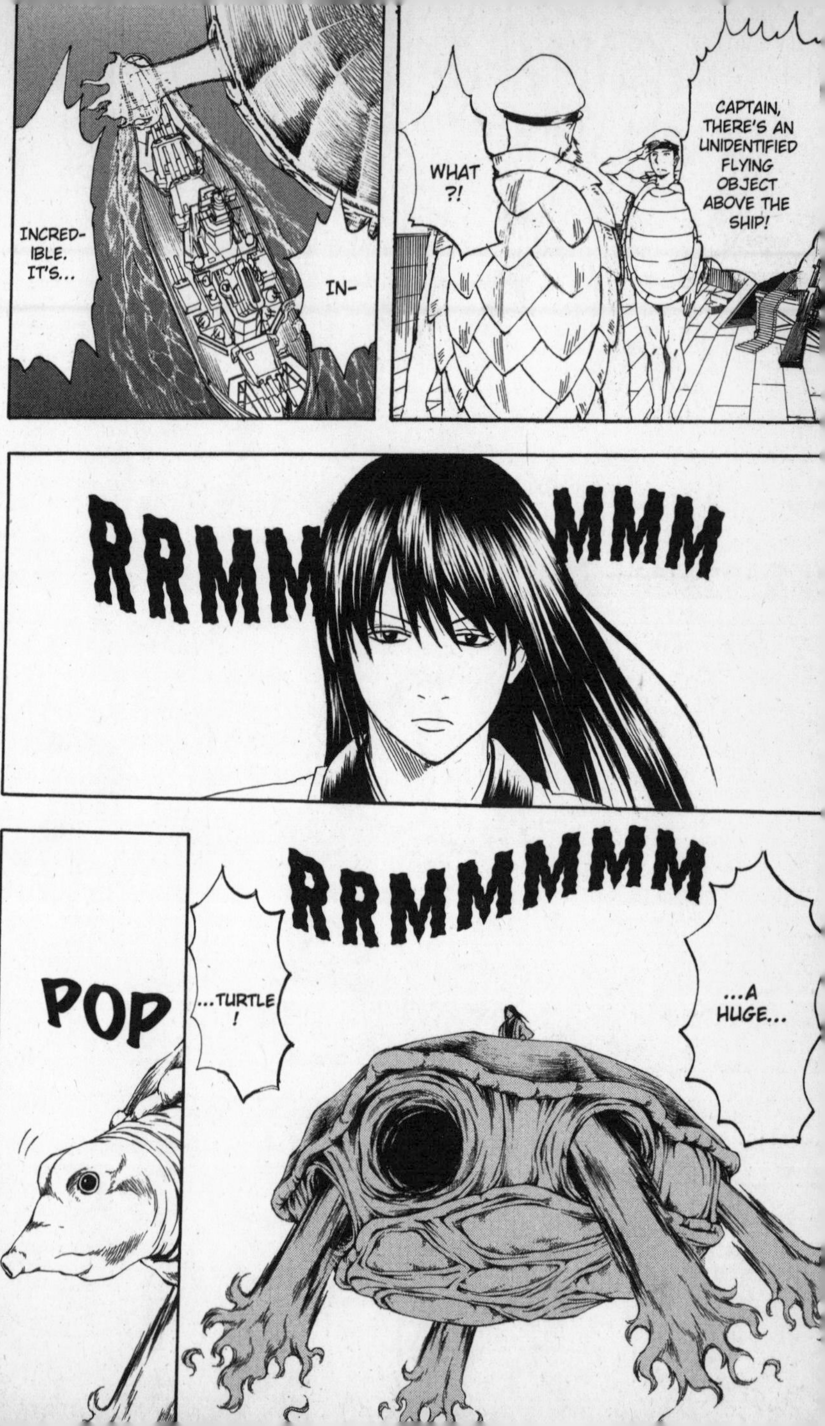
CAPTAIN, THERE'S AN UNIDENTIFIED FLYING OBJECT ABOVE THE SHIP!
WHAT ?!
INCRED-IBLE. IT'S...
IN-
RRMMMMM
RRMMMMMM
...A HUGE...
...TURTLE !
POP

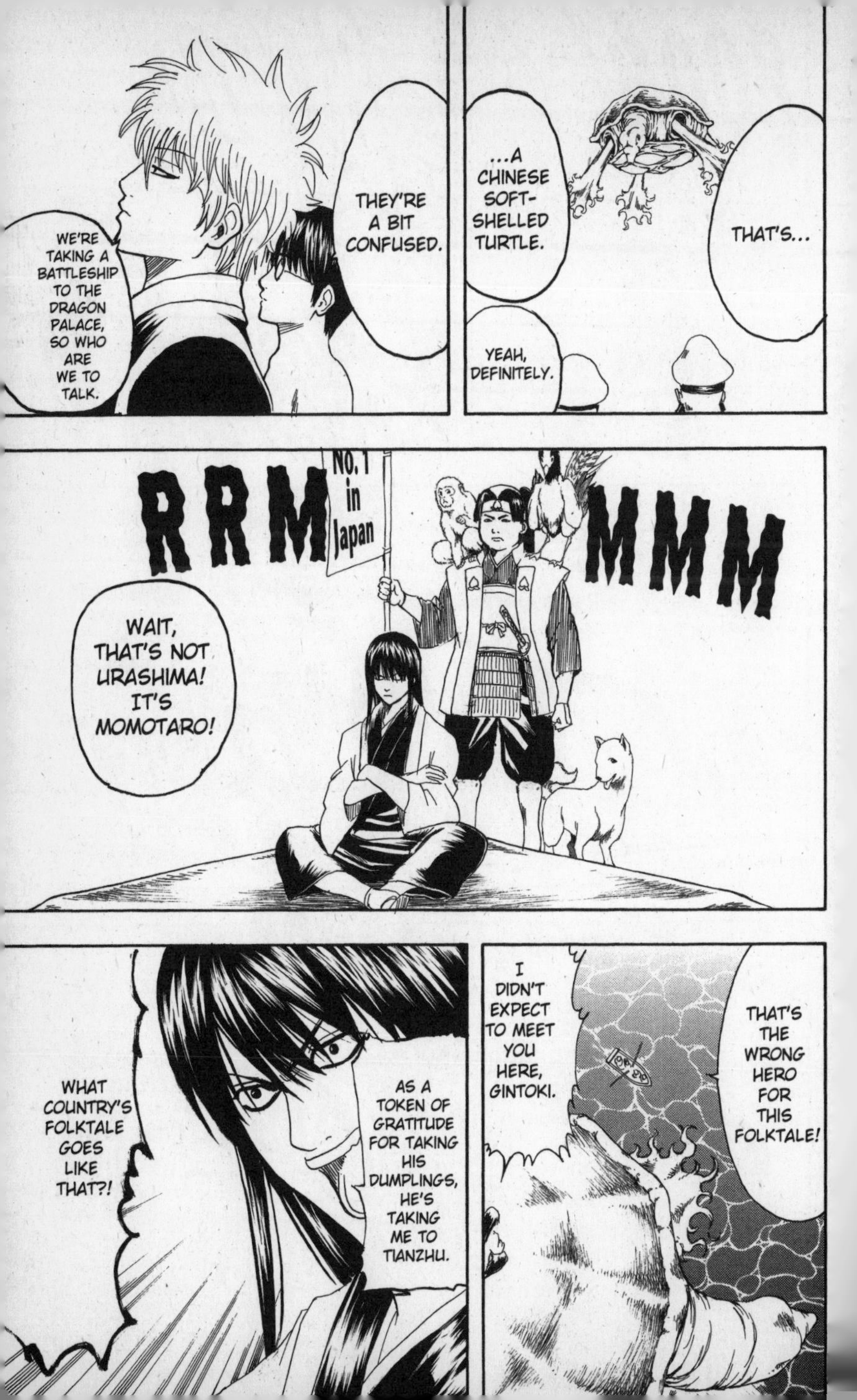
THAT'S...
...A CHINESE SOFT-SHELLED TURTLE.
YEAH, DEFINITELY.
THEY'RE A BIT CONFUSED.
WE'RE TAKING A BATTLESHIP TO THE DRAGON PALACE, SO WHO ARE WE TO TALK.
RRM MMMM
No. 1 in Japan
WAIT, THAT'S NOT URASHIMA! IT'S MOMOTARO!
THAT'S THE WRONG HERO FOR THIS FOLKTALE!
I DIDN'T EXPECT TO MEET YOU HERE, GINTOKI.
AS A TOKEN OF GRATITUDE FOR TAKING HIS DUMPLINGS, HE'S TAKING ME TO TIANZHU.
WHAT COUNTRY'S FOLKTALE GOES LIKE THAT?!

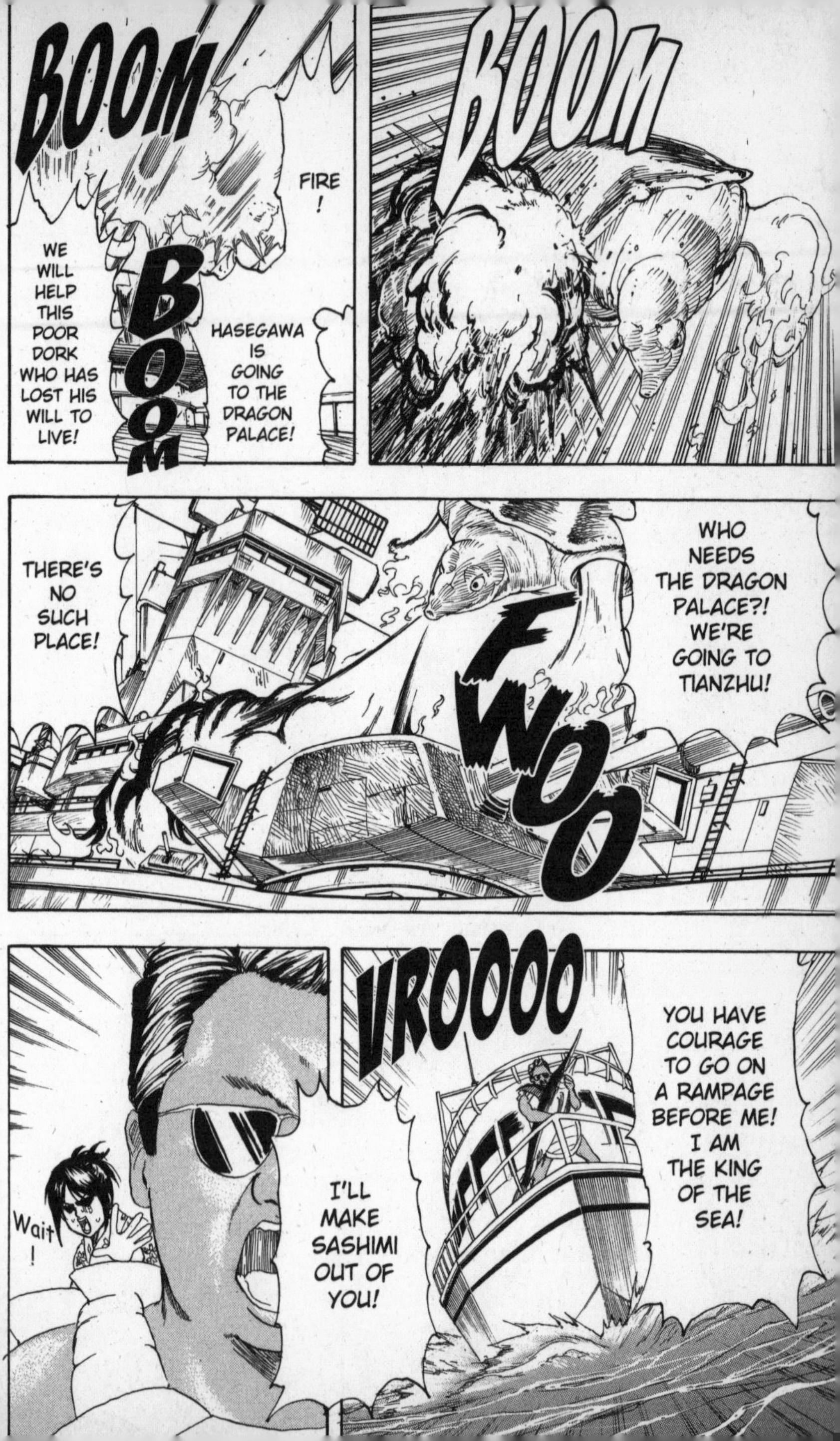
BOOM
BOOM
FIRE!
HASEGAWA IS GOING TO THE DRAGON PALACE!
WE WILL HELP THIS POOR DORK WHO HAS LOST HIS WILL TO LIVE!
BOOM
WHO NEEDS THE DRAGON PALACE?! WE'RE GOING TO TIANZHU!
FWOO
THERE'S NO SUCH PLACE!
VROOOO
YOU HAVE COURAGE TO GO ON A RAMPAGE BEFORE ME! I AM THE KING OF THE SEA!
I'LL MAKE SASHIMI OUT OF YOU!
Wait!

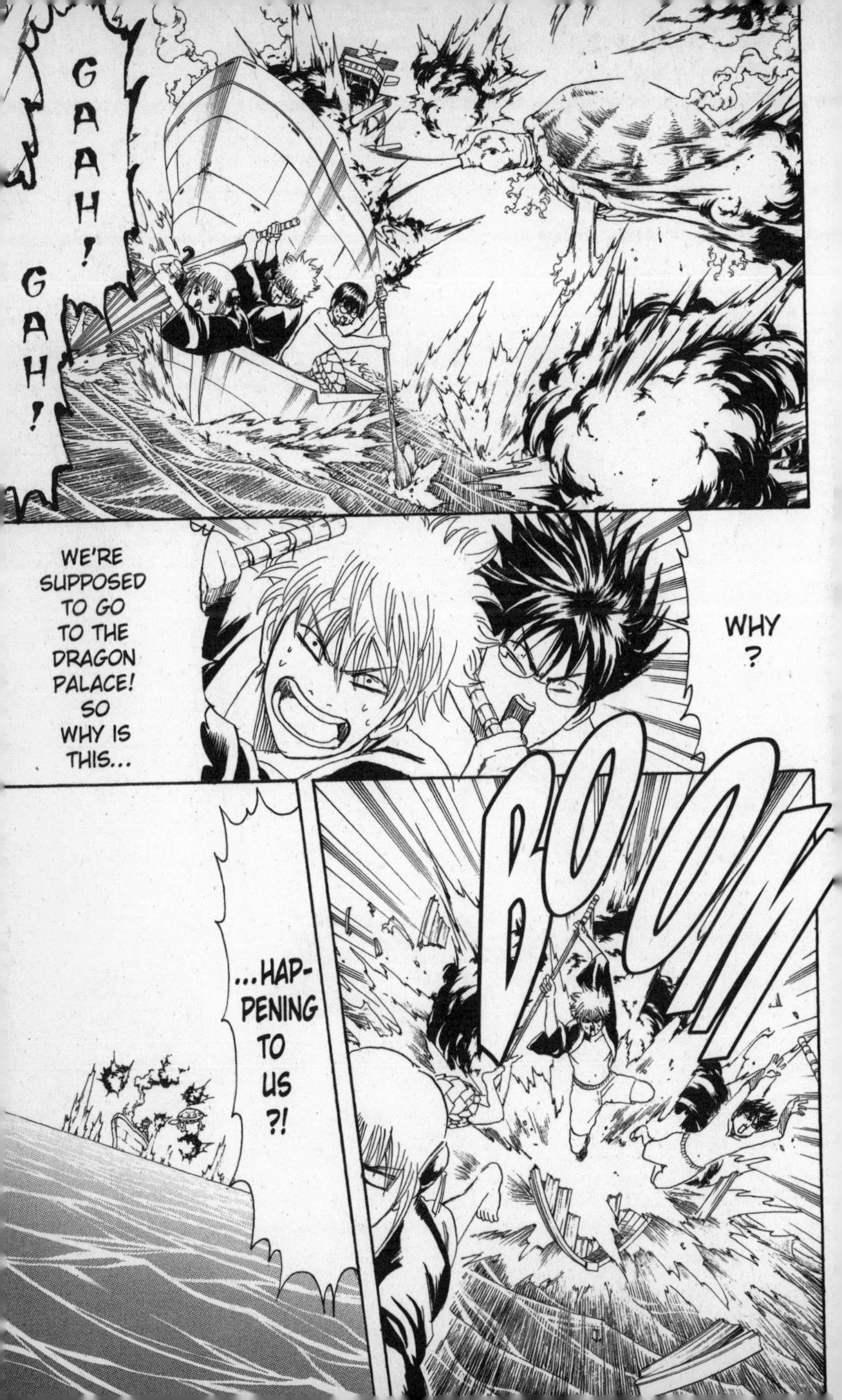
GAAH!
GAH!
WHY?
WE'RE SUPPOSED TO GO TO THE DRAGON PALACE! SO WHY IS THIS...
BOOM
...HAPPENING TO US?!

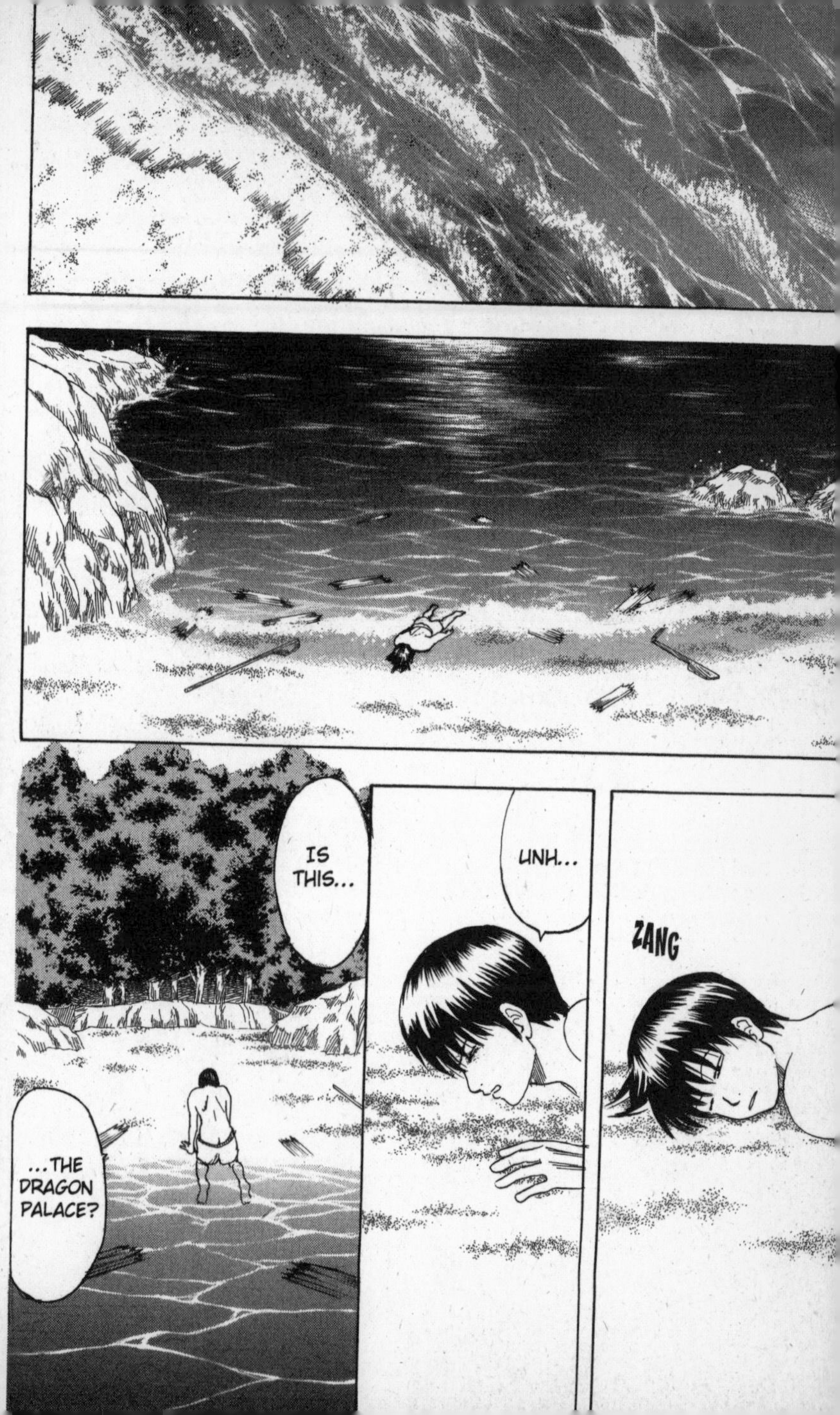
ZANG
UNH...
IS THIS...
...THE DRAGON PALACE?

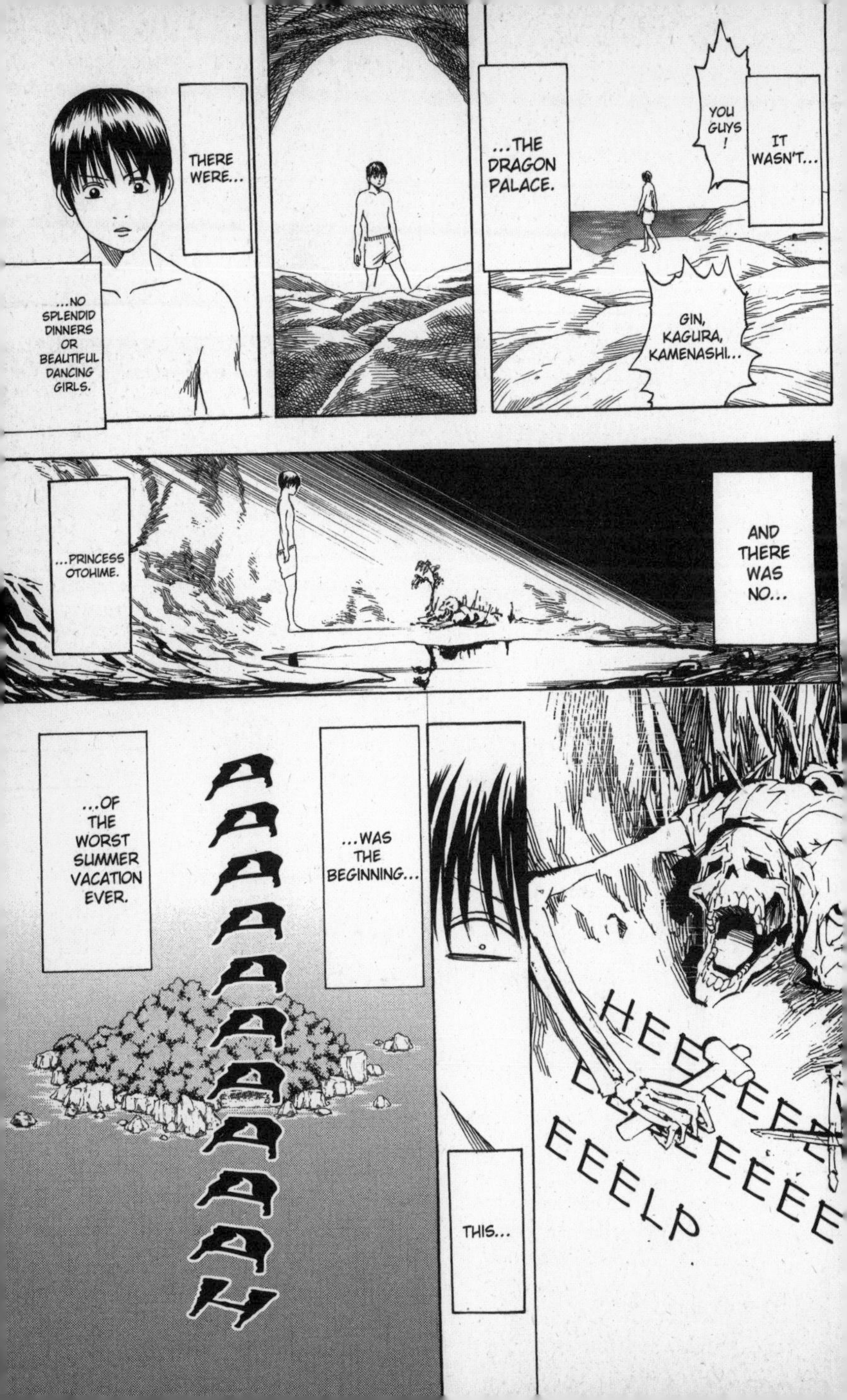
IT WASN'T...
YOU GUYS!
...THE DRAGON PALACE.
GIN, KAGURA, KAMENASHI...
THERE WERE...
...NO SPLENDID DINNERS OR BEAUTIFUL DANCING GIRLS.
AND THERE WAS NO...
...PRINCESS OTOHIME.
HEEEEEEEEEEEEEEEEELP
THIS...
...WAS THE BEGINNING...
...OF THE WORST SUMMER VACATION EVER.
AAAAAAAAAAAH

● Published on the cover of *Weekly Shonen JUMP*, 2007, Volumes 36 & 37 joint issue

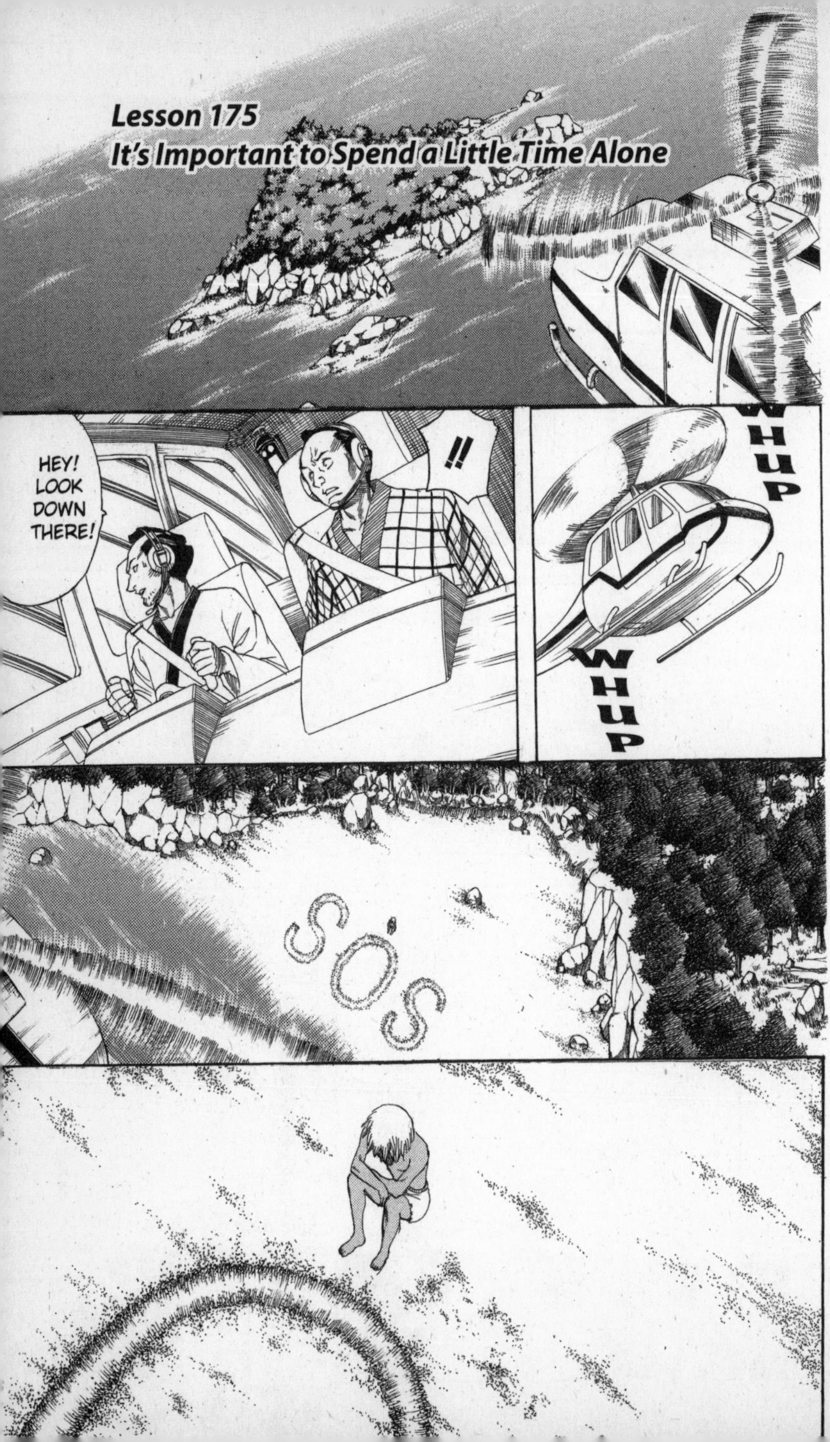
Lesson 175
It's Important to Spend a Little Time Alone
WHUP
WHUP
!!
HEY! LOOK DOWN THERE!
SOS

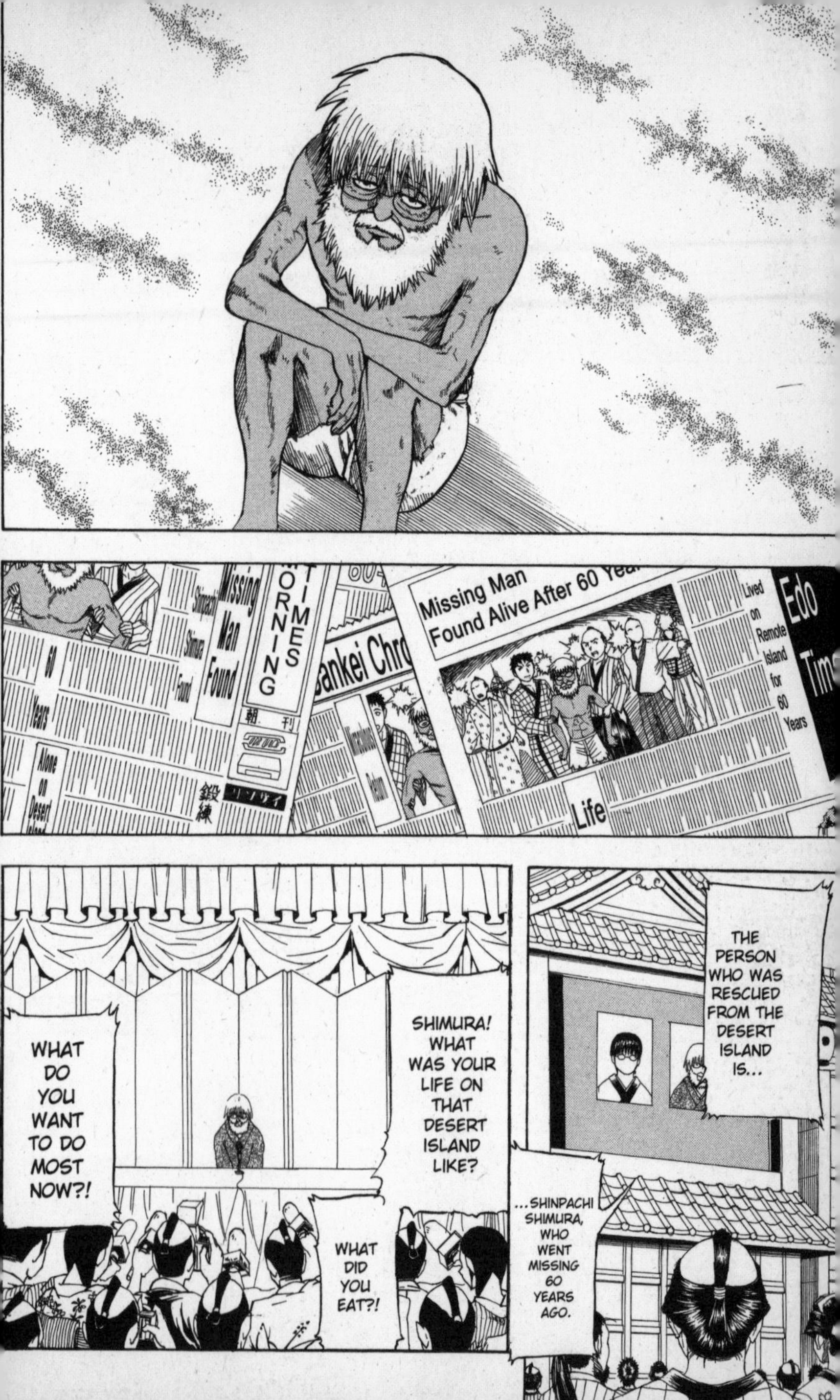
Lived on Remote Island for 60 Years
Missing Man Found Alive After 60
Life
MORNING TIMES
朝刊
Missing Man Found
Shinpachi Shimura Found
60 Years
Alone on
THE PERSON WHO WAS RESCUED FROM THE DESERT ISLAND IS...
...SHINPACHI SHIMURA, WHO WENT MISSING 60 YEARS AGO.
SHIMURA! WHAT WAS YOUR LIFE ON THAT DESERT ISLAND LIKE?
WHAT DO YOU WANT TO DO MOST NOW?!
WHAT DID YOU EAT?!

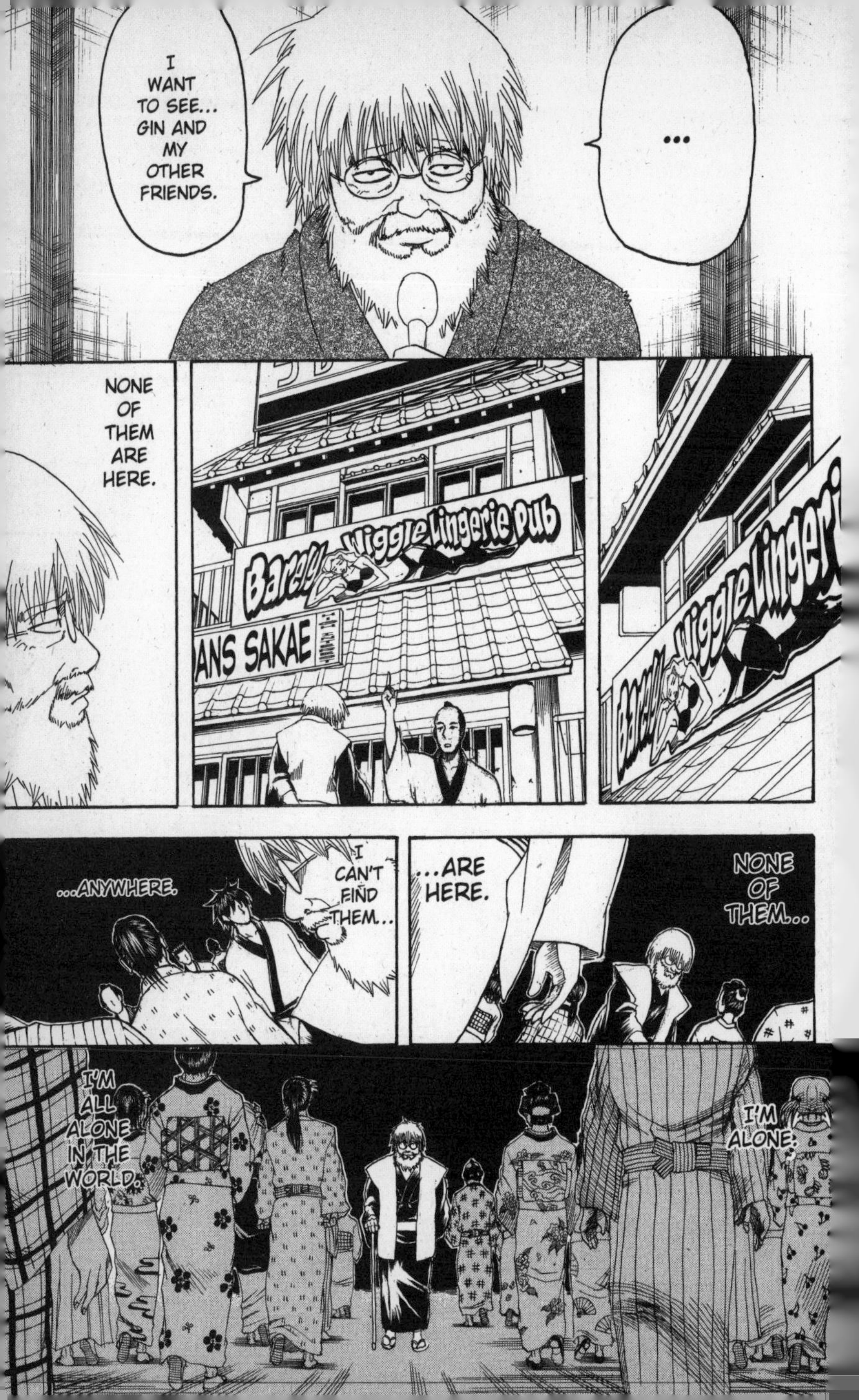
...
I WANT TO SEE... GIN AND MY OTHER FRIENDS.
Barely Wiggle Lingeri
Barely Wiggle Lingerie Pub
ANS SAKAE
NONE OF THEM ARE HERE.
NONE OF THEM...
...ARE HERE.
I CAN'T FIND THEM...
...ANYWHERE.
I'M ALONE.
I'M ALL ALONE IN THE WORLD.

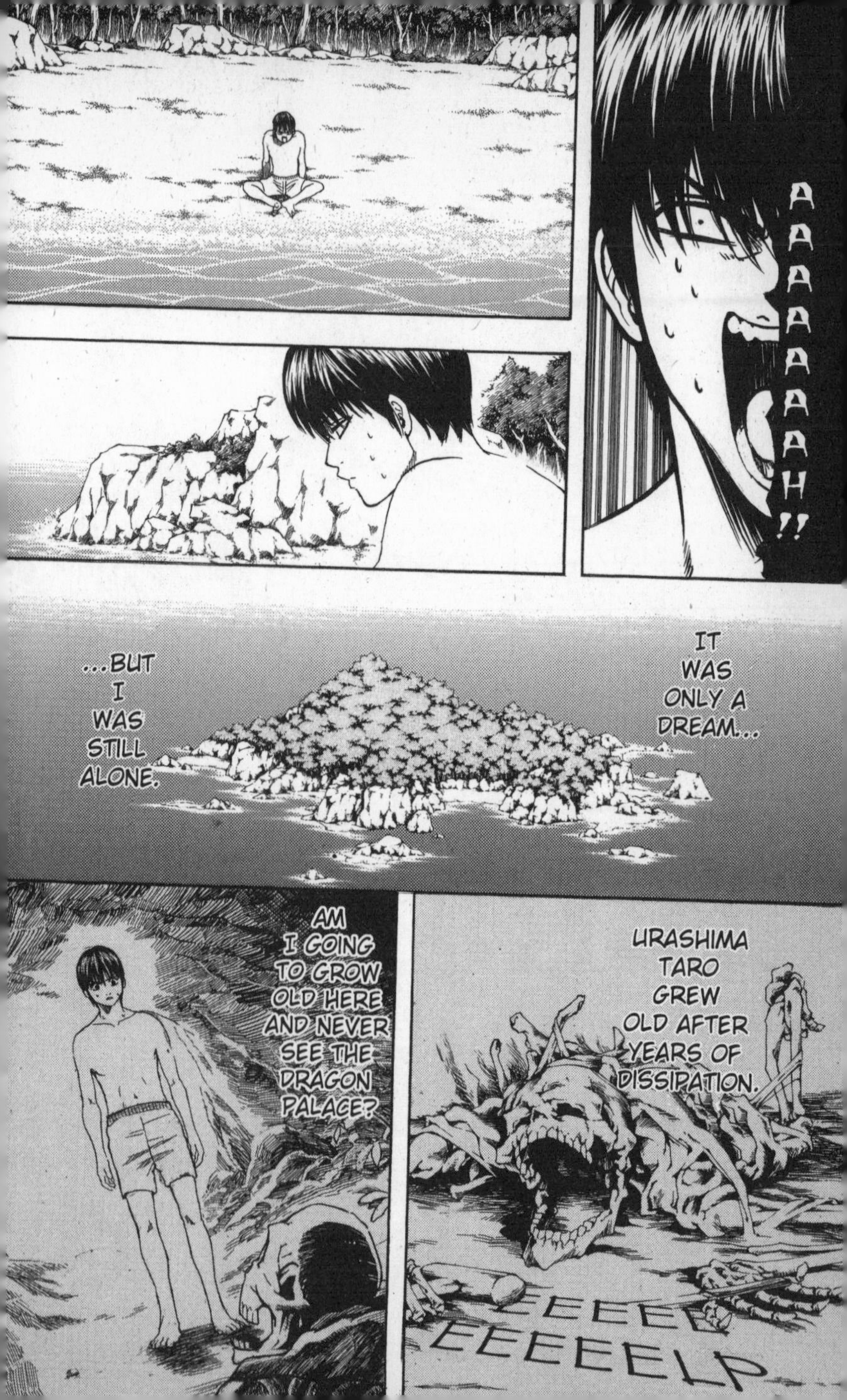
AAAAAAAH!!
IT WAS ONLY A DREAM...
...BUT I WAS STILL ALONE.
URASHIMA TARO GREW OLD AFTER YEARS OF DISSIPATION.
EEEEE
EEEEELP
AM I GOING TO GROW OLD HERE AND NEVER SEE THE DRAGON PALACE?

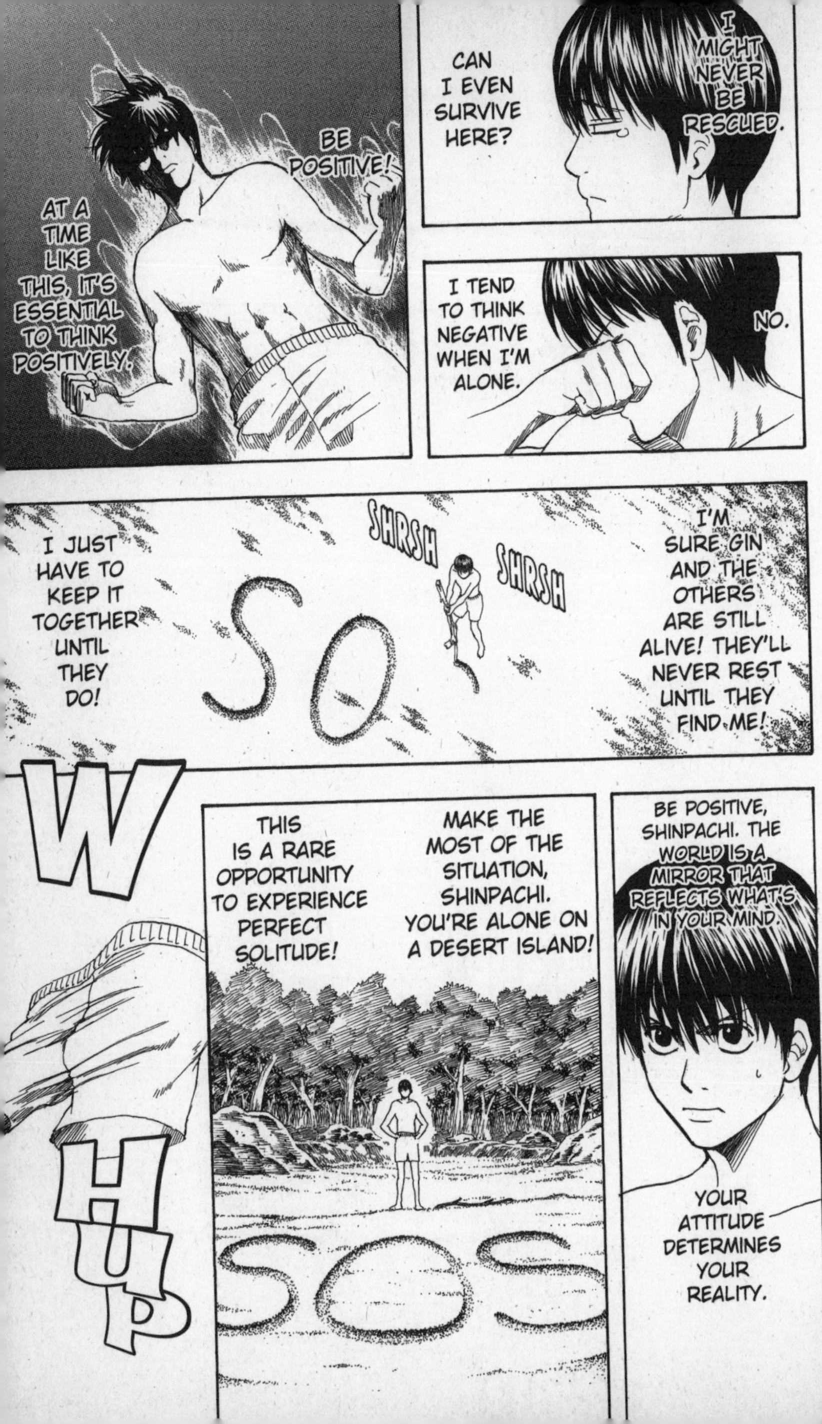

I MIGHT NEVER BE RESCUED.
CAN I EVEN SURVIVE HERE?
NO.
I TEND TO THINK NEGATIVE WHEN I'M ALONE.
BE POSITIVE!
AT A TIME LIKE THIS, IT'S ESSENTIAL TO THINK POSITIVELY.
I'M SURE GIN AND THE OTHERS ARE STILL ALIVE! THEY'LL NEVER REST UNTIL THEY FIND ME!
SHRSH
SHRSH
I JUST HAVE TO KEEP IT TOGETHER UNTIL THEY DO!
BE POSITIVE, SHINPACHI. THE WORLD IS A MIRROR THAT REFLECTS WHAT'S IN YOUR MIND.
YOUR ATTITUDE DETERMINES YOUR REALITY.
MAKE THE MOST OF THE SITUATION, SHINPACHI. YOU'RE ALONE ON A DESERT ISLAND!
THIS IS A RARE OPPORTUNITY TO EXPERIENCE PERFECT SOLITUDE!
WHUP

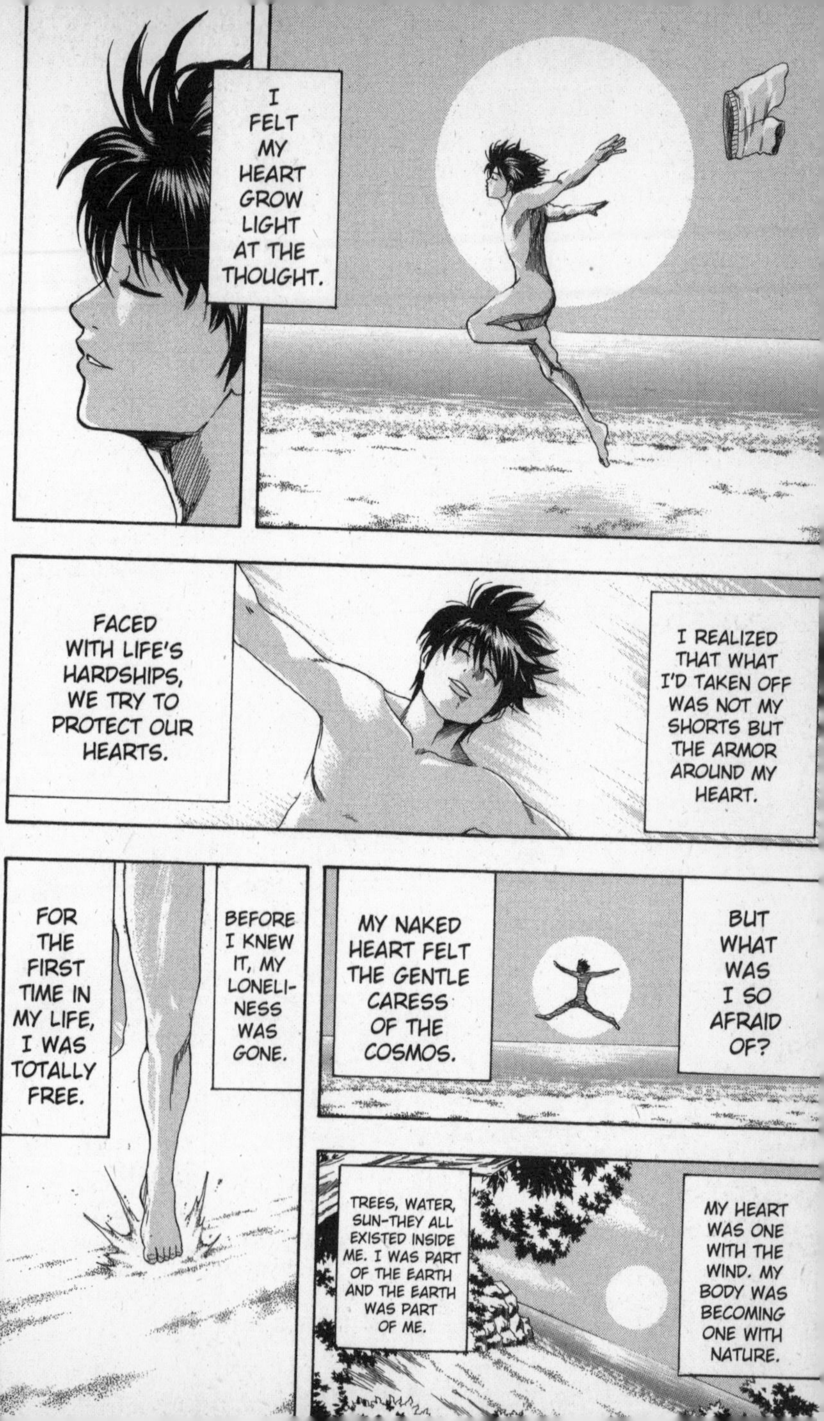
I FELT MY HEART GROW LIGHT AT THE THOUGHT.
I REALIZED THAT WHAT I'D TAKEN OFF WAS NOT MY SHORTS BUT THE ARMOR AROUND MY HEART.
FACED WITH LIFE'S HARDSHIPS, WE TRY TO PROTECT OUR HEARTS.
BUT WHAT WAS I SO AFRAID OF?
MY NAKED HEART FELT THE GENTLE CARESS OF THE COSMOS.
MY HEART WAS ONE WITH THE WIND. MY BODY WAS BECOMING ONE WITH NATURE.
TREES, WATER, SUN–THEY ALL EXISTED INSIDE ME. I WAS PART OF THE EARTH AND THE EARTH WAS PART OF ME.
BEFORE I KNEW IT, MY LONELI-NESS WAS GONE.
FOR THE FIRST TIME IN MY LIFE, I WAS TOTALLY FREE.

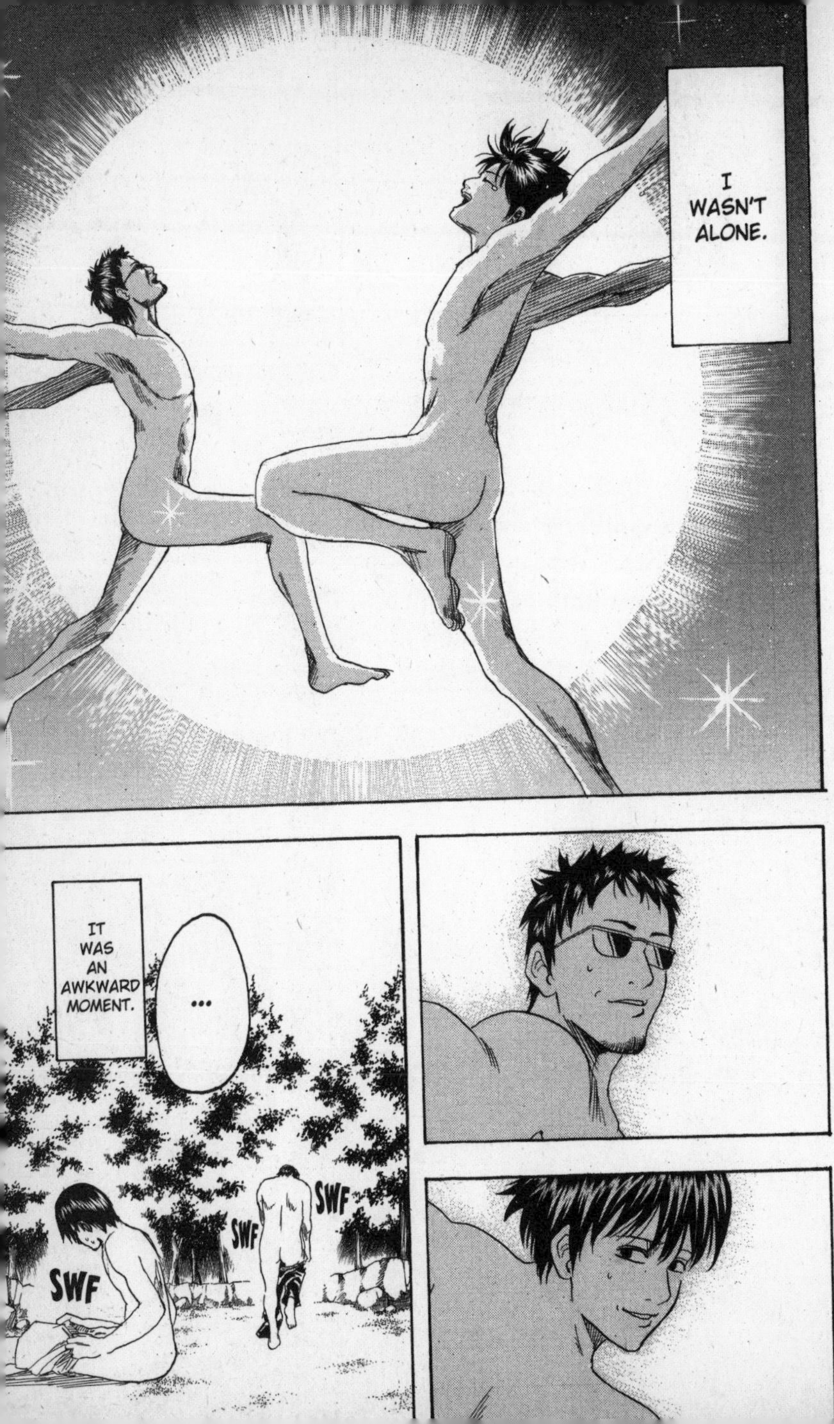
I WASN'T ALONE.
...
IT WAS AN AWKWARD MOMENT.
SWF
SWF
SWF

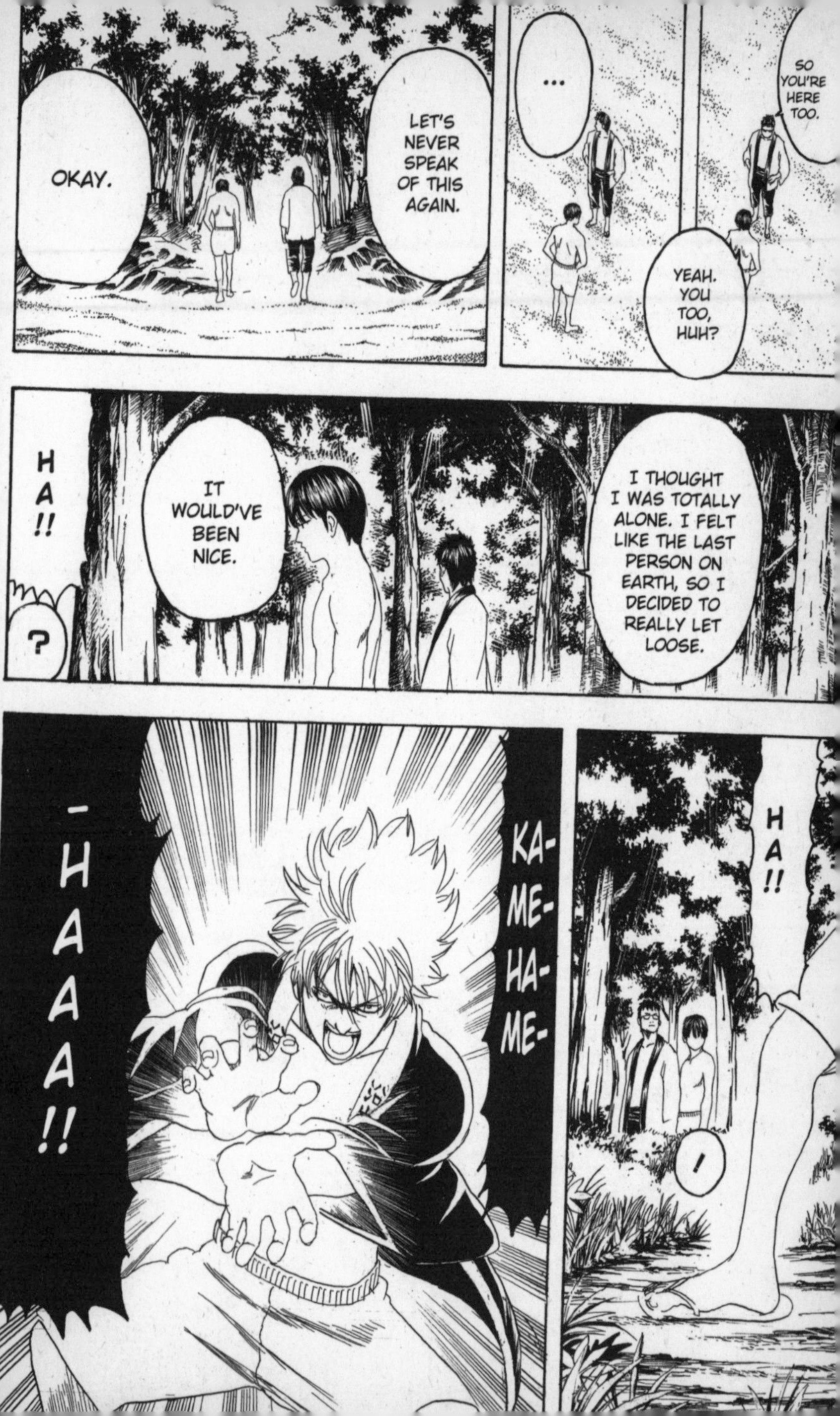
SO YOU'RE HERE TOO.
YEAH. YOU TOO, HUH?
...
LET'S NEVER SPEAK OF THIS AGAIN.
OKAY.
I THOUGHT I WAS TOTALLY ALONE. I FELT LIKE THE LAST PERSON ON EARTH, SO I DECIDED TO REALLY LET LOOSE.
IT WOULD'VE BEEN NICE.
HA!!
?
HA!!
!
KA-ME-HA-ME-
-HAAAA!!

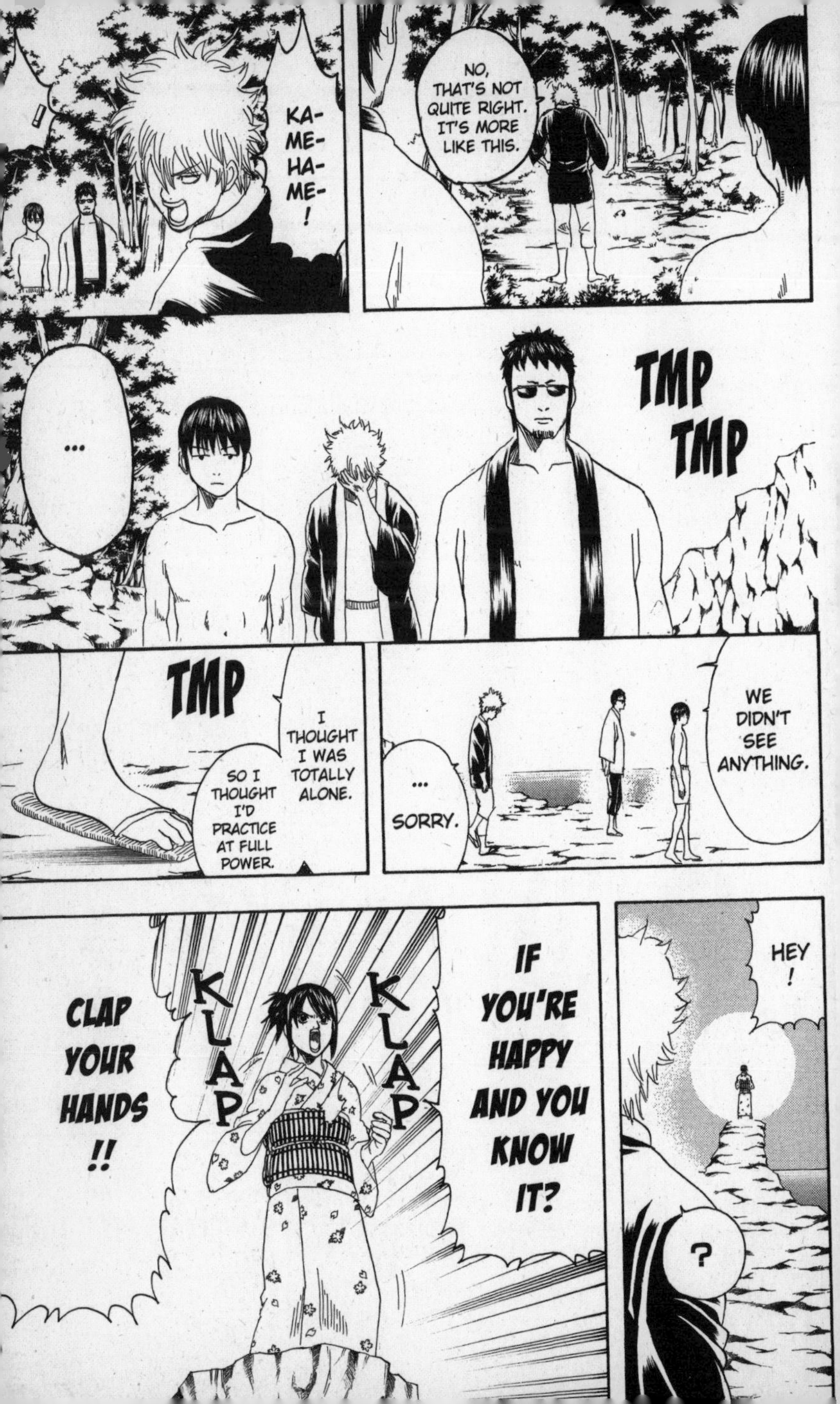
NO, THAT'S NOT QUITE RIGHT. IT'S MORE LIKE THIS.
KA-ME-HA-ME-!
!
TMP TMP
...
WE DIDN'T SEE ANYTHING.
... SORRY.
TMP
I THOUGHT I WAS TOTALLY ALONE.
SO I THOUGHT I'D PRACTICE AT FULL POWER.
HEY!
?
IF YOU'RE HAPPY AND YOU KNOW IT?
KLAP
KLAP
CLAP YOUR HANDS!!

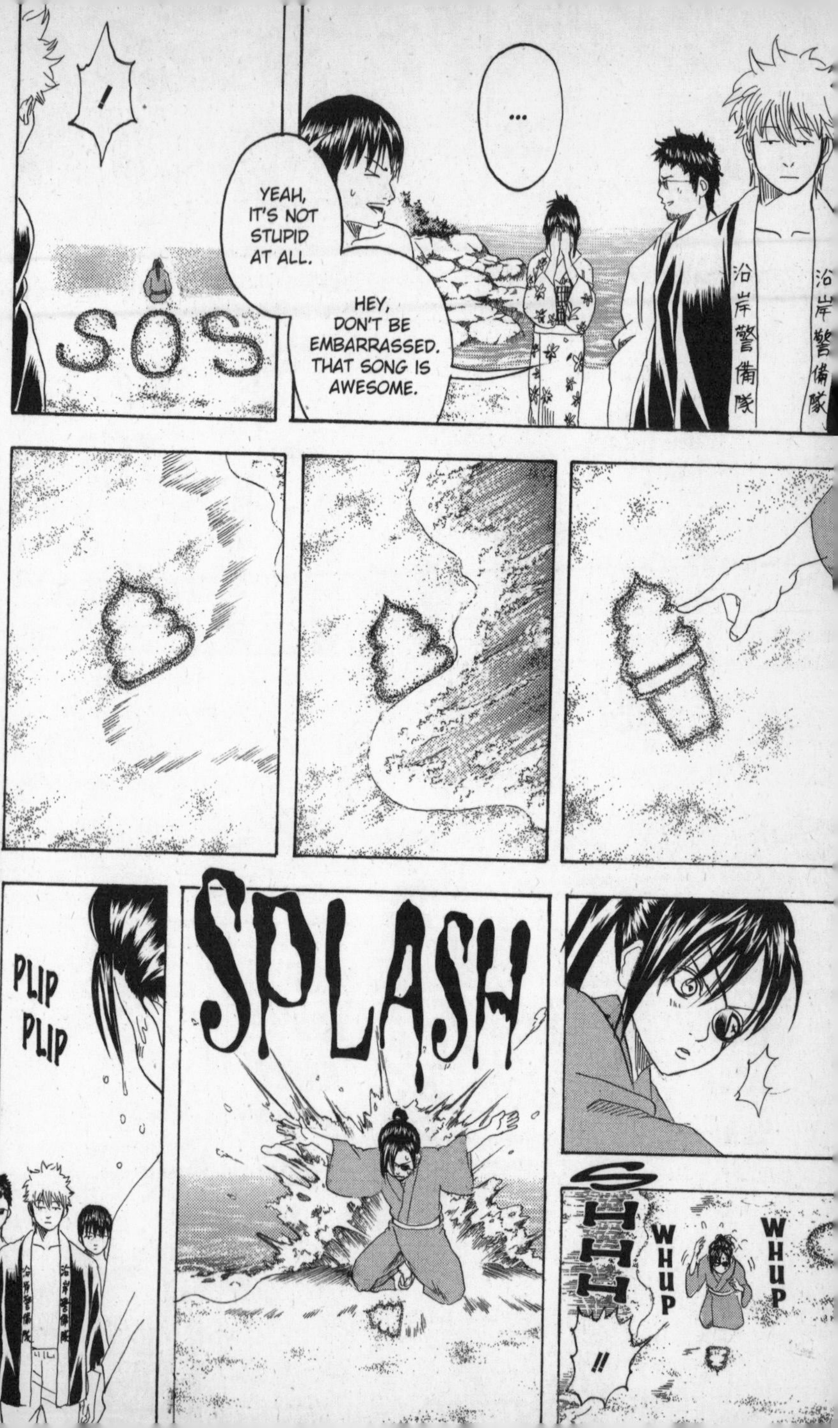
...
沿岸警備隊
沿岸警備隊
YEAH, IT'S NOT STUPID AT ALL.
HEY, DON'T BE EMBARRASSED. THAT SONG IS AWESOME.
!
SOS
SHHH
WHUP WHUP
!!
SPLASH
PLIP PLIP

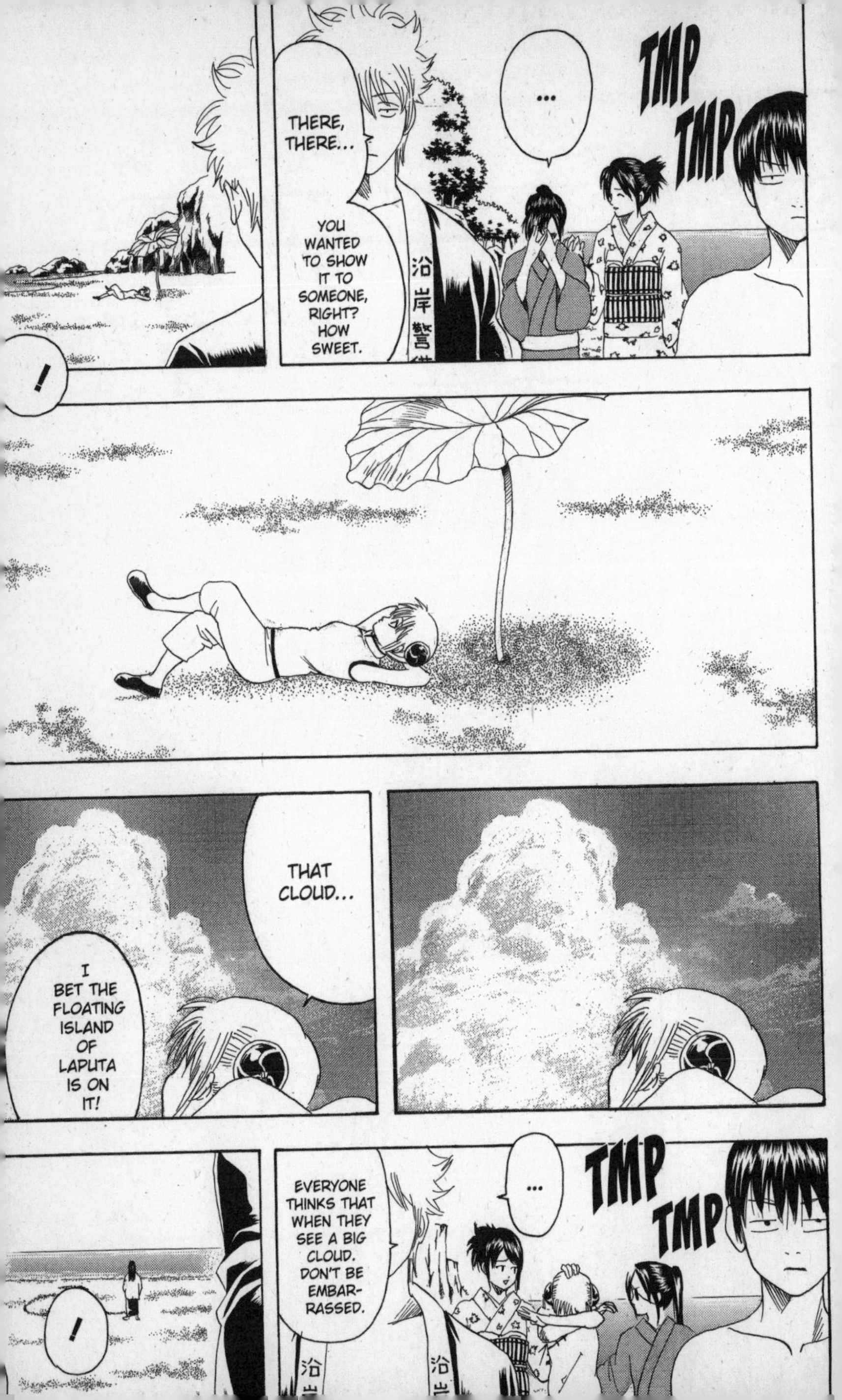
TMP TMP
...
THERE, THERE...
YOU WANTED TO SHOW IT TO SOMEONE, RIGHT? HOW SWEET.
!
THAT CLOUD...
I BET THE FLOATING ISLAND OF LAPUTA IS ON IT!
TMP TMP
...
EVERYONE THINKS THAT WHEN THEY SEE A BIG CLOUD. DON'T BE EMBARRASSED.
!

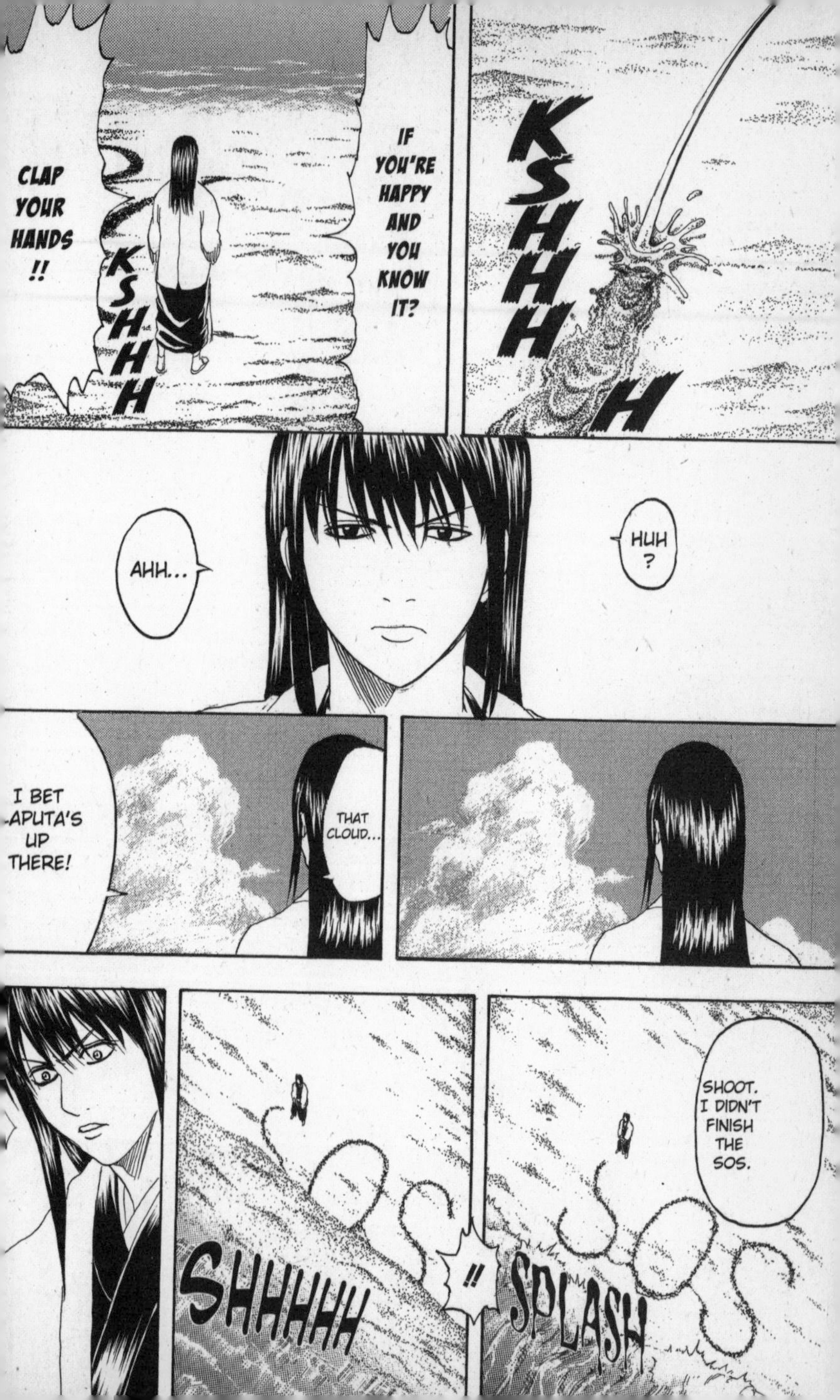
KSHHHH
IF YOU'RE HAPPY AND YOU KNOW IT?
CLAP YOUR HANDS !!
KSHHH
HUH ?
AHH...
THAT CLOUD...
I BET APUTA'S UP THERE!
SHOOT. I DIDN'T FINISH THE SOS.
SPLASH
!!
SHHHHH

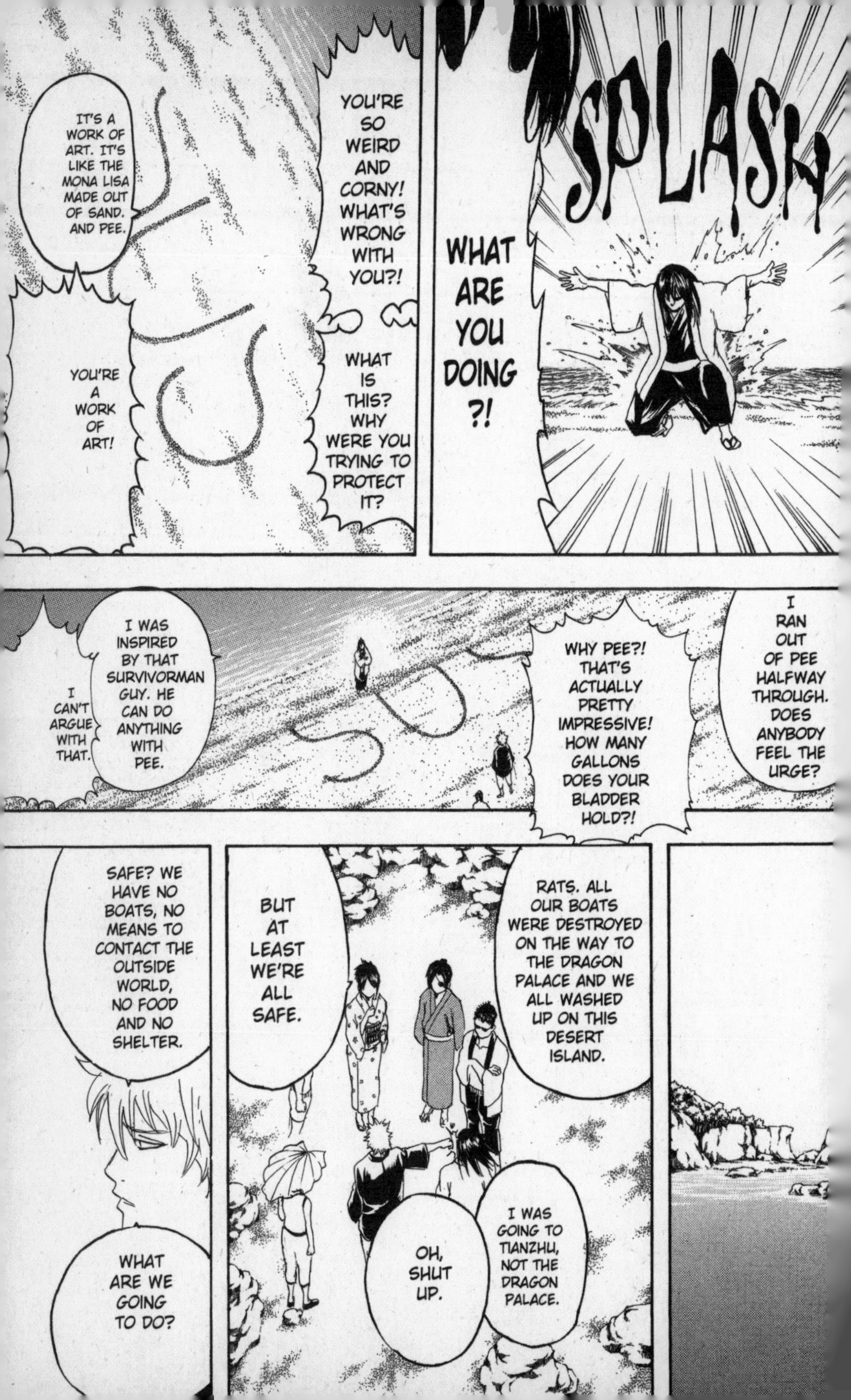
SPLASH
WHAT ARE YOU DOING ?!
YOU'RE SO WEIRD AND CORNY! WHAT'S WRONG WITH YOU?!
WHAT IS THIS? WHY WERE YOU TRYING TO PROTECT IT?
IT'S A WORK OF ART. IT'S LIKE THE MONA LISA MADE OUT OF SAND. AND PEE.
YOU'RE A WORK OF ART!
I RAN OUT OF PEE HALFWAY THROUGH. DOES ANYBODY FEEL THE URGE?
WHY PEE?! THAT'S ACTUALLY PRETTY IMPRESSIVE! HOW MANY GALLONS DOES YOUR BLADDER HOLD?!
I WAS INSPIRED BY THAT SURVIVORMAN GUY. HE CAN DO ANYTHING WITH PEE.
I CAN'T ARGUE WITH THAT.
RATS. ALL OUR BOATS WERE DESTROYED ON THE WAY TO THE DRAGON PALACE AND WE ALL WASHED UP ON THIS DESERT ISLAND.
BUT AT LEAST WE'RE ALL SAFE.
I WAS GOING TO TIANZHU, NOT THE DRAGON PALACE.
OH, SHUT UP.
SAFE? WE HAVE NO BOATS, NO MEANS TO CONTACT THE OUTSIDE WORLD, NO FOOD AND NO SHELTER.
WHAT ARE WE GOING TO DO?

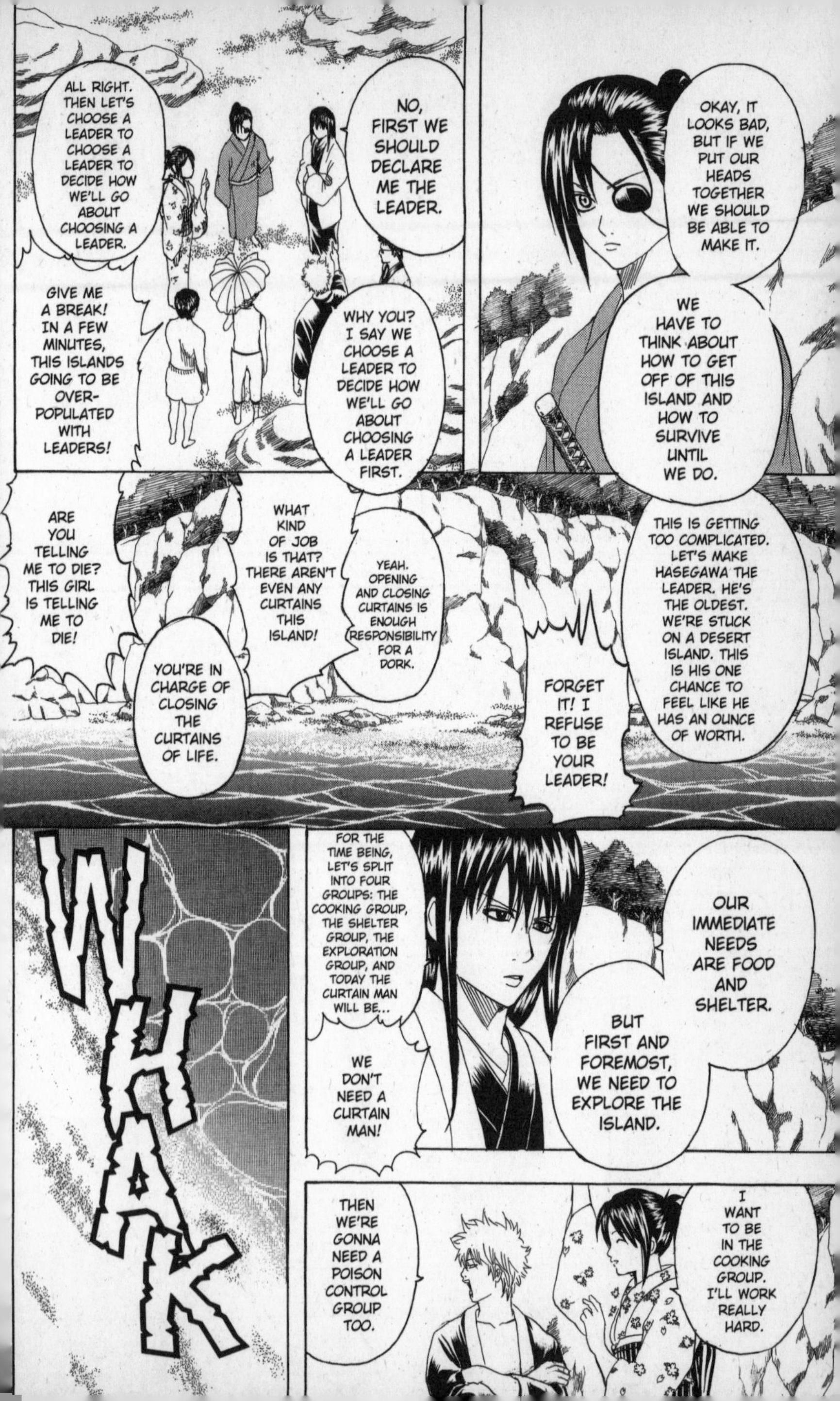
OKAY, IT LOOKS BAD, BUT IF WE PUT OUR HEADS TOGETHER WE SHOULD BE ABLE TO MAKE IT.
WE HAVE TO THINK ABOUT HOW TO GET OFF OF THIS ISLAND AND HOW TO SURVIVE UNTIL WE DO.
NO, FIRST WE SHOULD DECLARE ME THE LEADER.
WHY YOU? I SAY WE CHOOSE A LEADER TO DECIDE HOW WE'LL GO ABOUT CHOOSING A LEADER FIRST.
ALL RIGHT. THEN LET'S CHOOSE A LEADER TO CHOOSE A LEADER TO DECIDE HOW WE'LL GO ABOUT CHOOSING A LEADER.
GIVE ME A BREAK! IN A FEW MINUTES, THIS ISLANDS GOING TO BE OVER-POPULATED WITH LEADERS!
THIS IS GETTING TOO COMPLICATED. LET'S MAKE HASEGAWA THE LEADER. HE'S THE OLDEST. WE'RE STUCK ON A DESERT ISLAND. THIS IS HIS ONE CHANCE TO FEEL LIKE HE HAS AN OUNCE OF WORTH.
FORGET IT! I REFUSE TO BE YOUR LEADER!
YEAH. OPENING AND CLOSING CURTAINS IS ENOUGH RESPONSIBILITY FOR A DORK.
WHAT KIND OF JOB IS THAT? THERE AREN'T EVEN ANY CURTAINS THIS ISLAND!
YOU'RE IN CHARGE OF CLOSING THE CURTAINS OF LIFE.
ARE YOU TELLING ME TO DIE? THIS GIRL IS TELLING ME TO DIE!
OUR IMMEDIATE NEEDS ARE FOOD AND SHELTER.
BUT FIRST AND FOREMOST, WE NEED TO EXPLORE THE ISLAND.
FOR THE TIME BEING, LET'S SPLIT INTO FOUR GROUPS: THE COOKING GROUP, THE SHELTER GROUP, THE EXPLORATION GROUP, AND TODAY THE CURTAIN MAN WILL BE...
WE DON'T NEED A CURTAIN MAN!
I WANT TO BE IN THE COOKING GROUP. I'LL WORK REALLY HARD.
THEN WE'RE GONNA NEED A POISON CONTROL GROUP TOO.
WHAK

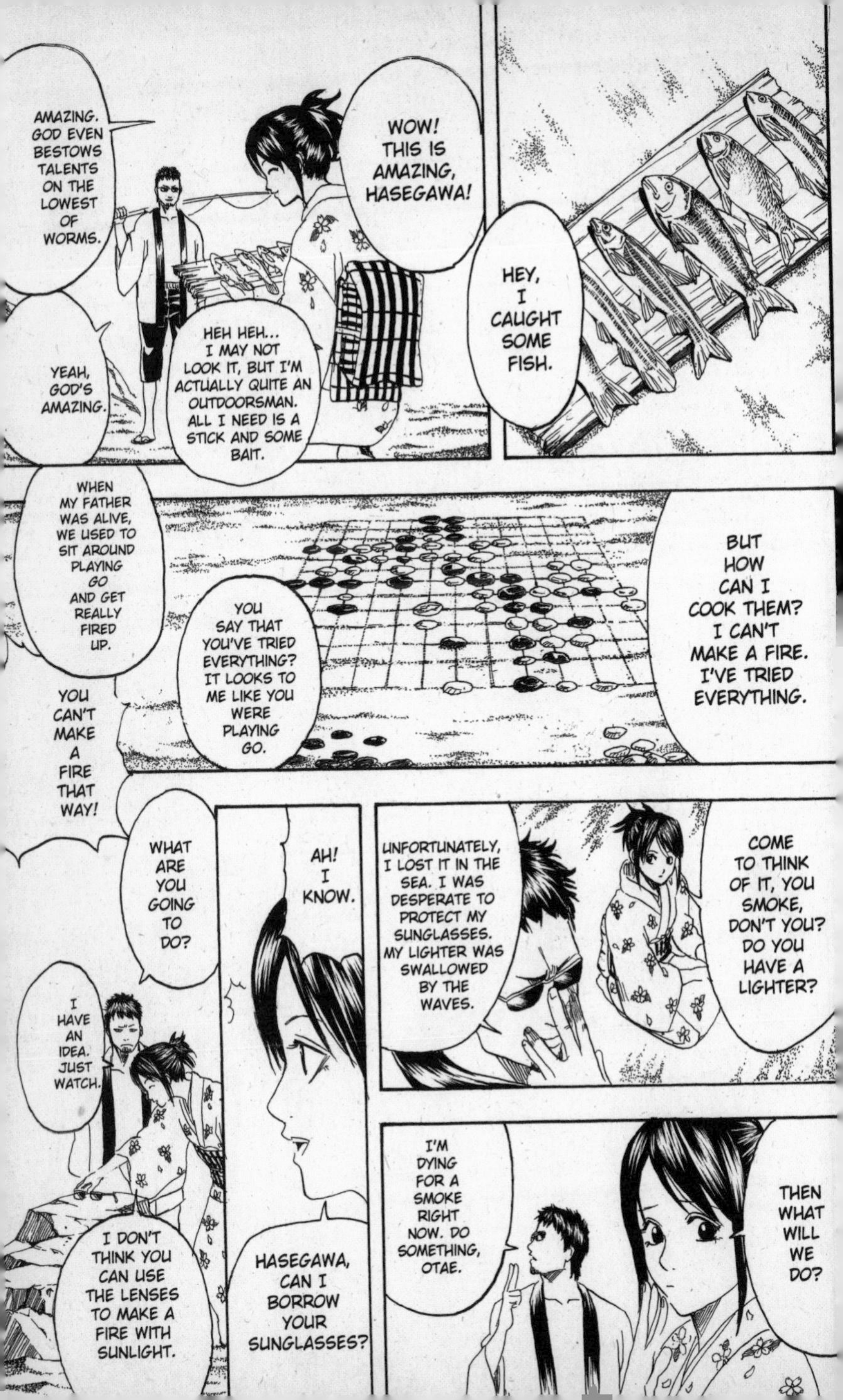
HEY, I CAUGHT SOME FISH.
WOW! THIS IS AMAZING, HASEGAWA!
HEH HEH... I MAY NOT LOOK IT, BUT I'M ACTUALLY QUITE AN OUTDOORSMAN. ALL I NEED IS A STICK AND SOME BAIT.
AMAZING. GOD EVEN BESTOWS TALENTS ON THE LOWEST OF WORMS.
YEAH, GOD'S AMAZING.
BUT HOW CAN I COOK THEM? I CAN'T MAKE A FIRE. I'VE TRIED EVERYTHING.
YOU SAY THAT YOU'VE TRIED EVERYTHING? IT LOOKS TO ME LIKE YOU WERE PLAYING GO.
WHEN MY FATHER WAS ALIVE, WE USED TO SIT AROUND PLAYING GO AND GET REALLY FIRED UP.
YOU CAN'T MAKE A FIRE THAT WAY!
COME TO THINK OF IT, YOU SMOKE, DON'T YOU? DO YOU HAVE A LIGHTER?
UNFORTUNATELY, I LOST IT IN THE SEA. I WAS DESPERATE TO PROTECT MY SUNGLASSES. MY LIGHTER WAS SWALLOWED BY THE WAVES.
THEN WHAT WILL WE DO?
I'M DYING FOR A SMOKE RIGHT NOW. DO SOMETHING, OTAE.
AH! I KNOW.
HASEGAWA, CAN I BORROW YOUR SUNGLASSES?
WHAT ARE YOU GOING TO DO?
I HAVE AN IDEA. JUST WATCH.
I DON'T THINK YOU CAN USE THE LENSES TO MAKE A FIRE WITH SUNLIGHT.

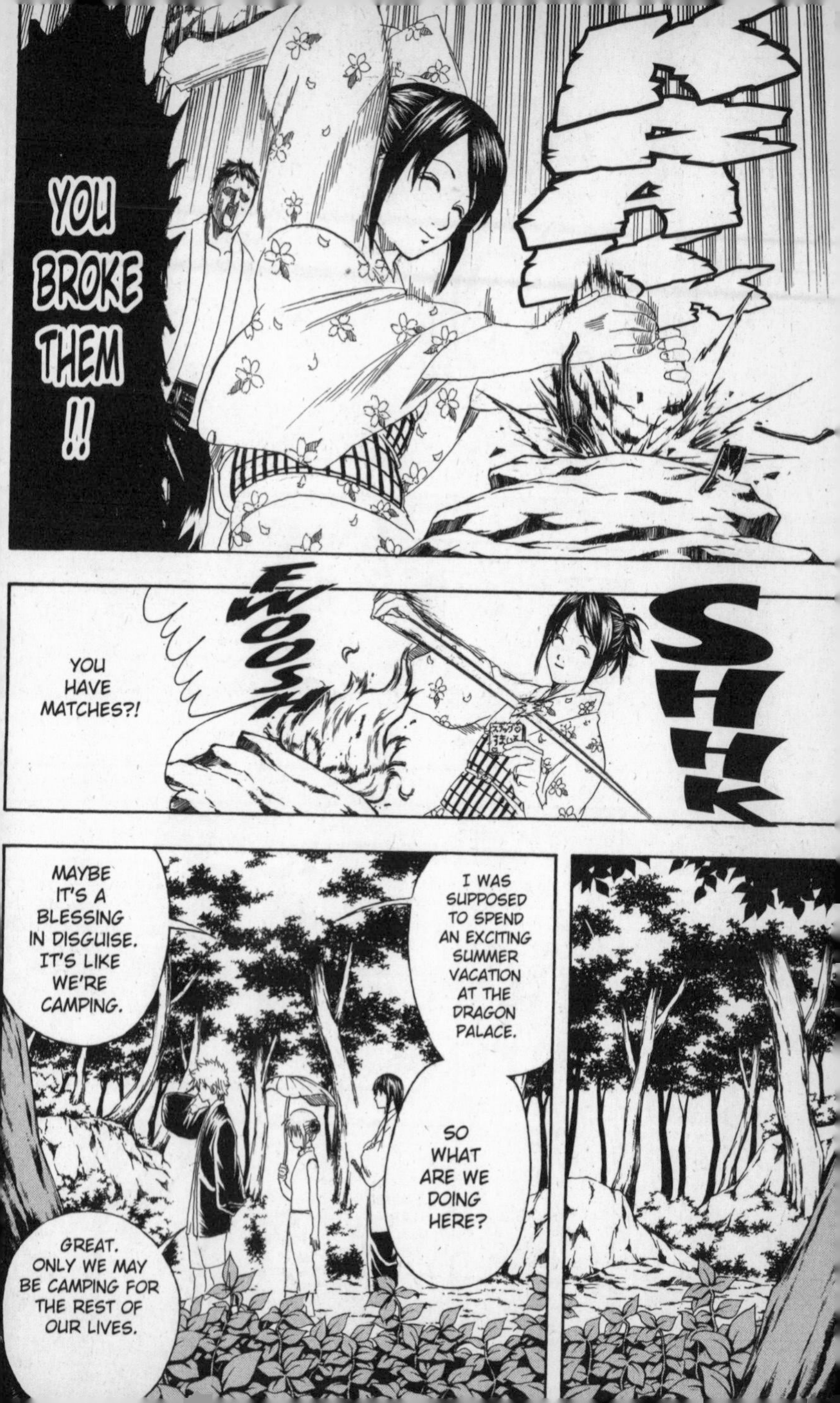
YOU BROKE THEM !!
SHK
WOOSH
YOU HAVE MATCHES?!
I WAS SUPPOSED TO SPEND AN EXCITING SUMMER VACATION AT THE DRAGON PALACE.
SO WHAT ARE WE DOING HERE?
MAYBE IT'S A BLESSING IN DISGUISE. IT'S LIKE WE'RE CAMPING.
GREAT. ONLY WE MAY BE CAMPING FOR THE REST OF OUR LIVES.

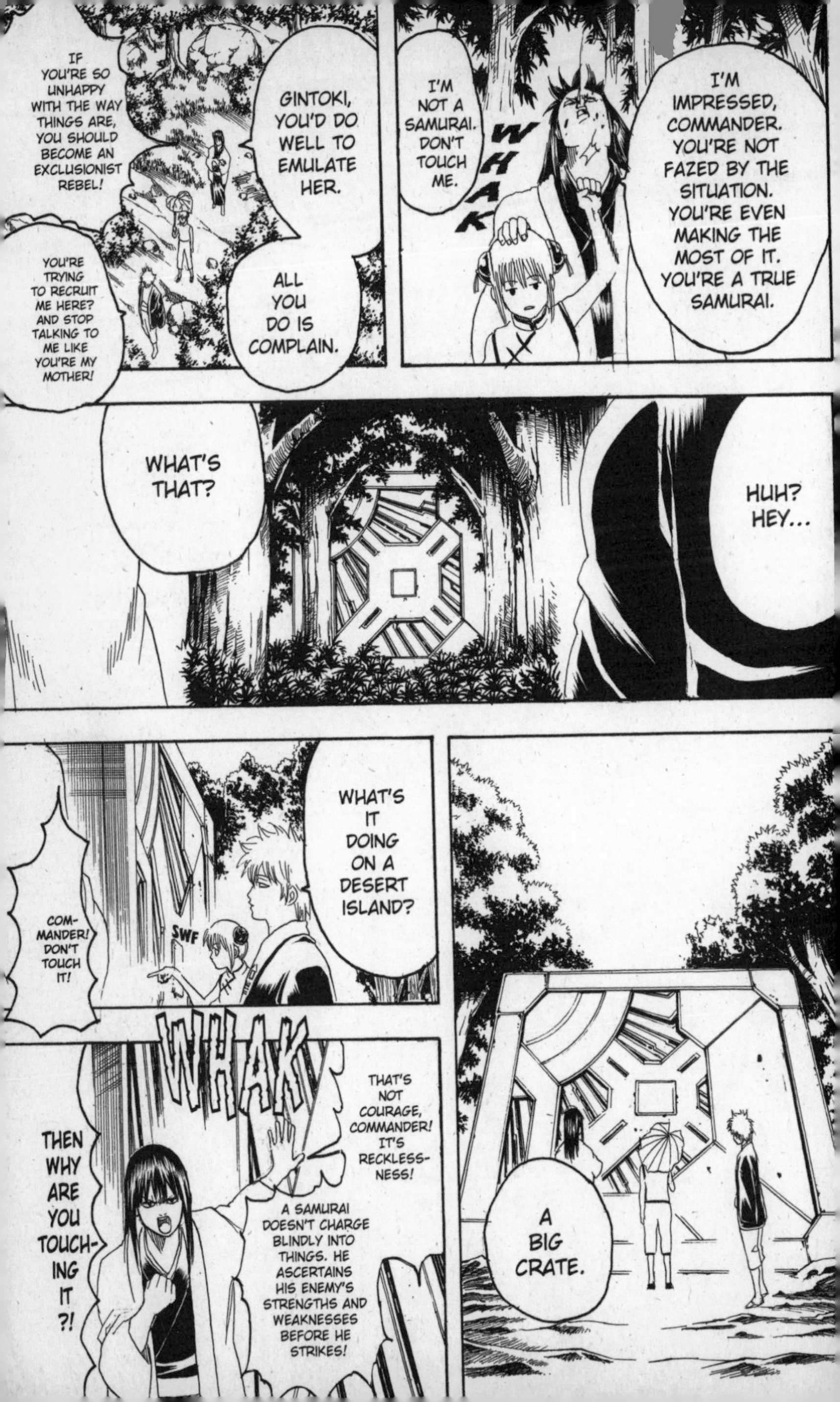
I'M IMPRESSED, COMMANDER. YOU'RE NOT FAZED BY THE SITUATION. YOU'RE EVEN MAKING THE MOST OF IT. YOU'RE A TRUE SAMURAI.
WHAK
I'M NOT A SAMURAI. DON'T TOUCH ME.
GINTOKI, YOU'D DO WELL TO EMULATE HER.
ALL YOU DO IS COMPLAIN.
IF YOU'RE SO UNHAPPY WITH THE WAY THINGS ARE, YOU SHOULD BECOME AN EXCLUSIONIST REBEL!
YOU'RE TRYING TO RECRUIT ME HERE? AND STOP TALKING TO ME LIKE YOU'RE MY MOTHER!
HUH? HEY...
WHAT'S THAT?
A BIG CRATE.
WHAT'S IT DOING ON A DESERT ISLAND?
SWF
COM-MANDER! DON'T TOUCH IT!
WHAK
THAT'S NOT COURAGE, COMMANDER! IT'S RECKLESS-NESS!
A SAMURAI DOESN'T CHARGE BLINDLY INTO THINGS. HE ASCERTAINS HIS ENEMY'S STRENGTHS AND WEAKNESSES BEFORE HE STRIKES!
THEN WHY ARE YOU TOUCH-ING IT?!

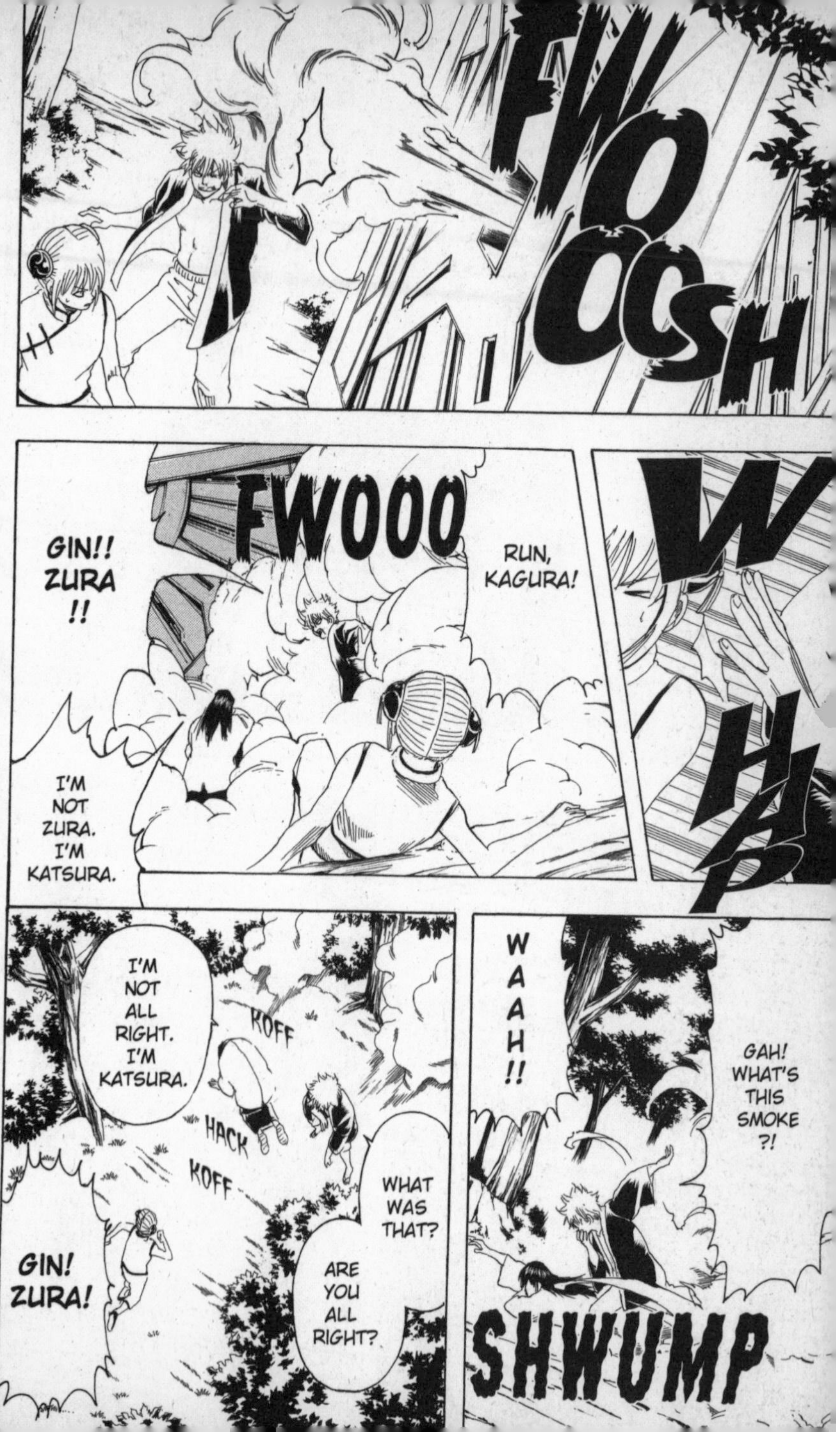
FWOOOSH
WHAP
FWOOO
RUN, KAGURA!
GIN!! ZURA!!
I'M NOT ZURA. I'M KATSURA.
WAAAH!!
GAH! WHAT'S THIS SMOKE?!
SHWUMP
WHAT WAS THAT?
ARE YOU ALL RIGHT?
I'M NOT ALL RIGHT. I'M KATSURA.
KOFF
HACK
KOFF
GIN! ZURA!

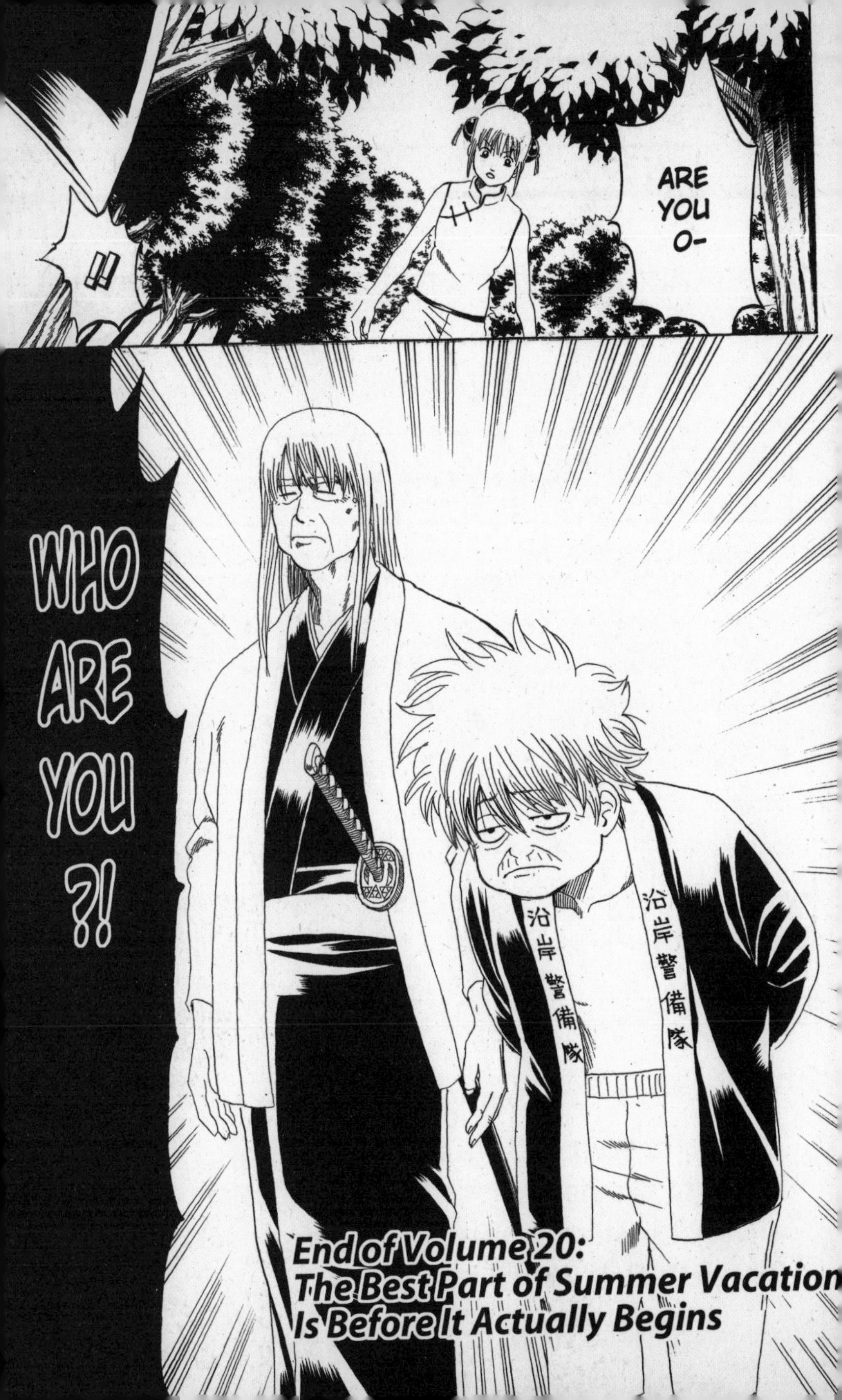
ARE YOU O-
!!
WHO ARE YOU ?!
沿岸警備隊
沿岸警備隊
End of Volume 20:
The Best Part of Summer Vacation
Is Before It Actually Begins

Due to my busy schedule and inability to come up with a story that wouldn't offend my editor's fiancée, I was unable to finish the marriage proposal episode in time for the wedding reception. So I thought, "Good! I should leave it up in the air and pretend the plan never existed." But on the day of the wedding, I heard Oonishi's father say in disgust, "What's *Gin Tama*? Never heard of it." So I started feeling the desire for revenge and thought about whether there was a way I could entertain my readers and cause damage to the Oonishi family, so that's how that episode was born. If you read the episode again, keep this behind-the-scenes information in mind. You'll have an entirely different perspective on it. Please read it again. Read it with your family and be embarrassed, Oonishi.

Send your letters and fan art to:
VIZ Media
Attn: Mike Montesa, Editor
P.O. Box 77010
San Francisco, CA 94107

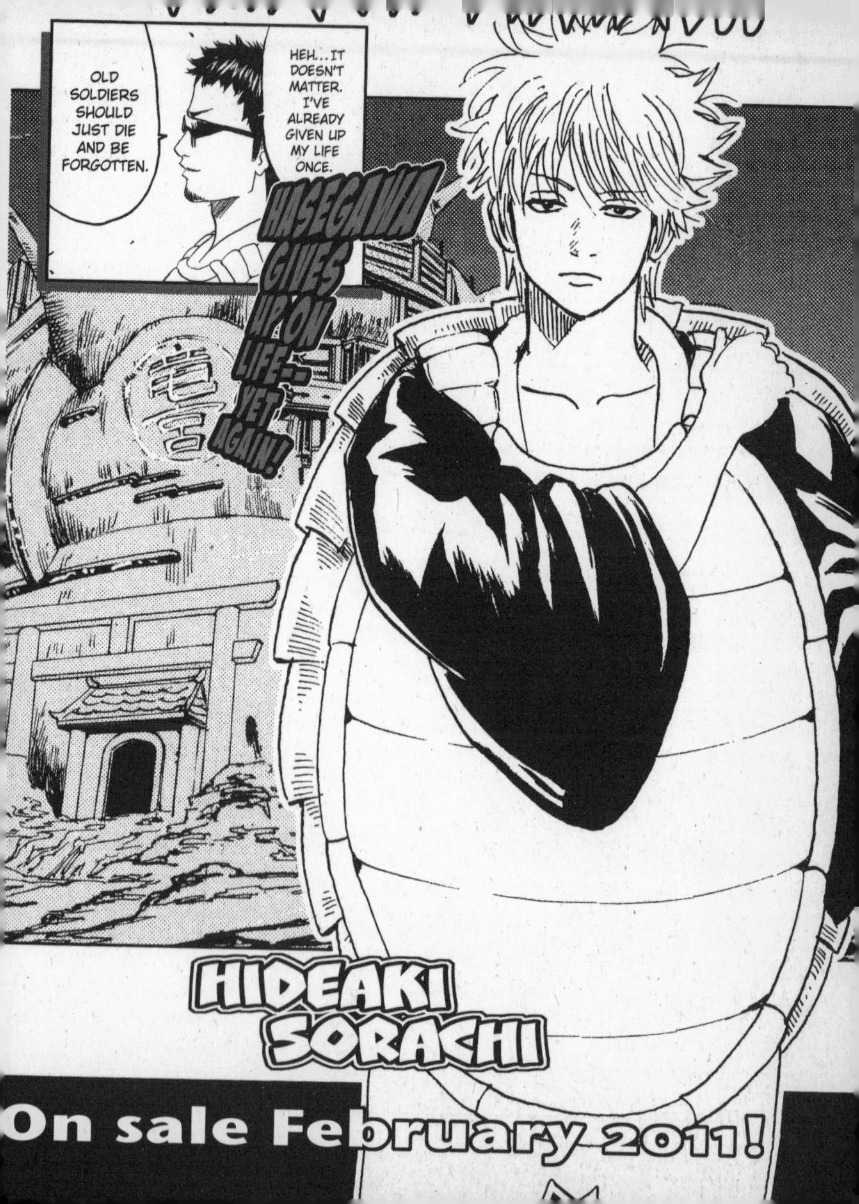
HEH...IT DOESN'T MATTER. I'VE ALREADY GIVEN UP MY LIFE ONCE.
OLD SOLDIERS SHOULD JUST DIE AND BE FORGOTTEN.
HASEGAWA GIVES UP ON LIFE... YET AGAIN!
HIDEAKI SORACHI
On sale February 2011!

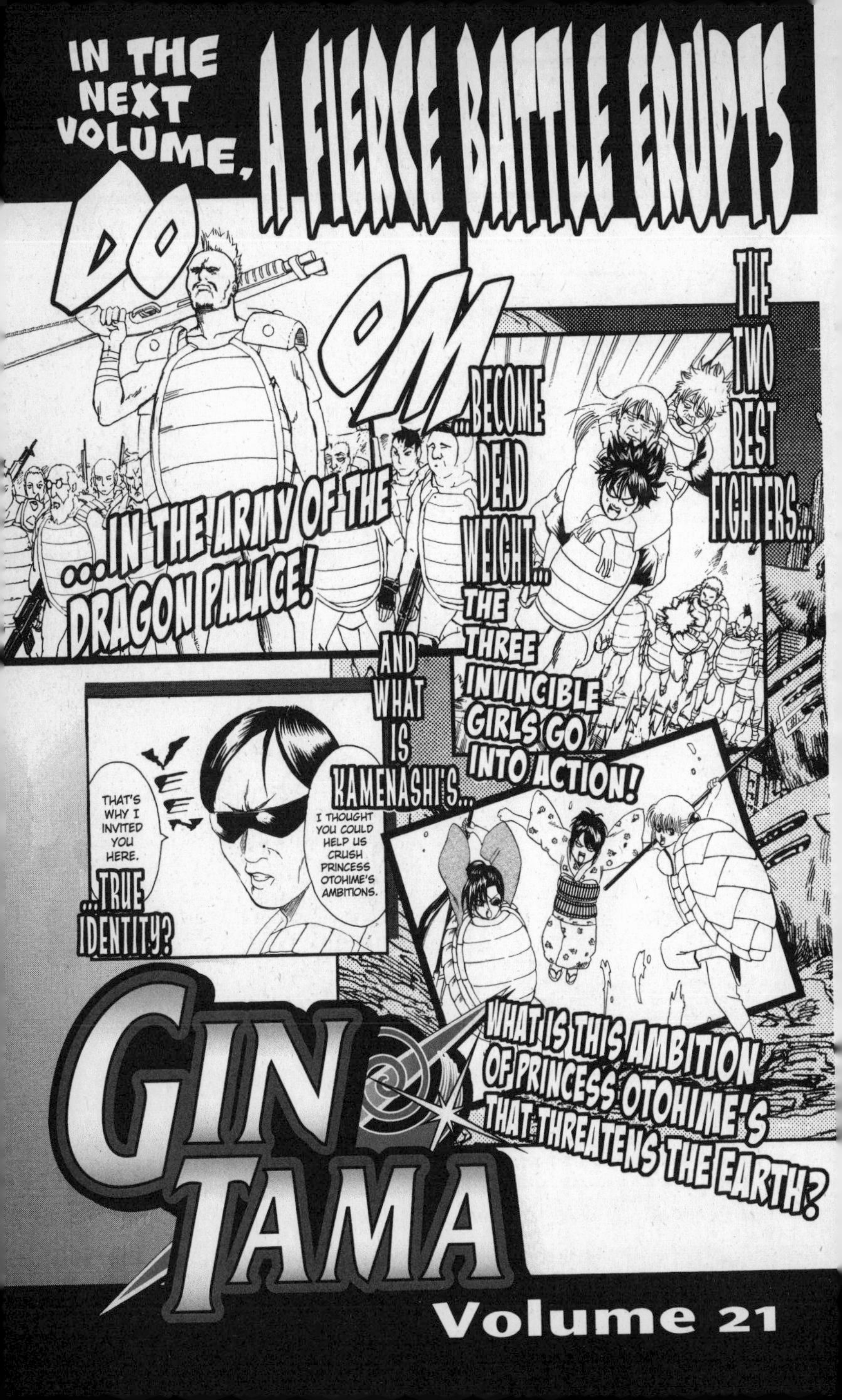
IN THE NEXT VOLUME,
A FIERCE BATTLE ERUPTS
DOOM
...IN THE ARMY OF THE DRAGON PALACE!
THE TWO BEST FIGHTERS...
...BECOME DEAD WEIGHT...
THE THREE INVINCIBLE GIRLS GO INTO ACTION!
AND WHAT IS KAMENASHI'S...
I THOUGHT YOU COULD HELP US CRUSH PRINCESS OTOHIME'S AMBITIONS.
VEEN
THAT'S WHY I INVITED YOU HERE.
...TRUE IDENTITY?
WHAT IS THIS AMBITION OF PRINCESS OTOHIME'S THAT THREATENS THE EARTH?
GIN TAMA
Volume 21

SHONEN JUMP

THE WORLD'S MOST POPULAR MANGA

BLEACH

STORY AND ART BY
TITE KUBO

ONE PIECE

STORY AND ART BY
EIICHIRO ODA

Tegami Bachi
LETTER·BEE

STORY AND ART BY
HIROYUKI ASADA

UMP INTO THE ACTION BY TELLING US WHAT YOU LOVE (AND WHAT YOU DON'T)

LET YOUR VOICE BE HEARD!

HONENJUMP.VIZ.COM/MANGASURVEY

HELP US MAKE MORE OF THE WORLD'S MOST POPULAR MANGA!

www.viz.com